"Communazis"

"Communazis"

FBI Surveillance of German Emigré Writers

A L E X A N D E R   S T E P H A N

Translated by Jan van Heurck

Yale University Press   New Haven and London

Original German-language edition: Alexander Stephan, *Im Visier des FBI:
Deutsche Exilschriftsteller in den Akten
amerikanischer Geheimdienste,* published by J. B. Metzlersche Verlags-
buchhandlung, Stuttgart, Germany, copy-
right © 1995.

The translation of this work was made
possible through funding from Inter
Nationes, Bonn.

Printed in the United States of America

Library of Congress Cataloging-in-
Publication Data

Stephan, Alexander, 1946–
[Im Visier des FBI. English]
"Communazis": FBI surveillance of
German emigré writers / Alexander
Stephan; translated by Jan van Heurck.
    p. cm
Includes bibliographical references and
index.
ISBN 0-300-08202-9 (alk. paper)
1. Authors, German—20th Century—
Political and social views. 2. Au-
thors, Exiled—20th Century—United
States. 3. Authors, Exiled—20th
Century—Mexico. 4. German litera-
ture—20th Century—History and Crit-
icism. 5. Politics and literature—
United States—History—20th Century.
6. United States. Federal Bureau of
Investigation—History—20th Century.
I. Title.

PT405 .S741713 2000
830.9′973′09043—dc21   00-021107

A catalog record for this book is available from the British Library.

10 9 8 7 6 5 4 3 2 1

Contents

3
The FBI and the Exiles in New York

4
The FBI and the Exiles in Mexico

5
The FBI Today: Obtaining the Files   279

Preface

POLICE AND INTELLIGENCE CORPS NORMALLY give access to their files only under duress from an external enemy or internal coup. Among the few exceptions are agencies of the United States of America, where the Freedom of Information Act and the Privacy Act have for years afforded limited access to files of the Federal Bureau of Investigation (FBI), the military intelligence services, the Central Intelligence Agency (CIA), and other bodies. These organizations released to me more than fifty dossiers with some fourteen thousand documents on German-speaking writers who fled the Gestapo and sought asylum in the United States in the thirties and forties. Nearly one thousand pages treat Nobel Prize–winning author Thomas Mann and his family, four hundred the dramatist Bertolt Brecht; a thousand each are devoted to best-selling novelists Lion Feuchtwanger and Anna Seghers, the author of *The Seventh Cross* who fled to Mexico after being barred from the United States.

These dossiers reveal a previously hidden picture of America the land of immigrants, which despite its deep-rooted principles of democracy deployed a massive spy apparatus to oversee the new arrivals from Europe. Agency censors blacked out many passages before releasing the files. Notwithstanding this and the wide variation in the size and significance of the files, they extend our knowledge of the personal and working lives of writers driven from Europe by Adolf Hitler following 1933; of their political schemes, their relations with their American hosts, their literary projects, financial hardships, and love affairs. And they say much about the relationship between state power and literature in the twentieth century.

When the Nazis began to occupy large areas of Europe in 1939 and 1940, the United States and, to a lesser degree, Mexico became by far the most important countries of asylum for the writers forced by their racial or political backgrounds to flee Germany, Austria, and Czechoslovakia. Whereas emigré authors previously had bridged the geographical and cultural gap between the Old and New Worlds only as scattered individuals, in the forties they formed sizable colonies on the East and West coasts of the United States. Heinrich and Thomas Mann, Bertolt Brecht, Lion Feuchtwanger, Erich Maria Remarque, and Franz Werfel were lured to Los Angeles by the possibility of work in the film industry and the pleasant California climate. Oskar Maria Graf, Hermann Broch, and occasionally Klaus Mann stayed in or near the more "European" New York City, the cultural and publishing center of the United States where most exile organizations were based, as were publications like *Aufbau* and *Decision*.

Once war broke out, the normally tight U.S. immigration laws, made even more restrictive in response to the hordes of refugees from Europe, became relatively generous when applied to prominent exiles. Aid organizations like the Emergency Rescue Committee, the European Film Fund, and the Exiled Writers Committee, which was a branch of the League of American Writers, provided ship's passages and sworn statements of support, as did numerous private individuals. The big Hollywood film studios offered the newcomers modest aid in the form of "lifesaver contracts." President Roosevelt and his wife, Eleanor, were kindly disposed to the exiles. Public opinion polls show that until 1942–43, the average American still drew a clear distinction between Nazis and Germans.

But the American public's interest in the refugees and their experiences was largely limited to rescuing them from Europe. After that, the new arrivals were expected to adapt rather than to give literary accounts of events in far-off Germany. Publishers and film studios quickly tired of the antifascist propaganda that was a central topic of exile literature. The majority of exile organizations with their particular political leanings, like the American Guild for German Cultural Freedom, the German-American Writers Association, and the Council for a Democratic Germany, were fairly short-lived. The rare attempts to build magazines and emigré publishing houses to circulate German literature could not be sustained for very long. German plays were performed mostly in exiles' living rooms or in small local or campus theaters.

Relatively few emigré writers achieved success and recognition in the American book market. Thomas Mann and Lion Feuchtwanger were already known in the United States before 1940. Scriptwriters like Frederick Kohner, George Froeschel, and Gina Kraus managed to adapt to Hollywood work methods. Younger authors like Klaus Mann and Stefan Heym were readier than their older colleagues to tackle new tasks and the language of their host country. Among the major works of modern German literature that were produced in the United States but went largely unnoticed there were Thomas Mann's *Lotte in Weimar* and *Doctor Faustus,* Hermann Broch's *The Death of Virgil,* Bertolt Brecht's *The Caucasian Chalk Circle* and a version of *Galileo,* Franz Werfel's *The Song of Bernadette,* and Carl Zuckmayer's *Des Teufels General.*

The refugees' reactions to their country of asylum were correspondingly mixed. Those like Billy Wilder and Curt Siodmak who were successful in Hollywood disengaged fairly quickly from their home country. The same was true of the majority of Jewish exiles, who if they had not already taken steps to settle permanently in the United States dismissed the idea of returning to Germany once the atrocities of the concentration camps were revealed. Best-sellers and film contracts enabled Thomas Mann, Feuchtwanger, and Werfel to achieve a measure of prosperity, but in both form and content the older, established writers stayed tied to the European cultural tradition. Others, including Brecht, Alfred Döblin, and Heinrich Mann, remained alien to their host country, and the consistency with which they ignored the theme of the United States in their writings says a lot about the intellectual inflexibility of exile society.

Yet even during the war years, when as "enemy aliens" they were subject to certain restrictions, exiles found conditions favorable to artistic production. American publishers and theaters were not forced into compromise, as they had been in Switzerland and Czechosklovakia, by their proximity to an all-powerful Germany. German-Americans who had settled in the United States offered a good-sized body of readers for German texts, although for the most part they were politically more sympathetic to the new Germany than to the refugees. And unlike the Soviet Union, which also harbored exiles, the United States exercised no direct censorship or overt state control, although virtually all the refugees were kept under surveillance by the FBI and other U.S. government agencies, both secret and public, for many years.

U.S. secret services and agencies might track refugees from Hitler (almost always without their knowledge) because they were foreigners; because they were Germans and thus enemy aliens, citizens of a country with which the United States was at war twice within a short span; because most were considered Communists or "fellow travelers"; and, after 1943, because they were potential opponents in the policy debate on the new Germany that would be formed after destruction of the Third Reich. The scenes of this drama of espionage were the three centers of exile life in the Americas: Los Angeles, New York, and Mexico. The players included, on the side of the government, the FBI, the OSS (Office of Strategic Services, the forerunner to the CIA), the Immigration and Naturalization Service (INS), the Office of Censorship, which intercepted and examined mail, army and navy intelligence, the Department of State, which was mainly active in Mexico, the House Un-American Activities Committee (HUAC) in Washington and its offshoot in the California state senate, and other national and local authorities. Surveillance methods ranged from opening mail and tapping telephones to "tailing" individuals, burglarizing homes, searching luggage and garbage ("trash cover"), and installing listening devices. The FBI's concern was to prevent subversive activities, not to sponsor government-approved poetry. Thus, although writers and the content of their works came under the investigative spotlight, the form and style of literature were not scrutinized as they were, for example, by East Germany's Stasi. Nor was Hoover interested, like his counterparts in Moscow and in other branches of the U.S. government, in recruiting followers among the exile writers so as to exert a direct influence on political processes in postwar Germany. An FBI file was closed, if at all, only upon the subject's death or return to his former homeland.

Three recurrent themes guide the reader through the welter of files, which although uniform in their appearance differ markedly in content. First, the blanket surveillance of exiled writers in the United States needs to be viewed in terms of U.S. history at the time. Instead of turning directly to the files with their jumble of disconnected facts to gain new information on the lives and work of the exiles, I propose to emphasize the context in which surveillance operations took place, that is, Franklin D. Roosevelt's "big government" policies and his taste for centralized mega-agencies; the history of the FBI and the ideology of its director J. Edgar Hoover, which remained fixed on xenophobia and anti-Communism from 1917 onward; the plans that the German exiles and their host nation formed for postwar Germany; and the roots of the un-American activities witch hunt, which former FBI informant Ronald Reagan continued to describe decades later as a manifestation of patriotic duty.

A second theme is the special feature that sets each major file apart, despite a general similarity. The case of Thomas Mann's son Klaus, for example, shows the FBI and the army's Military Intelligence Division (MID) taking particular interest in his homosexual leanings. Bertolt Brecht's dossier is full of references to the playwright's contacts with left-wing culture in the United States. Heinrich Mann is observed for his correspondence with the Communist exile group in Mexico, while his famed brother Thomas comes under scrutiny by the State Department and OSS when he participates in planning for postwar Germany. Anna Seghers runs afoul of the FBI when they connect her with a series of mysterious coded letters, and Erika Mann, Thomas's eldest child, is the sole example I know of a prominent exile who volunteered to give the Bureau information.

The third theme is the combination of high efficiency with grotesque overkill in agency operations. What else to call it but absurd that dozens of government employees were set to monitor pillow talk between the little-known Brecht and his Danish co-worker Ruth Berlau, at taxpayers' expense, in the middle of a world war? Or that agents followed the car of Lion Feuchtwanger's gardener, or asked the mailman about the mailbox at Thomas Mann's villa? Yet despite the extravagant investment in tracking a mere handful of scattered exiles, agencies surprisingly warped only a few lives in a serious way, and in no case were able to achieve threatened deportations and internments.

The sheer bulk of the material amassed by the FBI and other government agencies made it necessary to limit the scope of this book and to exclude certain topics. Of the more than two hundred writers who sought asylum in the United States, only the most prominent are discussed: the Mann family, Bertolt Brecht, Lion Feuchtwanger, the Bavarian popular novelist Oskar Maria Graf, and theater and film director Berthold Viertel, with shorter segments on

Franz Werfel, Erich Maria Remarque, Bruno Frank, Emil Ludwig, Leonhard Frank, Alfred Döblin, F. C. Weiskopf, Hans Marchwitza, Alfred Kantorowicz, Ernst Bloch, Ferdinand Bruckner, Erwin Piscator, Fritz von Unruh, Hans Habe, Hermann Broch, Carl Zuckmayer, and others. For the exile colony in Mexico, the case studies are limited to Anna Seghers and, in summary, Egon Erwin Kisch, Bodo Uhse, and Ludwig Renn. Files kept on emigré politicians, scientists, musicians, and filmmakers must be reserved for a future study. The difficult but appealing task of comparing the U.S. files with similar files from Nazi, Stasi, and Soviet archives, and drawing up a typology and aesthetics of modern intelligence records, must likewise be postponed, as must a comparison of the exile files with the relatively meager and uninformative dossiers on leading American authors. Considerations of time and expense prevented me from bringing the protracted legal actions required to try to obtain documents that had been withheld or passages that were blacked out by the censors.

Those interested in learning more about the writers in exile and their experiences in the United States and Mexico are referred to the extensive body of material on the exile phenomenon, some important examples of which are listed at the end of this volume. The material includes introductions to the history of the German exiles, ranging from the persecution of left-wingers, Jews, and "decadent scribblers" that began immediately after the Nazis came to power, to questions like whether the exile ended in 1945, why so many of the refugees preferred to remain abroad after the war, and why others felt that their exile was a journey from which one could return but never return home. Several studies treat the emigré colonies in Europe, including Czechoslovakia, Switzerland, Britain, and the Soviet Union, where the refugees sought shelter when they still hoped to go home again soon and the United States seemed too alien and far away. Exile research, a field that developed in Germany and the United States only after the Cold War thawed and the study of literature was politicized in the sixties, has devoted much attention to issues like the exiled writers' loss of language and identity, problems with publication and sale of their works, lack of a readership while abroad, and the tension between eyewitness accounts of the Third Reich and less political forms like the historical novel and poetry. More recent studies focus on the question of cultural adaptation that was central to the exiles in America—whether and how European writers and intellectuals could attune themselves to a different artistic setting keyed more to teamwork than to the originality of individual ideas, and more to commercial considerations, upbeat endings, and an appeal to a wide audience than to cultural criticism and political issues.

I began this project before the collapse of East Germany and the years of nonstop revelations about the Stasi and the writers and other informants who served them. These disclosures further diminished my interest, never strong to begin with, in reconstructing names (often names of informants) that were routinely blacked out by the FBI before releasing its files. To preserve the original tone of the documents, I have not corrected the misspellings of German (and sometimes English) names, places, and literary works but have kept intact the language of the special agents, warts and all. Because emigré memoirs and academic writings both reflect little awareness of the exile community's relations with intelligence agencies,[1] there is no need to devote a separate chapter to the few specialized studies that have recently been published in this area.

Political shorthand terms like "left-wing," "right-wing," "liberal," and "conservative," although their meaning has recently become more blurred than ever, have been used in the absence of something better. Besides, abbreviations of this kind fit the mentality of FBI bureaucrats, who used problematic words like "subject," "subversive," "un-American," and "brown bolshevism" without much concern for what they really meant. In fact, one of these terms, "Communazi," so well reflected the public mood following the

Hitler-Stalin pact and throughout the Cold War that it seemed appropriate for the title of this study. The well-known exile journal *Das Neue Tage-Buch* and feuding leftist groups in Mexico denounced a number of exiles who had just arrived in the New World, among them Klaus Mann and Oskar Maria Graf, as "Communazis," a term useful for those who were convinced that Nazis and Communists belonged to the same empire of evil and differed only in insignificant details. Immediately after joining the anti-Communist camp, Jack B. Tenney, chairman of the California Senate Fact-Finding Committee on Un-American Activities, began to publish a newspaper column with the title "Commu-Nazism." J. Edgar Hoover and the State Department used the term repeatedly during World War II, although the United States and the Soviet Union were allies in the fight against the Nazis. And those German exiles in the United States who at the time were trying to define the concept of "totalitarianism" saw no reason to object to the term "Communazi."

Of the many individuals and institutions that supported my work, I can here name only a few. My thanks go first and foremost to those members of the U.S. Congress who proposed the Freedom of Information Act and the Privacy Act, making possible the release of the files. The unknown employees of the Freedom of Information and Privacy Acts Division of the FBI who had to read, censor, and copy thousands of documents on my behalf deserve my sympathy. Susan Rosenberg, first as an FBI historian and later a freelance researcher, advised me on many details, as did former FBI agents Elmer F. "Lindy" Linberg, Ernest J. van Loon, and Robert J. Lamphere. In 1995, Johannes Eglau and I produced a television documentary, with the same theme as this book, that has been shown a number of times in Germany and internationally. Interviews for the film and book were kindly granted by, among others, Eric Bentley, Egon Breiner, Hilde Eisler, Franklin Folsom, Stefan Heym, Harold von Hofe, Konrad Kellen, Robert Lamphere, Minna E. Lieber,

Elmer F. Linberg, Ernest van Loon, Elisabeth Mann Borgese, Ruth Radvanyi, and Will Schaber. R. B. Hood, who in the forties became the first exile researcher by virtue of his role as special agent in charge of the FBI's Los Angeles Field Office, was in poor health and did not wish to be consulted.

This book was supported by grants from the Alexander von Humboldt Foundation, the American Philosophical Society, and the German Academic Exchange Service.

Readers familiar with German who are interested in a more detailed analysis of the FBI, secret service, and government files reviewed here are referred to my earlier study on which the present abridged volume is based, *Im Visier des FBI: Deutsche Exilschriftsteller in den Akten amerikanischer Geheimdienste* (Stuttgart: Metzler 1995).

Note on the Sources

ALL NOTE REFERENCES ARE TO FILES AT FBI headquarters unless otherwise specified. The file name is stated ("FBI file, Lion Feuchtwanger") if not clear from the context. The type, place, and date of documents are listed ("FBI Report, New York, 5/5/43" or "SAC, Los Angeles, Memorandum to Director, FBI, 13/3/45") rather than the file and numerical designations in the FBI register, so as to supply temporal and geographical reference points. FBI dossiers are always filed under the subject's name and normally are in chronological order, so that quotations can be traced easily if the originals are consulted.

Quotations from exiles' letters, which almost without exception came to the FBI through the Office of Censorship, are identified by name and date ("Walter Janka, Letter to Heinrich Mann, 29/7/42") and by the context. Files of the Immigration and Naturalization Service are identified by "(INS)" only if the text does not make the source clear. State Department documents in the National Archives are designated by their file numbers ("862.01/6-2645") and come from Record Group 59 unless otherwise indicated. Files of the Foreign Nationalities Branch of the Office of Strategic Services are listed by their original numerical designations (OSS, 867), which were retained by the CIA when it released OSS files several years ago, and are so listed in the microfiche catalog. OSS files in this book come from group INT-13GE, if not stated otherwise. Other sources, the Office of Naval Intelligence (ONI), the army's Military Intelligence Division (MID), the Central Intelligence Agency (CIA), and so on, are identified by the appropriate abbreviations.

Senders and addressees of agency memoranda and letters are listed as "Director, FBI," "J. Edgar Hoover," or "Secretary of State," although this does not necessarily mean that a communication went to the organization head personally. At FBI headquarters a stamp of Hoover's signature was regularly used by other senior staff members. Titles of correspondents are listed only if needed for clarity.

The FBI practice of writing proper names in all capital letters has been discarded to make quotations more readable. Typographical errors and misspellings of foreign (and English) names and quotations are replicated as they appear in the files and are not followed by any special indicator, such as "[*sic*]." Bracketed numbers refer to works listed in the Bibliography at the end of this volume: "[32, p. 95]." Brackets within quotations contain my explanatory notes. The bracketed phrase "[blacked out]" indicates deletions by the FBI.

All quotations from the German are translated by Jan van Heurck unless otherwise stated.

Abbreviations

AFL	American Federation of Labor
Amguild	American Guild for German Cultural Freedom
AST	Abwehrstelle (German espionage organization in World War II)
BBC	British Broadcasting Corporation
BI	Bureau of Investigation (FBI forerunner)
CIA	Central Intelligence Agency
CIC	Counter Intelligence Corps
CIG	Central Intelligence Group (CIA forerunner)
CNDI	Confidential National Defense Informant
COI	Coordinator of Information (OSS forerunner)
Comintern	Communist International
Comsab	Communist sabotage
CP	Communist Party
Detcom	Detention of Communists
DF	Distrito Federal (government district of Mexico City)
EBF	Enclosure Behind File (oversized attachment to FBI dossier)
ERC	Emergency Rescue (Refugee) Committee

EWC	Exiled Writers Committee
FBI	Federal Bureau of Investigation
FGM	Free Germany Movement
FNB	Foreign Nationalities Branch (of OSS)
FOIA	Freedom of Information Act
FOIPA	Freedom of Information and Privacy Acts
GAWA	German-American Writers Association
GDR	German Democratic Republic (East Germany)
Gestapo	Geheime Staatspolizei (Nazi secret police)
GID	General Intelligence Division (FBI forerunner)
G-Men	Government men (nickname for FBI agents)
GPU (OGPU)	Soviet secret police
G-2	*See* MID
HUAC	House Un-American Activities Committee
IFTU	International Federation of Trade Unions
INS	Immigration and Naturalization Service
IRC	International Rescue Committee
IRRC	International Rescue and Relief Committee
IRS	Internal Revenue Service
KGB	Committee for State Security (Soviet security and intelligence agency)
KPC	Czech Communist Party
KPD	Kommunistische Partei Deutschlands (German Communist Party)
LAC/LAFGC	Latin American (Free German) Committee
Legat	Legal Attaché (code for FBI agents working from embassies abroad)
MGM	Metro-Goldwyn-Mayer
MID (G-2)	Military Intelligence Division (U.S. Army)
Misur	Microphone surveillance
NFGC	National Free Germany Committee
NKVD	People's Commissariat of Internal Affairs (Soviet secret police)
OGPU	*See* GPU

ONI	Office of Naval Intelligence (U.S. Navy)
OSS	Office of Strategic Services
OWI	Office of War Information
PA	Privacy Act
PEN	Poets, Essayists, Novelists (Writers' Association)
R&A	Research and Analysis (OSS branch)
RSHA	Reichssicherheitshauptamt (Nazi/SS Bureau of Internal Security)
SA	Special Agent
SAC	Special Agent in Charge (of an FBI field office)
SED	Sozialistische Einheitspartei Deutschlands (East German Communist Party)
SIS	Special Intelligence Service (U.S. agency in Latin America), *also* Secret Intelligence Service (British)
Stasi	Staatssicherheitsdienst (secret police of the GDR)
Tass	Soviet News Agency
USAREUR	United States Army Europe

1

J. Edgar Hoover's America

The Red Scare and Enemy Aliens

"I AM VERY HAPPY TO HAVE BECOME AN American," Erich Maria Remarque, famed German author of the best-selling novel *All Quiet on the Western Front*, told *Newsweek* magazine in 1957. "I have met exceedingly cultivated people in America. Americans have an innate sense of freedom" [165]. Klaus Mann, like his sister Erika, predicted that a democratic, united postwar Europe was bound to follow the American model, and in 1942 he applied to join the U.S. Army. "I want to notify you of my willingness, indeed, eagerness to join the United States forces," he wrote. "It is my honest desire to serve your country and our case in whatever capacity the Board may deem appropriate."[1] Communist Anna Seghers, trapped in occupied France in 1940–41, wished for nothing so ardently as to be able to get to the United States. And even Bertolt Brecht, inveterate critic of America, confessed in a weak moment that Americans "move more freely, more gracefully" than "German petty bourgeois" with their "pinched neurotic natures," their "obsequiousness" and their "arrogance" [20, vol. 23, p. 48f].

What the refugee writers scattered from New York to Los Angeles did not know and for the most part did not even guess was that almost all of them, admirers and critics of the United States alike, were under surveillance by secret agencies of their host nation, especially the FBI and the forerunner of the CIA, the Office of Strategic Services, along with the Immigration and Naturalization Service, the State Department, the army's Military Intelligence Division, the Office of Naval Intelligence, the Un-American Activities Committee of the House of Representatives, and its counterpart in the California state senate, the Tenney Committee. Few exiles suspected that their telephone conversations were being recorded and their mail not only opened and read but translated, summarized, cataloged, photographed, and passed to other government bureaus. Hardly any guessed that the men parked in cars outside their homes were FBI special agents recording everyone who went in and out. In the diaries, autobiographies, correspondence, *romans à clef,* and interviews of the exiles we find virtually no references to the FBI burglaries of private homes and offices or the luggage searches. Even the activity of spies and informers, perhaps the least known chapter in the history of the emigré Germans, seems scarcely to have been mentioned in exile circles.

In the background of FBI surveillance lay a widespread public fear of foreigners, especially German spies and saboteurs, combined with deep distrust of liberal or socialist ideas, and a need bordering on religious zeal to defend the "American way of life," however undefined that might be. Since the late thirties, one of the masterminds of these increasingly powerful trends was FBI boss J. Edgar Hoover.

Hoover had begun his career in the Department of Justice toward the end of World War I by tracking German aliens along with anarchists and dissidents. By the start of World War II twenty years later, he had established himself with American politicians, press, and public as a highly qualified and successful policeman, and he was rapidly assuming the role of unchallenged watchdog over the nation's political and moral hygiene. Presidents, Cabinet members, and journalists relied on facts and rumors collected legally or illegally by his agents. Public prosecutors, investigative committees like the House Un-American Activities Committee headed by Martin Dies, the INS divisions that dealt with deportations and petitions for naturalization, the military intelligence services, the Office of Strategic Services, boards that examined federal employee loyalty—all depended on cooperation with the FBI. An ingenious system of card indexes and files, telephone tapping, mail interception, and a wide network of spies and informers supplied Hoover with information that allowed him to steer the decisions of other agencies, intervene in political developments, and influence legal proceedings. In countless speeches, leaflets, and books, America's "top cop" propagated his ideology of the American Way, as vague as it was influential. He made smear attacks on Communists and liberals while preaching traditional moral, religious, and family values and loyalty to his country.

When the emigré writers came to the United States around 1940, Hoover and his liberal president, Franklin D. Roosevelt, were at the pinnacle of their power. Public trust in the banks and the American economy, shattered by the crash in 1929, had been restored, and reduced unemployment allowed the unions to launch a series of strikes to gain a minimum wage, a forty-hour work week, and more humane conditions for assembly-line workers. Roosevelt fearlessly attacked "business and financial monopoly," "speculation," "reckless banking," and "organized money" [115, p. 143] to achieve his New Deal social reforms, which were supported by a majority of the population. Instead of threatening the countries of Central and South America with a "big stick" as his predecessors had, the president advocated a "good neighbor" policy and further reduced the already weak armed forces. Joseph E. Davies went to the Soviet Union as U.S. ambassador, and in his book *Mission to Moscow,* which later was made into a film, he reported that Stalin's show trials had eliminated Hitler's fifth column in Russia. The United States tried to stay out of Europe's internal quarrels for as long as possible. In 1938, over 80 percent of Americans polled expressed the wish that Russia would defeat Germany in the event of an armed conflict, but until late in the war they continued to draw a distinction between Germans and Nazis, as the German exiles themselves did.

Roosevelt had been reelected in 1936 by the largest landslide vote in American history, then was reelected again in 1940 and 1944 to become the only four-term president. John Steinbeck's saga of impoverished farmers, *The Grapes of Wrath,* was published in 1939, soon followed by *For Whom the Bell Tolls,* Ernest Hemingway's novel about the Spanish Civil War. Writers, artists, and intellectuals in the "red thirties" talked about social change, art as a weapon of progress, and how best to portray the new themes of social criticism: by realist or experimental forms. In the Spanish Civil War and at various writers' congresses, German refugee writers met progressive colleagues from America who, like the unconventional Eleanor Roosevelt, were not afraid to criticize their country and question the principles of their own society. When news came in 1933 about the persecution of Jews in Germany and the laws boycotting Jewish businesses and barring Jews from working in certain professions, Roosevelt's new labor secretary pushed for a liberalization of immigration laws. Six years later, there began a surge of private aid for the refugees who had fled to southern France and Britain and were waiting for rescue. Many American writers and almost all the new arrivals from Europe were out of sympathy with the nationalistic tones of the America First movement, which tried to close the door of the New World to refugees, abused Roosevelt as "another Stalin," and sought to undermine the transatlantic alliance with Britain, then the last bulwark in Europe against the Nazis.

But the stereotype of America as a freedom-loving nation open to the world did not reflect the whole reality of that time. Another,

darker side of America, marked by xenophobia, political narrow-
ness, and blinkered ideology, continued to gain strength until well
into the fifties, although it existed largely on an official level and almost never affected the exiles in their private relations. Immigration
to the United States had almost dried up since the quota laws were
passed in the early twenties, and the latent hostility to foreigners
flared up as immigrants started to pour in again from a Europe torn
by racism and war. Foreigners were blamed for both left-wing and
right-wing subversive activities, as they had been during the "Red
Scare" after World War I. As the provocations of the Axis powers in
Czechoslovakia and Austria threatened war in the late thirties, warnings from American isolationists—Republicans, the rising phalanx
of southern Democrats, and political amateurs like transatlantic
flyer Charles Lindbergh—intensified. The Hitler-Stalin pact of
1939 split the political left, not strong to begin with, and reminded
the American public of the separate peace the Bolsheviks had made
with Germany in 1918. This peace was still regarded as a betrayal
and gave rise to a theory of "totalitarianism" that led Americans to
group "Huns" and "Reds" together under blanket terms like "Communazi" and "Red Fascism."

The House Un-American Activities Committee (HUAC) was
founded in 1934 to investigate Nazi and Fascist groups, but after
1938, led by congressmen Martin Dies of Texas and, later, J. Parnell
Thomas of New Jersey, it decided that the real enemy was not on the
political right but on the left, was foreign controlled, and supported
the New Deal as a "cross between Communism and Fascism" [46].
Americans who had fought against Franco in Spain were threatened
with confiscation of their passports; Mexico, which had opened its
doors to those who had fought Spanish Fascism, among them several German intellectuals, was watched with suspicion. Moreover,
during the years when German refugees were fleeing to the United
States, a large majority of Americans believed that any foreigners
living on welfare should be sent home, and "aliens . . . who came

here from the Axis countries" [161, p. 947] should be deported or interned even if their conduct was loyal and peaceable. The Gallup Poll revealed that 67 percent of Americans wanted more power and money to be given to HUAC, and 75 percent opposed allowing the Communist Party USA equal time on the radio to put its views before the electorate. Half the population believed that Communists were directed from Moscow [101; 102], but 39 percent admitted not being informed about the Communist Party [63, vol. 1]. By contrast, 66 percent thought in December 1939 that Germans were "essentially peace-loving and kind" [161, p. 500] although easily led astray by power-hungry leaders.

Roosevelt himself contributed to making his period in office memorable for other things besides its liberal climate. Americans saw their rights curtailed by the Hatch Act of 1939, which barred federal employees from belonging to organizations that advocated overthrow of the government. A deep-rooted distrust of foreigners, who were indiscriminately suspected of being un-American and subversive (67 percent of Americans believed in 1938 "that 'with conditions as they are we should try to keep them out'" [240, p. 47]), meant that attempts to relax the strict quota laws failed in Congress despite a Democratic majority. The transfer of the Immigration and Naturalization Service from the Department of Labor to the Department of Justice in 1940 underlined the fact that immigrants were no longer viewed as a strain on the labor market but as a security risk.

The German immigration quota, which had been halved in response to the worldwide economic crisis that began in 1929, was never completely filled during the war years. Many U.S. consular officials regarded Nazi terrorism as a passing phenomenon or a welcome shield against Communism. The already high rate of unemployment in the United States made trade unions take a dim view of the 300,000 Germans trying to enter the country. And government officials like Breckinridge Long, head of the Special War Problems Division in the State Department and in charge of the visa section, erected new bureaucratic barriers that impeded if not prevented the entry of refugees suspected of being radicals or Communists. The President's Advisory Committee on Political Refugees, set up after the defeat of France, was not even able to distribute the three thousand emergency visas that the State Department had approved, much less to rescue en masse the victims of political and racial persecution in Europe. Xenophobia was the impulse behind another law that cleverly blended the supervision of foreigners with limitation of the civil rights of American citizens, the Alien Registration Act (Smith Act) of 1940.

The Hatch and Smith Acts opened the door to censorship and the principle of guilt by association, reminding liberal Americans of the dark days of Attorney General A. Mitchell Palmer's Red Scare campaign of 1919–20, which had shaped the young J. Edgar Hoover. But refugees seeking asylum from Hitler in the United States were more at risk from a "big government" enterprise launched by Roosevelt, who ordered construction of a "domestic intelligence apparatus" [160, p. 180] that was used against foreigners, especially if they were "enemy aliens" like the Germans, and against anyone perceived as subversive or un-American. Three of Roosevelt's mega-agencies that were essential to this apparatus are also central to this book: the FBI, which in the forties took on an increasingly political, ideological role in addition to that of combating crime; the Office of Censorship, which operated during the war years; and the Office of Strategic Services, known as "America's first central intelligence agency" [184].

Roosevelt laid the foundation for an American national security state on 24 August 1936. Troubled by reports of the United Front coalition policy of the Communists, the work of foreign intelligence in the United States, and the activities of the Soviet embassy in Washington, he called FBI chief Hoover to a confidential meeting at the White House and assigned him to gather information about "subversive activities in the United States, particularly Fascism and

Communism" [160, p. 229]. Hoover, who on his own initiative had for years been keeping an index file on twenty-five hundred politically suspect individuals, obediently set to work, and by the end of the war he had expanded his small troop of agents who specialized in hunting bank robbers and kidnappers into a powerful agency that justified its existence by continuously discovering conspiracies against democracy and the American Way. The number of special agents assigned to political duties zoomed from three hundred in the mid-thirties to some five thousand by the end of the war. Between 1941 and 1943, Hoover hired almost seven thousand employees to help catalog the flood of information, type reports, and maintain the Custodial Detention Lists of suspicious foreigners like the German exiles. In the same period, the budget of his bureau rose from $6 million to more than $30 million a year.

To secure the southern flank of the United States, Hoover assigned the several hundred agents of the Special Intelligence Service (SIS), founded in 1940 especially to monitor Latin America, to watch out for German spies and, increasingly, for actual or potential Communists. Detailed SIS analyses, often drawn up in cooperation with navy and army intelligence or U.S. embassies, kept the State Department up to date about the plans of the Free Germans for postwar Germany and the internal quarrels of the Communists in exile in Mexico. Gustave ("Gus") Jones, the first FBI agent to maintain surveillance of the exile colony in Mexico City [54, p. 335], set the pattern for agents disguised as legal attachés who operated under cover of U.S. diplomatic and military missions abroad, and who long after 1945 continued to supply Hoover with information from Bonn, Heidelberg, Vienna, and Paris about exiles who had returned home. In short, a small crime-fighting organization had turned in a brief span into a sort of political police force whose boss, notwithstanding all his protestations that the FBI was merely a "fact-gathering agency,"[2] treated opinions as facts and convictions as deeds, who equated immorality with crime and regarded lawbreakers as "aliens."

The criticism of Hoover in liberal circles intensified in 1940–41 because of policies like "preventive detention," telephone eavesdropping, illegal break-ins (known as "black bag jobs"), and an FBI operation to arrest and imprison members of the Abraham Lincoln Brigade that continued for years after the Spanish Civil War was over. Union leaders openly spoke of the FBI as the American equivalent of OGPU, the Soviet secret police. Eleanor Roosevelt compared Hoover's men to the Gestapo, and the ugly nickname "J. Edgar Himmler"[3] started making the rounds. But the president, who despite ideological differences valued his top cop for his organizational talent and the information he supplied, stayed on the path to a national security state. Instead of limiting the political missions of the FBI, Roosevelt created two more mega-agencies in the early forties: the Office of Censorship, which targeted groups like the exiles, and, with the help of British intelligence, the Office of Strategic Services, the predecessor of the CIA headed by Hoover's archrival General William ("Wild Bill") Donovan. Although the OSS primarily operated abroad, one of its missions was surveillance, interrogation, and analysis of "enemy alien" groups and others of foreign nationality in the United States, which of course included the refugees from Nazi Germany.

Hoover was protected by "big government" advocate Roosevelt because of his remarkable organizational gifts and his lifelong faith in bureaucratic structure. But equally important to Hoover's success was the fact that, like his counterparts in other countries, his worldview was in tune with the times, which destined him to become guardian of the American Way against radical, subversive, and foreign elements.

Hoover's image of America was shaped by the conservative, Puritan, and Victorian ideals of the white middle class and the conviction that hard work and orderly conduct guaranteed security and advancement; by a religious upbringing that included Sunday school, church choir, and grace at mealtimes; and by a family background of generations of civil servants who were loyal to the state as an institution and as their provider. When the illness of Hoover's father threatened the family with social and financial decline, "J.E." (as he was known to his domineering mother) took a job in the Library of Congress and attended a local night school to earn his law degree. The twenty-two-year-old Hoover gained his first solid post in the Department of Justice in 1917, where he rapidly worked his way up to become director of the Bureau of Investigation (BI), then still a small organization; he remained loyal to that office until his death forty-eight years, sixteen attorneys general, and eight presidents later. Intellectual curiosity, openness to the unfamiliar, travel, and the risks of experiment had no place in his world. He systematically suppressed abnormalities and instincts in himself as in others and interpreted change as threatening.[4] Sorting file cards and cataloging dossiers with endless cross-references was a means to control the randomness of history. The human being, as the source of insecurity, was as much as possible kept to the norm within the director's domain by hierarchical structures of command and organization, standardized training, the demand for absolute loyalty, and strict rules of conduct.

Hoover's career followed a straight course founded on experiences that ideally suited him to monitor the German and Austrian exiles in the forties. When the United States had entered World War I, the young Hoover, preferring to avoid military action in Europe, worked as an "intelligence clerk" and "permit officer" who spied on German "enemy aliens," processed internment and deportation cases, issued travel permits, and examined foreigners who volunteered for military service to obtain U.S. citizenship.

When this work finished at the end of the war, Hoover smoothly shifted to a similar field: the surveillance, internment, and expulsion of foreign anarchists, union members, and Communists. All summer, while the first great Red Scare was looming, young Hoover read every left-wing publication he could find, from the *Communist*

Manifesto to the pamphlets of the Socialist Party of America, and then presented the fruits of his reading to the House Rules Committee in the form of a detailed memorandum. The aim of his report was to establish "that the Communist Party of America . . . openly advocates the overthrow of the Government of the United States by force and violence,"[5] and that its non-American ringleaders could therefore be deported. Hoover described Communism as a doctrine supported only by a few "intellectual perverts"[6] and Communist writings as "atheistic in tendency and immoral."[7] A well-organized team under his direction translated and analyzed hundreds of radical newspaper and magazine articles from home and abroad.

As head of what was known as the Anti-Radical Division (later the General Intelligence Division) of the Bureau of Investigation, Hoover worked with Palmer in 1919–20 staging operations against the Union of Russian Workers. A short time later he engineered the departure from Ellis Island of the ship known as the "Red Ark," which deported to Russia the anarchists Emma Goldman and Alexander Berkman, along with 247 other "blasphemous creatures who not only rejected America's hospitality . . . but also sought . . . to ruin her as a nation of free men."[8] And even after public opinion had shifted against the view that Communism was a German invention and that anarchists who had set off bombs in the United States in 1919 were Bolshevists "aided by Hun money,"[9] Hoover continued to defend the Palmer Raids, a series of night-time police and Bureau forays on the homes and businesses of left-wing activists in which thousands of people, many not even foreigners, were rounded up simultaneously in thirty-two cities, imprisoned, interrogated without trial, and often beaten.

To justify the Red Scare campaign, Hoover dredged up three emergency laws that he would invoke again twenty years later for his surveillance of the German-speaking exiles: the Immigration Act, by which it became a deportable offense for a foreigner to belong to a radical organization; the Espionage Act, which made it illegal to obstruct the military draft and, under certain conditions, to practice political dissent; and the Sedition Act of 1918, which defined it as a crime "to . . . utter, print, write, or publish any disloyal, profane, scurrilous, or abusive language about the form of government of the United States . . . or any language intended to . . . encourage resistance to the United States, or to promote the cause of its enemies" [quoted in 148, p. 14]. Hoover, who all his life was a master at getting around laws and the directives of his superiors, quickly grasped that the vague way these laws were formulated gave him wide latitude for individual interpretation. He used the fuzzy term "loyalty" however the need dictated, defined foreign organizations as enemies of the U.S. Constitution, especially if they supported trade unions, and combined robust police measures like mass arrests, technical surveillance, break-ins, deportations, and the systematic collection of smear evidence with a hazy ideology phrased in colorful language and more concerned with moral and religious than political categories.

Attorney General Harlan Stone no doubt was wise to make Hoover promise, before appointing him director of the Bureau of Investigation in December 1924, that the BI would wage no more campaigns against radicals and Communists and would limit itself to cases involving "violation of the Federal statutes" [quoted in 209, p. 105]. But a decade and a half later, when Thomas Mann, Bertolt Brecht, Lion Feuchtwanger, and other refugee writers were driven by Hitler out of Europe, Hoover discarded this promise, which he had never kept very strictly anyhow. Faced by the bloody conflict in Spain, the Hitler-Stalin pact with its fateful reminders of the Brest-Litovsk Treaty of World War I, and the threat to the United States from the Axis powers, Hoover perceived a fresh need to warn against "alien groups . . . , foreign oppressions and noxious 'isms'" [83, p. 555], which joined with writers "who decry religion and argue that distance from God makes for happiness" [ibid., p. 556] to threaten the American home with a "social world filled with frivolities and surrounded by a confusion of silly theories" [ibid., p. 555]. Once again, Germans were cast in the role of hated "enemy aliens" in whose ranks lurked saboteurs, spies, and agitators who could be brought under control only by keeping close watch on them and threatening them with internment or deportation. If, in addition, these Germans were political liberals, fellow travelers, or genuine Communists, people who in their own countries had been in concentration camps or as refugees had been kept in internment camps or been in trouble with the police in their countries of asylum, that made them doubly or triply suspect in Hoover's eyes.

What Hoover's America was like in the forties, and how readily he could revert to his experiences of the twenties, is apparent from his own speeches and essays. "Vile and vicious forces are today seeking to tear our America asunder," he warned women's clubs, students, the Daughters of the American Revolution, his colleagues in the International Association of Chiefs of Police, and anyone else who would listen, "killing freedom, ravishing justice, and destroying liberty" [quoted in 110, p. 357]. "Foreign interlopers," "international swindlers," and the "espouser of alien philosophies" could not be permitted to hide "behind masquerading fronts" [ibid., p. 360]. "The subversive group—those termites of discontent and discord" [84, p. 736], could be neutralized only by a "holy war" of the kind the FBI waged day and night. "I charge," the FBI boss told the archconservative Daughters of the American Revolution meeting in Washington, "that accusations indicating a purpose on the part of the Federal Bureau of Investigation to become an Ogpu, a Gestapo, a national police, or anything resembling such bodies, emanate . . . from certain anti-American bodies who hope to discredit the FBI as a step in a general plan to disrupt the entire United States" [110, p. 356]. Moreover, his audience would find these "anti-American bodies" among foreigners and writers: "Foreign 'isms' are seeking to engulf Americanism . . . in the underworld of literacy . . . by oral and printed attack, numerous thinly camouflaged organizations of questionable background and endeavor have sought to wash away our national foundation in an ink stream of vilification" [ibid., p. 357].

But the innermost circle of Hoover's Hell was peopled by those "disciplined brigades of . . . conspirators" whom he had always regarded as the chief danger to the American way of life, namely Communists. All members and friends of the Communist Party were "anti-democratic and godless," "treachery" and "deceit" were their tools, "tyranny and oppression" their goals [87, p. 30], and "the slimy wastes of lawlessness" their hiding-place" [82, p. 508]. "No trick is too low for them. They are masters of the type of evasion advocated by that great god of Communism, Lenin" [87, p. 30]. Communists and Fascists were "materialistic, . . . totalitarian, . . . anti-religious, . . . degrading and inhuman. In fact, they differ little except in name. Communism has bred Fascism and Fascism spawns Communism" [85, p. 11]. "Red Fascists," said Hoover, were "akin to disease that spreads like an epidemic" [86, p. 2692] and were now attacking the American government, "which has stood for almost two centuries as a beacon light amid world conflicts" [87, p. 30]. And like an epidemic (as he stated in his lecture before the House Un-American Activities Committee, using his characteristic medical-biological terminology), Communism could be stopped only by quarantine, the best antidote being "vigorous, intelligent, old-fashioned Americanism with eternal vigilance" [86, p. 2692].

By 1945, Hoover had achieved all he only dreamed of in 1920. The young Justice Department clerk had become head of America's most powerful police force, admired by the public and feared by the president. German spies and saboteurs, who had managed to do some damage to the United States in 1917–18, were quickly neutralized in World War II. The FBI, with its typically twentieth-century combination of crude ideology and refined technology, had been aligned with the fears and hopes of Americans, who had little to counter the threats of Fascism, Communism, and foreigners ex-

J. Edgar Hoover with presidents Harry S. Truman *(above)*
and Dwight D. Eisenhower *(following page)*

cept the largely undefined and rapidly crumbling values of the
American Way. The Hatch Act gave Hoover the weapon against subversive elements that he and Attorney General Palmer had once
looked for in vain. And Hoover was ready to tackle the one enemy
that he had not yet overcome: the Communists and their "fronts" and
fellow travelers, whom history itself seemed to have brought back
into his line of fire.

Indeed, the Cold War, atomic espionage, and the Korean conflict made the director's experience in this field more in demand
than ever. The FBI expended great money and effort amassing material in the *Amerasia* magazine spy case [102], the investigation of
government officials like Harry Dexter White and Alger Hiss, and
the case of Ethel and Julius Rosenberg, who were executed for
atomic espionage. They were aided by informants and denun-

ciations from ex-Communists or anti-Communists like Whittaker
Chambers, Elizabeth Bentley, and Louis Francis Budenz. The Los
Angeles Field Office was assigned to feed information to HUAC to
help its investigation of the Hollywood film industry, including its
hearings on Bertolt Brecht and the composer Hanns Eisler, because
the committee acted on the principle "that one of the most effective
weapons against un-American activities is their continuous expo-
sure to the spotlight of publicity" [218, p. 1]. The threat of a third
world war gave Hoover a pretext to step up his efforts to institute a
program of preventive detention.

The FBI boss did not like President Harry Truman, who was uneasy about the HUAC hearings, which he called a "red herring"
[209, p. 273], and about the general political atmosphere during his
term in office. Truman commissioned a study on hysteria and witch
hunts in the history of the United States[10] and warned his country-

men against setting up a police state in America ("We must . . . be on our guard against extremists who urge us to adopt police state measures," he argued).[11] After establishing loyalty boards to investigate the political credentials of federal employees, Truman struggled with Hoover over who would control the investigations. Again and again in speeches and essays, America's top cop played the role of his country's savior from subversive elements. "I do fear," Hoover declared, "so long as school boards and parents tolerate conditions whereby Communists and fellow travelers under the guise of academic freedom can teach our youth a way of life that eventually will destroy the sanctity of the home, that undermines faith in God, that causes them to scorn respect for constituted authority and sabotage our revered Constitution" [86, p. 2692].

Once World War II was over, refugee surveillance quickly became secondary to the domestic witch hunt, and Germany and the Germans vanished from public mention almost overnight. But the refugees, the majority of whom had become naturalized Americans, were not let off the hook, if for no other reason than because the FBI rarely closes a file once it is opened. Bertolt Brecht and the brothers Hanns and Gerhart Eisler were summoned before HUAC hearings in 1947, and the internment of Gerhart, a Communist politician, led to press campaigns and a public stir topped off by his spectacular escape. Five years later, Thomas Mann left the United States for Switzerland after he was repeatedly attacked in right-wing news articles—articles that then found their way into his FBI files—as an "upholder of Soviet amorality"[12] or as "America's Fellow-traveler No. 1."[13] The names of Brecht, Feuchtwanger, Mann, Stefan Heym (author of *Hostages*),[14] and others continued to appear regularly in the annual reports of the Tenney Committee in California. Jewish novelist Lion Feuchtwanger was still watched in his southern California home in the mid-fifties, by HUAC member Richard Nixon among others.

Thomas Mann was one of the last exile authors to leave the New World and return to the Old. Not long after, the frightening spooks of the McCarthy era largely stopped haunting the country. J. Parnell Thomas, who had interrogated Brecht before HUAC, was imprisoned for embezzlement in the same prison where he had sent some of the Hollywood Ten. Joseph McCarthy became politically isolated after his overblown attacks on the U.S. Army, which he claimed had been infiltrated by Communists. Democrat Harry Truman, who had not managed the balancing act between Americans' need for strong internal security and the hysterical excesses of McCarthy, was replaced in the White House by Republican and former general Dwight Eisenhower. Other public figures like Nixon and FBI informant Ronald Reagan used the years of the Communist witch hunt as a springboard for their political careers. The only one for whom nothing changed was Hoover, who, after smashing the Communist Party USA by public hearings and secret measures, found fresh enemies he could interpret as pro-Communist in the civil rights movement of the sixties, opponents of the Vietnam War, and groups advocating social change, which he combated with clandestine operations in a series of counterintelligence campaigns until his death.

Hoover died in 1972 after almost five decades in office. Nixon, in his graveside address four weeks before the Watergate break-ins, summed up the life's work of the FBI chief: "The trend of permissiveness in this country, a trend which Edgar Hoover fought against all his life, a trend which was dangerously eroding our national heritage as a law-abiding people, is now being reversed. The American people today are tired of disorder, disruption and disrespect for law" [quoted in 65, p. 722].

Secret Agencies, Government Bureaus, Surveillance Methods
FEDERAL BUREAU OF INVESTIGATION

The principle of intelligence agencies is to gather as much information as they can. They need a correspondingly extensive apparatus, in both staff and technical aids, and possession and expansion of this apparatus in turn depends on the quantity and importance of data they collect. That the FBI was caught in this vicious circle is evident from its booming expansion in the politically turbulent forties, and from the range of surveillance techniques it learned to deploy. In other words, the scattered handful of refugee writers in the United States and Mexico, whose presence was almost undetectable to the public, came under fire from the FBI not just because they were Germans, and more or less left-wing to boot, but because the Bureau, after its successful campaigns against gangsters like Machine-Gun Kelly, Baby Face Nelson, and Pretty Boy Floyd, was expanding rapidly and needed new enemies. A further motive was that the asylum-seekers talked publicly and proudly of their resistance to state power in their own countries, and sometimes in other countries as well, such as France under the Vichy government that collaborated with the Nazis. This attitude did not recommend them to Hoover's Bureau, whose members had met with the state police of Europe at international congresses in the thirties and swapped experiences in friendly visits with them, at a time when the exiled writers were already on the wanted lists of these very same police.

Since the twenties, Hoover had systematically tightened the dragnet that his agency spread across the United States in its hunt for criminals and subversives. Branches of the Bureau known as field offices were set up in almost every good-sized city, the largest being in New York and Los Angeles, the two main centers of the exile community in America. A small army of employees in the field offices and in Washington was kept busy storing files according to an ingenious numerical system that included more than two hundred categories and is still used in more or less the same form today. The designation 100, for "Domestic Security," was by far the most common one applied to the exiles; 105 stood for "Foreign Counterintelligence," 65 for "Espionage." Without computers or modern copy machines, the G-men wrote endless reports on old-fashioned type-

writers and stored biographical data on index cards—a procedure
that lends itself to mistakes and in one case allowed work at the Los
Angeles Field Office to break down when an earthquake mixed up
the contents of filecard boxes.

"Physical surveillance"—the direct observation of persons,
vehicles, and buildings—was applied to discover how long the
lights stayed on at night when male friends of Klaus Mann visited
his room at New York's Bedford Hotel. Special agents, discreetly
referred to in the files as "confidential national defense informants," spent months eavesdropping on the telephone conversations of Brecht, Berthold Viertel, and others. In at least one case,
agents debated whether to use Misur, short for "microphone surveillance"—planting a bug—in a hotel room to hear the pillow talk
between an exile and his mistress. In so-called pretext interviews,
agents used an excuse to speak to a subject, or to family members,
friends, neighbors, or co-workers, and then more or less adroitly
turn the conversation to political issues or the subject's travel plans.
The notebook of Gregory Kheifetz, the Soviet consul in California
who was often in the company of the German exiles, fell into the
hands of the FBI in an unspecified manner.[1] A "trash cover" (search
of household garbage) was applied to Ruth Berlau in New York in
the hope of uncovering secrets about Brecht. And even in their
homes and offices, refugees like Berlau, Leonhard Frank, Erwin
Piscator, and Ludwig Renn could not feel safe from burglaries and
searches.

Physical and technical surveillance were supplemented by another classic source of information: signed or anonymous denunciations and reports from informants. However, care should be taken
not to attach moral opprobrium to terms like informant or informer,
because what in retrospect may look like smears or betrayal may
have looked like patriotism during the hot and cold wars of the forties and fifties. Ronald Reagan, for example, in later years made no
secret of having supplied the FBI with information about people in

ALIEN

| LEAVE THIS SPACE BLANK |

Name .... MANN, ... Heinrich Ludwig .... Classification ....
(Surname)   (First)   (Middle)

(PLEASE TYPE OR PRINT PLAINLY)

Nationality ..Czech.. .... Color White .... Sex Male .... Reference ....

RIGHT HAND

| 1. Thumb | 2. Index finger | 3. Middle finger | 4. Ring finger | 5. Little finger |

LEFT HAND

| 6. Thumb | 7. Index finger | 8. Middle finger | 9. Ring finger | 10. Little finger |

Impressions taken by: Paul Blott
(Signature of official taking prints)
Date impressions taken ..3/28/41..

Note amputations

Heinrich Ludwig mann
(Alien's signature)

FOUR FINGERS TAKEN SIMULTANEOUSLY

| Left hand | | Left thumb | Right thumb | Right hand |

PLEASE DO NOT FOLD THIS CARD

Hollywood while he was president of the Screen Actors Guild. He reported to the Bureau under the code name T-10; his wife at that time, actress Jane Wyman, was informant T-9 [238, pp. 245ff]. Walt Disney, who gave Thomas Mann's name to the FBI [52, p. 291], and actors Robert Taylor, Robert Montgomery, and Gary Cooper were proud to appear as so-called friendly witnesses before the same House Un-American Activities Committee that interrogated Bertolt Brecht and Hanns Eisler. FBI documents refer to informants by abbreviations like "T-1" or phrases like "reliable confidential informant," which in many cases indicate not a person but another agency. Where names were used, they are blacked out before the release of files.

The dossiers nevertheless indicate that there were spies among the refugees too, who deliberately infiltrated exile circles to collect information. And there were informants, exiles willing to tell the FBI what they knew. Not only for us looking back but for people there at the time, it was sometimes hard to distinguish between statements made without harmful intentions, evidence stemming from real or misguided patriotism, and deliberate betrayal. In the diaries and letters of Thomas Mann, for example, are repeated references to routine visits from FBI and State Department employees asking Mann for information about fellow exiles who had applied for U.S. citizenship, or who had to prove loyalty for some other reason. A more unsavory case was that of staff members at the Bedford Hotel in New York who were asked to tell the FBI about the homosexual contacts of the hotel's permanent guest, Klaus Mann. It is disquieting to read how Thomas Mann allowed himself to be questioned about the famous meeting of a "'Russian-German Committee'" at the home of Austrian theater director Berthold Viertel ("According to Thomas Mann, who was questioned concerning this meeting");[2] how ex-Communist Karl August Wittfogel gave evidence about colleagues to a Senate committee; or conservative journalist and novelist Friedrich Torberg, known to the FBI as "Source A," told the Bureau "that Subject [Brecht] and Eisler were co-authors of a march known as the 'Song of Solidarity'"[3]—a piece of information that HUAC used against Brecht years later. And finally, it is unclear why Erika Mann a number of times voluntarily contacted the FBI between 1940 and the early fifties to give information, a liaison that is without parallel in the files released to me.

On the other hand, no doubt exists about the motives of ex-Communist Ruth Fischer ("Mrs. Fischer asked me to submit to my superiors her offer to supply them with intelligence in return for funds").[4] Also obvious is the activity of a certain Source D, who ap-

pears to have been highly regarded in exile circles and was assigned
to watch Brecht.

> Source D telephonically contacted Special Agent Sidney E.
> Thwing on September 20, 1944 at which time he agreed to
> contact Bert Brecht and question him in regard to his ac-
> tivities in the Free German movement in Mexico and New
> York. . . . In response to direct questions put to him by
> Source D, Brecht stated that he was not connected with the
> Free German movement in Mexico City, nor was he con-
> nected with the Free German movement in Moscow, his
> only connection being with the Council for a Democratic
> Germany in New York. . . . Source D remarked here that he
> personally believed Brecht to be stating the truth in regard
> to the activity of the Free German movement in Los Ange-
> les because he said if there was any organization of that na-
> ture in Los Angeles, Brecht, Feuchtwanger and Thomas
> Mann would have solicited his aid in the formation of such
> an organization because they know that he likes Germany
> as Germany without Nazism, and that he is not a Commu-
> nist. They thus would desire his aid as a "front."[5]

Repeatedly the dossiers include more or less unequivocal statements like "will contact [blacked out], New York City, a German
refugee, who has furnished information about the subject,"[6] "you
are . . . instructed to . . . recontact all of the informants and persons
who have furnished information to you in the past which would be
of value in the deportation proceedings,"[7] or "your cooperation in
furnishing this information to this Bureau is appreciated and a Special Agent from our Detroit Field Office will call upon you in the
very near future to discuss this matter further with you."[8]

And, finally, there is another source of information that tends to
be overshadowed by more spectacular methods, although it takes up
considerable space in the files: printed matter, including more or less

publicly available documents from archives and official agencies. In fact, the magazine articles, books, and biographical and biblio-graphical sketches written by the exiles themselves were often the most important and reliable source of data about their lives, works, and political activities. The files contain frequent notes indicating that the major newspapers routinely and unhesitatingly opened their archives for FBI inspection: "Special Employee [blacked out] ex-amined the morgue of the New York 'Times' on September 23, 1947, and advised that File 780392 is Feuchtwanger's file and it is quite voluminous."[9] Banks informed the FBI about the financial affairs of clients, such as the transfer to Mexico of royalties from Anna Seghers' best-selling novel *The Seventh Cross,* or the payments made by Brecht to his mistress Ruth Berlau, or by Helene Weigel-Brecht to their son Stefan. And even in far-off Mexico, FBI agents had access to government documents: "Subject's file at the Secre-taría de Gobernación," Ludwig Renn's dossier states unabashedly, "is #4/355/1166666."[10]

It became clear to Hoover early in his career as FBI director that his high-quality special agents and wide-ranging surveillance meth-ods could not by themselves win the fight against crime and sub-version. He therefore relied equally on a less spectacular and less publicized arm of his Bureau, the Central Record System, and a sys-tematic reporting format that he organized to maximum efficiency. The system involved standardized "Character of Case" designa-tions like "Alien Enemy Control" that corresponded to classifica-tion numbers. In the numerical classification 100-18112, for exam-ple, 100 stood for "domestic security" and 18112 was the individual file. Photos, carbon copies, books, and oversized documents were stored in "EBF"'s, or Enclosures Behind Files. FBI headquarters used the notation "On Yellow Only" to designate file notes contain-ing particularly confidential or compromising information intended for internal use only. In short, hierarchical thinking was central to the filing system because, given the welter of documents, this was the only way to insure rapid access to the data and the ability to cross-reference the files. Hoover's blend of vague ideology with precise and efficient organization resembles a mindset highly valued since the twenties by totalitarian systems on both sides of the political spectrum.

OFFICE OF STRATEGIC SERVICES (FOREIGN NATIONALITIES BRANCH)

While the FBI almost always acted covertly in gathering information, operations by the Foreign Nationalities Branch of the OSS were overt. Also, the FNB, unlike the FBI, drew conclusions from its material, although not such far-reaching conclusions as the Research and Analysis (R&A) branch of the OSS, which was the organization's "think tank." A third difference between the FNB and the FBI was that OSS director Donovan was sophisticated, a war hero and ladies' man who was friendly with British agents like Ian Fleming, creator of James Bond. He thought in different and more global categories than did Hoover, who never left the United States in his life except for day trips and a short holiday in the Caribbean. Donovan, founder of the Office of Coordinator of Information in July 1941 and OSS director from June 1942, was less interested in short-term counterintelligence work than in creating a modern intelligence agency that would wage a permanent worldwide campaign of subversion, propaganda, and psychological warfare, carry out paramilitary operations, support resistance groups, and work to overthrow governments disliked by the United States.

To fulfill these tasks, Donovan had to furnish political decision makers with the most exact and complete information and analysis. Besides intelligence gathering in other countries, the OSS relied on observation of foreigners who came to the United States as immigrants and exiles and who continued to be publicly active in unions, political organizations, or the arts. At the time, the United States did not yet have specialists with a secret-service background to fill the gaps in the intelligence network. Also, many Americans, including leading members of Roosevelt's government, felt that the tactics of espionage violated the tradition of American democracy and their own sense of fair play. If "Wild Bill" wanted to set up an efficient service to monitor foreign nationals in America and do it fast, he had to draw on sources that his rival Hoover had never tried: former civil servants with experience abroad, academics from the elite East Coast universities, and the leaders of emigré and exile communities.

Thus John Wiley, who had served as a diplomat in the Baltic states and was posted in Austria at the time of the *Anschluss,* was Donovan's choice to lay the groundwork for the Foreign National-ities Branch in autumn 1941, when Donovan was still Coordinator of Information. And DeWitt Poole, who after Wiley's transfer headed the FNB from its founding in late December 1941 until it was disbanded in autumn 1945 and later led the CIA-affiliated Na-tional Committee for a Free Europe, came from a background as a consular official and then as director of the School of Public Affairs at Princeton University. Members of Germany's Frankfurt School for Social Research who had been driven out by the Nazis worked in the famed R&A branch of the OSS, while other German exiles la-bored shoulder to shoulder with American FNB employees and a small army of "volunteer helpers" [231, vol. 1, p. 65] at U.S. uni-versities, drawing up hundreds of reports, summaries, and manuals. Emmy Rado and Charles Friediger (originally Karl B. B. Friediger), whose names appear over and over in the FNB files on Thomas Mann and the Council for a Democratic Germany, came from Switzerland and Austria, respectively.

OSS files hold abundant material on the exiled writers that has not to my knowledge been previously evaluated by researchers. A few examples will show how the FNB operated.[11] Its reports on leading literary figures like Brecht emphasize interpretation rather than facts, as in this analysis from America's "first coordinated intelligence service":[12] "He is primarily a poet and has no knowledge of the political inside story of men and parties."[13] FNB agents and informants, themselves often members of exile or immigrant communities, would attend exile-sponsored public meetings in New York just like the FBI special agents, and like them would read the exile press and pick up information from insiders and informers. OSS agents interrogated prominent exiles about political issues, as will be described below in the chapters on individual writers. One G-man described the publisher Kurt Wolff as "extremely pleasant and quite talkative"[14] in a conversation in which Wolff expressed the view "that the jews now in Germany in the US service, were being so tough and awful with the population that they were stimulating anti-Jewish feeling perhaps the *first time* in Germany!"[15] And Franz Ullstein, formerly one of the most powerful publishers in Germany, who "now lives very simply, in a rather dirty, poorly furnished apartment," was likewise sharply critical of the GI's stationed in his homeland ("conquerors," not "liberators") and of General Eisenhower: "He was *not* complementary to the General, and said that we suffered from a certain form of Fascism ourselves over here, and did not realize it as yet."[16]

The FNB's main interest in the refugee writers was to know if they planned an organizational merger of the various "Free German" groups. The FNB focused on Thomas Mann as the representative of a different, better Germany; the links between the exile colonies in the United States and Mexico; the mixed reactions of the exiles to the founding of the Communist-dominated National Free Germany Committee in Moscow; and the unhappy history of the New York–based Council for a Democratic Germany. Agents regularly evaluated exile publications like *Freies Deutschland,* printed in Mexico; *Aufbau,* published in New York; and New York's German-American newspaper, the *New Yorker Staatszeitung und Herold.* It seems an irony of history that in 1946, director Fritz Lang made the film *Cloak and Dagger* celebrating the work of the OSS, only to be blacklisted a short time later by anti-Communist witch-hunters, while two of his co-workers on the film were screenwriters Albert Maltz and Ring Lardner, both brought to trial as members of the Hollywood Ten.

IMMIGRATION AND NATURALIZATION SERVICE

Whereas the FBI and OSS could decide which exiles to investigate and why, the Immigration and Naturalization Service had the automatic duty to keep a file on every foreigner entering the United States. The immigration laws, with their quotas, restrictions, and controversial asylum policy, defined the main part of INS duties. But the INS forms, which at first glance look like dry formalities, hold a wealth of biographical detail and give insight into the background and everyday lives of the exiles, thus making a valuable addition to the records of the secret services. Three features should be noted. First, the INS section that processes applications under the Freedom of Information Act and Privacy Act blacks out little information before releasing files. Second, although the INS relied on its own investigators and on information from outside sources, it was flooded with material from the exiles themselves, who filled in quantities of forms and were interviewed for hours or days at a time. Finally, because the INS worked with hard data, it played an important role in investigations by the FBI, ONI, and MID.

Exiles seeking asylum in the United States or passing through New York on their way to Mexico encountered the INS at Ellis Island—the infamous "Isle of Tears" where fugitives from Europe normally first set foot—and sometimes in Los Angeles, where the main job of the agency was to deal with refugees seeking a visa extension or applying for citizenship. At desolate spots along the U.S.-Mexico border like Nogales, Arizona, and San Ysidro and Calexico in California, novelists like Feuchtwanger, Heinrich Mann, and Döblin returned to the United States with immigrant visas that prolonged their stay indefinitely and were required before applying for citizenship. Mann family members traveled back into the United States through Canada for the same purpose. The ports of entry at Laredo and Eagle Pass in Texas played a role in the histories of Egon Erwin Kisch, Bodo Uhse, and Anna Seghers.

The INS opened files on the exiles as soon as they arrived in the United States. Preliminary visas or transit permits were obtained from U.S. embassies abroad, which unlike the INS worked for the State Department. Normally, INS files were closed when an exile became a naturalized citizen or left the country again. Naturalized Americans remained under INS investigation if their political activities might give cause to revoke their citizenship. Emigrés had to deal with the INS or State Department if, like Brecht and others, they applied for a "reentry permit" upon leaving the country, or if, like Spanish Civil War veteran Alfred Kantorowicz, they met with barriers when they tried years later to revisit their former host nation.

For most exiles, Ellis Island was their first point of contact with the much-feared INS. Suspicious inspectors would hold embarrassing interviews with people who had just narrowly escaped the Gestapo, asking them about their imprisonment under the Nazis or their internment in French camps, their financial and family affairs, and their health. A maze of interdepartmental investigative committees, review committees, and a board of appeals (with representatives from the FBI, State Department, and military intelligence as well as the INS) examined the political background of the new arrivals and threatened them with deportation. The relatively small group of exiles like Thomas Mann or dramatist Carl Zuckmayer who had fame, money, or contacts to ease their paths faced few hurdles once they entered the country, except to report for the draft, which became compulsory during the war, to apply early for permission to travel, and to wait out the five years until they could seek naturalization.

But most exiles left Ellis Island with a short-term visa that might expire in as little as thirty or sixty days, often burdened with further restrictions like being forbidden to take a job. For them, life in the New World meant a never ending stream of applications for visa extensions—Hans Marchwitza's sixth extension was approved in 1946— of uneasy waiting for the decisions of review and appeal boards, of petitions and letters to influential Americans asking for a recommendation. A few of the most unlucky, like Anna Seghers and her family, were turned away and had to catch the next steamer to other destinations, in this case Mexico. Those who waited their five years and then applied for U.S. citizenship not only had to fill out the required INS forms, find three sponsors, and furnish documents that could only rarely be obtained from Nazi-occupied, bombed-out Europe, but also to undergo investigation by the INS working closely with the FBI, military intelligence, HUAC, and the State Department. Even exiles who had been naturalized years earlier but whose loyalty was still in question were kept under observation and threatened with loss of their citizenship, as was Viertel, or with deportation like Thomas Mann.

INS files, interview records, and forms tend to be factual because serious penalties attached to making false statements, and interviews took place under oath. The INS forms contain information about parents, national origin, and dates of birth that is often difficult to glean from other sources, especially for lesser known authors. The INS learned that Klaus Mann used to be paid $50 to $125 for a lecture, and when Klaus chattered on about his parents' finances and the monthly allowance they gave him, the INS wrote it all down. One section of the forms was devoted to physical peculiarities, like the mole on Viertel's cheek and the scar on Brecht's face. Jewish exiles evidently felt no hesitation about listing themselves as "Hebrew" on the line referring to race, except for Feuchtwanger who wrote "white." Little inaccuracies about the refugees' height and weight on INS forms and in interview records mostly result from the fact that the new arrivals were unfamiliar with the American system of measurement.

Finally, it should be said that apart from spectacular cases like those of Communist politician Gerhart Eisler and his brother Hanns, which were widely reported by the press, and a relatively small number in which petitions for naturalization or reentry permits were refused, no exile writers were brutally treated or seriously hurt by actions of the INS. All the same, Thomas Mann's decision to return to Europe seems at least in part to have resulted from the notorious Immigration and Nationality Act[17] (the McCarran-Walter Act), which he believed could result in revocation of his U.S. citizenship: "K. prefers to get our passports renewed at once. Not unlikely that I may be expatriated, traceable back to the Weimar trip" [132, p. 296]. Other exiles may have hesitated, based on their experiences with the INS, to revisit the United States once they had gone back to Germany. Yet in the three dozen or so dossiers that the INS turned over to me, I found no indication that any deportation, long-term internment, or attempt to revoke U.S. citizenship was actually carried out.

DEPARTMENT OF STATE

Exiles were watched and if necessary controlled by the State Department as well as by the FBI, OSS, and INS. Assistant Secretary of State Adolf Berle was a useful contact for Thomas Mann, among others. The Division of Mexican Affairs in the State Department's Division of American Republics and the Division of Foreign Activity Correlation were intensively involved with the exile colony in Mexico. Secretary of State Cordell Hull intervened personally over important issues like mail censorship, the international role of the various Free German groups, and petitions from the highly respected Thomas Mann. The numerous letters and documents that Hoover sent to Berle labeled "personal and confidential" or "secret" are evidence that the FBI chief did not limit himself to intelligence gathering as he liked to claim but took an active role in politics, just as Berle, whose domain in theory was foreign affairs, did not hesitate to ask the FBI to monitor "subversive activities" on the domestic scene.

Predictably, besides refugee aid the concerns of the State Department were identical to those of the FBI and OSS: the organizing activities of the Communist exile group in Mexico and emigré writers' plans for Germany's future. Lengthy reports by U.S. embassy staff in Mexico, especially embassy secretary William K. Ailshie, witness the close cooperation between the State Department, the FBI's Special Intelligence Service operating in Latin America, and army and navy intelligence in monitoring the politically and culturally active exiles in Mexico who were grouped around Anna Seghers, Ludwig Renn, Bodo Uhse, and Egon Erwin Kisch. The U.S. embassy in Sweden, where Free German groups were active as in other unoccupied countries of Europe, reported that detailed conversations had taken place between Free Germany and Willy Brandt, later chancellor of Germany, about their country's future.[18] The American legation in Ankara forwarded a letter to Thomas Mann from Ernst Reuter, later mayor of West Berlin from 1950 to 1953, containing an emotional appeal to Mann to rally the forces of a better Germany. In autumn 1943 the OSS and the State Department sabotaged the preparations to form a committee under Mann's leadership.

Following the successful Allied landing in Normandy, the attention of the State Department shifted from the exiles' schemes for a new Germany to what they would contribute if they returned home. The department kept files on writers like Brecht, worker-author Hans Marchwitza, and the refugees in Mexico, who planned to return to Europe as fast as they could. Records were made of the travel plans and speeches of writers in exile, especially if, like Thomas Mann, they had any relations with the Soviet Occupation Zone or, later, East Germany. The State Department continued to track exiles like F. C. Weiskopf, who took a diplomatic post in

Czechoslovakia after 1945, and those who played a public role in East Germany, as did Seghers, Renn, and Uhse. And the department was officially required to keep records of cases in which refugees who returned to their homeland gave up their U.S. citizenship, or lost it automatically after five years' absence, like Ferdinand Bruckner, Viertel, and Zuckmayer.

OFFICE OF NAVAL INTELLIGENCE AND MILITARY INTELLIGENCE DIVISION OF THE U.S. ARMY

In contrast to the State Department files in the National Archives in Washington, which for the most part are available to the public without restriction, the archives and practices of the two military intelligence services, the Office of Naval Intelligence and the Military Intelligence Division of the U.S. Army, are largely secret, and relatively few files are released.

Traditionally, the ONI and MID operated abroad, including in Mexico and, after 1945, Germany. ONI attachés were given four-week training courses by Hoover's "top Communist-hunter Kenneth McIntire" [50, p. 11]. More than two hundred naval reserve officers served as mail censors during the war [222, p. 399]. A series of military-service reports preserved in State Department files, and cross-references in the FBI files, indicate that military attachés in Mexico monitored the exiles there, concentrating on the Free Germany Movement, just like their colleagues from the SIS and State Department. The INS, when processing petitions for naturalization, routinely asked ONI and MID if they had any negative information on the candidates. MID put considerable effort into investigating the loyalty and associates of exiles like Stefan Heym and Klaus Mann who, after entering the United States, applied for military intelligence training to serve in the army.

After 1945, U.S. Navy and Army intelligence became active in Germany, where they monitored homecoming exiles. A special "Political (or Counter Subversion) Team" was set up by the Counter Intelligence Corps (CIC) to watch "targets dealing with right- and left-wing political activities in all the Zones of Germany" [173, p. 273], a group that of course included others besides the writers in exile. In Berlin, the 66th CIC Group of the U.S. Army in Europe collected data about Heinrich Mann's contacts with East Germany's Aufbau publishers and the German-Czech novelist Weiskopf, who "has written . . . 'Party Line' books for Dietz Verlag."[19] The "Security Group" of the U.S. Army in Frankfurt fantasized that Alfred Kantorowicz had traveled illegally from Bremen to Berlin to meet "secretly" with Stalin's chief of security Lavrenty Beria.[20] And as long as fifteen years after the war ended, U.S. Army and Air Force intelligence still tracked the movements of Oskar Maria Graf, Leonhard Frank, and Fritz von Unruh.

OFFICE OF CENSORSHIP

The Office of Censorship was founded immediately after Pearl Harbor in December 1941 to monitor "mail, cable, radio or other means of transmission passing between the United States and any foreign country."[21] The legal basis for the office was the first War Powers Act of 1941, which—a bad omen for German exiles—was passed unchanged from the similar anti-German act of World War I vintage. In two years, an enterprise that had begun with a few retired soldiers "sitting around a table in the Post Office building, slitting open a few letters at random" [79] turned into a gigantic apparatus stretching from Balboa in Panama to Miami, Los Angeles, and the Postal Censorship Station in New York. It grew from 728 to 1,678 "examiners" between March and December 1942 alone, and commanded the services of 2,006 translators in 73 languages. Agents of the Office of Censorship were sent to Mexico in June 1942 to coordinate surveillance of postal traffic crossing the border and to stay informed about Mexico's mail censorship, which was allowed by Mexican law. The FBI, INS, and Office of Censorship worked with Mexican authorities to stop "mail drops" and couriers at the border crossings in Texas, New Mexico, Arizona, and California. Executive Order 8985 of 19 December 1941 provided that mail between third-party countries was subject to censorship if it came into contact with U.S. sovereign territory, for example on board a ship. (The FBI's call for a law to control homing pigeons presumably did not affect exile history!)

To censor a refugee's mail, the FBI merely petitioned to have him placed on a "National Censorship Watch List" for thirty, sixty, or ninety days. A vague suspicion of subversive or un-American activities sufficed for placement on the list. Renn, Seghers, and others were put on a "Special Watch List" on suspicion of smuggling information in letters that were coded or written in invisible ink. Since all correspondence with foreign countries was automatically subject to strict censorship in wartime (for Americans as well as foreigners), anyone in Mexico or the United States who corresponded with an exile across the border knew that his mail was not safe from prying eyes. But exiles in Mexico probably did not suspect that cooperation between the Mexican authorities and their powerful neighbors to the north went so far that even correspondence with third countries—letters from Mexico to Chile or the Soviet Union—landed on desks in the Office of Censorship.

Of all the intelligence and surveillance networks that were expanded or built during the Roosevelt administration, the Office of Censorship reached most directly into the daily lives of the exiles. Letters with important personal and business information lay on the censors' desks for days or weeks at a time, and books and magazines were not delivered because their contents were classified as subversive. Intimate communications ended up in the files of the FBI and other agencies in the form of summaries or translations by the mail censors. Political debates were waged publicly, so to speak, in full view of agents and the State Department who read the mail im-

Los Angeles - 13 - California
May 18, 1944

Director, FBI

RE: FREE GERMAN ACTIVITY IN
THE LOS ANGELES AREA;
INTERNAL SECURITY - R

35583

Dear Sir:

REFER 5 IS

Since correspondence between the Free German group in
Mexico and persons in the Los Angeles area has been carried on as
reflected in previous reports in this case, it is recommended that
the following subjects be placed on the National Censorship Watch
List for ninety days:

1. HEINRICH MANN, 301 South Swall Drive, Los Angeles.

2. BERTOLT BRECHT, 1063 - 26 Street, Santa Monica,
California.

3. LION FEUCHTWANGER, 520 Paseo Miramar, Pacific
Palisades, California.

4. ▮▮▮▮▮▮▮▮▮▮▮▮▮▮▮▮▮▮▮▮▮▮▮▮▮

5. ▮▮▮▮▮▮▮▮▮▮▮▮▮▮▮▮▮▮▮▮▮▮▮▮▮

6. ▮▮▮▮▮▮▮▮▮▮▮▮▮▮▮▮▮▮▮▮▮▮▮▮▮

7. ▮▮▮▮▮▮▮▮▮▮▮▮▮▮▮▮▮▮▮▮▮▮▮▮▮

b7c

Very truly yours,

RECORDED

100-5143-25

FEDERAL BUREAU OF INVESTIGATION
SAC

AUG 16 1944

U. S. DEPARTMENT OF JUSTICE

KFL:AH
100-21367

7 SEP 13 1944

DECLASSIFIED ON 2-2-81
BY SP1 CSK/abb

mediately or after it had passed through Hoover's office. An attempt by the State Department to isolate the Free Germans in Mexico by totally annihilating their mail failed less for legal or moral reasons than political considerations: Washington feared that Moscow might resent its ally severing postal communication between Mexico and the Soviet Union, and also the Office of Censorship jealously refused to be regulated by another agency.

The efficiency of the Office of Censorship, and the requests of the FBI and other agencies for censorship watch lists, insured that few letters exchanged between exiles in Mexico and the United States between 1942 and 1946 arrived at their destination without first being read by others. Censors checked the names of correspondents using an ingenious indexing system, and in 1944 they processed some twenty thousand letters a day in Los Angeles alone. Special departments investigated selected mail from Mexico and South America looking for coded material or secret writing, and they occasionally made mistakes that destroyed the letters: "Since the submitted specimens have been permanently stained in the course of secret ink examination . . . they are being retained in the files of the laboratory."[22] To make work more efficient and pleasant for the censors, who although "sincerely patriotic" were for the most part hastily trained, the Miami office set up a so-called ABC system ("Alphabetically by Countries") in which a particular censor was assigned to track the mail of specific individuals for an extended period so as to become thoroughly familiar with their affairs.

For the FBI, the forms filled in by the mail censors seem to have been among the best sources of detailed, reliable information about the political activities, literary work, private and professional relations, and human strengths and weaknesses of their "subjects." The files of Heinrich Mann, Brecht, Seghers, and others, for example, show that a careful record was kept each time one of them received exile publications like *Freies Deutschland* and *Internationale Literatur,* or Russian publications like *Pravda* and *Moscow News.* The

G-men tried to monitor Thomas and Klaus Mann by talking with the post office in Princeton and the postman in Pacific Palisades. Censors who read German translated letters from Seghers about the deportation of her Jewish mother from Mainz to a concentration camp. Ruth Berlau's correspondence with Brecht gave the FBI information about the playwright's love life: "o, bertolt, your letter! if you only could know, how much good it has done. again this time you understood everything. again this time you have been so very kind. and to think, that I was afraid, that you might have thought it terrible to find that I had a round-trip ticket. bertolt. my dear bertolt . . . it was a good thing from you to let me travel this way with a sleeper and with meals . . . it is snowing now . . . it blends well with the furcoat . . . I have to thank you for all the clothes."[23] One examiner at the Office of Censorship made the first English translation, and not a bad one either, of Seghers' story *The Excursion of the Dead Girls* as an attachment to Laboratory Report D-15460 C4. His colleague no. 12198 in New York had the dubious pleasure of having to read a 452-page manuscript by Hans Marchwitza and summarize the contents in a few lines.

HOUSE UN-AMERICAN ACTIVITIES COMMITTEE

The FBI, OSS, State Department, military intelligence, and the Office of Censorship were the most significant collectors of information on the German-speaking exiles in the United States and Mexico. Their work was supplemented by other government bodies, most of which scanned the exile community only sporadically or in response to a specific inquiry. Most prominent of this group were the Un-American Activities Committee set up by the U.S. House of Representatives and its equivalent in the California state senate, the Tenney Committee.[24] HUAC merits special attention for two reasons: first, because its declared goal was to cleanse the United States of liberal, left-wing, and Communist ideas, which many of the exiles represented, and, second, because the committee had its own staff of intelligence gatherers who amassed files not only on Brecht and Eisler but on exiles like Stefan Heym and Thomas and Erika Mann.

The House Un-American Activities Committee flourished between 1938 and 1944 under the leadership of Martin Dies, and when the Cold War broke out it was revived by John Rankin, J. Parnell Thomas, Richard Nixon, and their political confreres in the House. The two opponents that Dies targeted—at least officially—during HUAC's first term of operations were the German American Bund, a Nazi organization, and the Communists. By the time of the Cold War only the Communists remained, and their "fronts,"[25] as defined by HUAC, included the Hollywood film industry. Exiles like Brecht and screen composer Hanns Eisler were summoned to Washington as "unfriendly witnesses" (although Brecht turned out to be quite willing to talk and not especially unfriendly) and questioned in a blaze of cameras and microphones by HUAC chairman Thomas and his assistant Robert Stripling, who asked them again and again the notorious question, "Are you now or have you ever been a member of the Communist Party?" to which the only acceptable answer was yes or no. Other writers, like Thomas Mann and Erwin Piscator, lived in constant fear of being called to testify before the committee.

Hoover, who was as suspicious of HUAC as he was of any competing organization in the "internal security" arena, signaled that he was willing to cooperate once he realized that fellow travelers were exposed and stripped of influence more effectively in public hearings than by the covert activity of his special agents. From then on he cautiously and deliberately fed the committee selected files, including some on the German exiles. Former FBI agents offered HUAC their services as "investigators." Jack Tenney, the regional witchfinder-general in California, headed the Senate Fact-Finding Committee on Un-American Activities, HUAC's counterpart in Sacramento, where he compiled lists of suspicious persons and organizations and expressed his gratitude that Hoover had exposed the godless philosophy of Communism during the war by stressing the difference "between respecting our ally Russia, and respecting those within our country who would destroy all that we believe in."[26]

The FBI lent the same sort of official help to other government bodies as to HUAC. On the local and regional level, city police forces sometimes had "Alien Squads" and "Red Squads" [49; 169] that cooperated with Hoover's G-men. These monitored Free German activities in the Los Angeles area, for instance ("files of the Anti-Subversive Detail of the Los Angeles Police Department were checked").[27] Local draft boards, where all men fit for military duty had to report, gave the FBI a sample of F. C. Weiskopf's signature, and the information that philosopher Ernst Bloch was working on his doctorate at Harvard. The Los Angeles Coroner's Office supplied data about the suicide of Heinrich Mann's wife.

The tangle of bureaucracies and information sources grows denser moving from the local to the national level, where official and semi-official government agencies seem to proliferate endlessly. Security or loyalty tests had to be passed by any exile who worked with such an agency, for example German-Czech author Johannes Urzidil when he assisted the Voice of America, Alfred Kantorowicz in the Office of War Information, and Berthold Viertel in the Office of the Coordinator of Information. The FBI procured from the much-feared Internal Revenue Service copies of Feuchtwanger's tax returns for 1941 to 1945, and it learned from the Alien Property Custodian what royalties Seghers had earned from *The Seventh Cross* and the MGM film based on it. Information on other exiles was traded between the FBI and James G. McDonald's President's Advisory Committee on Political Refugees, the Senate Judiciary Committee's Internal Security Subcommittee (known as the McCarran Committee), the Special Defense Unit of the Justice Department, and after the war with the Office of the U.S. Political Advisor to Germany in Berlin. On the other hand, the files released to me show no evidence that the FBI, CIA, or military intelligence services cooperated with official agencies in postwar Germany in keeping tabs on exiles who returned home, although this does not necessarily preclude such activity.

Anatomy of a File

The FBI and secret services may at times have showed imagination in handling their targets; but the number and format of the forms where they recorded and exchanged the results of their investigations were intentionally limited. Three of the most important and frequently used forms will be described briefly in this section, using concrete examples from FBI files on Bertolt Brecht and Heinrich Mann.

The first two documents shown here (pp.42–43) are the cover and end page of an FBI report—forms that can be found in almost all FBI dossiers. Reports were prepared at irregular intervals by a special agent assigned to a case by a field office, which would pass any new information to FBI headquarters and other field offices. The regional Special Agent in Charge—at the L.A. Field Office it was R. B. Hood (15)—was responsible for signing reports to headquarters. Because his work was often passed on to other agencies, the reporting agent protected his most important sources of information with code names like "LABB-1" or "Source J" (22). The names of additional informants (11, 14) and the name of the special agent handling the case (6) were blacked out by the FBI before the files were released to me.

The Los Angeles Field Office (1) was responsible for Brecht's case and prepared the report on him on 22 May 1943 (4, 3). The period of observation was 19 April to 15 May 1943 (5). The subject's name was routinely accompanied by all known variations, pseudonyms, nicknames, variant spellings, and so on (7). The "Character

FEDERAL BUREAU OF INVESTIGATION

Form No. 1
THIS CASE ORIGINATED AT LOS ANGELES (1)   FILE NO. 100-18112 (2)

REPORT MADE AT	DATE WHEN MADE	PERIOD FOR (5)	REPORT MADE BY (6)
LOS ANGELES (3)	5/22/43 (4)	5/15/43	CVB

TITLE	CHARACTER OF CASE
BERTOLT EUGEN FRIEDRICH BRECHT, with aliases, Eugen Berthold Friedrich Brecht, Bert Brecht, Berdat. (7)	ALIEN ENEMY CONTROL - C (8)

(9) SYNOPSIS OF FACTS: Confidential National Defense Informant ▓▓▓▓ advises Subject made moving picture with Communist tendencies, which he showed in Moscow in 1932. Source ▓▓▓▓ advises Subject is friend of numerous persons in SALKA VIERTEL's circle, who are known to have Communist tendencies. BRECHT's radical poetry is known to have been used recently by foreign group on program in New York. Advertisements in refugee weekly "AUFBAU" indicate BRECHT still active in New York, although Source ▓▓▓▓ advises he is expected to return to Los Angeles soon.

(10)
(11)

- P -

(12) REFERENCE: Report of Special Agent ▓▓▓▓▓▓▓▓ Los Angeles, dated March 30, 1943.
(13)   Letter to Bureau dated April 16, 1943.

DETAILS:

On April 19, 1943, Confidential National Defense Informant ▓▓▓▓ advised that to his knowledge Subject was in Moscow in 1932 to show a picture with Communist tendencies, entitled "KUHLEWAMPE". Informant stated that this picture had as its subject the unemployed who lived in a tent colony near Berlin. HANNS EISLER wrote the music accompanying this picture. Informant saw Subject in Moscow at that time, although he was not positive that he had seen EISLER as well.

(14)

On April 19, 1943, Source ▓▓ advised that Subject's wife was frequently invited to social affairs put on by SALKA VIERTEL, 165 Mabery, Santa

APPROVED AND FORWARDED (15)	SPECIAL AGENT IN CHARGE	DO NOT WRITE IN THESE SPACES (17)	RECORDED
(16) COPIES DESTROYED 5-11-			INDEXED
COPIES OF THIS REPORT 5 Bureau 1 New York (Info) (18) 4 Los Angeles			

JUN 9 1943

42

LA 100-18112

(19)

UNDEVELOPED LEADS

THE NEW YORK FIELD DIVISION

AT NEW YORK CITY, will identify the occupants of 8 East 41st
Street, from which address BERT BRECHT receives letters regularly, one of
which is known to have contained a document relating to the political economy
of Postwar Germany. (20)

(21)
Will spot check the activities of BRECHT and BERLAU while in
New York City. It is desired that this office be advised in advance of the
return of BRECHT and BERLAU to Los Angeles. This lead has previously been
furnished the New York Office by letter.

THE LOS ANGELES FIELD DIVISION

AT LOS ANGELES, CALIFORNIA, will continue to report the results
of the mail cover and censorship stops on BERT BRECHT. Will maintain contact
with Confidential Informants ████████ LA BB-1 and Source J. (22)

Will maintain contact with ████ CONF INFT ████ for information concerning
████████ BERT BRECHT ████████. Will examine the United States
District Court records concerning the naturalization status of RUTH BERLAU.

For future reference it is to be noted that the local office of (23)
Immigration and Naturalization Service is unable to locate its files pertaining
to BERLAU. These files are identified as 23/109276 and 23-L-9280.

Will ascertain the identity of K. L. CERTAIN, 237½ West 5th (24)
Street, whose telephone was called from the BRECHT residence on August 13 and
September 22, 1944.

AT LONG BEACH, CALIFORNIA, will check the Immigration and (25)
Naturalization records of RUTH BERLAU at the Immigration and Naturalization
Service at Terminal Island, California.

Two copies of this report are being furnished the San Francisco
Field Division inasmuch as BERT BRECHT is a suspect in the Comrap Case, of
which the San Francisco office is the office of origin.

A copy of this report is being furnished the New Orleans
Field Division inasmuch it contains information concerning KARL KORSCH, (26)
Professor at The Tulane University of Louisiana, New Orleans.

of Case," here listed as "Alien Enemy Control - G" (8), with "G"
standing for "German," helped the reader classify the file quickly
and might be changed a number of times during an investigation.
Two file designations are shown on the report: the Los Angeles "File
No." 100-18112 at upper right (2), and the headquarters number
100-190707, bottom center and almost illegible in this copy (17).

Every report begins with a "Synopsis of Facts" (9) summarizing the most important information. If necessary, the "Reference" section (12) lists older documents or other dossiers that are relevant. "Details" (13) then leads into the actual report. A notation on the lower left cover page states how many copies are going to other FBI offices (18). The official stamp "Copies destroyed" with the date 11 May 1954 (16) refers to routine FBI disposal of excess paperwork, mostly duplicates and lengthy appendices, and occasionally of entire files. A handwritten notation signed "FOIA/Ed" on the left-hand border (10) shows that in 1974 Brecht's file was released to other researchers, including his biographer James Lyon.

Almost every FBI report concludes with an "Administrative Page," or sometimes just "Undeveloped Leads" (19). Here the reporting agent sets out under geographical or other systematic headings the steps that he believes should be taken to follow up the investigation. In Brecht's case, the agent recommends that the New York office identify the occupants of a building from which letters are being sent to Brecht (20), and that periodic checks be made on Brecht and Ruth Berlau while they are in New York (21). In Los Angeles, he recommends continued monitoring of Brecht's mail and telephone conversations ("Confidential Informant [blacked out] LABB-1" [22]), the collection of information from the INS about Berlau (23, 25), and investigation of K. L. Certain, who received two phone calls from Brecht's home (24). Also, the New Orleans Field Office is to be kept informed because Karl Korsch, who is teaching in that city, is known to be an associate of Brecht's who discussed Marxist ideas with him in the twenties (26).

The third document here is an Office of Censorship form on Heinrich Mann summarizing a letter to him from Communist Party official Paul Merker. This form, which the Office of Censorship passed to the FBI, shows the attention and expertise that were devoted to examining the exiles' mail. Three features are distinctive. First is the discrepancy between the small-print "Special Notice" from Director Byron Price at the bottom of the form (16), which

OFFICE OF CENSORSHIP
UNITED STATES OF AMERICA

CONFIDENTIAL
POSTAL CENSORSHIP

(1) Record No. SA-184304

Page 1 of 2 pages

FROM:

PAUL MERKER)
TAMAULIPAS 129-6)(FROM INSIDE)
MEXICO, D.F.

(2) LIST: SWI/23 -Bfn-4600

TO:

MR. HEINRICH MANN
301 SO. SWALL DRIVE,
LOS ANGELES, CALIFORNIA. **(3)** L.B.L WATCH LIST

LIST: NONE

Date of communication	Date of postmark	Kind of mail	Mail No.	Register No.	Serial No.
(4) OCT. 11, 1943	**(5)** OCT. 13, 1943	AIR			

Language	Previously censored by	Station distribution	**(7)**	SECURITY DIVISION DISPOSAL ORIG. ORIGINAL COMMUNI-
ENGLISH **(6)**	NONE	/		Mr. Watson

Previous relevant records	For interoffice use			H	Mr. Alden
			DR	R	Mr. Buckley
SA-183183	To be photographed	Photo No.	To whom photograph is to be sent	C	Mr. Burton
EP-5579					MB. Callan
	(8)			RS	Mr. Carson
	NO			Sent with comment to	Mr. Cunningham
					Mr. Fletcher
					Mr. Strickland

Division (or section)	Table	Examiner	D. A. C.	Reviewer	Examination date	Typing date
REG.	**(9)** 3	**(10)** 2258	2039	**(11)** 2025	OCT. 16, 1943	**(13)** 10/18/43

DR
use only
(14)

1-IC
6-IC
1-EPC
1-SC
1-FBI
1-CNI
2-SD
3-OSS
7-MID
2-OWI
1-C.IA
1-CAH(IR)
27)

COMMENT

RESIDENT OF MEXICO (SWI-23, Bfn 4600) DISCUSSES BOOKS AND A NEW GERMAN NEWSPAPER

Writer acknowledges and thanks addressee for his letter of Sept. 26 article enclosed. Writer states that on July 29, he sent addressee a letter and enclosed a check to cover the balance due addressee for his fee in connection with the Terror Book.

Writer says "Lidice" will be published Oct. 18, 1943. Writer advises that a recent Government decree prohibits future exportation of clothbound books; therefore addressee's copies will have to be paper-bound. Writer will send addressee sufficient copies immediately after publication. Writer states (Quote): "The proposal concerning your autogram was meant this way: We would like you to write your name on small slips of paper and send us these slips, which would then be pasted into the books. Two further copies of the Black Book Against The Nazi Terror' will be sent to you immediately. Likewise I have arranged that after publication of No. 12 of the 'Free Germany' a bound annual set will be sent to you. The delivery of the magazine has been rather irregular lately and unpleasant interruptions have occurred." Writer reminds addressee of his proposal that "El Libro Libre" (Bj 4600) would like to publish "Lidice" in Spanish writer says friends of the publishing house believe a large number of copies could be sold.

Writer states (Quote): "The movement has made further good progress. Meanwhile, as you probably know, a committee in London has been founded, so that the pioneer work that could be done from here with your kind support evidently begins to bear fruit. I hope that you, Dear friend Heinrich Mann, have received meanwhile the protocol of the first national conference of the movement, which will give you a comprehensive picture of its development in Latin-America. Meanwhile we have started here another small newspaper in the German language, the 'Democratic Post', which is being distributed in Central-America. We will send you the paper regularly."

Writer sends best wishes to addressee's wife along with addressee.

(15) EXAMINER'S NOTE: Writer is secretary of Comite Latino Americano De Alemanes Libres (Ban 4600), Mexico, D.F., which is active in publishing the monthly magazine "Freies Deutschland," operate's a German publishing house "El Libro Libre (Bj 4600), and sponsored the first congress of the movement Free Germany (Ban 4600-7000-1064). The publishing house has published numerous German books from various writers, including addressee. (SA-183183) On July 29, 1942, addressee was informed by Walter Janka, The Free Book, Aptdo 10214, Mexico, D.F., calls for confidential treatment of the private contents of Mann's letters, and the "Security Division Routing" stamp (7) and long list of agencies being sent copies: the FBI, ONI, OSS, MID, OWI, and so on (14). Second, it is impressive how skillfully the report combines quotations with summaries of the key passages in Merker's letter, and how familiar "Examiner 2258" (10) and "Reviewer 2025" (11) appear to be with the exile communities in Mexico and the United States. For example, the "Examiner's Note" (15), which is typical of such notes, shows knowledge of the backgrounds of Merker and Mann, points out the significance of the organizations referred to, and mentions previous reports on censored mail. Third, and important for authors and recipients of letters, the Office of Censorship showed exceptional efficiency compared with other agencies investigating the exiles, as the work of the censors at "Table 3" (9) amply demonstrates: Merker's letter, dated 11 October (4), was stamped by the Mexican postal authorities just two days later (5), by the 16th it had been opened (12), and processing was completed within forty-eight hours (13).

Other data listed on the cover page are self-explanatory: "Record No." (1) and "List" (2) ensure that this summary can be located at any time in the archives of the Office of Censorship. No translator was needed because Merker wrote in English (6), probably to make the censors' work easier and thus to speed delivery of the letter. The notation that Form OC-8a was recently revised (17) makes clear that the Office of Censorship, a fairly new agency, was still having teething problems. And the stamp "F.B.I. Watch List" (3) indicates that the letter was not opened as part of a routine operation but because Hoover's Bureau was actively interested in the mail of Merker and Mann.

2

The FBI and the Exiles
in Los Angeles

Witch Hunts in Paradise

WITH THE OUTBREAK OF WORLD WAR II, Los Angeles rapidly became the leading center for German writers in exile in the Americas
and, with New York and Mexico, a key area for exile surveillance.
After the annexation of Austria and the occupation of Czechoslovakia in 1938, new floods of refugees had poured into France,
Britain, and Switzerland, and after 1939 these countries too were
under threat from the Germans. Exiles who had just managed with
great difficulty to escape from French internment camps into unoccupied southern France now tried desperately to obtain exit and
transit visas and ship's passages for themselves and their families so
they could flee to the United States, which was reluctant to accept
them. Vessels transporting exiles or camp internees out of Great
Britain were increasingly at risk from German U-boats. Refugees
headed for the sea route out of Portugal first had to pass through the
Spain of General Franco, a Nazi sympathizer. Aid organizations

like the legendary Emergency Rescue Committee, for which Varian Fry was working in Marseilles, could not begin to meet the demand. Gestapo squads that hunted refugees, extradition orders to France's Vichy government, the lack of opportunity to work, and a dependency on handouts from exile self-help organizations like the American Guild for German Cultural Freedom, the European Film Fund, and the Exiled Writers Committee combined to make desolate the lives of those struggling to survive.

Heinrich Mann, leader of the refugee colony in France in the thirties, and Franz Werfel, who was soon to write *The Song of Bernadette* (1941), fled France in September 1940 to escape the victorious army of their countrymen, pursuing an adventurous route by foot across the Pyrenees, and headed for California. Bertolt Brecht, about to attract the interest of Hoover's G-men for his left-wing views, followed an almost equally dangerous path from Finland through Stalin's domain to Japan and on to San Pedro, California. Other writers landed in Hollywood because one of the great film studios had offered them a so-called lifesaver contract, which gave them a U.S. visa and an income for one year, but, as Ludwig Marcuse recalled, no real job: "There they were in the film factories, Heinrich Mann, Alfred Döblin, Leonhard Frank, Alfred Polgar, Walter Mehring, unable to speak English, knowing nothing of filmmaking, full of contempt for the industry" [138, p. 275].

Many exiles were drawn to Los Angeles by the mild climate and low cost of living compared to New York. Still others, like Bruno Frank and a handful who knew how to write filmscripts, had already moved to the Southwest before the war began. Successful authors like Thomas Mann, Lion Feuchtwanger, and Franz Werfel were able to transfer to the Pacific Coast and Beverly Hills the same lifestyles they had enjoyed in Europe, keeping stately villas, surrounded by rare books and cultivated companions. Alfred Döblin, Heinrich Mann, and Leonhard Frank, who either could not or would not adapt to the conditions of literary production in America, eked out a poverty-stricken existence in the western suburbs of the metropolis, often living off handouts from their wealthier colleagues or from aid organizations.

Southern California in the forties was justly regarded as the capital of German literature and was dubbed "Weimar on the Pacific" [234]. In his description of how he wrote *Doctor Faustus*, Thomas Mann contentedly described a party at his home in Pacific Palisades: "Neither Paris nor turn-of-the-century Munich could have offered a more companiable, lively and amusing evening of art" [127, p. 743]. Werfel and his wife felt that they had come to a "paradise" where life meant simply living in the "glorious day" [114, p. 275]. But screenwriter and dramatist Curt Goetz spoke critically of his time in California. Acknowledging that he had been comfortable physically and lived in sunshine and affluence, his "emotional isolation," he said, prevented him from enjoying it [66, p. 278]. Others complained of the lack of "culture" ("The taste of the producers for cheap mass-produced goods . . . made every effort an illusion" [47, p. 355]) and the "never-ending springtime" of "artificially watered gardens, . . . chlorined swimming pools and neo-Hispanic castles" [241, p. 486]. Brecht, unsuccessful in his attempts to establish himself in Hollywood and on Broadway, described Los Angeles in a series of famous elegies, one called "Reflections on Hell" *(Nachdenken über die Hölle)*.

Paradise or hell, riches or unsuccess, the dossiers show that J. Edgar Hoover, who often had tracked exile writers while they were still under way from Europe, had them watched more closely than their American writer colleagues once they arrived in Los Angeles [143]. The number and length of the files devoted to lesser known writers show how seriously the FBI director and his competitors in the OSS and California's Un-American Activities Committee took the threat they thought the refugees posed. R. B. Hood, Special Agent in Charge (SAC) at Los Angeles in the forties and fifties, can justly be called the head of the world's first center for German exile research.

Hood and his special agents were the first to know who phoned whom about what in the exile colony; which cars parked how often and how long on Paseo Miramar outside Feuchtwanger's villa, or in Mabery Road near the Viertels'; and what was said in letters exchanged by the groups in Los Angeles, New York, Mexico, and Moscow. It is Hood's signature that appears on orders to shadow recent escapees from the Gestapo, observing their contacts with Americans and with suspicious foreigners like Soviet diplomat-spy Gregory Kheifetz. Hood was informed when Heinrich Mann's wife drove a car while drunk; and when she committed suicide in December 1944, he sent his agents to the Los Angeles Police Department to try to find out why. Informers, some themselves exiles, carried scraps of party conversation to Hood, and through him to Hoover. Hood's agents burglarized the home of Leonhard Frank, searched the luggage of Brecht's mistress Ruth Berlau, and organized "pretext interviews," and Hood's men in southern California recorded trips and changes of residence, and the attempts of refugees to return to Europe.

Not just daily life among the California exiles but their views on international politics were monitored by Hood in the forties and fifties. The SAC knew when exile groups met to plan the future of Germany, a theme that became central to government agencies as the war neared conclusion [233]. When Feuchtwanger dined at the Soviet consulate, or the Russian vice-consul met Brecht in Santa Monica ("on October 25, 1943, Gregori Kheifets . . . visited the residence of Bert Brecht from approximately 1:45 p.m. to 3:05 p.m."),[1] Hood's men were watching. From California's Un-American Activities Committee, Hood acquired lists of individuals and organizations that "lovers of freedom" like political agitator Jack Tenney [29, p. 98] claimed were "part of a lying, scheming, pernicious army of international gangsters, determined to destroy and desecrate human dignity and civilization."[2]

Hood was motivated by the same fear as his boss and many other Americans: "The Communist movement," according to Hoover, "stands for the destruction of our American form of government; it stands for the destruction of American democracy; it stands for the destruction of free enterprise."[3] Politically uncontroversial exiles like Werfel ended up in the files of the Los Angeles Field Office as surely as "lefty" Brecht, of whom Hood said in a report on "Brecht's Communist History"[4] sent to Washington in February 1948, after the playwright had already left the country: "A confidential source, referred to as 'Source B' . . . reveals that: 'In reality, Brecht has always acted and written as a propagandist of Communism and Sovietism.'"[5] Parking your car on a street near the Communist Party office in Los Angeles would land you in Hood's files, as it did Johanna Kortner, wife of the actor Fritz Kortner. Writers like Heinrich Mann who fell silent in the United States would be pursued by the FBI as zealously as Feuchtwanger, who continued to write and publish his historical novels.

Despite occasional mistakes, Hood and his special agents did an efficient job of monitoring the exile colony in southern California. Their work was supplemented by the Tenney Committee, the OSS, and the INS. Fundamental to them all was material supplied by the Office of Censorship, whose records have largely disappeared except for photocopies, translations, and letter summaries preserved in the files of other agencies. Army and navy intelligence, the Justice Department, and the State Department specialized in foreign operations and were rarely in evidence in southern California.

Of these organizations, the most notable in some respects was the Tenney Committee, which was active long before the McCarthy era. While Hoover's Bureau worked under cover so that subjects were unaware of being observed, the Tenney Committee regularly publicized its collections of fact and opinion in the form of thick reports to mobilize the press and public against political dissidents, "communist fronts," and "stooges." "It was found," Tenney crowed to California voters in his annual report for 1943, that "the elastic powers of your committee were exceedingly helpful to other law enforcing agencies. The committee, . . . not being bound by the rules of evidence and armed with the power to punish for . . . perjury in the event that crime might be established, cuts through the technical restriction of other investigative units which are primarily law-enforcing in character rather than fact-finding" [10, p. 27f].

As chairman and chief ideologue of the committee from 1941 to 1949 and author of four of its five reports, Tenney was among that group of witch-hunters, similar to former liberal Ronald Reagan, whom Hannah Arendt, analyst of totalitarianism, described figuratively as "ex-Communists." "The ex-Communists," she wrote, "have become prominent on the strength of their past alone. Communism has remained the chief issue in their lives" [8, p. 595f]. "Although a registered Republican until 1933," Tenney wrote in a 1952 retrospective, describing himself in the third person and unwittingly confirming Arendt's definition, "like many others who did not know the truth, . . . Tenney . . . succumbed to the vicious propaganda directed at President Hoover in 1932" [207, p. 2], speedily joined the Democratic Party, made political capital with left-wing legal submissions as a member of the California assembly, and attacked Washington's Dies Committee at a public meeting of Hollywood's Anti-Nazi League in 1938 where Bruno Frank was also a featured speaker. "Fellow subversive elements," Tenney said, "I have just heard that Mickey Mouse is conspiring with Shirley Temple to overthrow the government and that there is a witness who has seen the 'Red' card of Donald Duck."[6]

Two years later, after losing a union election, Tenney began to regard his old friends as his new enemies, the "Communazis,"[7] and sought to purge them at considerable personal effort for nearly a decade. Besides left-wing Americans, the state senator preferred to target foreigners. In 1941, his committee demanded that California censor foreign-language media and revoke the citizenship "of any former alien who, since receiving citizenship, has been a member of any subversive organization," with the Tenney Committee and similar organizations deciding (of course) what was subversive. This part of the purge affected many German exiles.

How serious the threats were became clear to exiles whose names appeared on one of Tenney's lists. "*Forty-nine* . . . sponsors" of the Scientific and Cultural Conference for World Peace, went one of his reports, "have been affiliated with from 11 to 20 Communist-front organizations, and include . . . Albert Einstein . . . Lion Feuchtwanger . . . Thomas Mann. . . . *Two hundred and seventy* have been affiliated with from 1 to 10 Communist-front organizations," among them Erika Mann and Stefan Heym, who was one of the very few exiles writing in English.[8] Feuchtwanger's name appears nearly thirty times in the Tenney Committee's reports for 1947–49, for offenses like membership in the "Committee of Welcome for 'Red' Dean of Canterbury"[9] and for supporting the National Council of American-Soviet Friendship, along with Thomas Mann and Einstein. Mann's involvement in politics earned him fifty-two mentions in committee reports by 1951.

Edward L. Barrett, the first historian of the Tenney Committee, admitted in 1951 that although he presumed there were close links between the committee and Hoover's Bureau, he was unable to determine the exact extent of their cooperation. Today, after the release of the FBI files, it is clear that the FBI, INS, and other agencies routinely and often made use of Tenney Committee material on the German exiles.

Compared with the FBI and the Tenney Committee, the OSS paid little attention to the exiles in southern California. One reason may be that although Donovan's service was very interested in political groups of German and Austrian exiles, such groups were based almost entirely in the East, whereas the role literature and media played in politics held no interest for the OSS. Thus "Californians" like Heinrich and Thomas Mann, Brecht, and Hanns Eisler came under OSS scrutiny only if they became involved with the Free Germany Movement in Mexico, helped found organizations like the Council for a Democratic Germany in the United States, or like the Eisler brothers were caught in the trench warfare between left and right.

In 1944–45, an OSS agent from the San Francisco office came to Los Angeles to interview Feuchtwanger, Emil Ludwig, and novelists Alfred Döblin, Bruno Frank, and Alfred Neumann. The interviews were dominated by a single political theme: the future of Germany after the war. The questions focused on topics like the "dismemberment of Germany," "the idea of an Austro-Bavarian *Anschluss*,"[10] German "re-education,"[11] decentralization, the nationalization of German industries, and of course "the treatment of war criminals."[12] It was suggested that the OSS take a closer look at "Communist political cells in Hollywood," but the organization disbanded soon after without ever following the proposal.

The Immigration and Naturalization Service, the Justice Department, and the State Department played an even more marginal role than the OSS in keeping an eye on the California exiles. Since almost all the refugees had entered through Ellis Island, the Los Angeles INS office had little contact with them unless they applied for naturalization.[13] A Justice Department representative for Los Angeles, Assistant Attorney General Attilio di Girolamo, proved unexpectedly liberal when deportation proceedings were brought against Brecht. Exiles encountered diplomatic agents of the State Department when they applied to alter or extend their visas and had to reenter the United States from Mexico via Tijuana or Nogales. The LAPD had no dealings with the exiles except occasionally to supply the FBI with information when requested and to issue certificates of good conduct for several exiles applying for citizenship. Military intelligence (ONI and MID) appears from the files not to have been active with the West Coast exiles but confined itself to checking the reports of the Tenney Committee [10, p. 79].

Six case studies of writers in exile in California follow. Because the Mann family was central to FBI and secret service investigations, it seems reasonable to examine the dossiers of Thomas Mann's son and daughter Klaus and Erika alongside those of Thomas and Heinrich, even though the younger Manns lived in New York more than in California. Bertolt Brecht was kept under intensive FBI observation for several reasons, including his political views and his widespread contacts with American writers and artists. Hoover worked successfully for almost two decades to prevent Lion Feuchtwanger from being granted American citizenship. Other cases— Leonhard and Bruno Frank, Franz Werfel, Erich Maria Remarque, Emil Ludwig, Alfred Döblin, Vicki Baum, Alfred Neumann, Ludwig Marcuse, Curt Goetz, and Ernst Toller—whose government files are qualitatively and quantitatively sparse by comparison, are summarized at the end of the chapter.

The Mann Family Files

THOMAS MANN

Thomas Mann was by far the best-known writer in exile in the United States. Alfred Knopf had been publishing English editions of his books for years. In 1935, on his second visit to the United States, the Nobel Prize–winning author met with President Roosevelt, and he stayed in touch with him afterward. An honorary doctorate from Harvard, a guest professorship at Princeton, and the post of "Consultant in Germanic Literature" at the Library of Congress added to his prestige. A popular and expensive public speaker, Mann was elected to the governing boards of numerous committees and organizations, and in 1951 he was made a member of the American Academy of Arts and Letters. In his radio addresses, lectures, and essays, the uncrowned king of the German exile colony in America expressed his views about Germany's future, the presidential elections in his host country, and later the aberrations of the Cold War. State Department officials, even the secretary of state himself, pondered how to make use of Mann for their own ends. Members of Free Germany in Mexico, under close surveillance by U.S. government operatives, tried to recruit their renowned fellow exile's support for their democratic anti-Fascist movement, rooted in the United Front coalition of the thirties.

Many of Mann's friends, his brother Heinrich, and his children Klaus and Erika were regarded as "enemy aliens" and Communist sympathizers and kept under surveillance by U.S. agents. Mann himself was routinely visited by "FBI gentlemen" who asked his views about the "group in Mexico, Katz, B. Brecht" [128, p. 614]. Or they wanted to know—usually in connection with citizenship applications—about actor Ernst Deutsch, sociologist Leo Matthias, publisher Felix Guggenheim, or literary scholar Curt von Faber du Faur ("gave unfavorable opinion" [129, p. 116]). In short, Hoover and his colleagues thought they had every reason to give serious attention to the case of "Thomas Paul Mann, Security Matter - C."[1]

With meaningful exceptions, the material the FBI and INS amassed about the German exile most familiar to Americans seems largely routine compared with FBI files on other prominent exiles, and with the important Mann files of the State Department and OSS. Thomas himself was never the target of an official FBI investigation, and his FBI documents comprise only 54 pages on relatively insignificant events. The remaining 153 pages of FBI material are copies of publicly available news articles that inattentive staff members sometimes mistakenly filed more than once, or that have nothing to do with the German exiles. The 93 pages released by the INS are likewise routine, that is, they consist of numerous forms that repeat identical facts and personal details, along with a half-hearted INS move toward deportation.

More important to understanding Mann's role in his U.S. exile, and largely ignored until now, are the files of the State Department and the Foreign Nationalities Branch of the OSS, which was assigned to monitor the refugees. Over one hundred pages on Mann at the State Department focus on letters, petitions, and discussion notes concerning two topics: his family's entry into America, and the political aspects of his attempt in 1943 to establish himself as the acknowledged leader of the exile community in the West with the official blessing of the U.S. government. The OSS files are of a similar length and once again revolve around Mann's bid for political leadership of the emigrés, but they also contain such intriguing items as the transcript of a previously unknown conversation between Mann and an OSS official.

Looking first at the State Department files, we see that an exile's typical concerns about papers and travel permits (not grave in Mann's case), soon blend into his intentional association with political decision makers. On 4 November 1936, "Tomas Mann" cabled his "joyful and sincere congratulations" from Küsnacht to President Roosevelt on his reelection.[2] A month later, the well-informed U.S. ambassador in Berlin, William Dodd, sent to the State Department in Washington a report of Nazi Germany's "Proscription of Additional Enemies of the Regime," in which he states: "The proscription of Thomas Mann has caused some surprise inasmuch as it was understood that the authorities about a year ago were endeavoring to facilitate his return so that he might assume his rightful position as an ornament to German literature. Herr Mann has never been a violent opponent of the Nazis and in a letter published in the *Neue Zürcher Zeitung* at the beginning of this year he refused to associate himself with the rabid German emigré press."[3] In the next few years, trying to aid refugees and victims of Fascist persecution, Mann wrote petitions with Albert Einstein to Secretary of State Cordell Hull asking him "to help and probably save the life of the German refugees in Prague,"[4] and with American journalist Dorothy Thompson he petitioned Roosevelt "to protest the announced intention of General Franco to deliver back to Germany . . . prisoners of war who will most certainly be tortured to death in their countries."[5]

In every case the results were the same: Mann was told that the

U.S. government could not intervene in the affairs of other nations unless the safety of American citizens was involved, and any public intervention on behalf of German exiles individually or as a group would be contrary to "long-established practice."[6]

Mann's contacts with the State Department proved more successful when he appealed for visas for himself and his family. Documents relating to this topic go back to 1934, when he made his first visit to the United States. The publisher Alfred Knopf had petitioned the State Department to let Mann enter the country even though his German passport had expired in 1933, because "the purpose of the visit would be entirely literary, and I am sure Mann would agree in advance . . . to say nothing whatever of a political nature."[7] The State Department also responded favorably when Mann approached it in 1938 through a petition from Mrs. Eugene Meyer, wife of the owner of the influential *Washington Post,* asking for "German non-preference quota immigration visas" for himself, his wife, and their children Elisabeth and Michael.[8] Mrs. Meyer described him as a "great artist" and "very distinguished man,"[9] and the authorities replied that they would do everything permitted by law for him. As Hull said in his letter to the publisher's wife, "I am, as you know, not unmindful of the plight of those unfortunate people, who, like Dr. Mann, find themselves in such a distressing situation."[10]

Central to the State Department files on Mann, however, are not petitions and visa requests but a project that alarmed the OSS and led it to prepare scores of analyses, reports, and background studies: the exiles were trying to form an official organization with Mann as their leader. Like the United Front coalition of the thirties, this organization aimed to bring together as many individuals and groups as possible from the cultural and political exile. First called simply the "German Committee,"[11] then the "Provisional Thomas Mann Committee,"[12] and finally the "Free Germany Committee or Council,"[13] its most important goal was the creation of a sort of German government-in-exile headed by Mann. As its official representative, he would mediate between the opposing views that were forged in the Weimar Republic of the twenties and carried into exile.[14] But the project went awry almost from the start.

The sequence of events shows that not Mann but the OSS, cooperating with the State Department, was the real decision maker in this critical phase of exile history and U.S. policy on Germany. "On October 27, 1943 Paul Hagen came . . . to talk over 'an idea' he just had. . . . Thomas Mann was in town for the Free World Congress and . . . one should use this opportunity to 'rope him into some German Committee,'"[15] read the opening lines of an internal OSS memorandum dated 29 October 1943 in which agent Emmy Rado, assigned to investigate the exiles, introduced the "Mann case" to DeWitt Poole, director of the newly founded Foreign Nationalities Branch of the OSS. By the time Mann came to Washington a month later to confer about the project with Assistant Secretary of State Adolf Berle, Donovan's OSS had long since completed maneuvers to thwart it.

In fact the FNB had been suspicious of the plan to form a German exile group since it was first proposed by Paul Hagen of the Social Democrat splinter organization "New Beginning," and their suspicions were not allayed when Mann accepted leadership of the nascent committee on the evening of 27 October 1943. "General Donovan . . . was rather anxious about the whole matter," Rado reported after speaking with the OSS chief,[16] and went on to say, "the General felt quite strongly that it was undesirable for this Committee to take the field at this time."[17] Other FNB agents took a similar view: "We all, including General Donovan, feel that word should be gotten quickly to Mann and others, that the Government would rather see nothing done in this connection for the moment," and in an analysis labeled "secret" they listed their arguments against the German Committee: "Firstly, we do not like some of the personalities involved. Secondly, the Committee is not wisely constituted and a bad action at this time would detract from the effectiveness of a better effort later. Thirdly, and most important, Thomas Mann is extremely important and useful for any Group which might be needed later, and he should not be permitted to expend his usefulness now by an action of this kind. If you can get a quick expression of opinion from the State Department in this matter we can arrange to have Mann contacted and we will do the necessary."[18]

The last sentence in this OSS assessment shows what a small step it is for a secret service to move from the collection of information to political intrigue.[19] Even clearer evidence is an FNB message sent to Berle on November 10 by Poole, an ex-diplomat and anti-Communist ("The real danger to our civilization is Soviet Russia" [185, p. 212]), politely but firmly telling the assistant secretary of state what to do:

> It is likely that within the next few days Thomas Mann . . . will—quite on his own responsibility—call you on the long-distance telephone and ask your advice in connection with the project. . . . If you are willing to speak with Mr. Mann it is recommended that you say simply that the question of a German National Committee is naturally an important one and ought to be carefully considered with an eye to both the American and German interest and with that in mind you would be glad at some future mutually convenient time to receive Mr. Mann in your office and have a talk with him. If you do find it suitable to speak to Mr. Mann in that vein it is our understanding that the exigencies of the present situation will have been met and that Mr. Mann will defer any definite action on his part until he has had an opportunity of conferring with you. In our handling of the matter emphasis has been placed upon the need to avoid creating a situation in which it might appear that the State Department had actively intervened in a negative way.[20]

Mann, unaware of the OSS plot, stepped blindly into the trap. A week after the OSS had made its arrangements and three days after Mann spoke with "diplomatic agent, Pool[e]" about the "Free Germany question in relation to the results in Moscow" [128, p. 648], he offered Berle his services. Employing the abstruse language of diplomacy, Mann tried to sound out whether exile leaders like himself might be expected to take on more important jobs in the future, instead of serving in the initial provisional administration after the war where they would ruin their good reputations both with Germans and with the Allies. The terse "Memorandum of Conversation" that Berle dictated and filed right after his lunch with Mann shows that the State Department stuck to the scenario assigned by the OSS, a scenario that in any case suited the plans of Berle and his colleagues, who were extremely cautious in matters concerning "Free Germany": "Mr. Thomas Mann . . . stated that he had difficulty in accepting the chairmanship of any committee designed to intervene in German politics because he had applied for American citizenship and expected to spend the rest of his life here. I told him I thought indeed that would place him in a difficult position. I told him also that his own name was very highly regarded in German circles, and that I rather felt that he might not wish to enter the tangled and controversial field until the issues became considerably clearer. With this he agreed."[21]

But Mann's withdrawal from the German Committee did not end the controversy. "After Thomas Mann's meeting with Secretary of State Berle and his subsequent refusal to form a Free German Committee," OSS official C. B. Friediger[22] wrote somewhat inaccurately to FNB director Poole on 8 January 1944, "I have been watching to see what new initiative will be taken by the German political exiles." He concluded that "the recognized Stalinist Germans . . . Wieland Herzfelde and Bertolt Brecht are in a victorious mood," because the growing prestige of Russia was leading to what the conservative Friediger regarded as the dangerous situation "that all these pro-German activities including the Social-Democratic ones must drift sooner or later in the direction of the Moscow Free Ger-

HOTEL
BEDFORD

118 EAST 40 STREET · NEW YORK (16) N.Y.
EAST OF PARK AVENUE · CALEDONIA 5-1000

November 18. 1943

My dear Mr. Ber...

    May I take the liberty to submit to you a problem
the solution of which will largely depend for me on your
advice.

    Among the politically interested groups of the
German émigrés there is a general feeling that the time
has come for the formation of a Free Germany Committee
or Council in this country. Such a committee could serve
a double purpose: it could, in support of the political
warfare, try to influence the people inside Germany, and,
in view of its knowledge of the German mind, it might
prove useful to the American authorities in an advisory
capacity. It should consist, as far as possible, of all
the political groups from the right to the left. From
various directions it has been suggested that I should
take the initiative in bringing about such a cooperation
of the different parties, probably with the idea that I,
as an independent German born writer committed to no
political party, would be the most suitable person for
this purpose.

    I am in no way a man of action or diplomacy, and I
would prefer certainly to carry on my personal work un-
disturbed. Nevertheless, out of a feeling of responsibility, I would, under certain conditions, come to the conclusion, that I ought not to shirk such a task. The essential
condition would be that the formation of a committee of
this kind would meet with the approval of the authorities in Washington. This is, first, a natural expression
of my loyalty toward the country whose citizen I am
about to become, and further I am convinced that only an
organization acknowledged and in some way backed by
official America could be of any use.

862.01/523

PS/CF
FILED

DEC 23 1943

62

HOTEL BEDFORD

118 EAST 40 STREET · NEW YORK (16) N.Y.

EAST OF PARK AVENUE · CALEDONIA 5-1000

Therefor what I ask you,my dear Mr. Berle,is whether you think the formation of such a committee altogether desirable and,if so,whether this is the right moment to form it.

It is perhaps not misplaced to use this opportunity in order to express the following idea. Naturally, all kinds of guesswork and suggestions,in the form of rumors, and also of comments in the press,are going about regarding the personalities who may be called upon to play a leading and representative part in a future democratic Germany. To my way of feeling all these speculations and "nominations" are premature and futile. There can be no doubt that decisions about the near future of Germany after the defeat have already been reached, and it would be of the greatest interest to me to know whether you agree with me,that in a country in the particular circumstances in which Germany will be,there will be,in the beginning,no place for a"government" in the genuine sense of the word. What will be needed is merely a body of men experienced in administration business,taken from inside Germany and also perhaps from the Emigrés,which,as a mediating and executive organ,would cooperate with the occupation authorities. For this job,which can only be a thankless one,there is certainly no need of personalities with whose names hopes are connected for a leading part in a reorganized democratic Germany. By taking part in the first provisional administration by the victorious powers they would doubtless lose a great deal of their credit and influence in Germany.and,on the other hand their relations to the Allies might easily become precarious. Such men should therefore be spared and saved for the future. How far this principle of sparing and saving should also be applied to the plan I developed earlier is an other question which I would like to submit to your judgment.

I would very much appreciate it if you could let me have your opinion about these problems at your earliest convenience,because my stay in New York is to last only until November 27. and I am to return then to the West Coast.

Respectfully yours

man Committee."[23] A brief exchange of views between Poole, who had come to the OSS from the Institute for Advanced Studies at Princeton, and Franz Neumann, who arrived in Donovan's Research and Analysis Department by a left-wing route when Frankfurt's Institute for Social Research transferred to the United States, shows that in early 1944, OSS personnel thought Mann might be influenced by his daughter Erika to support a "hard peace" in the right-wing group around "F. W. Foerster and [T. H.] Tetens."[24] And the "case" of Thomas Mann continued to resurface in FNB reports on the Council for a Democratic Germany.

Berle in the State Department and leaders in the OSS realized that Mann, "as perhaps the best-known German scholar and cultural leader outside Germany,"[25] occupied a special position among the exiles, and the information their agencies collected on him and his political contacts was correspondingly extensive. Thus even before the founding of Moscow's National Free Germany Committee, Berle learned from an FBI "confidential informant" that a provisional German government-in-exile in Moscow planned to offer Mann the office of minister of education.[26] In November 1943 the U.S. embassy in Ankara relayed the translation of a five-page letter from Ernst Reuter to "Dr. Thomas Mann, America," in which the future mayor of West Berlin begged his fellow exile to issue an appeal uniting "all the Germans in the world." "My plea, our plea to you, Thomas Mann, is this: Please try to unite all Germans whose voices are heeded to in Germany and issue a common appeal to the German people."[27] Other influential Germans also saw Mann as a leader, and the New School for Social Research [105] offered his services to the OSS and the Office of War Information, next to those of Hans Sahl for "Propaganda Techniques," as an expert in "Artistic and Intellectual Life," in a memorandum titled "Experts on Germany Available Through the New School for Social Research Classified by Field."[28]

Did the New School ask Mann's permission before recommending his services to the OWI and the OSS? The documents do not say, but they do tell us that Mann willingly answered questions on a wide range of topics in a long interview with the OSS, and then omitted all mention of the event from his normally elaborate diary. The OSS office in San Francisco wrote up the interview for Poole shortly before he went to Germany as a State Department special envoy. Agent John Norman, who questioned Mann, evidently was so impressed by the atmosphere in the writer's home that, shedding officialese and professional taciturnity, he began his drily titled "Report of conversation with Thomas Mann in Pacific Palisades, California, 8 December [1944]"[29] by launching into a small mood piece:

Thomas Mann's retreat is an author's paradise. . . . We were received in a spacious, comfortable room, one side of which . . . was lined with books. Mr. and Mrs. Mann invited us to sit around a coffee table to sip coffee and liqueur while we talked. We got the coffee but not the liqueur, though glasses were set for it. Mr. Mann poured some for himself but absentmindedly neglected to offer us any. He lit a long cigar which he wielded with deliberate, graceful gestures, somewhat like a baton, to help him drive home a point, meanwhile sprinkling the cigar-ashes liberally on the carpet. Mr. Mann is a gray-haired, mustached, middle-sized person of slender build looking every bit like his published photographs. His manner forms the perfect prototype of the leisurely, gentlemanly, continental man of culture. Mrs. Mann is white-haired and somewhat queenly in bearing.[30]

Although Norman and his unnamed companion apparently were disappointed that they got no liqueur, they could not complain that Mann failed to answer the eighteen prepared questions they had brought with them from San Francisco. On the contrary, he was outspoken in his replies, such as to question 1, why he had postponed his next lecture tour ("his decision was owing to his desire to await further developments before committing himself publicly"),[31] and to question 17, his opinion of Emil Ludwig ("'wrong,' 'tactless,' and 'one-sided' in his arguments against Germany . . . sounded too much like 'Jewish resentment'").[32] Mann said bluntly, when asked about the important issue of "guilt for the war," that when the Allies came to punish war criminals, they ought not to overlook the responsibility of "'theoretical' men like [Karl] Haushofer and [Ewald] Banse" who were "even more guilty than more active Nazi leaders," and that it would be good "to blacklist such writers."[33] Asked his views of the territorial claims of Germany's neighbors, Mann spoke against partitioning Germany but took a positive view of the plan to deport Germans from Czechoslovakia and to internationalize the Ruhr and the Saar. His reply to question 14 was short and to the point, if not especially realistic: "Asked about the feasibility of returning Jewish refugees to Germany, Mr. Mann asserted that 'As a whole, Germans would not object to Jewish return. The Germans were not really anti-Semitic. They are even less anti-Semitic now!'" Other issues of world politics were polished off between the coffee and the liqueur: "Stalin is not anxious to communize Germany" (Mann said) because he feared that the Germans would create a better Communism than Russia.[34]

How seriously Washington and the OSS took Norman's interviews with Mann and other exiled writers in Los Angeles is unknown. That the conversations were not ignored is evident from a summary the FNB prepared for OSS chief Donovan on 18 January 1945.[35] This does not mean that other OSS employees were kindly disposed to Mann. "In respect of politics he is a child," says a biographical note written right after the FNB was founded, "his German is over edged, his order of thoughts . . . strange, . . . the language unpopular . . . and . . . the pamphlets . . . broadcasted via short-wave to Germany . . . go far beyond the understanding of the German average listener."[36] Emil Ludwig, whom Mann criticized for his right-wing views, informed the OSS that the novelist was, like many of the exiles, "incapable for 1945" because in Germany they would be laughed at as "Pan-Germanists."[37] In short, Mann figured in OSS files as "the outstanding literary figure of contemporary Germany" and as "benevolent" and "social-minded," but despite all his efforts in the political realm, not as an "'homme politique.'"[38]

If we turn from the files of the OSS and State Department to the relatively thin FBI dossier on Mann, it will be evident that Hoover either did not consider Mann's political position especially un-American or, as FBI agent Elmer Linberg remembers it, that he showed special caution in his surveillance of the Nobel Prize winner.

Mann's FBI dossier departs in several ways from the usual pattern. For instance, it does not contain a single report of the kind that the field offices supplied on other targets—Feuchtwanger, Brecht, Graf, Heinrich and Klaus Mann—summarizing the most important findings and passing them on to headquarters in Washington. Nowhere in the pages released to me did the FBI mention surveillance of the subject's home and person, although this was routine in other cases, and a notation in Brecht's file reveals that Mann's telephone conversations were recorded: "In the report of Special Agent Richard C. Thompson, dated April 15, 1943, entitled Otto Katz with aliases, it was stated that a telephone listed to Eva Landshoff, 79701/4 Sunset Boulevard, Los Angeles, had been called several times from the residence of Thomas Mann."[39] Mail censorship was limited to one letter intercepted by "Imperial Censorship Bermuda" in which an exile in Switzerland asked Mann for support in founding a Free Germany organization: "As emigrants living in Switzerland, we are unable to undertake any political activity. All that we can do for the moment for a 'Free Germany' is to canvass members."[40] Special Agent Linberg, who was temporarily assigned to Mann's case, said in an interview with me that he remembered a long conversation with Mann in which he asked the writer about other exiles, Communists, and political topics; but half a century later he no longer recalled whether he had visited Mann to get a specific statement or for some more general purpose.[41] Spies and informants among Mann's associates either never completed reports or these were destroyed later. A six-page "summary memorandum," based on some two hundred entries on Mann in the FBI archives up to 1941, turned out to be nothing more than standard cross-references to the files of other subjects, not to Mann's own case file, and the same is true of an additional "600 references"[42] from later years.[43]

Other parts of Mann's FBI dossier, although meaningful, relate only indirectly to the exile or are isolated fragments. Once, the SAC in Los Angeles appears to have confused the two Mann brothers after receiving a report from an informant "whose name should be protected" concerning a conversation with "Mrs. Thomas Mann relative to the Heinrich Ludwig Mann estate": "The inference is being entertained that Thomas and Katia Mann were or still are expecting funds from [blacked out] to finance their return to the Soviet controlled Eastern Sector of Germany."[44] So many words or phrases are blacked out that the file leaves unclear the identity of the informant who sent a negative article about Mann from the *New Leader* to "My dear Mr. Hoover"[45] in the summer of 1951, and in a follow-up conversation with an FBI agent stated his readiness to make available his collection of "several hundred clippings, letters, speeches, articles, etc. relating to Mann."[46] Finally, Mann's file contains a brief correspondence labeled "secret" between FBI agents in Paris, Heidelberg, and London in the fifties, about Mann's visit to East Germany to attend a Schiller Festival on the 150th anniversary of the poet's death: "According to G-2, Headquarters, USAREUR, the East German radio, on January 4, 1955 announced that Thomas Mann would attend the Schiller Festival on May 9, 1955. This festival will be held in Eastern Germany, probably at Weimar."[47]

J. Edgar Hoover left no clue why he did not order his G-men to keep closer watch on "subject" Mann, by then a U.S. citizen, throughout the Cold War. By the standards of those days, Mann was a suspicious enough character to warrant surveillance, as State Department files from 1950 and the reports of California's Tenney Committee both indicate. The FBI mentions only in passing, in its file on Erika Mann, that Thomas Mann signed the Stockholm "Appeal for the Interdiction of the Atomic Weapon"[48] in 1950, whereas the State Department procured a telegram on Mann's arrival in Paris confirming that his signature on the peace appeal had been "prominently reproduced"[49] in the French Communist Party newspaper *l'Humanité*. California witch-hunter Jack Tenney and his successors regularly investigated Mann as a member of what they considered Communist covert organizations like the Hollywood Independent Citizen's Committee of the Arts, Sciences, and Professions, and the American Continental Congress for World Peace held in Mexico in September 1949, and then turned over their blacklists to Hoover's agency.

While the FBI kept itself precisely informed about arrangements between Heinrich Mann and the East German publishing house Aufbau Verlag, it was left to the State Department to worry about the spectacular struggle between Aufbau and West Germany's S. Fischer Verlag over copyrights to the books of Heinrich's brother Thomas. At least it is the State Department archive, not the FBI's, that holds several letters and a detailed legal opinion about the brutal business tactics of East Germany,[50] showing how agreements between Walter Janka, Aufbau's executive director in the early fifties, and S. Fischer were withdrawn a short time later, how East Berlin refused to transfer fees payable in U.S. dollars because "the USA's economic boycott of the GDR . . . obviates any currency trade with dollar nations,"[51] and how books were printed in East Germany without any contractual agreement, by order of the GDR's Ministry of Public Education ("with a view to the public interest based upon the ordinance on the arts passed on 16 March 1950 by the government of the German Democratic Republic, the collective of editors . . . ordered . . . the printing of the volume *Buddenbrooks*").[52]

Low key as Thomas Mann's FBI dossier appears compared with the Mann files of the State Department and OSS, his INS file surpasses it in bureaucratic humdrum. Mann, or sometimes "Mrs. Thomas Mann" as his proxy,[53] filled in a plethora of INS forms— Declarations of Intention, Applications for a Certificate of Arrival and Preliminary Form for Petition for Naturalization, Statements of Facts . . . in Making and Filing My Petition for Naturalization—repeating the same information over and over: "Occupation: writer & lecturer, . . . complexion dark, color of eyes grey, color of hair mixed, height 5 feet 9 inches; weight 150 pounds; visible distinctive marks Wart on right temple, race German; nationality German."[54] The petitioner obediently (if not always quite accurately and completely) listed his trips, residences, employers ("Library of Congress, Washington D.C., Consultant, 1942–now; University of Princeton, Princeton N.J., Visiting Professor, Sept. 1938–July 1940"), and membership in "organizations, lodges, societies, clubs, or associations": "American Author's League, New York, 1939–now; American Academy of Arts and Letters, New York, 1939–now; Committee for Christian Refugees, Center Street, New York, 1938–now; Phi Beta Kappa, 1944–now; Emergency Rescue Committee, New York, 1940–now."[55] Asked what he had done to further the U.S. war effort, the future American stated: "I bought warbonds, donated several manuscripts to the Treasury Dpt. for the purchase of War Bonds, wrote articles and broadcasted for the Government. Furthermore I am broadcasting every month to the German people."[56] And of course Mann recorded a simple "yes" when asked if he believed fully and completely in the U.S. form of government and whether, if necessary, he would take up arms to defend the country, but answered "no" to whether he had ever been in a mental hospital, or belonged to organizations that taught anarchy or aimed to overthrow the existing government or to damage property. (This last being a topic that would get the Marxist Bertolt Brecht in trouble with the FBI through his poem "Demolition of the Ship Oskawa by the Crew.")

We know that Mann had the support of prestigious sponsors in his petition for citizenship: Robert Sproul, president of the University of California at Berkeley; Eugene Meyer, "Washington Post editor";[57] Dean Christian Gauss of Princeton University; the philosophy professor Charles Henry Rieber from Pacific Palisades; and fellow exiles Max and Rose Horkheimer, and "Miss Eva Hermann, Artist-Painter."[58] We also know, because his file holds a copy of the document, that "Thomas Paul Mann, then residing at 1550 San Remo Drive, Pacific Palisades,"[59] applicant no. 6178188, became a citizen in Los Angeles on 23 June 1944, after what was more or less the normal waiting period.

The INS evidently found no grounds to deny or delay the popular writer's petition for American citizenship. Mann conscientiously turned over to the INS a certified copy and English translation of his Czech citizenship papers: a document that saved him from the unpleasant status of enemy alien after the United States entered the war. In January 1944 the INS sent a form asking the FBI for any information it had on "subversive activities or tendencies," "pro-Nazi sympathies," or infringements of the Nationality Act of 1940 committed by Mann, and on the form appears this laconic notation by an INS official: "No derog. info held by F.B.I., however, they are interested in him."[60] The fact that Mann built a home in Pacific Palisades indicated to the authorities that he did not intend to return to his country of origin. Routine questioning of Mann's acquaintances and neighbors from 6 to 8 April 1944 brought uniformly positive replies: the petitioner was "attached to the principles of the constitution," "not in any way subversive,"[61] and "a man of excellent moral character."[62] And even a neighbor who considered the foreigner "'arrogant' in his manner" and "not a very social person"[63] could find nothing worse to say about him than that he had visitors at all hours of the day and night.

At a hearing of the Select Committee Investigating National Defense Migration held in Los Angeles in March 1942 at the behest of the House of Representatives in Washington, Mann was moderate in his responses: No, in his opinion the refugees from Hitler in the United States were not "enemy aliens" but "the most passionate adversaries of the European governments this country is at war with."[64] Thus regulations that might be applied to Japanese on the West Coast ought not to be simply transferred to Germans. If necessary he, Thomas Mann, would make himself available to the government at any time ("I am only awaiting a call from the Government" [219, p. 11732]) to protect loyal anti-Fascists from deportation or internment. He had, he said, no doubt "that the Federal Bureau of Investigation has carefully observed all aliens for quite some time, and has proven to be very well informed about their behavior and intentions" [ibid., p. 11727].

Not until the fevered years of the McCarthy era did a clear change take place in the INS's attitude toward the writer, and even then no visible consequences were borne by "subject Mann."[65] Alarmed by newspaper reports, including an article about his work with the American Committee for Protection of the Foreign Born, and by ex-Communist Ruth Fischer's denunciation of him before a Senate investigating committee, the INS in spring 1951 asked the Security Division of the FBI to investigate "whether the naturalization of Thomas Paul Mann is amenable to cancellation or whether he may be subject to denaturalization and deportation."[66] When Mann's dossier in the Los Angeles Field Office was judged too "voluminous"[67] to cope with—it may have been destroyed later, because it certainly is not the one released to me—the case was referred to "Central Office level," that is to Washington.[68] Washington's examination of files, indexed cross-references, and publications of the "Un-american Activities committee of Calif. of 1847 [i.e., 1947], 48, and 49" produced a list of recent press notices and of "movements or fronts, or files"[69] in which Mann's name appeared, including the National Council of American-Soviet Friendship, the Citizens Committee for Motion Picture Strikes, and the Hollywood

Writers Mobilization. Finally, an FBI man, or possibly an INS employee, wrote a cramped two-page summary of what he considered the most important facts: "After a trip to the Soviet Zone of Germany, Mann wrote a glowing account of the growth of democracy in that area. . . . Subject was a signer of a Brief to the United States Court of Appeals protesting the Los Angeles Witch Hunt Trials . . . and . . . of a petition urging Attorney General Clark to drop deportation proceedings against Hans Eisler . . . and . . . was scheduled to appear in the proposed radio program entitled 'Hollywood Ten,'" a program the Bureau thought was boycotted by the "major networks."[70]

The INS and FBI appear not to have followed up their overtures to deport Mann, although the charge of "Communist-front associations & activities consistantly since 1920's"[71] resurfaced in his file in March 1955, and Mann himself, as evidenced by his diaries, had felt for some time that he was no longer safe in the United States. "Conversation with K[laus] and Erika about the situation in America and our future there," he wrote, "amid intensifying chauvinism and persecution of any nonconformity. Passport fairly certain to be revoked" [131, p. 223]. That the two bureaus failed to pursue the deportation may in part have been because the twice-exiled Mann had been living outside the United States since June 1952. "Mann has announced his intention of remaining in East Germany permanently,"[72] a handwritten note in his files, dated 21 January 1953, states inaccurately, since he had in fact moved directly to Switzerland. Also, Mann's advanced age made him appear incapable of inflicting harm on Hoover's American Way ("Reasons for Placing Case in Deferred Status: Age 79").[73] "Mr. Mann paid warm tribute to America," the U.S. consul said in June 1953, reporting on a lecture Mann had delivered at the University of Hamburg, "but went on to say that the longer he remained in America, the more he became aware of being a European. . . . He . . . felt that he had fulfilled an obligation in renouncing the comforts and conveniences of

America in order to return to the 'battered old continent of Europe.'
. . . In private conversation later, Thomas Mann stated that he 'deplored the apparent rise of right-wing tendencies' in the U.S. at the present time. . . . Although making no definite statement to the effect, he gave the impression that this 'atmosphere' might have been one of the things influencing his leaving the United States."[74]

A final laconic notation concludes Thomas Mann's FBI file on 10 August 1956: "1600/104917 Subject deceased, to file."[75]

HEINRICH MANN

"You are what circumstances make you," Heinrich Mann wrote in his autobiography in 1943–44, during his California exile. "Today I am highly regarded in a far-off empire [i.e, the Soviet Union], but I count for nothing here where I set my foot upon the ground" [119, p. 258]. Five years later, Thomas Mann expanded on his elder brother's self-portrait in "Letter on the Death of My Brother Heinrich": Heinrich spent his last years in Los Angeles "unrecognized" and "solitary"; he wanted to be "left in peace"; he had become "indifferent of late" and "very old."[1]

No new facts have lightened this picture. America took no interest in Heinrich Mann, who had been an exile leader in France up to 1940. Warner Brothers Studio canceled his contract after he had worked there for one year, without ever seriously examining any of his filmscripts. Around the same time, in October 1942, he had to abandon plans to leave California and move to New York. His wife, Nelly, wrote resignedly to Friedel Kantorowicz: "We have now given up all hope and have reconciled ourselves to going silent here. Heinrich Mann cannot undertake any project from here. We cannot even struggle to find a publisher or agent. We are living in a grave" [124, p. 54]. "Heinrich Mann was always very much interested in political life," the OSS reported in a biographical sketch late in 1943. "He now lives in one of the suburbs of Los Angeles and seems to have renounced all political activities."[2] Neither literary critics nor scholars of German literature in America gave attention to Heinrich's work. His books went unpublished; his political and organizational projects fizzled out. "America knows almost as little about me as I know about it,"[3] the seventy-seven-year-old wrote to a friend in 1949, and that same year he lamented in a letter to novelist F. S. Grosshut, whose work is still largely unknown today: "For the most part I am met nowadays by a meaningful silence" [71, p. 359]. This realization was confirmed a few weeks later by Mann's obituary in the *New York Times,* which devoted just a hundred lines to the author of *The Patrioteer* and *Professor Unrat,* on which the film *The Blue Angel* with Marlene Dietrich was based: more or less the same space allotted to a Pillsbury Mills board member and a newspaperman on the *Norfolk Virginian-Pilot* who died the same day.

Heinrich Mann's problems with the culture industry in America have often been described. What few people know is that a more hidden side of American society—the FBI's Special Intelligence Service, the Office of Censorship, army and navy intelligence, the OSS ("Heinrich is . . . eager to play a role in social life and to be in the foreground . . . he is . . . less philosophically minded"),[4] the attorney general, the INS, the Intelligence Section of the Internal Revenue Service, and branches of the State and Treasury departments— all directly or indirectly took a keen interest in the elderly exile.

This interest is documented by 312 file items in the archives of the FBI, 241 of which were released to me with the usual mutilations after several years of waiting. The Intelligence and Security Command of the U.S. Army in Arlington, Virginia, gave me 19 pages, the INS 31. A further 90 items were withheld by the FBI and INS. The OSS files hold scattered reports and notes focusing mainly on Mann's role as honorary president of the Latin American Committee of Free Germans in Mexico and his support of the National Free Germany Committee in Moscow.

Heinrich Mann's FBI file was compiled in the forties and early fifties by the L.A. Field Office in cooperation with special agents in New York, San Francisco, El Paso, Mexico City, and elsewhere. Material was classified as File No. 100-166834 and the "Character of Case" as "Internal Security - R," a designation applied to all activities that at the time fell into the category "un-American," which was never precisely defined by the FBI or any other agency. Cross-references to other files make clear the general type of the offense: "Comintern Apparatus," "German Communist Activities in Western Hemisphere," "Free German Activities," "Communist Infiltration of the Motion Picture Industry," "National Council of American-Soviet Friendship," and so on.

The data in L.A. dossier 100-18229 reflect a wide range of sources. By 1942, letters to and from Mann were routinely intercepted by the Office of Censorship and by the Special Intelligence Service set up at the U.S. embassy in Mexico City when war broke out, and translated or summarized for the FBI. FBI reports, in this case seventeen totaling 135 pages, refer to "confidential" or "highly confidential sources," some probably from exile circles. Agents regularly consulted *Freies Deutschland,* the exile magazine published in Mexico, of which copies evidently were available in the L.A. Field Office, and the *Los Angeles Times* and other American newspapers and magazines. Brecht's file indicates that the telephone of his "companion subject" Heinrich Mann was tapped.[5] And predictably, agents sometimes watched Mann's apartment, monitoring everyone who came and went.

The first document in Mann's FBI file is a letter dated 1 June 1942 from writer Ludwig Renn, who had fled from the Nazis to Central America and wrote to Mann on behalf of the Free Germany Movement in Mexico. The last item is an office memo from the SAC in New York to FBI headquarters in Washington, discussing the identity and credibility of an informant—five years after Heinrich's death. In autumn 1945 the Los Angeles Field Office tried to

NAME: HEINRICH LUDWIG MANN
RESIDENCE: 301 South Swall Drive, Los Angeles, California;
                    Telephone CRestview 19823.
DESCRIPTION: Age 75, born 3/27/71 at Luebeck, Germany; 5' 7";
                    165 lbs; hunched shoulders, stooped build; gray
                    hair; blue eyes, glasses; fair complexion.
OCCUPATION: Writer.
PRINCIPAL CONTACTS: Soviet Consular officials and Communists connected
                    with film industry.
MAIL DROP: None known.
ORGANIZATION: Latin-American Committee for Free Germany.
                    Probably VOKS.
SURVEILLANCE NOTES: Not surveilled.

ALL INFORMATION CONTAINED
HEREIN IS UNCLASSIFIED
DATE 2/11/86 BY _____

RECORDED
&
INDEXED
100-_____
F B I
15 JAN 31 1948

52 FEB 6 1948

close Mann's case, citing "apparent lack of activity."[6] His name was dropped from the National Censorship Watch List, but it was not crossed off the Security Index listing individuals to be interned in the event of a national emergency. Although the Los Angeles office had known for years that Mann was "elderly, in ill health, and . . . inactive in Communist matters"[7] and even though he was now almost eighty, 1949–50 saw a new wave of operations against him, no doubt resulting from his plan to return to East Germany.

Turning first to the eighty-nine pages of censored correspondence preserved in the FBI file, we find extracts and English translations of eleven letters and telegrams from Mann and thirty-three to him, with five letters exchanged by other parties that mention his name: evidently only a fraction of Mann's correspondence in the California years. Seven letters are addressed to Communist activist Paul Merker and his colleagues in the Free Germany Movement in Mexico; twenty-one were sent from Mexico to California. They belong to the same group from which East German exile researcher Wolfgang Kiessling, using other archives, published sixty-five items, although I have nine letters that are missing from his collection. These include reports on the founding of the publishing firm El Libro Libre and on the revision of Mann's novel *Lidice* by Walter Janka, whose antigovernment political activities in East Germany led to the suppression of his work there from 1956 to the end of 1989 [91]. Other parts of the correspondence treat the activities and internal quarrels of various exile groups in Latin America, the death of Nelly Mann, and Heinrich's relations with Europe.[8] From May 1944 we find a letter that the Office of Censorship intercepted by mistake, from a Heinrich Mann residing at "139 Ad. Hitler Str. Bellheim . . . Germany" to Herbert Mann, a P.O.W. in "Camp 20, Canada."[9]

The FBI's cache of letters tells us nothing new about relations between Heinrich Mann and the Free Germany Movement in Mexico, but the selection of passages the censors chose to copy, and the explanatory notes that translators sometimes added, give us clues to what the Bureau was looking for in the correspondence between Mann and his fellow exiles to the south. Ludwig Renn (the mail censor states in June 1942, quoting file "LA-7798 and numerous") is "a communist suspect in Mexico."[10] A month later, Examiner 2006 submitted a report on "Communistic Activity in the Americas" with passages translated from the first installment of a "'Free German Newspaper for Chile,'" and added a note saying that "the whole movement of 'Free Germany' is merely a cover for communistic activity . . . newspaper . . . released to Keep Channels open."[11] In spring that year, Paul Merker sent speeches from the first congress of the Free Germany Movement to Heinrich Mann and to the editors of *Internationale Literatur* in Moscow, adding a note to the U.S. censors on the stationery of the Comite Latino Americano (Latin American Free German Committee), but the censor who intercepted the note did not see the humor and confiscated it: "This letter was also condemned."[12] In March 1945, when Heinrich sent the manuscript of his famous appeal "To the People of Berlin" from Los Angeles to Mexico, the censor summarized passages, emphasizing the relations between the German population and the Allied victors, and the need Mann saw to expel the "common money grabbers," "'Junkers,'" and members of the "'Grand General Staff'" who had financed Hitler and his "blond beasts and supermen."[13]

Anti-Communism, the exiles' plans for a new order in postwar Germany, and Heinrich Mann's contacts with East Germany in 1949–50 are also the focus of the second main group of documents in his file: seventeen reports drawn up between September 1944 and September 1950 by the FBI field offices in Los Angeles, San Francisco, and New York. The first report (at thirty-three pages also the longest) comes from R. B. Hood's office and sets the tone and purpose of the file. It begins with a sort of political curriculum vitae, lists among Mann's contacts the exiles Brecht and Feuchtwanger, who were also under FBI surveillance, and details the political platform of organizations like Free Germany in Mexico. "This investigation," states the "synopsis of facts"[14] in another report by SAC Hood, "is being instituted for the purpose of keeping abreast with the activities of Heinrich Mann, 301 South Swall Drive, Los Angeles, in connection with the Free German Movement, some of which are already known to this office."[15] The same report, stamped "personal and confidential," offers this summary:

> Heinrich Mann, 73 years old Czech citizen of German descent, born 3/27/71, Luebeck, Germany is exiled German author who was allegedly assisted by underground in departing from France in 1940. Entered US as visitor 10/13/40 at New York City, and reentered for permanent residence 3/29/41 at San Ysidro, California. . . . Has been affiliated in Los Angeles with Bert Brecht and Lion Feuchtwanger, communistically inclined German refugee writers. These three are very active in Free German Movement, aim of which is establishment of postwar German government favorable to Russia. Heinrich Mann is Honorary President of Latin American Committee For Free Germany, the organization under which all Free German movements in Western Hemisphere united. He attended meeting for purpose of endorsing Moscow Manifesto, announced by Free German Committee in Mexico in July, 1943 [blacked out] . . . he signed declaration of the Council For a Democratic Germany, which is also concerned with the government of postwar Germany.

Phrases like "communistically inclined," the reference to those who aided Mann's escape from Europe as members of the "underground" (rather than "the French resistance"), and the emphasis on plans of the "Free German Movement"[16] for a pro-Russian postwar government in Germany leave no doubt that despite the war against Germany and the U.S. alliance with Russia, the FBI like the Office of Censorship was less concerned by the threat of Nazi saboteurs and spies than by the "Red menace" that Hoover since 1918–19 had seen as the real danger to the "American Way."

The "Red menace" in fact was the recurrent theme of reports on the Free Germany Movement, which the FBI and State Department suspected was another attempt, like the failed "Thomas Mann Committee," to form an exile government, this time under Communist leadership and headed by Heinrich Mann. In a summary of his "Activities in the United States—1942,"[17] the FBI announced confidently "that the Free German Movement as its ultimate purpose has the establishment of a postwar German government favorable to Soviet Russia. . . . Information available to this office indicates that at least some of the individuals involved in this movement contemplate transferring their activities to Europe or Germany as soon as this is possible."[18] When a group of exiles the FBI called the "Russian-German Committee" met a year later at the home of stage director Berthold Viertel, a longtime resident, to consider an inquiry from the Soviet news agency Tass to Thomas Mann asking his views on the newly founded National Free Germany Committee in Moscow, Thomas appears to have told the FBI or one of their informants that the group planned to release a public statement supporting the Moscow Manifesto: "According to Thomas Mann, who was questioned concerning this meeting, the statement to be drawn up was to be a declaration to be published in American papers expressing agreement with the policy of the Free Germany movement in Moscow and backing the Moscow Manifesto."[19] Later, in 1944, the FBI was concerned about Heinrich's ties to the "Council for a Democratic Germany," a group of "nineteen individuals, considerable of whom are Communists," because "during the period of the organization of the new Council in New York Mann's name was frequently mentioned as future chairman,"[20] and because the Council, the FBI believed, was interested "in shaping the postwar government of Germany."[21]

But postwar developments in Germany quickly took a different turn. The Soviet Union withdrew from the Free Germany Movement [192], and quarrels within the New York–based Council for a Democratic Germany destroyed it, so the Los Angeles Field Office broke off its first series of reports on Heinrich Mann in October 1945. After that, instead of burrowing into Mann's private correspondence and recent issues of *Freies Deutschland,* L.A.'s special agents preferred to busy themselves with the Hollywood Ten and with leads that actor Ronald Reagan and other informants supplied on allegedly left-wing colleagues in the entertainment industry. Also, Hoover's attempt to expand his operations outside the United States failed permanently at the end of the war with the founding of the Central Intelligence Group, renamed the CIA in 1947, and his agents curbed their intensive monitoring of foreigners.

Hood's men actively watched Heinrich again only when his plan to move to East Germany took concrete form. Their interest may have been triggered by Thomas Mann's attendance at the Goethe festival in Weimar, which troubled Washington and California. "Heinrich Mann . . . is an older brother of Thomas Mann also an eminent author who was admitted to the Soviet zone of Germany early this year and who was at that time exploited for propaganda purposes by the Soviet authorities,"[22] Hoover reported in October 1949, citing a "highly confidential and reliable source." In January 1950 he used virtually identical language in letters to Assistant Attorney General Peyton Ford, to Jack Neal, associate chief of the State Department's Division of Security, and to the director of intelligence for the Army General Staff. Alternatively, the FBI may have been alarmed by letters from Heinrich to the exile F. C. Weiskopf, who became a Czech diplomat after the war: "I am contemplating my move to Berlin, the Soviet Zone. Too many places have claimed me, I'm no longer at peace. . . . I can't tell people here my destination, that would immediately cause inquiries and delays. I'd like to pretend that I'm traveling to Prague and actually go there to begin with. I'm entitled because I have a Czech passport. . . . May I send you my passport, now expired? Would you arrange to renew it, and also arrange a visa for me if required?"[23]

Whatever the cause, renewed interest in Heinrich's case led the FBI to issue several memos, one "confidential by special messenger" to the Bureau of Internal Revenue,[24] the contents of which were almost entirely blacked out before their release to me but which evidently had to do with the transfer of $2,000 to Mann via East Germany's government-controlled publishing house, Aufbau Verlag.[25] On 9 March 1950, three days before Mann's death, the Counter Intelligence Corps of Region VIII stationed in Germany drew up a detailed background report on the history of Aufbau Verlag ("Soviet licensed" and "under the auspices of the Communist controlled Kulturbund")[26] and the circumstances of the suspicious money transfer. Other agencies investigated the bank that made the transfer and concluded that two of the bank directors were Soviet Russians. Despite the crisis in Berlin shortly after the blockade, the CIC took the time to calculate whether the $2,000 in question could be royalties from Mann's novel *The Patrioteer*, which Aufbau had published shortly after the war ended: "In terms of dollars twenty-thousand (20,000) copies of Der Untertan selling retail at 8.40 DM East would realize only a little more than six-thousand dollars ($6,000.00)."[27] But, the report went on, it was also conceivable that Aufbau, which received an "enormous subsidy from the Soviet Control Commission," was passing special payments to Heinrich Mann "as a favored author" for a book "which may be regarded as an excellent propaganda weapon." In any case, the CIC said, it planned to pursue the matter further "in an effort to determine whether or not Mann has arranged with Aufbau Verlag for publication of any further writings and whether or not payment of the money to Mann's account may have been occasioned by the need to finance his proposed trip to Germany."[28]

So much for the more or less "public" aspects of Mann's career as reflected in his FBI dossier. Other items relate to the private life of Heinrich and Nelly Mann. Here, the many INS forms that Mann filled out when he arrived in the United States on 14 October 1940, and when applying for a visa extension and then for permanent residence in March 1941, were the FBI's main source. The forms told them that the exile had arrived via New York with a visitor's visa[29] on the Greek steamer *Nea Hellas* and reentered from Tijuana, Mexico, by "private automobile"[30] carrying a "German Quota Immigration Visa" despite his Czech citizenship. Mann listed Warner Brothers as his employer, and under "Occupation" he stated: "I wrote books edited by the publisher Knopf at New York."[31] Like all the exiles, he unhesitatingly signed the declaration that he had not been active during the previous five years in any organization that aimed to influence any foreign government.[32] The only unusual entry is by Herbert Hadley, who handled Mann's visa affairs in 1941 and who, when filling out a form, first listed "Hebrew" under "Race" and then "German," apparently unaware that Mann was not a Jew.[33]

The files show interest by special agents when Nelly Mann was twice arrested for drunk driving by the Beverly Hills police. "She pled guilty and was to be sentenced on January 4, 1944."[34] Shortly after, SAC Hood, "in an effort to develop possible information of interest concerning the reason for Mrs. Mann's suicide," ordered his men to examine the report of the LAPD and File 17943 in the Los Angeles coroner's office, which listed the "reason or motive for Mrs. Mann's decease" as "despondent." "The basis for this reason was not shown, however . . . Heinrich Mann did not see Mrs. Mann commit suicide and was unable to give any information. No suicide notes were left by the deceased."[35]

FBI agents watching Mann's apartment noted the models and license numbers of cars parked outside: once a 1939 Hudson Sedan, another time a 1940 Oldsmobile Coupe or a 1941 Mercury Convertible Coupe.[36] The FBI wanted to know if Heinrich had applied for American citizenship[37] and who in Beverly Hills was selling his books ("it was ascertained through this source as of July, 1943, that the books of Heinrich Mann and various other German leftist writers are being sold by Reinhard [illegible] Braun, 9269 Burton Way, Beverly Hills, California, who describes himself as a representative of the Free German publication of 'Today'").[38] In a long letter to Marxist writer Johannes Becher in July 1945, right after Becher had returned from exile to Berlin but mistakenly sent to his old address in Moscow, Heinrich Mann, himself living at subsistence level, asked Becher to have all payments for Russian editions of his books sent to his daughter and first wife in Prague: "My daughter and her mother were both in a Concentration Camp, the mother is ruined, the child is better off (my God, she will be 29), but they are without funds. The consul here has promised to cable to Moscow but please do whatever you can. I cannot write from here yet."[39] Hood several times included in his reports descriptions of Mann's physical appearance, giving him "hunched shoulders, stooped build,"[40] "rimless glasses," "fleshy jowls," and a "Hitler-type mustache."[41] And of course the FBI did not neglect to investigate the circumstances of Mann's death: "death due to cerebral vascular accident and chronic pulmonary fibrosis on 3/11/50 . . . at 11.28 p.m."[42] "Sole heiress" was "Henrietta Leonie Azkanasy, Subject's daughter, who resides at Praha . . . , Czechoslovakia."[43] "In view of the death . . . it is recommended that the Bureau cancel his Security Index Card."[44]

That the left-wing Heinrich Mann ended up in the FBI files is hardly surprising given the anti-Communist atmosphere in the United States since the end of World War I, an atmosphere that was embodied in a systematic and influential form in J. Edgar Hoover. What is surprising is the intensity and tenacity with which investigators pursued until death and beyond one whom their own informants and reports repeatedly described as elderly, weary, resigned, and ailing. Because the FBI, like Heinrich and Thomas, saw that "upon entering the United States where he was relatively unknown, [Heinrich] Mann found life rather difficult and not entirely pleasant. He was short of funds, at times verging on near poverty, and was unable to bask in his former wide acclaim."[45]

But such realizations did not stop Hoover's Bureau from tracking Heinrich's left-wing or Communist ties and expressing concern that a liberal author like him might, by his works and reputation, support a postwar German government and society that differed from American concepts of democracy and free-market economics. "Heinrich Mann, from the very beginning, appeared to be a liberal and 'fellow traveller' as well as a friend and admirer of the Russian people," Hood wrote in his penultimate report dated 16 August 1950, summarizing the statement of an informer who had known Mann for years and who said of himself "that he has an excellent insight into the workings of the subject's mind."[46] Admittedly, the report goes on, Mann's admiration "for the liberals of all races and for the Russian people" had always remained theoretical and intellectual, but books like *The Patrioteer* were "well-received by the Russians" and "of considerable timely interest."[47] Or in the words of the New York SAC, who in a letter to the FBI director in January 1952, almost two years after Mann's death, made a last attempt at a political and literary characterization of "Subject Heinrich Mann, Internal Security - C": "Heinrich Mann is more radical than Thomas Mann, according to [blacked out] Heinrich Mann was one of the figure-heads in United Front Committees, which the German Communist Party had created in Paris when it was exiled due to Hitler's persecution. Heinrich Mann was not a member of the CP but was a fellow traveller of absolute obedience and had the full confidence of the CP. He is very prominent in German literature today and has been in the past. [Blacked out] stated it is a matter of discussion as to who is the better in literary work between the two brothers."[48]

KLAUS MANN

Klaus Mann, author of novels on Nazi Germany *(Mephisto)* and the exile experience *(Der Vulkan),* editor of the anti-Fascist journal *Die*

Sammlung, and the antithesis to his father in his bohemian lifestyle, constant travels, and drug consumption, entered the FBI's files by the same route as many other exiles: an anonymous denunciation. He and his writer sister Erika were "very active agents of the Comintern," claimed a letter with no return address, signature, or date sent to the U.S. embassy in London in spring 1941. "They were very active in Berlin before Hitler seized power. Klaus Mann was an active agent of Stalin in Paris, for many years." Mann was publishing an English-language magazine called *Decision* in the United States, the informer continued, which claimed to be a "neutral anti-Nazi publication" but in reality was one of the "camouflaged Communist propaganda-instruments": "The first thing these Soviet propagandists do, is to secure highly unsuspected international personalities, who sign their appeals and declarations in the launching-period of their publication. In this case, besides a number of prominent American people unsuspected of Communist connections, they also obtained the name of Benes, President of the Czechoslovak Government in London." The letter, which also denounced "Dr. Radvanij" and his wife, Anna Seghers, ended with the friendly phrase, "I hope this information may be of some use to you."[1]

The U.S. embassy dutifully passed the letter to Washington, giving no clue to its author or source. Nevertheless the State Department immediately suggested "that the Bureau might desire to index this material for future reference."[2] The bureaucratic avalanche thus triggered did not subside until the words "Subject deceased"[3] were entered in the files fifteen years later, long after Klaus Mann had returned to Europe and killed himself. "Please be advised that the information concerning the subject's activity in Germany was received from an official of the State Department on May 17, 1941," the FBI SAC in Los Angeles wrote in an internal memo in September 1951, "it was not possible to determine the writer of the original document."[4]

The mystery in which the State Department and FBI shroud

their informant is surprising, since both the Office of Censorship and the OSS had known for some time who was behind the letter. "Klaus" and "Erica" were mentioned in a 1943 "Postal and Telegraph Censorship" report by the OSS on "Free Germans": "Son and Daughter - were alleged by Schevenels, to have been active agents of the Comintern in Berlin before the advent of the Nazis. . . . Klaus was active for Stalin in Paris for many years."[5] The censorship report gave no details about "Schevenels" but presumably referred to Belgian union leader Walter Schevenels, who had fled to England in 1940 and as a high official in the powerful International Federation of Trade Unions in the United States had influential contacts in the American Federation of Labor and in the White House itself.[6]

The files on Klaus Mann compiled by the FBI, MID, ONI, and INS from 1940 to 1956 comprise more than two hundred pages. Of these, 109 are held by the FBI, which released 77 to me, with parts blacked out so that only a few words are visible. U.S. Army Intelligence in Arlington, Virginia, gave up 71 pages after their administrator for the Freedom of Information and Privacy Acts examined them and also blacked out passages. The INS released 33 pages after several years' wait.

Klaus Mann's files are mainly INS and FBI reports made between September 1940 and summer 1943, when Mann joined the U.S. Army. After extensive investigation of his loyalty, the two agencies closed their files with the finding that the "discretion, integrity and loyalty of Subject"[7] were no longer in question and that no obstacles barred his service in the army or his petition for naturalization. The FBI assigned its material to File 65-17395, "Internal Security - C." In the Central Records Classification System, 65 normally stood for espionage and C for Communist. Hoover himself more than once took a hand in the investigation, either personally or through his closest aides. Besides Washington, the New York and Los Angeles field offices actively investigated Klaus, while the MID inquiry was led by its offices at Governor's Island and Los Angeles.

As usual, information was gleaned from every imaginable source and with scant regard for how accuracy might suffer along the way.[8] Reports of "confidential informants," some from exile circles, mingle with multipage interviews with Klaus himself. Relatives were questioned, including his father Thomas and mother "Catherine" (this being the Americanized version of Katia's name favored by Military Intelligence). So were fellow exiles and acquaintances Fritz Landshoff, Bruno Frank, Gerhart Seger, and Thomas Quinn Curtis; the staff at the Bedford Hotel in New York who blabbed intimate details concerning the "sexual perversion"[9] of their long-term guest; neighbors of the Mann family in Pacific Palisades, California; and the postman assigned to 1550 San Remo Drive: "[Blacked out] stated that Klaus Mann had received mail at his father's address and that he had a discussion with Klaus Mann as to where the mail box should be placed at the Thomas Mann residence."[10] The FBI and MID consulted intercepted letters[11] and news clippings. Immigration forms were analyzed and police records checked. A physical description that the immigration authorities prepared to accompany a ten-page interview with Klaus reads like a wanted poster:

Height: 5 ft. 11 in.
Weight: 145 lbs.
Eyes: Blue
Hair: Dark Brown
Nose: Sharp
Complexion: Light
Face: Oval
Mouth: Medium
Distinctive marks: Hair grows high on each side of forehead[12]

The Bureau even knows, courtesy of "Confidential Informant T3," the exact location of Klaus's room at the Bedford Hotel: "Subject occupies room 1403 which faces the front of the hotel and is the fifth window in front from the east side of the building."[13] We have the same report to thank for telling us Mann's precise activities on the afternoon of 28 May 1942 between 12:32 and 1:30 P.M.: "On that date and at the doctor's office as above noted, Klaus Mann entered [blacked out] Street at 12:32 P.M. at which time he was wearing a gray suit, no hat, horn-rimmed glasses and brown shoes. He left the doctor's office at 12:47 P.M. and took a Lexington Avenue subway to 86th Street. At this point, he left the subway and walked over to Geiger's Restaurant at 206 East 86th Street and made a purchase of some pastry. It was 1:06 P.M. at this time. He thereafter returned to the Lexington Avenue subway and took an express train to Grand Central Station. Leaving Grand Central Station, he stopped and made a purchase at 'Filing Equipment and Office Supplies,' on the south side of 42nd Street off Lexington Avenue. He thereafter returned directly to the Hotel Bedfort at 1:30 P.M."[14] An INS "Report of Investigation Under Immigration Laws" states that Klaus was arrested on a minor charge by the LAPD in September 1940: "Q[uestion] Why were you arrested? A[nswer] I was driving without lights, and did not have the ownership papers, and they found out that the car was registered under my sister's name."[15] The FBI seemed disappointed to report that "subject" had "no credit record" in Los Angeles.[16] And extensive questioning of the Manns' former neighbors in Los Angeles, even then a fast-living and anonymous town, turned up little of interest: "The Negro domestic servant at 449 North Rockingham, recalls that the Mann family lived at 449 North Rockingham during the summer of 1940, but had no further information."[17]

The persistence with which the FBI, MID, and INS pursued the not especially successful refugee writer in the middle of a war, notwithstanding the meager results, is notable, as is the range of information they gathered. The government snoopers appear to have focused on two themes: Klaus Mann's professional activities, which they scanned for overt or covert hints of anything un-American, and his private life, where they looked for weaknesses and dependencies in the time-honored style of secret agents everywhere.

Regarding Klaus's public and political activities, the FBI and MID agreed from the start that he was a left-wing intellectual whom they assumed to have contacts, even close relations, with Communists and "Communist front organizations."[18] Isolated hints of pro-Nazi activities reflected public hysteria about Nazi sabotage and could not disguise his real convictions. MID references indicate that the INS, to whom the exile had to report frequently for permission to extend his stay, was suspicious of Klaus's petition for naturalization as a "military petitioner," not only because he had accepted fees without having a work permit and then not paid taxes on them, but also because FBI files listed him as a "well known sexual pervert" and "connected with various Communistic activities."[19] The professional Communist-hunters kept records of the writer's lecture tours and work as a journalist, and they noted how, filling in a preliminary request for naturalization, he answered "no" to the question of whether he had ever made "political speeches or propaganda speeches in the United States." Klaus's work as publisher of the magazine *Decision,* which was in print from January 1941 to January–February 1942, was regarded by the FBI and MID as a "most radical activity."[20] This was despite the information from experts consulted by the MID, including the exiled social democratic politician Gerhart Seger and Charles Henry Rieber, professor emeritus at the University of California in Los Angeles, who told the agents that *Decision* showed at most an "undercurrent of Communistic influence"[21] or a mere propensity to "'screwball' philosophical ideas."[22] Naturally both agencies scrutinized the magazine's financial decline: "'Decision' . . . had never been successful for the reason that Subject and his associates writing for the magazine had remained essentially Teutonic in their thoughts and expressions."[23]

FBI and MID interest in Klaus's professional and political activities was due at least in part to his attempt to volunteer for the U.S.

Army as soon as the United States entered the war ("impatient to join the army, as if the American uniform were a talisman against the evil spirits that pursue and harass me" [123, p. 96]). But the unusually comprehensive scan of his private life (homosexual relations, money problems, and his relationship with his father Thomas) must have originated in other factors, for one thing the narrow moral convictions of the time, and for another the hope of finding weakness in a potential opponent of the "American Way" that could be used to discredit him or—a recurrent motif in his INS file—as grounds for deportation.

Predictably, homosexuality was the topic that drew most attention in the sometimes ambiguous male world of intelligence agencies [cf. 205]. Informant T3 confidently blurted out to the FBI "that unquestionably Klaus Mann is a sexual pervert" and for good measure threw in the tidbit that when Klaus's sister Erika stayed at the Bedford Hotel, she occasionally spent the night with a doctor who had a practice at the corner of Park Avenue and 86th Street. A soldier from Governor's Island slept in Klaus's room two or three times a week, T3 went on—"a large 6 foot heavy set individual with fair complexion and dirty-blond hair. . . . Informant . . . advised . . . that the only suitable sleeping place in Mann's room is a single bed. . . . Informant further advised that quite a number of 'longhairs' go in and out to see Mann, but that he does not know the names of them."[24] In a four-page report from the New York Field Office dated 4 February 1943, an FBI agent speculates minutely how severe a case of syphilis Klaus might have: "At the request of Local Board 15, subject went to the New York City Board of Health, which . . . diagnosed subject's physical disability as syphilis and stated that from examination it appeared that 13 arsenical and 39 heavy metal injections had been received by subject."[25]

An MID special agent, Paul Abrahamson, mercilessly probed Mann's private life in a lengthy interview. The exile made a statutory declaration to Abrahamson that his syphilis test had produced "a dubious 'plus-minus' reaction."[26] And if he even had syphilis at all, Klaus declared, he had not contracted it through "any form of perversion" but simply "from a prostitute in New York."[27] "Slanderous . . ., most fantastic and false rumors" about "alleged homosexualism or perversion"[28] were attributed by Klaus to Nazi propaganda, to his novel about Alexander the Great, and to the delayed publication of Thomas Mann's Wagner-inspired novella about incest, *The Blood of the Walsungs,* and he coolly claimed "that he had never engaged in any sex practices other than those normal to a young unmarried man, who was more or less 'sewing his wild oats.'"[29]

Perhaps even more embarrassing than the interview with Klaus himself, in content and style, was an interrogation of his friend Thomas Quinn Curtiss by two MID agents that was riddled with suggestive questions: "He [Klaus] is pro-Communist, isn't he?"[30] "Question: He used to entertain a lot of soldiers in his room, didn't he?"[31] "Question: [Y]ou have no indication whatsoever that he is a homosexual?"[32] Other friends and acquaintances had similar experiences: "Informant stated" (an FBI agent said about a "drinking party" in New York) "that at this meeting were Vincent Sheean and his wife, Morris Samuels and his daughter, Strelsin and Erica Mann and Klaus Mann. Informant stated that Vincent Sheean seems to be pre-occupied sexually and that there was little doubt in his mind but that Erica Mann and Vincent Sheean had separated themselves from the group that night to indulge in sexual pastimes."[33]

Finally, the FBI and army intelligence took special interest in Klaus's financial and family situation. Informant T3 estimated that Klaus ran up a $500 debt at the Bedford Hotel in spring 1942, adding "that Confidential Informant T4 would be better able to give information concerning money matters at the Hotel."[34] Klaus himself admitted to the INS in a long interview, "I occasionally make some money with my own work," but immediately modified the statement by saying "I live as my parents' guest."[35] "Q. Has your father advanced you any money since you have been here? A. Yes. Q. Has

On May 26, 1942, Confidential Informant T3 advised that subject MANN is still residing at the Hotel Bedford, 118 East 40th Street and that at this time he owes the hotel about $500., which debt accumulated over the past several months. Informant advised that he usually gets money from his mother when he is hard-pressed. Informant stated that subject's magazine has folded and that it was MANN, himself, who told informant so. Informant also stated that MANN had told him that he had money.

Confidential Informant T3 further advised that Confidential Informant T4 would be better able to give information concerning money matters at the Hotel Bedford. Informant T3 advised that KLAUS MANN had signed checks as principal in the magazine, "Decision." This informant further stated that unquestionably KLAUS MANN is a sexual pervert and that two or three night each week, a soldier by the name of ███████ from Governor's Island spends the night with MANN in his room. Informant stated that the soldier appears during the evening and leaves MANN's quarters after 9 o'clock in the morning.

67c+D

Informant further stated that the soldier, known as ███████ is a large 6 foot heavy set individual with fair complexion and dirty-blond hair. He advised that ███████ stayed the night of May 25, 1942 and that the only suitable sleeping place in MANN's room is a single bed.

Informant further stated that subject MANN, has received his draft call; that he does not usually leave his room before 10 or 11 o'clock in the morning and that he usually goes to bed rather late. Informant further advised that quite a number of "longhairs" go in and out to see MANN, but that he does not know the names of them, Informant further advised that subject occupies room 1403 which faces the front of the hotel and is the fifth window in front from the east side of the building.

Informant T3 further stated that ERICA MANN was in the hotel on the evening of May 24, 1942 and that she was expected back again either on May 27th or during the following week. He advised that she stays in the Bedford Hotel when she is in New York, but that she is frequently away on lecture tours.

67c+D

Informant further stated that when ERICA MANN does spend the night in the hotel that ███████ occasionally spends the night with her, which doctor is alleged to have an office on Park Avenue near 86th Street. Informant stated that indications were strong that the doctor had spent the night because he was seen there very early the next morning. Later, the same day, informant T3 telephonically advised agent that at 6 P.M. that day, the man from the army known as ███████ had just arrived at the hotel and was presently up in subject, MANN's room with the subject.

Confidential Informant T4 was also interviewed on this

- 9 -

he given you any cash? A. Yes. Q. Approximately how much? A. In cash $1,500 or $2,000 within the two years. He pays my bills."[36] A New York Field Office report on Klaus's INS files lists in detail the financial institutions in Princeton (then the Manns' residence) where Thomas had accounts in 1940–41. In another interview Klaus told the INS that he estimated his father's annual income to be around $25,000.

The Manns seem generally to have presented themselves as a harmonious family with no differences of opinion about either politics or money. Thus Thomas, who now and then was himself accused by informants of being "docile to any plans of the Communists,"[37] confided to H. Ward Dawson, Jr., an MID agent who held a lengthy interview with him at the family home on San Remo Drive on 4 June 1943, that he and his son shared the same moderate political views. "Mann stated," Dawson summed up in a two-page document, that "his son had the same democratic ideas that he had, and during 1940 was enthusiastic about 'Aid for Britain.' He continued, his son was an ardent Nazi-hater. . . . To be sure, Mann averred, his son was liberal-minded but had never evidenced any radical tendencies"—a statement that "Mrs. Catherine Mann, Subject's mother . . . , interviewed on June 6, 1943, at her home" confirmed: her son Klaus was "quite like his father." He found the Nazis "unbearable" and no one had ever accused him of being a Communist. On the contrary, according to Katia Mann, "Subject's last book had been given a writeup in the Daily Worker (a New York Communist paper), and . . . this review had been adverse to the book and Subject." Thomas Mann "concluded by saying his son . . . joined the Army in January of 1943 in New York, and that from the tone of his letters Subject was enjoying being in the service very much."[38]

The information of Klaus's parents was supported by the interviewing agent: "This Agent believes that Thomas Mann would prefer not to answer a question than to answer it dishonestly,"[39] and by other sources. "Subject had come from a fine family, sound stock, and his home life had been excellent," testified a family friend whose name was blacked out by the FBI, and went on: "He had been a well-behaved child . . . , adoring his father, very seldom in the past having gone contrary to his wishes."[40] Neighbors of the Manns in Pacific Palisades said unanimously that Klaus had never in their presence made any remarks about "governmental or economical problems" and that they had observed "nothing un-American in his statements or conduct."[41] The FBI and MID heard mostly positive remarks from other exiles. Klaus "would do nothing to in any way cast suspicion or doubt upon his father or his belief in democracy,"[42] one anonymous interviewee told the MID. Exile Bruno Frank, never accused of being Marxist, said in a Beverly Hills interview dated 7 June 1943 that Klaus was a "capable writer, clever psychologist with high character and abilities."[43] Other named or anonymous informants expressed similar views.

Sexual perversion, a sympathy to Communist thought, syphilis, dubious friends, financial problems, and reports from his army trainers that neither his discipline nor his mode of dress were quite what they should be ("Mann appears on company punishment records as having been restricted . . . for one week for mixed uniform"):[44] none of it could dissuade the War Department, responsible for Klaus once he had been inducted, from accepting "Private Mann" as a soldier and supporting him in his ardent appeal for American citizenship. ("But if my application were straightaway *rejected,*"he wrote, "SUICIDE actually would be the only logical response, would be almost inevitable" [123, p. 147].) "Loyal; trustworthy; honest; discreet; persevering; choosey in friends" was the verdict of a comprehensive investigation of Mann's loyalty that ranged from New York to Los Angeles, and it added that he was of good family, "well-behaved; anti-Nazi; extremely democratic; liberal in ideas; not Communist."[45] The harsh judgment of fellow emigrés Gerhart Seger and Rudolf Katz that Klaus was "shallow and degenerate"[46] was now forgotten by agents, and forgotten too was that first letter, sent to the U.S. embassy in London, that had denounced Mann for links with the Comintern, Stalin, and the "Guépéou" (the GPU, or Soviet secret police).[47] "This agent is of the opinion," Abrahamson concluded his investigation, "that citizenship should be allowed Subject,"[48] and Dawson recommended, "if no further or other adverse information is uncovered, that Subject be favorably considered for assignment as a student in Military Intelligence Training Center, Camp Ritchie, Maryland."[49]

Whether democratic attitudes finally prevailed to the advantage of the accused in a case where there was reasonable doubt; whether the army's examining agents were actually impressed by Klaus's personal qualities ("highly intelligent and possesses a wonderful command of the English language"); or whether, in view of the imminent assault on Hitler's Fortress Europe, what triumphed was the pragmatic view "that Subject would be very useful in combat propaganda"[50]—U.S. citizenship was conferred on Klaus Mann ("single, former nationality Czechoslovakian")[51] on 25 September 1943, he was admitted into the military intelligence service soon after, and his FBI and MID files were closed.

ERIKA MANN

Erika Mann's FBI dossier differs from the other files primarily in that for more than a decade she was not only a subject of investigation but volunteered information to Hoover's Bureau.[1]

Mann first contacted the FBI in spring 1940, and she remained under surveillance for more than ten years, until her return to Europe. The FBI released some one hundred pages from its files on her in New York, Los Angeles, Newark, and Washington, including interview notes and data on her personal habits, lecture tours, friends, acquaintances, and relatives.[2] The INS gave me 30 pages but refused to part with an astonishing 375, citing "exemptions" to the Freedom of Information Act.[3] Transcripts and records of mail and telephone surveillance, which clog many exile dossiers, were not preserved. A half dozen FBI reports, the longest one 16 densely filled pages, summarize and update data for 1941–43 and 1951–54. A list of aliases beginning with "Erica Mann" and including "Mrs. Wystan H. Auden" and "Erika Julia Hedwig Auden, nee Mann" was used to trace cross-references, indicating how tight a net was cast over exiles whose political views or personal conduct attracted the Bureau's attention.

But Erika Mann, author of a formidable list of books and essays in German and English, among them *School for Barbarians* and, with Klaus Mann, *Escape to Life* and *The Other Germany,* was not just an FBI target. From 1940 until the early fifties, independent of shifts in the U.S. political climate, she repeatedly supplied information on various topics, including members of the emigré colony.

In 1940, she offered Hoover the opportunity to choose from among her many acquaintances in German exile organizations in New York two "very responsible people who would be willing to give us their reactions concerning any of the German leaders in Europe or the United States today."[4] "I talked with Miss Erica Mann and [blacked out] today," a report from December 1941 quotes T. J. Donegan, assistant special agent in charge of the FBI's New York office. "The purpose of Miss Mann's visit . . . was to introduce [blacked out] to me," who, although he did not speak especially good English, was by his knowledge of Germany "in an excellent position to furnish information regarding refugee activities." "[Blacked out] agreed that he would be available whenever we desired and would be glad to furnish any information."[5]

Ten years later, in a greatly changed political situation, the SAC in Los Angeles described Erika Mann as cooperative, after an interview "concerning the case [blacked out]," and proposed in a report to the "Director, FBI": "In view of the fact that the subject appeared to be cooperative in the interview mentioned above, you should consider the advisability of requesting Bureau authority to interview the subject concerning her Communist activities."[6] Another agent reported, after an interview with Erika at her father's home in Pacific Palisades, that not only would she "probably be cooperative if interviewed" about "Communist Party activities" but also "about other matters of which she has knowledge." Given her positive attitude, she ought therefore to be questioned as soon as she returned from her next trip to Europe: "In view of Mann's attitude, it is requested that the Bureau grant authority for interview with Mann concerning her knowledge of Communist Party activities upon her return from Europe in September, next."[7] "Agents stated," the director summed up in September 1951 in a passage marked "On Yellow Only," meaning an internal memo for Washington headquarters, "she . . . indicated a desire to be of assistance to that Office," and recalled that "the best known daughter of Thomas Mann" had already willingly and frequently supplied information on various matters for many years: "During the past war, she was frequently contacted by the New York Office on her own initiative and furnished information regarding German matters."[8]

In contrast to many exile files, Erika Mann's dossier does not begin with a denunciation or publication that makes her a suspected Communist but with a series of memoranda between Francis Biddle, the U.S. deputy attorney general, and high-ranking FBI officials.[9] The first memo discusses whether and how to make use of Mann's offer to tell the FBI what she knows. "I informed the Solicitor General," Hoover's deputy E. A. Tamm told the director on 4 June 1940, "that I would arrange to have an Agent of our New York City Office get in touch with Miss Mann there to arrange a mutually convenient time for a meeting." Tamm stressed the importance of receiving the information from "Miss Mann and her friends" in a way that would not involve "any official recognition"[10] and that would keep Thomas and Heinrich Mann out of the investigation: "Particular discretion was urged in the investigations of Erika Mann and her brother, Klaus Mann. The Bureau also instructed that no investigation was to be conducted of Thomas Mann or Heinrich Mann."[11]

Hoover did not let slip the opportunity to tap a source so highly placed in the exile community. "I told [FBI agent] Mr. Foxworth," Tamm reported in a memo to his boss in mid-June 1940, "you desired him to contact Miss Mann and try to establish a liaison which might be of possible value."[12] Next day, Erika sent a first sample of her work to Hoover through the journalist Walter Winchell, who worked closely with the director,[13] a letter from a soldier addressed to Thomas Mann. With it was a note from go-between Winchell that said, "She thought you should see it and maybe check this writer."[14]

Erika Mann's activity as a cooperative and credible source of information ("interviewing agents stated she was most cooperative")[15] continued until the early fifties when she moved back to Europe for good. Periodically she would drop by FBI headquarters in New York to reveal, for example, that a refugee was "very suspicious" because although not a Jew, he had slipped past the British authorities by marking a "J" on his German passport. Another exile (whose name of course was blacked out by the FBI before giving me the files) was, Erika claimed, the "chief German saboteur for the Nazis" in France.[16] From a friend in Florida she learned that an acquaintance now involved in shady business dealings in America had been "a German adventurer during the Polish invasion."[17] She unselfishly recommended to the FBI a "Miss [blacked out] who she stated had been her personal secretary for four years,"[18] praising her as an able and reliable translator, and at the same time offered her own services: "She also volunteered to do any German translation work which we might desire and she stated that she would handle such matters in an absolutely confidential way."[19] And when the Office of Naval Intelligence questioned her after she returned to Boston from France, she gave information not only about her work ("was employed as a War Correspondent for Liberty Magazine")

JOHN EDGAR HOOVER
DIRECTOR

Federal Bureau of Investigation
United States Department of Justice
Washington, D. C.

EAT:JJW   June 10, 1940

2:30 P.M.

MEMORANDUM FOR THE DIRECTOR

    While talking to Mr. Foxworth at New York
City, I advised him that Erika Mann, daughter of the
exiled German writer, was recently in to see the
Solicitor General and stated she thought she might
be in a position to furnish information about Germans.
Her address is 118 East 40th Street, which is the
Bedford Hotel.

    I told Mr. Foxworth you desired him to con-
tact Miss Mann and try to establish a liaison which
might be of possible value.

                            Respectfully,

                            E. A. TAMM

CC: Mr. Clegg

N   55-17395-1

RECORDED
&
INDEXED

but about her private affairs: "She has no real estate in this country . . . and . . . has a nearly defunct bank account."[20]

Two closely related incidents make clear how tenaciously the FBI pursued sources like Erika Mann once they proved useful. First, in spring 1951 the New York office sent out a barrage of telegrams marked "Top Secret" and "Secret" trying to locate her, hoping she could shed light on the mysterious disappearance of British diplomats Guy Burgess and Donald MacLean. Burgess, who alarmed Western intelligence by fleeing to Moscow in May 1951, had belonged to the same circle as Erika's former husband W. H. Auden. But the Mann-Auden-Burgess connection turned out to be a dead end. Much time and effort were spent tracing the missing Erika, who had been hospitalized in Chicago and was found when she returned to her father's home ("discharged Billings Hospital Chicago, Illinois, on May 28 . . . returned to her home at 1550 San Remo Drive Pacific Palisades, Calif."). But although she willingly told what she knew, the information sent back to Hoover in a telegram marked "urgent"[21] cannot have been much help. "Mrs. W.H. Auden" could hardly remember Burgess but thought that he was rarely sober when she saw him at parties in London; and since he used to spend time with writers Christopher Isherwood and Stephen Spender, who were also members of Auden's group,[22] it was possible ("Erica" said) that he was homosexual and that, like Spender and others, he subscribed to the "aims and purposes of the CP."[23] She could provide no more definite "leads" than that, she said,[24] because she had not even known of the Burgess-MacLean affair until the special agent told her about it.

An unpublished and undated manuscript fragment from this period, found among Mann's papers after her death, contains the following description of the episode: "The F.B.I. have been here again. . . . I had just returned from a Chicago hospital. . . . The man in question, it turned out, was Guy Burgess, one of the 2 British diplomats who are said to have escaped to Russia last summer. . . .

Wasn't it odd that I should so completely fail to remember him? Perhaps with a little help . . . ? I thought hard. And true enough—there it was, a bloke by the name of Guy. . . . Hadn't he been working for the B.B.C. at the time of the big 'Blitz' . . . ? They nodded patiently—not quite trusting my haziness of course. . . . As I proved unable [or unwilling?] to name any one in this [illegible] likely to possess additional information, they departed leaving me wondering whether there wasn't, after all, something I knew, and which it would have been my duty to report."[25]

The interview about the British spy scandal, unproductive though it was, started the FBI thinking about questioning Erika again concerning her ties to the Communist Party. On 24 October 1951, during this second episode of FBI contacts, she was questioned in her father's home and claimed that she herself, the former wife of the poet who headed the "Auden Group,"[26] "has never been remotely connected with the Comintern or the Communist Party of any country, and . . . has never knowingly espoused a Communist Party cause." Moreover, Otto Katz, "an avowed Communist" and "probably a Comintern agent" whom she had met in her exile in Paris in 1937, gave her a thorough distaste for working with Communists. Concerning America's Abraham Lincoln Brigade, which had fought on the Republican side against Franco in the Spanish Civil War, she claimed to know that it was "definitely a Communist inspired and dominated organization," whereas she herself had been entirely "unbiased" in her own reporting from Spain. The Communist Party, "Miss Mann volunteered," was nationally and internationally "an extreme menace to the freedom of the democracies," just as Fascism had been in the thirties and forties. This was the reason she and her father had stayed out of all organizations, "because of their fear that the organization might be a Communist dominated one."[27]

Reports from East Germany claiming that Thomas Mann supported the Stockholm Peace Petition, and information that she and

SAC, Los Angeles

Director, FBI

September 13, 1951

ERICA MANN, was.
SECURITY MATTER - C
Your file 100-7804
RECORDED-20 Bufile 65-17395 — 46

**ALL INFORMATION CONTAINED
HEREIN IS UNCLASSIFIED
DATE 7-19/85 BY sp-2545/byy**

EX. - 105

Reurlet dated August 15, 1951.

In view of the fact that the subject appeared to be cooperative during the interview with her concerning the disappearance of Guy De M. Burgess, you are authorized to interview her concerning her Communist activities.

You should take appropriate steps to assure being promptly advised of her return to the United States.

Please be advised that the information concerning the subject's activity in Germany was received from an official of the State Department on May 17, 1941. At the time that this information was received, the State Department was unable to obtain any additional identifiable data concerning the original communication received by them and it was not possible to determine the writer of the original document which sets forth the allegations regarding the subject's activity in Germany.

In view of the interest of the Immigration and Naturalization Service in this matter, the results of your interview should be set forth in report form suitable for dissemination. A copy of this report should be disseminated locally to the Los Angeles Office of the Immigration and Naturalization Service.

(On Yellow Only) Subject is the best known daughter of Thomas Mann, novelist, professor, and refugee from Hitler's Germany. During the past war, she was frequently contacted by the New York Office on her own initiative and furnished information regarding German matters. She has been a frequent visitor to the U. S. and is not a U. S. citizen. She is a citizen of England.

During an extensive investigation no information has ever been developed that she has been a member of the CP in the U. S., although she has been active in and loaned her name to some Communist Front organizations. In 1950, in Los Angeles, California, she addressed some meetings sponsored by the Jewish Peoples Fraternal Order which is part of the International Workers Order which in turn has been cited by Attorney General. She was interviewed by agents of the Los Angeles Office in June 1951, concerning the disappearance of Guy Burgess, an English scientist. At that time the interviewing agents stated she was most cooperative and indicated a desire to be of assistance to that Office. Los Angeles has requested permission to interview her specifically regarding her Communist activities. INS has also expressed interest in the subject and has not as yet obtained sufficient evidence upon which base the issuance of a warrant of arrest in deportation proceedings.

JRH:jas

COMM-FBI
SEP 14 1951
MAILED 13
SEP 19

her father had worked for the Cultural and Scientific Conference for World Peace in New York, which at the time was being attacked as a Communist "party-line assembly" [211, p. 397], were simply false, she said ("he . . . had definitely refused to sign it").[28] Moreover, when her father had been asked in 1948 to support Henry Wallace, the presidential candidate of the liberal Progressive Party of America, Mann had immediately distanced himself after Erika asked the candidate why he only criticized the United States but not the USSR and Wallace replied that there were already enough people expressing negative views of Russia.

The FBI files I examined permit no other interpretation than that, for whatever reasons, Erika Mann seems to have talked with U.S. agencies like the FBI more openly and over a longer period than any other exile writer, with the exception of "ex-Communists" like Ruth Fischer and Karl August Wittfogel [168] or the shady adventurer Richard Krebs, alias Jan Valtin. This is not to deny that the journalist, lecturer, and writer was simultaneously under close surveillance by the Bureau while she fed it information, as she herself evidently sensed with disquiet. "Were it not for my fierce dislike of the comrades and virtually all that they stand for, I should—out of sheer stubborn courage—promptly commence to fellow travel like mad," she wrote. "For, neither the 'Un-American Activities Committee' nor the 'Loyalty Checks' nor any of the activities of the F.B.I. and related bodies are at all funny, and it takes considerable mulishness not to be intimidated."[29] The reason for the surveillance was the same as for other refugees from Central Europe: without any concrete evidence ("her activities in Los Angeles have not indicated any un-American leanings"),[30] the daughter of Thomas Mann, "the famed exile,"[31] was suspected of being a Communist or at least a fellow traveler, and at other times of associating with conservative critics of Germany like Friedrich Wilhelm Förster and T. H. Tetens. Like almost all the writers in exile, she was listed on a Communist index card. Even the methods of information gathering were the same in her case as for other exiles: mail interception and telephone tapping (although no records of her mail or calls have been preserved), questioning of hotel staff and acquaintances, news clippings, rumors.

The surveillance of Erika Mann, who lectured widely in America denouncing Nazi policies in her homeland, began with the same undated and unsigned letter of denunciation sent in 1941 to the U.S. embassy in London that set the State Department and FBI to watching Klaus: "Klaus and Erika Mann are very active agents of the Comintern."[32] Ten years later almost to the day, Louis Budenz, a former Communist and *Daily Worker* employee [24, 25], put U.S. intelligence in an uproar with a list of "400 Concealed Communists," but he soon crossed off Erika's name and others because he could not "positively"[33] identify them as Communists. Finally, three years later, on 23 July 1954, an FBI employee in London, who without realizing it may have come across the old undated letter from 1941, noted in a last report on Erika, who had long since moved back to Europe: "An anonymous communication received by American Embassy, London, suggests subject (a communist) be investigated thoroughly."[34]

The FBI treated Erika more or less as it did all the exiles in 1941–54 when she was under surveillance. True, agents cannot have "come once a week to interrogate [me]" as she claimed to remember in an interview in 1965.[35] But "confidential informants" expressed outrage "that Klaus and Erica Mann were having affairs together" and that one of the books by their father described these affairs, while other informants said they were shocked by the "sexual perversions"[36] of the group that included Erika and Klaus Mann, Auden, and Isherwood. A personal description by the FBI emphasized that "subject" wore her hair "in short mannish bob with part on right side."[37] An FBI report of October 1941 expounds at length on INS files (now lost or at least not released to me) that told how Erika's Peppermill political revue, which in Europe had been perhaps the most successful theater enterprise of the exiles, toured the United States in the winter of 1936–37 ("Erika Mann . . . described the production as being in intimate European style to bring the audience and players together, making the audience almost a part of the production"[38]) and described the lives of the Peppermill players, all "members of the Hebrew race."[39]

In Princeton the FBI tackled the "city directory, phone book, and post office records," plus the *Princeton Herald* and *Princeton Packet* newspapers, but learned nothing more than that the Mann family had remained "very aloof from the townsfolk"[40] and had not made any left-wing statements, "as any such statements would be quite noticeable and remembered in a town like Princeton."[41] FBI Confidential Informant #1 at New York's Bedford Hotel brought word of Erika's "associates"[42] and lists of incoming and outgoing phone calls. The FBI learned from reports of HUAC and California's Tenney Committee that she was a member, among other organizations, of the Non-Sectarian Committee for Political Refugees, "an avowed affiliate of the International Labor Defense, 'legal arm of the Communist Party.'"[43] FBI special agents, in routine cooperation with the INS, stumbled on newspaper clippings that in part described Erika's problematic attitude toward U.S. policies on Germany, an attitude that had also worried the State Department: "Miss Mann declared that 'denazification of Germany has failed entirely' . . . , that re-education and rehabilitation programs have ceased, and that occupation forces are not in Germany because of the Germans, but because of the Russians."[44]

Thomas Mann, interviewed by FBI officials under pretext, told them details of his daughter's travel plans, not knowing that he himself was under observation: "He and Mrs. Mann . . . purchased the property on the corner of Monaco and San Remo Drives, buying the land, which approximates one acre in area, for $6,500. The building permit as issued was in the amount of $23,000."[45] Other informants described Erika as a "very vicious person who has played ball with

Communists for years";[46] blamed her for having a bad influence on Thomas and Heinrich Mann ("[Blacked out] stated that . . . subject was responsible for the 'leftist' writings attributed to her father and her uncle"); accused her of having been for a long time "an outstanding 'pro-Communist' and 'fellow traveler' and a Communist Party front organizer";[47] recalled long-ago meetings in Berlin in 1924 and in Barcelona during the Spanish Civil War ("[Blacked out] described this congress as a Communist thing staged by Willy Munsingberg")[48] and an attempt to found a United Front newspaper in Paris in 1937. These informants justified their statements, in the style of the times, by claiming to repent of their own left-wing past: "[Blacked out] . . . stated that he was in the Communist Party in Germany from 1923 to 1926. . . . He stated that he has seen the subject on a few occasions, the last being at the Russian Institute at Columbia University. He concluded that he considered the subject to be a 'fellow traveler.'"[49]

Like other dossiers, Erika Mann's is riddled with errors that range from the misspelling of her husband's name ("Audan,"[50] her partner in a "marriage . . . of convenience"),[51] to a reference to Thomas Mann as "perhaps the most publicized of all Jewish refugees from the Nazi regime,"[52] to an FBI man's credulous acceptance of an informant's claim that the Motion Picture Guild was founded in 1939 expressly to perform Erika's "'School for Barbarians.'"[53]

The FBI was not the only agency investigating Erika Mann ("Height: 5′ 9″, Weight: 120, Hair: Brown, Eyes: Brown . . . No scars or marks").[54] The Office of the Coordinator of Information, forerunner of the OSS, employed her services briefly,[55] and the OSS also took an interest, albeit minimal, in the daughter of the famous Thomas Mann but was never to my knowledge in direct contact with her. Central to OSS concerns was the influence that she allegedly had on her father's decision to withdraw from a Free Germany committee of exiles. Donovan's agents also monitored real or alleged shifts in her political views ("Erica Mann had now joined Foerster and Emil Ludwig in the Society for the Prevention of World War III"),[56] and the everyday gossip in the exile colony ("Erika Mann, unlike her father, Feuchtwanger continued, was a Vansittartist. Then he confided that Erika's sister, the wife of Professor Giuseppe Borgese, was 'much more intelligent' than Erika").[57]

Whether the CIA continued to take an interest in Erika Mann after the OSS was dissolved is unknown. But the INS, which released only thirty pages of its extensive files and those only of fairly unimportant news clippings, did ask for FBI assistance several times around 1950, when it hoped to institute deportation proceedings against her, a matter about which she apparently had some knowledge.[58] "INS has . . . expressed an interest in the subject and has not as yet obtained sufficient evidence upon which to base the issuance of a warrant of arrest in deportation proceedings," the FBI reported.[59] The released files do not say how far the INS and FBI pushed these proceedings, for which Hoover found there was not "sufficient admissible evidence" despite the "extensive investigation of subject" up to June 1951.[60] On the other hand, an FBI note confirms that Erika Mann, "Title of Case: Internal Security - C," "Espionage - C," and "Security Matter - C," withdrew her application for U.S. citizenship at the start of the fifties. Considering that for more than ten years she had been not only a victim but also a source of information for the FBI, the reasons she listed for taking this step may strike us as a little strange: "ruined career, reduced means of livelihood and considerable embarrassment resulting from investigations into her loyalty."[61]

Dossiers

BERTOLT BRECHT

Bertolt Brecht's exile in America was marked by paradox from the start. Disappointed by his first visit to New York in 1935–36, he nevertheless applied for a U.S. immigration visa shortly after, from his refuge in Scandinavia. In transit through the Soviet Union, he did not for a moment hesitate to turn his back on the world's first Communist state and his friends in Moscow to enter the "hell" [20, vol. 12, p. 115] of Los Angeles and to revisit New York, where previously he could stand the life only with a "gulp . . . of whiskey" [27, p. 234]. He did not have one good thing to say about Hollywood, "the market of lies" [20, vol. 12, p. 122] or about Broadway, which lacked "tradition."[1] Yet he at once set about making contacts in the American film and theater industries and selling his "wares" [ibid., vol. 15, p. 78] cheaply to the "dream factories" [ibid., vol. 12, p. 115]. He commented ironically on both the political views of fellow refugees and the naïveté of Americans he met with to plan a new, improved Germany. His outstanding lack of influence as an author, stage producer, and teacher while in the United States contrasts sharply with the long list of plays, poems, filmscripts, and theoretical writings that he completed there.

As an exile Brecht may have had an ambivalent attitude about his host country, but the most powerful police agency in the United States had no problem figuring out its opinion of the refugee, his views, and his activities from 1941 to 1947: "Subject's writings . . . advocate overthrow of Capitalism, establishment of Communist State and use of sabotage by labor to attain its ends."[2]

Two features typify Brecht's FBI file, more than four hundred pages of which were released to me:[3] Hoover's intense distrust of exiles preparing their return to Europe within the framework of the Free Germany Movement, and the unusually well-documented record of surveillance techniques used to monitor Brecht's private life. An additional feature is that the FBI and the House Un-American Activities Committee took more than customary interest in the literary work of their "subject," "Bertolt Eugen Friedrich Brecht, with aliases."[4]

The close link between Free Germany, government surveillance, and literature is established in Brecht's dossier in a memo dated 16 April 1943, when an unnamed special agent and Los Angeles SAC R. B. Hood tried to persuade Hoover to start internment proceedings against Brecht through the "United States Attorney." Citing two FBI reports from March 1943, Hood told the director that his office had learned from informants "that subject is a writer of Communist and revolutionary poetry and drama . . . and . . . looked upon by German Communists as their poet laureate."[5] A translation of Brecht's poem "Demolition of the Ship Oskawa by the Crew" was made by FBI agents, who were unaware that it was based on an American event described in Louis Adamic's *Dynamite* [2; cf. 144]. They cited it as evidence that Brecht supported not only construction of a "Communist state" but sabotage and the destruction of American property: "The poem . . . specifically refers to a United States steamer which was destroyed by its crew since they were paid too small wages. It specifically refers to the expense to the United States of this act of sabotage." Without comment (although it is clear what they thought), Hood and his subordinate quoted an article in the April issue of *Freies Deutschland* magazine about a Brecht performance in New York. Finally, Hood examined a Brecht text that allegedly showed the political unreliability of the exiles in the Free Germany Movement: "Furthermore, the author, and subject of this case, does not consider himself, according to his writings, an immigrant, but rather an exile from Germany, his native country. The poem 'On the Designation "Emigrant"' . . . expresses this point of view."[6]

Many documents show how seriously the FBI took the links between Brecht, the Free Germans in Mexico and Moscow, *Freies Deutschland* and the movement's policy on Germany. One example is a memo, "Free German Activities in the Los Angeles Area," that Hood sent to Hoover's office on 18 May 1944: "Since correspondence between the Free German group in Mexico and persons in the Los Angeles area has been carried on . . . it is recommended that the following subjects be placed on the National Censorship Watch List

FEDERAL BUREAU OF INVESTIGATION

Form No. 1
THIS CASE ORIGINATED AT   !LOS ANGELES   FILE NO. 100-21367

REPORT MADE AT	DATE WHEN MADE	PERIOD FOR WHICH MADE	REPORT MADE BY
LOS ANGELES	10/21/44	9/4,19,20; 10/4/44	SIDNEY E. THWING GIF

TITLE	CHARACTER OF CASE
FREE GERMAN ACTIVITIES IN THE LOS ANGELES AREA	INTERNAL SECURITY - C

SYNOPSIS OF FACTS:

Inquiry among members of German organizations in
Los Angeles failed to disclose any efforts on the
part of leaders of Free German movement to influence
these organizations in favor of the Free German
movement. BERTOLT BRECHT in conversation with Source
D. stated no effort being made to form Free German
organization in Los Angeles area. BRECHT also stated
his sole connection with Free German movement was as
member of Council For a Democratic Germany in New York.
BRECHT also stated his purpose in joining this Council
was to make certain no member of German military clique
or Nazi Party has any part in formation of postwar
German government. LION FEUCHTWANGER continues to
write for "Freies Deutschland" in Mexico City. CNDI
LA 1461 unable to furnish any additional information
regarding Free German movement in Mexico City.

- P -

REFERENCE: Report of Special Agent RICHARD C. THOMPSON,
                  Los Angeles, August 19, 1944.

DETAILS:

AT LOS ANGELES, CALIFORNIA:

The following investigation was conducted by Special Agent
RICHARD C. THOMPSON:

APPROVED AND FORWARDED:	SPECIAL AGENT IN CHARGE	DO NOT WRITE IN THESE SPACES

COPIES OF THIS REPORT
5 Bureau
2 Chicago   2 Philadelphia
2 Milwaukee   2 San Francisco
2 New York   2 Los Angeles

U. S. GOVERNMENT PRINTING OFFICE   16—27962-1

112

for ninety days: 1. [blacked out]. 2. Bertolt Brecht, 1063 - 26 Street, Santa Monica, California. 3. [blacked out]."[7] Trying to reconstruct Brecht's "activities in the United States" in 1941–42, the FBI consulted copies of *Freies Deutschland* in its Los Angeles archives and summarized Brecht's relations with the Free Germans: "It is . . . known that the Free German movement has as its aim the establishment of a postwar German government favorable to Soviet Russia. . . . The Free German Committee in Mexico is the fountainhead of the movement in the Western Hemisphere."[8]

Brecht's support for Free Germany and the Council for a Democratic Germany took on new significance in 1944 when Hoover stepped up his warnings against the Communist threat, the invasions of North Africa and Normandy made the collapse of the Third Reich appear imminent, and the United States had to think about the reeducation of German POWs and about Germany's future. The OSS, while it paid scant attention to Brecht as a "gifted dramatist" and "poet of expressionistic vigor,"[9] listened with interest to an informant who told them that well-known Stalinist Germans like Brecht and Wieland Herzfelde felt their cause would soon be victorious in Germany ("They warn their non-Communist friends quite openly to make their peace with the CP if they want to 'obtain return visas'")[10] and that Brecht, while making himself available as an "adviser" to theologian Paul Tillich's Council for a Democratic Germany,[11] had refused to become a member. The FBI of course took a keen interest in the doomed efforts of Brecht, Feuchtwanger, the Mann brothers, and others to arrive at a joint position about Moscow's National Free Germany Committee:

> During July or August 1943, according to this source, Bert Brecht attended a meeting for the purpose of endorsing the Moscow manifesto issued by the National Committee for Free Germany in Moscow during July. The information furnished by this source was to the effect that on August 9,

1943, Lion Feuchtwanger had advised that Tass, the Russian news agency, had requested him and Thomas Mann, brother of Heinrich Mann, to express their opinions on a certain matter. Feuchtwanger claimed that he convinced Mann that he should accept Tass's request only after a long discussion, and that thereafter a meeting was held at the home of Berthold and Salka Viertel, 165 Mabery Road, Santa Monica, California, who have been mentioned previously, for the purpose of drawing up a statement. Persons present at the Viertel home and first agreed to sign such a statement, according to Feuchtwanger, were Thomas Mann, Bruno Frank, Ludwig Marcuse, Berthold Viertel, Bert Brecht, probably [illegible] Eisler, and a professor whose name could not be recalled by this source. However, on the following day Thomas Mann, Bruno Frank, Ludwig Marcuse, and the professor withdrew their names.[12]

The name of the informant who told the FBI about the meeting at the Viertels' home was blacked out before Brecht's file was released. So were names of sources who reported the planning talks in New York for the Council for a Democratic Germany, which Brecht attended as one of the "leading Communist Party functionaries."[13] And the person who put Special Agents Sidney Thwing and Howard Davis on Brecht's trail in 1944 also remains concealed behind a code-letter: "Source D . . . asked Brecht what the purpose of the Free German movement was and what his reasons were in helping it. Brecht replied, according to Source D, that the purposes of the Free German organization and his reasons for joining the Committee were one and the same, and that they were: (1) to see that no person who is a member of the German Military clique is placed in a responsible governmental position in the postwar German Government; (2) to see that no person who is a member of, or sympathetic to the Nazi Party in Germany is placed in a responsible governmental position in the postwar German government . . . whether the democratic governments or Russia dominate postwar Germany made no difference to him as long as the persons who belonged to the above mentioned groups gained no power."[14]

This is not the place for a thorough analysis of the extensive material the FBI gathered on the Council for a Democratic Germany. But another theme in Brecht's files warrants brief examination: the Bureau's schizophrenic attitude toward exiles associated with Free Germany, who on one hand were expected to return to Europe or were at risk of deportation, and on the other were denied permission to leave.[15] Thus the FBI noted that in 1936, Brecht was allowed to extend his German visitor's visa in New York [201].[16] A report from "C.N.D.I. [blacked out]," a Confidential National Defense Informant whom we will meet again, recorded with concern in 1944 "that Bert Brecht and Hanns Eisler had conversed with Benes (first name believed to be Bohus), then Czechoslovakian Consul at San Francisco about the possibility of obtaining Czechoslovakian passports. This informant advised that Brecht and Eisler are already concerning themselves with an early return to Europe. They apparently believe that possession of Czech passports will facilitate their travel, particularly their departure from this country." An FBI agent thickly underlined a passage from the same source stating that Brecht, who on all but one occasion cleared with U.S. authorities any trip he took inside the United States, and Hanns Eisler thought they could leave the country without an exit visa if necessary: "'Well, the border is close by.'"[17] The FBI was just as suspicious about Brecht's return to Europe in 1947: "It has come to the attention of this office that the above-mentioned subject intends to leave the United States in September of this year for Switzerland and then will proceed to Germany. . . . The Washington Field Office is requested to ascertain at the State Department if Brecht has applied for an exit visa and the type of passport on which he is travelling. . . . It is requested that Philadelphia and Washington Field expedite the leads set forth inasmuch as the Bureau may desire that Brecht be interviewed before his departure for Europe in case he does not apply for a re-entrance permit."[18]

The Bureau's planned interview with Brecht, which is mentioned in various documents, never materialized. Inadequate information about his whereabouts and date of departure ("it not being known definitely where he is at the moment"),[19] the slow transfer of information along official channels between the various field offices, and Hoover's concern not to disrupt Brecht's hearing before HUAC ("postpone plans to interview subject until after his appearance before House Committee on Unamerican Activities")[20] delayed the G-men until it was too late. When Hood reported to headquarters that the regional INS office believed that "deportation proceedings against Brecht may be instituted by Saturday, November 8, 1947,"[21] Brecht was already in Zurich doing just what the FBI feared he would: joining with prominent writers like Carl Zuckmayer, Erich Kästner, Werner Bergengruen, and Max Frisch to denounce the Cold War. "The expectation of a new war," they said, was preventing the "rebuilding of the world," and "the existence of two different economic systems in Europe" was being used by the politicians "for new war propaganda" [228, p. 117].

The drama over internment and deportation, expulsion, "reentry permits," and "custom stops," important to both sides in the light of new issues like German reeducation and postwar cultural policy, did not end when Brecht fled the United States. "According to recent column," the FBI's New York office said in an "urgent" telegram to the director on 20 March 1956, "subject is to appear at the open stage theatre, NYC . . . to review his play, 'Private Life of the Master Race.'"[22] Whereupon headquarters in Washington, evidently thinking Brecht worth the expense of a surveillance operation even in 1956, decided instantly: "He is of sufficient importance in international Communism that the Bureau should be aware of all his activities and his contacts."[23] But the times they were a-changing. The playwright did not appear at the New York theater, or anywhere else in the United States, on the appointed date, and the audience made fun of the FBI special agents, saying, "'we expected to see hordes of fbi men here,'" and "'we certainly fooled FBI this time.'"[24]

Despite occasional setbacks in monitoring him as a leader of Free Germany, the FBI successfully carried out a years-long intensive surveillance of Brecht, his family, women co-workers, friends, and acquaintances. What follows is a more detailed look at this second main feature of his file: the surveillance process, including techniques used in the attempt to intern or deport him, such as wiretaps, mail censorship, informants, the analysis of news reports, bugs, searches of luggage and household trash ("trash" or "scrap cover"),[25] and observation of residences, cars, and people by special agents.

In contrast to other files, we can no longer reconstruct exactly when and why Hoover's Bureau began to take an interest in Brecht. What is certain is that the first five reports made by the Los Angeles Field Office from 6 March to 10 July 1943 have one theme in common: the preparation of enough clear-cut evidence to determine "whether . . . the United States Attorney . . . will authorize the arrest of Subject as an enemy alien with a view to his internment."[26] For example, "Source 'A,'" who knew "Mr. and Mrs. Brecht" in Germany, said there was no doubt that "subject" was a Communist. "Source 'B,'" a T. W. Baumfeld of Arnold Productions in Las Palmas and Santa Monica who met Brecht in the United States and breezily parroted rumors about him, said, "Subject was imprisoned by the Nazis at one time and is believed to have been severely treated by them," and "found him still a radical and an enemy of Capitalism."[27] Also, the FBI believed that Brecht worked as "Technical Advisor concerning the Underground"[28] on Fritz Lang's anti-Nazi film *Hangmen Also Die,* produced in Hollywood in 1943. The film showed a familiarity "through personal experience"[29] with all the tricks of an underground movement: "never tell the police anything," "establish alibis so as to fool the police," "work very secretly," "guard against informers,"[30] skills bound to arouse the distrust of every police force in the world, whether Gestapo or FBI. The FBI also eyed other Brecht works with suspicion as they tried to prepare his internment. His play *Die Massnahme,* of which an FBI specialist made a translation, drew attention from the Los Angeles Field Office as "A self-styled 'educational play' which advocates Communist world revolution by violent means."[31] "The 'Control Committee' "[32] celebrated the USSR, the CP, and illegal activities. The actors were expected to teach and to learn during the performance; and the play (as attested by an attached letter from Brecht and Eisler) had already been rejected by the German censors [21, no. 7, p. 351]. However, Assistant Attorney General Attilio di Girolamo, to whom the FBI recommended Brecht's internment, felt reluctant to make the decision. Di Girolamo repeated the FBI's leading arguments in a report to his superiors in the Justice Department, but at the same time (something rare among U.S. officials) he pointed out the anti-Fascist attitude of the suspect, "which is compatible with the ideology of a government which is an ally of the United States." "Therefore, if internment were based solely on the possibility of subject's giving aid and comfort to the enemies of this country, there would be no proper cause for his internment."[33]

Hoover, who several times intervened personally or through his closest aides in the internment proceedings against Brecht ("this action should be taken without delay"),[34] had no way to counter this argument. Drily and without listing reasons, the Justice Department informed di Girolamo on 26 June 1943 that a "Presidential Warrant" would not be approved "at this time."[35] Brecht, who probably knew nothing of the whole affair, had escaped the FBI's clutches.

Setbacks were no reason for the FBI to relax its efforts. Barely a year after the quashing of the internment initiative, Hoover, Hood, and their colleagues began a new, more intensive round of operations monitoring Brecht's family and friends, which continued into

autumn 1946.[36] The new investigation began with the previously
cited 2 October 1944 report on the Free Germany Movement, which
is so voluminous that we can only sample its contents. It shows
agents making routine checks ("two FBI people came and looked at
my registration booklet, apparently checking up because of the [en-
emy alien] curfew")[37] but also committing break-ins and other serious breaches of law. These they disguised with casual phrases in
their reports ("his name appeared in the notebook of Gregori
Kheifets,"[38] the Russian vice-consul in California) or hid under the
heading "Undeveloped Leads" ("Will attempt to obtain [blacked
out] from the Brecht residence").[39] Various entries indicate that
early in 1943, Brecht was under surveillance not only in Los Angeles but in New York: "Source [blacked out] . . . advised that on February 12, 1943, Bert Brecht arrived in New York City, and upon arrival went to an apartment house located at 124 East 57th Street,
which was ascertained to be rented by Ruth Berlau, previously mentioned, and Ida Bachman, who were then both employed by the Office of War Information."[40] Wiretapping was used, a method that the
FBI normally mentioned only reluctantly and in coded language ("it
is suggested that it be suitably paraphrased in order to protect the
Bureau's coding systems"):[41] "This source reflects that in May
1943 telephone calls made from the Brecht residence for the previous three months had been ascertained. . . . Among the persons
called from the Brecht residence during this time were Peter Lorre,
Alexander Granach, Mrs. Heinrich Mann, Ludwig Marcuse,
William Dieterle, and Oscar Homolk."[42]

Little trace of the wiretapping operation of spring 1943 can be
found in the Brecht files released to me. Possibly, the reason for this
is not that the FBI destroyed the files later but that in the heat of the
chase, Hood and his men did not bother to get the usual permission
from FBI headquarters and the attorney general. In any case, when
in February 1945 Hood asked Director Hoover for official permission to tap Brecht's telephone ("Authority is hereby requested for

the installation of a technical surveillance of Bert Brecht, 1063 - 26th Street, Santa Monica, California, telephone Santa Monica 5-4943"), he made the mistake of referring to the successful results of "technical surveillance . . . previously had on Bert Brecht."[43] Whereupon Hoover's office wrote back in a slightly prickly tone that Washington had no documents indicating that permission had ever been issued to tap Brecht's phone. Challenged to give an immediate explanation, Hood had to resort to a fib: "Brecht was confused with Heinrich Mann, a companion subject on whom there was a technical surveillance. The records of this office fail to show that any technical surveillance has been maintained on Brecht."[44]

That Hood took a flexible view of the truth would have been clear to everyone at FBI headquarters from the L.A. Field Office report of 1 February 1945, which repeatedly refers to an evident wiretap source ("C.N.D.I. [blacked out]").[45] But as long as the right information kept flowing in the right amount and could be processed without revealing the source, Washington was not interested in knowing the exact methods of its field offices. "Approval granted to install technical surveillance on subject . . . provided full security assured,"[46] Hoover wired to Los Angeles on April 9, triggering an avalanche of monitoring operations that did not stop until the end of the year.

The more or less official wiretap operation on Brecht that was authorized by FBI headquarters ran from 18 April to 5 November 1945 under the FBI code CNDI LA BB-1.[47] It was conducted from the local telephone exchange and extended by Washington on a monthly basis, either for persuasive reasons like Brecht's relations with Hollywood left-wingers and with Soviet diplomat and potential atomic spy Gregory Kheifetz, or for flimsy reasons like the plans of Brecht's friend and co-worker Karin Michaelis, "the Danish writer of Communist tendencies,"[48] to return to her homeland.

Most important to the FBI in its wiretap operation was to monitor Brecht's associates and his plans to return to Germany. Among his contacts were Americans like Charles Laughton ("according to BB-1 . . . has had considerable contact with the Brechts during the past month, at least"),[49] Archibald MacLeish ("presently an Assistant Secretary of State, has been a follower of the Communist Party line for many years"),[50] Eugene Meyer ("according to BB-1, Brecht was visited by Eugene Meyer . . . of the Washington Post"),[51] and E. Y. Harburg ("one of the leading figures of the Communist movement among the motion picture people in Hollywood"),[52] as well as London-born Charlie Chaplin ("[Brecht's colleague and mistress Ruth] Berlau . . . wanted 'Chappy' to write a short speech for her which she was to make by shortwave radio to Denmark"),[53] and a number of more or less prominent exiles. Trivial events—scientist Hans Reichenbach and his family were moving and had stored their furniture in Brecht's garage—were reported alongside explosive news like visits to Brecht by Soviet diplomats in San Francisco and L.A., Stepan Apresyan [226, p. 355f], "Michael Vavilov,"[54] and "Eugene Tumantsev,"[55] as well as by Gregory Kheifetz. And of course the wiretap operation brought into the files a quantity of notes on political themes, including the exiles' concern about events in Germany: screenwriter-director Billy Wilder was working for the Office of War Information, Alfred Döblin was active in France, Soviet radio spoke of the partitioning of Germany, and the Labour Party had beaten Churchill in the British elections.

But those hoping through BB-1 to learn intimate details of Brecht's life and work reaped little for their efforts. In a telephone conversation on 11 or 12 May, the playwright coolly rejected Ruth Berlau's request to give her at least "a little part" in the production of *The Private Life of the Master Race,* on the grounds "that what he had in mind she could not do because it must be in English."[56] "This informant was able to gather from various conversations at which he was present," BB-1 reported in coded language in September 1945, that Brecht held "open house meetings" almost every Sunday and that on other days there were "meetings of a closed nature."[57]

And when "Mrs. Eisler" phoned Brecht's wife, Helene Weigel, in May 1945, asking her to get Brecht to fetch Mr. Eisler back from New York so that he would not lose his job in Hollywood, Weigel's curt reply— "Mrs. Brecht stated that the number is in the phone book under the name of Ruth Berlau"[58]—told no one anything they didn't already know about Weigel's attitude toward her husband's women associates.

Other surveillance techniques gave better results: mail interception, statements by informants, press notices on his works, the observation of contacts between Brecht and American artists and writers, and probably the most interesting part of his files, the surveillance of his mistress and co-worker Berlau, culminating in the search of her luggage and a bungled attempt to eavesdrop on conversations between the lovers by "bugging" the Chalet Motor Hotel in Santa Monica.[59]

The surviving documents do not allow us to fully reconstruct the scale and duration of the mail censorship. We know that Brecht's name repeatedly appeared on the National Censorship Watch Lists,[60] that his correspondence was opened by the FBI for a period of years, and that the Office of Censorship kept track of him even when he was traveling: "On June 13, 1945, a 30 day mail cover was placed on Bertolt Brecht at 124 East 57 Street, New York City, the residence of Ruth Berlau."[61] Anyone who like Karin Michaelis had mail delivered at Brecht's address in Santa Monica ended up in the FBI files. And frequently the mail of other exiles went into Brecht's files merely because they had mentioned the playwright's name: "Confidential Informant T-1 furnished the writer with a letter dated April 26, address to 'Dear Ruth' and signed 'Hanns and Lou,' presumably Hanns and Lou Eisler. The English translation of the letter is being set forth: 'Dearest Ruth, It looks as if Br. and Eisler are really coming to New York. I have to stay home on account of great poverty. . . . Hanns is unfortunately not very economic and the liquor cost also something.'"[62]

James Lyon, Brecht's American biographer, counted "half a dozen unknown Brecht letters and one telegram" that are reproduced "partly or completely" in the files [113, p. 379], and gives several examples: correspondence with Berlau; a telegram from film director Paul Czinner, who in August 1945 offered to stage Brecht's play *Galileo* with Charles Laughton; letters from Paolo Milano and Berthold Viertel in March 1945 about a plan by Italian anti-Fascist Ignazio Silone to stage Brecht's *The Good Person of Szechwan* in Rome; and an exchange with Karl Korsch about adapting "the Manifest,"[63] that is *The Communist Manifesto,* into a didactic poem in the style of Lucretius' *De Rerum Natura.*

Although much of the censored mail has undoubtedly been destroyed, the files make clear that Hoover's agents read, recorded, translated, indexed, and analyzed hundreds of letters to and from Brecht over the years. Traces of this operation remain as file entries that sometimes read like an address book of the exile community: "A letter postmarked February 7 was received by Brecht from W. H. Auden, 16 Oberlin Avenue, Swarthmore, Pennsylvania. . . . A letter postmarked February 17 was received from Stefan Brecht indicating that his address was Company A, Soc. III, 3663 SU (possibly SV), University of Chicago, Chicago, Illinois. A letter postmarked February 20, 1945 was addressed to Helen Weigel (Mrs. Brecht) by the Academy of Motion Picture Arts and Sciences, Suite 820, 530 WEst 6th Street, Los Angeles."[64] The letters recount trivial occurrences ("10-24-44. Mrs. Brecht, John W. [illegible], Electrical Contractor")[65] or politically significant events, such as the report from Charlotte Dieterle, wife of Hollywood director William Dieterle, to Bruno Frei, a refugee journalist who had fled to Mexico, on 20 July 1943: "At the present we have here a young Russian lady journalist from whom much information can be had of a kind which would be of much interest to you there. Recently there was a big social gathering at D's, where she spoke at a very interesting international gathering (Thomas Mann, Feuchtwanger, Brecht, Bruno Frank, Eisler,

⌐ 100-18112

C O N F I D E N T I A L

SOURCE A — A highly confidential source known to Special Agents D. NIEL F. CAHILL and ERNEST J. VAN LOON.

SOURCE B — LOUISE KLINKHAMER, Office of Superintendent of Nurses, Cedars of Lebanon Hospital, Los Angeles.

SOURCE C — FELIX GUGGENHEIM, 258 South Tower Drive, Beverly Hills, California.

SOURCE D — Report of Special Agent JOSEPH B. STEELE, dated January 25, 1945 at Los Angeles, entitled MARTIN HALL, was., Internal Security - R, L.A. File 65-1536-56.

SOURCE E — A highly confidential source known to reporting agent

SOURCE F — Postal Censorship, Los Angeles.

SOURCE G — CIELL H. ROGERS, 2312 Ivygrove, Venice, California.

SOURCE H — Mrs. ELSIE MAY BARNES and BETTE H. FREEMAN, 1241 6th Street, Santa Monica, California, proprietors of packing service.

SOURCE I — LDB No. 243, 700 Santa Monica Boulevard, Santa Monica, Calif.

SOURCE J — WILLIAM IBACH, manager, Western Union, Santa Monica, California.

SOURCE K — Memorandum dated April 28, 1945 regarding COUNCIL FOR A DEMOCRATIC GERMANY, INTERNAL SECURITY, by ROBERT M. W. KEMPNER, Special Employee of the Philadelphia Field Division.

SOURCE L — CONT. INFT. CONI L. 1138, L.A. file 100-18558-12.

SOURCE M — LDB No. 178, 6410 Van Nuys Boulevard, Van Nuys, California.

De Kobra, Lubitsch)."[66] Sometimes the FBI investigated addresses found in Brecht's mail: "It was determined that Room 701, 8 East 41 Street, New York, New York contained the offices of the Council for a Democratic Germany."[67] Brief clues informed examiners of the files who Brecht's correspondents were: "The New School For Social Research . . . has a reputation of being extremely liberal."[68]

Besides mail and telephone monitoring and the surveillance of

Brecht's home, the FBI collected evidence from a less reliable source: spies and informants whose identity is still protected today. An anonymous "Source B" reported that Brecht was "an associate of persons with Communist inclinations," "a radical and an enemy of Capitalism."[69] A four-page list attached to an FBI report of 1 February 1945 named Mrs. Robert Siodmak (among others) as a "Confidential Source," although it is not stated whether she knew she was supplying information.[70] Sometimes the FBI learned things it could only have found out through an informant from the Brecht-Eisler circle or through a listening device: "Informant [blacked out] . . . advised . . . that on October 7, 1943, Bert Brecht visited with Hanns Eisler. At that time Eisler inquired of Brecht as to whether he had heard anything from Sylvia Sidney, and Brecht replied that while he had heard nothing from her himself, he knew that she was coming to Los Angeles."[71] And the FBI naturally eavesdropped on Hollywood parties of the kind given for Billy Wilder before he left for Germany in spring 1945: "During the course of the gathering, Brecht discussed with Wilder the names of various individuals in Germany affiliated with the stage and movie industry . . . informant also overheard Brecht remark to someone that Otto Katz, alleged OGPU agent in Mexico, had no official connection and was of no political importance. Informant believes that this is another indication of Brecht's individuality in thinking which renders him incapable of being disciplined and hence the type of person whom the Soviets would not want in Russia."[72]

How unreliable informants often were is evident from the multitude of errors that riddle the Brecht files. One informant claimed to have overheard in conversation that Brecht had escaped from a concentration camp in 1933 dressed in women's clothing. Another said that Karin Michaelis was a relative of Helene Weigel. Hoover's special agents also made mistakes. One misread visa forms in 1935 and thought that Brecht's wife was named "A. Skovtastrand" and lived in "Svenborg, Denmark,"[73] and another misinterpreted names he heard ("Marianne Hopper" and "Gruentchen") while listening to a phone conversation between Weigel and the actor Curt Bois about a party given by Russian occupation forces in Berlin.[74]

Despite misinformation and errors, agents in Los Angeles, New York, and Washington showed familiarity with Brecht's literary works. In 1945 they attentively followed the performance and negative reception of *The Private Life of the Master Race* in New York ("neither play, propaganda nor good Red stalling").[75] They recorded Brecht's collaboration with Laughton in staging *Galileo* and Berlau's authorization to negotiate a film of the play after Brecht left America. When Warner Brothers filmed *The Three Penny Opera,* an informant told the FBI that one copy at the University of Illinois contained secret coded information that might be linked to espionage: "[Blacked out] reportedly told [blacked out] that the special characteristics in this particular copy of the film were extra words 'dubbed in' to the sound tract, which taken separately mean nothing but when considered as a group comprise some sort of secret message."[76]

The many Americans and naturalized citizens whose names appear in the files, and the quantity of news articles the FBI collected on Brecht, show that he did not isolate himself in the "hell" of California as was often assumed. Besides Laughton and Chaplin, the FBI took an interest in other Brecht associates like the producers of *Hangmen Also Die* (Arnold Pressburger, "a sympathizer with the Hollywood Communist element")[77] and *Galileo* ("Rod Geiger . . . and Brecht had been negotiating for months relative to the Galileo film contract").[78] The names of relatives ("DeWitt Bronard, . . . a cousin, and William Zaiss, . . . an uncle")[79] listed by Brecht on his visa application in 1935 landed in the FBI files. And British writer Christopher Isherwood, "one of the co-translators of Brecht's work"[80] who had lived in the United States since the late thirties, elicited FBI reports that he had joined the Hindu monastery of the Vedanta Society and that he took trips with W. H. Auden.

The scope and methods of surveillance on Brecht and his associates are especially clear in the case of Ruth Berlau. The Bureau's interest in Brecht's longtime co-worker and mistress had less to do with her being a writer in exile of Marxist leanings who was working for the Office of War Information ("she has . . . been said to be critical of the United States' policy and to advocate communism in this country")[81] than with the possibility of finding out about Brecht through her. Among other things, the FBI took a special interest in the photography work that he commissioned her to do in 1944–45. In a letter to Hoover dated 5 April 1945, Hood reported: "Recent investigation has indicated that Ruth Berlau . . . has acted in the capacity of a secretary to Bert Brecht. He is known to visit her almost daily at the Viertel residence and a recent examination of her effects . . . reflects that she has done extensive photographic copying of German language poems, etc. (no doubt the work of Bertolt Brecht)."[82] In the same report, Hood asked for "blanket authorization for the installation of a microphone surveillance in whichever unit of the Chalet Motor Hotel Berlau might reside upon her return."

The planting of a bug in Berlau's hotel room and the renting of a nearby apartment as a "Technical Plant"[83] (a listening headquarters) did not actually happen because her travel plans were postponed.[84] But it is still useful to examine the letters, papers, and other items that Hood's men picked up when they searched her luggage.

An FBI agent laconically recorded a message that Brecht scribbled to Berlau on a hospital envelope in autumn 1944, when Berlau was fighting for her life in Cedars of Lebanon Hospital after giving birth to Brecht's son, who died soon after: "Love, I am so glad that you are fighting so courageously. Don't think that I do not want to see you, when you are ill. You are very beautiful, then too. I am coming tomorrow before noon. Yours, Brecht."[85] Another special agent, carrying out a detailed examination of Brecht's telephone contacts, wrote briefly after the phone number "OLympic 2931": "Cedars of Lebanon Hospital, 4833 Fountain Avenue . . . Called

September 1 (twice), 3, 4 (twice), 5, 6, 7, 8, 9, 10, 11 (twice), 12, 13, 14, 15 (twice)."[86] Source A[87] listed without comment a series of unpaid medical bills from late 1944 and early 1945, apparently related to Berlau's pregnancy: $200 for Dr. Gordon Rosenblum and Dr. Eugene Melinkoff, $500 for Dr. Marcus H. Rabwin, and so on. With philological acumen, the Bureau decided that the line in a letter from Brecht, "In August your are beautiful too Ute" must be addressed to her—"Ute being a known nickname for Berlau, used by Brecht."[88] Entries in Berlau's address book were checked out by the FBI in its so-called "criss-cross directory."[89] Descriptions were made of news clippings and a record kept of rolls of film on which Berlau made photostats of Brecht's works: "Berlau's suitcase contained various supplies of photographic papers and 35mm. film. . . . There was much developed film scattered haphazardly through the bags."[90]

The information that the FBI gleaned from searching Berlau's luggage was supplemented by a mail search operation ("on June 13, 1945, a 30 day mail cover was placed on Bertolt Brecht at 124 East 57 Street, New York City, the residence of Ruth Berlau")[91] and by the "physical surveillance" of Berlau and Brecht by special agents.

Several letters from Berlau and Karin Michaelis were preserved by the mail cover and show their shocking degree of dependency on Brecht: "I have opened your letter, o you," Berlau wrote to her lover on 2 April 1945 while on a train from Los Angeles to New York. "I became so quiet. I am happy. I thank you, thank you. I will become just like you wish. . . . I know that I will be worried again now and then, it is mostly fear, that you might become unfaithful. . . . I thought that you would be thinking 'glad that she finally left, a good riddance,' and then you told me 'come back as soon as you can . . .'; of course, you were right again, when you told me that my photos are still 'dilletante' work . . . it is a good thing that you are so strict with me."[92] In another letter written the same day she continued: "Take care the first time you come . . . not to make it appear as if it has cleared the air, that I have left, and that you can come again there together with your wife now."[93]

Michaelis also, in two letters to Berlau containing "various references believed to relate to Berlau's pregnancy," is more concerned about Brecht than about Berlau: "You can always pretend you got it in your vacation. But I had my suspicions since that morning that Brecht went out without having had his morning coffee. . . . But how will it be with Helly (Brecht). Does she know it? Will that not make a rift between them? . . . And what does Brecht say about it?"[94] "You were pained by my questions about Brecht, and 'that he felt himself relieved' . . . you say that this is your child, but it is only yours if you develop it into a human being . . . and so I felt, involuntarily, that Brecht ought to hear about it, and so I used that word 'being relieved.' My sorrow in this regard for Helly (Brecht) will never allay, because . . . she has nothing left since Stef is in the Army and Barbara is not yet sufficiently grown to be able to talk with her."[95]

Notes in the files make clear that Hoover's agents not only read Berlau's and Brecht's mail but tracked his movements as he went about his business in Santa Monica and on visits to New York. The FBI in California learned from the staff of the Chalet Motor Hotel who regularly paid Berlau's bills in cash and who fetched her luggage in September 1944: "They described this individual as a little fellow with dark hair, who could hardly speak English, and who drove a 'wreck of an automobile.' This is undoubtedly Bert Brecht."[96] The manager of Berlau's apartment house in New York reported that he regularly saw Brecht in Berlau's apartment, "usually attired in lounging clothes."[97] The FBI learned about the exile's financial transactions from his bank: "This check bore a notation 'rent March-Mrs. Berlau, 124 E. 57th Street, New York.'"[98] When she was placed in the "Long Island Home" in Amityville in December 1945 following a nervous breakdown, he paid at least part of the cost.[99] One agent must have gotten cold feet outside Berlau's New York apartment in the winter of 1944, observing how Gerhart Eisler spent "one hour and a quarter" there with Brecht on January 17.[100]

Another agent reported that before Berlau began her return journey to New York on 31 March 1945 after one of her visits to the West Coast, he observed the couple all day while they packed, made final purchases, and said goodbye at the train station: "On March 31, 1945, Bert Brecht's car was again observed at the Salka Viertel residence at 10:15 A.M. . . . Ruth Berlau was observed by Special Agent [blacked out] and reporting Agent to load Brecht's car with various boxes, papers, etc. After delivering the bulk of this material to a packing service in Santa Monica, Berlau proceeded to Brecht's residence where she deposited two or three boxes of books, papers etc., and what appeared to be files. Bert Brecht assisted Berlau in unloading this material at his residence. . . . After stopping at the Eastman Kodak Store . . . at 202 Santa Monica Boulevard," where she got her photos developed for him, "Brecht and Berlau continued to the Union Station at Los Angeles where Berlau was observed to board the Union Pacific Challenger for New York City. She carried with her a suitcase and two briefcases which Brecht carried aboard the train for her."[101]

FBI records of Brecht's mail and telephone traffic, his many visitors, stage productions, translations, film projects, and the activities of him and his entourage indicate that the playwright lived a far from solitary life in the United States. No wonder he attracted notice from another agency that specialized in hunting real or alleged Communists: the House Un-American Activities Committee.

Brecht's subpoenaed testimony before HUAC has often been described, and the text of the questions and answers can be found on phonograph records and in printed form [22; 217, pp. 491–504; 210, pp. 207–25]. For this reason, my intention is to discuss only the FBI's role in preparing material used by HUAC at the hearing.

First and most important of the extant documents proving collaboration between Hoover's FBI and the Communist-hunters in the

House of Representatives is a report from the SAC in Los Angeles to FBI headquarters dated 14 May 1947, in which Hood says that he personally turned over memoranda on Brecht and other "individuals in the Hollywood area"[102] to Robert Stripling, HUAC's chief investigator, in response to a request from congressman and HUAC chairman J. Parnell Thomas. Hood stated that the documents were transferred at 6:15 P.M. on 13 May.

Hood's report, in the copy given me, is not completely legible, making it impossible to reconstruct the exact source and range of information on Brecht that was made available to Thomas, but the undated synopsis placed in Brecht's file along with Hood's letter of 14 May no doubt contains the bulk of it. Apart from biographical details, the synopsis lists virtually all the information that Stripling later referred to at Brecht's HUAC hearing. "In 1930 did you, with Hanns Eisler, write a play entitled, 'Die Massnahme'?" [210, p. 210] is the chief investigator's paraphrase of the almost identical phrase in the FBI report: "In 1930 Brecht together with Hanns Eisler wrote an educational play entitled 'Die Massnahme.'"[103] HUAC and the FBI both referred to an essay by the Russian dramatist and Stalin victim Sergei Tretyakov that was published in Moscow in May 1937 by the exile magazine *Internationale Literatur*. The FBI synopsis appears to be the source of Stripling's information that Brecht had been in Moscow and was visited in Santa Monica by Soviet vice-consul Gregory Kheifetz, whom the FBI regarded as an "espionage assistant to the chief of the N.K.V.D. [Soviet secret police] in the United States."[104] HUAC did not refer to compromising facts the FBI listed about Brecht's relations with the Free Germany Movement and his ties with "Communist" or "Russian sympathizers"[105] among the exiles who were active in the film industry and in refugee aid, like William and Charlotte Dieterle, Michaelis, Feuchtwanger, and Berlau. Also, HUAC's information about the times and dates of meetings between Kheifetz and Brecht on 14 and 27 April 1943 and on 16 June

1944 [210, p. 214f] was not in the synopsis and must have been funneled to the committee by other routes.

Stripling was apparently so well furnished with material on Brecht that his own information service collected only a few original pieces of information, and he had ordered a new translation of *Die Massnahme* for Hanns Eisler's hearing [217] that he then transferred to Brecht's. Some questions—"Mr. Brecht, are you a member of the Communist Party or have you ever been a member of the Communist Party?" [210, p. 209]—belonged to the standard repertoire. In any event, the case evidently was no longer of paramount interest to HUAC. Richard Nixon, John Rankin, and other committee members did not even turn up at Brecht's hearing. Stripling and Thomas meekly accepted Brecht's unclear and inaccurate replies, ignored his relations with other members of the Hollywood Ten and with his liberal associates in exile circles, and even praised the inveterate anti-American for his willingness to testify, saying he was a "good example to the witnesses" [210, p. 220].

On 31 October 1947, the day after his HUAC hearing, Brecht left New York for Paris and Zurich. His name did not vanish from FBI files as a result, not even after his Security Index Card was finally canceled in January 1949. Besides extensive material on the secret messages supposedly dubbed into the film of *The Three Penny Opera,* and surveillance of the 1956 stage production of *The Private Life of the Master Race,* the Bureau took an interest in a review of Brecht's *Selected Poems* printed in the *Daily Worker.* A personal description of the Brechts was made in Zurich and sent back to the United States without comment: "Age 48, . . . hair, cut short and combed forward, . . . married to Helene Weigel Brecht . . . brown hair, combed straight back and cut short; dark complexion; mannish looking; dresses very oddly at times, wearing ankle length skirts and peasant costume."[106] An undated CIA report from sometime after Brecht's death in 1956 listed the same attributes that had formerly attracted the interest of the FBI: "Bert Brecht was well known for his communist writings and associations while in this country. . . . Prior to his death in East Berlin . . . Brecht was known as the communist Poet Laureate of East Germany. . . . His literary works included the libretto for Kurt Weill's 'Three Penny Opera,' and royalties from . . . its theme, 'Mack the Knife,' are reportedly still paid to the Brecht estate."[107] Cause enough, the CIA thought, to set up yet another mail cover operation in the early sixties on "Helen Weigel," who was suspected of teaching American slang to the East German police, and on "son Stefan Sebastian Brecht": "Arrange for coverage of correspondence between persons in U.S. and Helen Brecht by Communications Intercept Service. This coverage should include correspondence to her son at Chausseestr. 125, Berlin."[108]

LION FEUCHTWANGER

Known in the United States as the author of readable and profitable historical novels like *Proud Destiny* and *Raquel, The Jewess of Toledo,* Lion Feuchtwanger arrived in New York in October 1940 amid headlines about his internment in France and his narrow escape from the Gestapo by fleeing on foot across the Pyrenees to Spain and Portugal. His suburban home in the hills of Pacific Palisades above the ocean became a meetingplace for the exile elite, especially friends of the USSR, about which their host had written a controversial travel report, *Moscow, 1937.* A large collection of expensive books reminded visitors of the atmosphere of his homes in Munich and the French Riviera. The interest of Hollywood and of American book clubs in his novels meant that he belonged to the small group of refugees who lived in relative comfort even in exile.

To examine the almost one thousand pages of Feuchtwanger's FBI and INS files is useful for three reasons. First, the large dossier with its forty-three FBI reports gives, like Brecht's, an especially detailed view of how the FBI operated in investigating the German exiles. Second, his files show particularly close cooperation between the FBI and INS in processing citizenship applications, a matter of special importance to many exiles. Finally, the more than 120 pages of transcripts of OSS interrogations of Lion and Marta Feuchtwanger are material for a sort of aesthetics of political interrogation: an international genre that, if examined more closely, would show strong similarities of form, regardless of the differing contents at different times and in different nations.

On the other hand, Feuchtwanger's FBI, OSS, and State Department files give us proportionally less new information on their subject than do many smaller exile files. Portraits of the writer are generalized: "is the arch-type of intellectual who believes in a patent solution for all problems . . . vain and not always reliable . . . has no physical or moral courage . . . should not be considered as an 'homme politique.'"[1] Apart from the important OSS interviews mentioned above, references to Feuchtwanger in OSS and State Department archives are limited to the helpful role of the President's Advisory Committee on Political Refugees in rescuing him and his wife from France ("these cases have the approval of the Department of Justice"),[2] the negative comments by Ruth Fischer and Leopold Schwarzschild about the political attitudes of their fellow exile, and Feuchtwanger's positive view of the Free Germany initiatives in Mexico, the United States, and Moscow ("no doubt the proclamation of the National Committee contributes to the cause of the United Nations").[3] The files give virtually no details about the writer's troubled private life, such as in the files of Klaus Mann, with one small exception: When Feuchtwanger was questioned for several days by three INS officials in 1958 concerning his application for American citizenship, the examiner at one point requested Feuchtwanger's secretary Hilde Waldo to leave the room and then asked about the nature of his relationship with the American cartoonist Eva Hermann: "Q. It has been reported that she had been your mistress. Is that true, Mr. Feuchtwanger? A. No. Probably it was reported, but she was not. Q. You deny that you have ever had any sexual relations with her? A. Yes, I do. (At this point, Miss Waldo is called back into the room.) *Questioning resumed.*"[4]

The core of Feuchtwanger's FBI files is a series of forty-three reports written mainly by the Los Angeles and New York field offices, with several from El Paso, San Francisco, Phoenix, Milwaukee, and Albany, between July 1941 and January 1959. The reports usually traced routine surveillance of contacts and activities, with occasional investigation of specific concerns. Their content thus is wide-ranging. Information about the writer's creative alias ("the name J. L. Watchek is being dropped as an alias, inasmuch as it was erroneously set forth in reference report")[5] mixes with the results of "spot surveillances": "It has . . . been determined in this investigation that this car," "a 1938 blue-green Willys Coupe,"[6] "belongs to [blacked out] who is believed to be a gardener employed in that capacity by Feuchtwanger."[7] A special agent who interviewed Feuchtwanger "under pretext" in July 1944 reported that the writer had spoken "freely" about the Council for a Democratic Germany but replied evasively when asked if he wished to return to Germany. Information from newspapers and magazines like the *New York Times,* the *Daily Worker, Atlantic Monthly,* and *Reader's Digest* is often cited, especially if it refers to Communist activities of the subject, or to a link between Communists, Nazis, and Chicago gangsters. Feuchtwanger, according to one report, "appears to take Russian pretense for reality still and to see a fundamental difference between the Hitler and Stalin regime. . . . the Germany and the Russia of today . . . are run by a gang of robbers and cutthroats with a hoodlum at the head. . . . Neither Hitler nor Stalin has any different ideals from Al Capone. Feuchtwanger is not sufficiently familiar with the Capone type to be able to recognize it."[8]

The files frequently quote from Feuchtwanger's writings, especially *Moscow, 1937,* showing that FBI agents and their informants read their target's books. Germans and Americans with whom the Feuchtwangers came in contact—Brecht, Thomas and Heinrich

Mann, Bruno Frei, Peter Lorre, Charlie Chaplin, Upton Sinclair, Dorothy Thompson, and publisher Benjamin Huebsch—routinely underwent a political check ("the names of individuals who were either contacted by the subject, or who contacted him . . . were checked against the indices").[9] The FBI painstakingly described a visit to Feuchtwanger by the Soviet vice-consul ("on February 11, 1947, the automobile bearing consular service plates #290 and belonging to the Russian consulate in Los Angeles was observed in front of the subject's house, staying from about five o'clock in the afternoon until 6:15 P.M.")[10] and an award he received from East Germany. The FBI declined to release several reports totaling almost a hundred pages about a cryptanalysis "with negative results"[11] carried out by the FBI lab in spring 1948 on orders from the SAC in Los Angeles to investigate Feuchtwanger's "possible espionage contacts."[12]

"Confidential informants" (a term that probably included Americans as well as exiles and simple cross-references to other files) told the Bureau that Feuchtwanger was "sympathetic to Communism, pro-Soviet, reliable in eyes of CP, and useful to the CP as a writer."[13] Other informants reported that Feuchtwanger and "Mr. and Mrs. Bert Brecht"[14] were together at a birthday party for someone whose name has been blacked out, and they made accusations colored by hatred and envy: "[Blacked out] described the subject as a clever writer whose success has been prodigious. . . . he . . . added that the subject is a potential enemy of this country and if given an opportunity would undoubtedly injure this country."[15]

How agencies obtained reports from informants, at least in some cases, is shown by a "sworn statement" from a former member of the Community Party USA named Paul Crouch, whose deposition was preserved uncensored in Feuchtwanger's INS file. After asking Crouch for the usual personal details, the examining officer, in his best secret agent manner, reminded the witness of his own political missteps, at the same time presenting him as an expert in the field of left-wing subversion: "member of the Communist Party of the United States . . . from 1925 until 1942," "County Organizer for the Communist Party in Alameda, California," and so on. At this point the witness was shown a picture of Feuchtwanger and asked if he recognized him or had "any knowledge of a person by the name of Lion Feuchtwanger." When Crouch gave an unsatisfactory reply ("only by his reputation both within and outside the Communist Party"), the examiner smoothly followed up with a leading question ("based upon your extensive knowledge . . . would you feel hesitant in forming the conclusion that Mr. Feuchtwanger was regarded as at least a consistent Communist Party sympathizer?"), and promptly received the answer he wanted: "Yes, he would have had to be regarded as at least a sympathizer, certainly."[16]

The "character of case" of the Feuchtwanger file was initially "Security G-R," with "G-R" standing for "German-Russian" or "German-Radical," and after being turned over to Los Angeles it was labeled "Security - C" for "Communist." Periodic attempts to lower the rating failed because of the stubbornness of an official, or the discovery of new documents that appeared to point to Communist activities. "It is recommended," the L.A. Field Office wrote on 9 March 1956, after head Communist-hunter Joseph McCarthy had already been censured and driven from office, that "Feuchtwanger be retained on the Security Index in view of his continuing expressions of pro-Soviet sympathy and his stature as an apologist for pro-Soviet activities."[17] His name was finally struck off the index one month after his death, when the FBI completed its final report—although the Bureau's passion for amassing data was not therefore satisfied. An FBI employee assured his boss after a visit to L.A.'s City Bureau of Vital Statistics, "death certificate Number 23929 reflects the death of Lion Jacob Feuchtwanger on December 21, 1958. . . . cause of death was shock due to gastric hemorrhage."[18] A clipping from the *Los Angeles Examiner* of 9 July 1959 in the file reports that "author Lion Feuchtwanger" "left an estate valued at $22,631.28" and bequeathed this sum to his wife. Later memoranda, the last dated 2 September 1960, were so mutilated by the censor that they no longer convey any information.

The second main group of documents in the FBI file contains forty reports on Feuchtwanger's mail, made by the Office of Censorship when he was put on the "FBI Watch List" for several months for reasons that are not clear. The censors regularly passed copies and translations to the FBI. FBI censors in turn blacked out many passages before releasing the reports, but to the extent that they are still decipherable they mostly concern publishing contracts, financial donations to relatives and friends, and publications by other exiles. They are less informative, though, than the mail reports on Anna Seghers or Heinrich Mann.

In spring 1944, for example, Feuchtwanger wired a Swedish publisher the rights to his novels *Die Brüder Lautensack* and *Exil*[19] (translated as *Double, Double, Toil and Trouble* and *Paris Gazette*) on the condition that both books be published by 1 January 1947. The Editorial Futuro in Argentina sent Feuchtwanger a bill for the translations of *Erfolg* (Success) and *Exil* and announced an edition of *Simone*. A correspondent whose name is blacked out asked Feuchtwanger to raise his allowance from twenty dollars a month to thirty. In February 1953, the writer cabled the Europa Verlag in Zurich, which had asked "if Lola Sernau Humm was authorized to make contract . . . concerning stage rights to play Sezuan," that "[blacked out] is authorized by this cbl [cable] to make contract with adse [addressee] for stage production and publication of works of sndr [sender] and Brecht."[20] The Office of Censorship captured even the small and sometimes embarrassing curiosities of exile, like the letter from a French insurance company in 1945 "announcing 'Stock Issue of 100,000 New Shares'" that were available provided "would-be subscribers"[21] made a statutory declaration that they were not Jews.

The third main feature of Feuchtwanger's dossier is a sporadic but significant exchange of letters between FBI headquarters in Washington, various Bureau field offices, the INS, State Department, CIA, G-2, and the IRS. This correspondence is interesting mainly for making clear that FBI chief Hoover or his closest aides intervened personally in Feuchtwanger's case from the start. "In view of the reported activities and affiliations of Lion Feuchtwanger," we first read on 4 June 1941 in a memo from Hoover stamped "Personal and Confidential" and addressed to Major L. R. Schofield of the INS, "it is suggested that all legal and proper methods be used to effect the deportation. This Bureau, at the present time, is conducting an investigation to ascertain whether Lion Feuchtwanger is engaged in any actions that would constitute a violation of existing United States statutes."[22] But FBI headquarters was not satisfied with the speed at which incriminating evidence was collected. In the ensuing weeks, the impatient Hoover several times admonished the assistant FBI director in New York and other SACs: "It is . . . believed that in view of the allegations against the subject this case is of the type that should receive preferred investigative attention and reports should be submitted to the Bureau without undue delay."[23] When even that did not bring the desired results, Hoover instructed his man in L.A.: "You will prepare without delay a 5″ × 8″ white card . . . for filing in your Confidential Custodial Detention Card File."[24]

Ten years later, Hoover realized that he could not achieve any final victory over the exile because Feuchtwanger neither let himself to be silenced as a writer nor felt compelled to change his views. One last attempt to drive the aging exile out of the country by putting him on the attorney general's "deportation list," and transferring the case to the "Espionage Section for further supervision and dissemination to INS,"[25] failed for lack of evidence. "The INS Office," the SAC in Los Angeles reported to Washington in December 1953, "advised that they do not feel the subject will make any attempt to obtain his naturalization and feel that should he do so they have

JCM:jlg

May 8, 1943

Special Agent in Charge
Los Angeles, California

35584

RE: CUSTODIAL DETENTION

Dear Sir:

Please be advised that a custodial detention card has been
prepared at the Bureau, captioned as follows:

FEUCHTWANGER, LION, WITH ALIASES   ALIEN   COMMUNIST
Leon Feuchtwanger
J. L. Wetcheek
James Wetcheek

13827 Sunset Boulevard
Pacific Palisades, California

The above caption should be checked immediately for accuracy
against the information contained in your files, and the Bureau should
be informed of any discrepancies. You will prepare without delay a
5" x 8" white card captioned as above and reflecting your investigative
case file number for filing in your Confidential Custodial Detention Card
File. In the event the above caption is not correct, the card you
prepare should be correctly captioned, and the Bureau should be informed
of the correct caption.

The caption of the card prepared and filed in your Office
must be kept current at all times and the Bureau immediately advised of
any changes made therein in that connection.

Mr. Tolson
Mr. E. A. Tamm
Mr. Clegg
Mr. Coffey
Mr. Glavin
Mr. Ladd
Mr. Nichols
Mr. Rosen
Mr. Tracy
Mr. Carson
Mr. Harbo
Mr. Hendon
Mr. Mumford
Mr. Piper
Mr. Quinn Tamm
Mr. Nease
Miss Gandy

Very truly yours,

E. Hoover 5/143-
NOT RECORDED

John Edgar Hoover
Director

COMMUNICATIONS SECTION
MAILED 3
MAY 8 1943 P.M.
FEDERAL BUREAU OF INVESTIGATION
U.S. DEPARTMENT OF JUSTICE

DECLASSIFIED ON 2-2-81
BY SP/GSK/abh

140

enough evidence to block his naturalization. They do not feel, however, that they have sufficient evidence at the present time to deport him."[26] This exchange of notes between FBI headquarters, the SAC in Los Angeles, and the INS shows a surprising frankness, and it leaves no doubt that while Feuchtwanger hoped to be granted an American passport and a certain freedom to travel, Hoover and his aides intended from the beginning to deport their unwelcome guest.

Two attempts by the Los Angeles Field Office to close Feuchtwanger's file "due to inactivity" were vetoed by Hoover, the first in April 1946. The reason for the veto is not clear, because the FBI would not release the reports from Los Angeles and New York on which Hoover based his decision. A second attempt was made in spring 1949, resulting in Feuchtwanger's removal from the "Key Figure List" for two years, only to be reinstated and placed under intensive surveillance because of a birthday telegram he sent to Stalin, "social functions"[27] he attended at the home of the Soviet vice-consul, and the National Prize for Literature awarded to him by East Germany.

Beginning in 1954, his name appeared on the weekly lists of the INS and the Criminal Division of the Justice Department together with "racketeers and subversives" "being considered under the Denaturalization and Deportation Program"[28] of the U.S. attorney general. Senator Thomas Kuchel and HUAC member Donald Jackson asked the FBI to fill them in on Feuchtwanger's case in the mid-fifties, and the special agents happily complied; leafing through their top-secret files, they concluded that the "Honorable . . . Senator Kuchel" "is highly regarded as both able and honest . . . , Bureau files contain no derogatory information identifiable with Kuchel."[29] Finally, Richard Nixon—who by the Watergate scandal opened the way to the Freedom of Information and Privacy Acts that today allow access to FBI files—took an interest in Feuchtwanger's case. "Delay of final naturalization hearings in these cases," the INS district director wrote reassuringly to the "Honorable Richard Nixon" in a reply dated 29 May 1952, "has been occasioned by an investigation contemplating possible action under the Internal Security Act of 1950."[30] The INS never approved Feuchtwanger's naturalization.

Compared with the FBI, the OSS's treatment of Feuchtwanger seems fairly innocuous. We have already noted that John Norman of the OSS interviewed the writer one Sunday afternoon at Feuchtwanger's "beautiful estate at 520 Paseo Miramar, Pacific Palisades."[31] As in other OSS interrogations, the examining agent asked questions about specific political issues, like Emil Ludwig's views of German collective guilt ("Emil Ludwig is lonely. We exiled writers all agree against him. I don't agree with Thomas Mann on many things, but we agree on Ludwig");[32] the German resistance against the Nazis ("'underrated'");[33] and the partitioning of Germany ("it would be wise to occupy three parts of Germany, but not wise to make three different countries").[34] Feuchtwanger, described as "a jolly little man with twinkling eyes . . . and a respectable paunch,"[35] had little respect for the exile politicians: "I don't like Bruening. I don't like Rauschning. Prince Hubertus zu Lowenstein has only a muddled mind and a title."[36] Some of his writer colleagues also got short shrift: "Vicki Baum . . . he did not consider a great writer"[37] and Ludwig wrote too much, was "'superficial,'" and lacked "'inhibitions.'"[38]

Feuchtwanger's four-hundred-page INS file is a melange of trivialities, disturbing details, and dubious procedures by his examiners. INS forms tell us that he put on only ten pounds of weight in his almost twenty years of life in America while, reassuringly, neither his date of birth nor his height changed (unlike those of Anna Seghers and Heinrich Mann, who were tempted to flights of creativity when filling in the same forms). But other entries give food for thought. Why did Feuchtwanger (or an INS official?) cross out "Jewish" under "Race" and write "white" instead? And in a two-page handwritten addendum to an Application for Certificate of

Immigration and Naturalization Service
Los Angeles, 13, California

52

246-P-135253
246-P-135254   Enf

March 4, 1952

Honorable Richard Nixon
United States Senate
Washington, D. C.

Dear Senator Nixon:

This is in response to your letter of February 27, 1952
making inquiry concerning the status of the naturalization cases of Lion Feuchtwanger and his wife, Marta.

Mr. and Mrs. Feuchtwanger filed their petitions for
naturalization some time ago. Their cases have been under investigation since that time for possible action
under the Internal Security Act of 1950.

It is believed that our investigation will be brought to
a close shortly and the matter will be presented to the
Naturalization Court.

Sincerely yours,

DISTRICT DIRECTOR

cc: Central Office, Washington, D. C.

AR 7510026 and AR 7510027 relate.

cc: Mr. Landon

ADG:BD

143

Identification, Feuchtwanger described his persecution by the Nazis: "I had to leave Germany in October 1932. My Berlin house was raided by the Nazis in Feb. 1933. On August 23, 1933, I was expatriated . . . and all my possessions were confiscated. Goebbels himself announced my expatriation over the radio."[39] He concluded, "Therefore I cannot feel to be an enemy alien."[40] Predictably, the file also contains material on the writer's possible left-wing activities and contacts, including a photo in which he is gazing with a serious expression at Josef Stalin.

More important than routine forms and reports are six INS interrogations of Lion and Marta Feuchtwanger conducted between 1942 and 1958, some of which went on for several days. This fourth major group of documents allows us to establish the typical pattern of an interrogation, because the language and structure of police interviews tend to be similar whether they are conducted by INS or OSS employees, FBI special agents, totalitarian bureaucrats of the Third Reich, the much-demonized Stasi, or Zurich security police [187].

The first of Feuchtwanger's interrogations under oath took place on 15 June 1942. It focused not on the exile himself but on the law firm of Button, Gayland, and Butts, which allegedly had helped Feuchtwanger reenter the United States through Nogales, Mexico, in 1941 for a substantial fee. More serious in its consequences for Feuchtwanger was a five-page document "subscribed and sworn to before" INS officer Ben J. Ginn in Los Angeles on 5 March 1948, which was attached to the writer's Petition for Naturalization. Besides the usual personal details ("served . . . in the German army, as far as I can remember from October 1914 to December 1914 as Private Second Class of the Infantry"), there were questions of a kind that made Feuchtwanger feel compelled to play down his political activity. He claimed not to recall public appearances or membership in "organizations, lodges, societies, clubs or associations" except those promoted by official bodies: "As far as I recall, I spoke for instance in Paris for the PEN Club under the auspices of the President of France and all the French Ministers; . . . I do not remember having attended meetings of any organizations if not requested to make a speech."[41] Asked "What, if anything, have you done or tried to do to further the war effort of the United States?" Feuchtwanger answered: "I bought war bonds, and I sent a voluntary contribution to the Treasury. . . . The novels which I wrote since I live in the United States, pursue, besides their literary aims, the purpose to fight fascism with all means and to inspire understanding for the institutions and the philosophy of the United States."[42] Asked if he had been associated with any "patriotic, civic or social welfare agencies,"[43] he named only the Jewish Club of 1933 in Hollywood.

Far more complicated, and more degrading, were the hours-long "conversations" that an INS team conducted at Feuchtwanger's suburban home in Pacific Palisades in 1957 and 1958. The interviews were led by two INS "examiners," Samuel Hozman and Sidney Gren, accompanied by a female stenotypist and, at the first interview, an INS investigator.[44] In addition, there was a fluctuating audience in the form of Feuchtwanger's lawyer Milton Koblitz, a "Miss Hilde Waldo - Witness," and sometimes Marta Feuchtwanger. Feuchtwanger was already seriously ill, which brought repeated pauses in the interrogation and at times discontinued it until the following day. Both Lion and Marta stated, in separate interviews, that they found the INS cross-examinations "very strenuous"[45] but not inhumane. For example, the examiners came to Feuchtwanger's home to ask him their "remarkably silly" questions when he told them he "did not feel well enough to take the long trip to the INS offices." They were polite and "extremely considerate," so that the whole thing did "not affect [him] very deeply."[46] "At the end," Marta recalled, "they said 'it's not our fault that we have to ask all those questions, to press you so much, because we have to do what Washington asked us to do' " [56, p. 1573].

Whether the examiners were assigned questions by Washington, and how restricted they were in what they could say, is not clear. The relatively random course of the 1957–58 interviews suggests that they were largely free to use their own discretion, although three central themes dominate the nearly one hundred pages of transcripts. First, who were Feuchtwanger's associates in the United States and why? The names mentioned are of prominent people, many themselves the focus of intensive FBI, INS, and HUAC investigations in the late forties: Hollywood couples like the Dieterles and the Viertels, Hanns and Gerhart Eisler, Brecht, the Mann brothers, Franz Werfel, and Charlie Chaplin. Occasionally Agent Hozman would read out lists of six, seven, or more names and ask Feuchtwanger if he knew them, to which he invariably replied "No." The examiners wanted to know when and where the exile had discussed Communism with Brecht, whether he had ever revealed to the Russian vice-consul in Los Angeles any secret that "was against the best interests of the United States,"[47] and whether he had been "intimately acquainted with Mr. Horskheimer"[48] (meaning Max Horkheimer of the Frankfurt School of Critical Theory). They used gambits typical of political interrogators, trying by surprise attack or a veiled indirect approach to lead Feuchtwanger from simple factual replies to biographical sketches of friends and acquaintances and then to statements about their political convictions, so that almost imperceptibly the interviewee turned into an informer. "Do you know that they [Hanns Eisler and Brecht] both collaborated in the writing of a play, 'Die Massnahme'? What was the theme of this play?" one agent asked, seemingly without ulterior motive. When Feuchtwanger replied evasively, the agent got to the point by asking a leading question: "Isn't it true that this play praised the Soviet Union and lauded Communism?"[49]

Feuchtwanger saw through INS tactics from the start. His use of phrases like "as far as I know," "I do not remember," "at several occasions," and "as far as I recall" guaranteed that if questioned in more detail he always had a way out. His name-dropping did not just reflect a measure of vanity but was his way of warding off potential criticism; and phrases like "according to the reviews of most American newspapers from the far Right to the far Left"[50] safeguarded him from political classifications before they were made. At other times he used passive resistance to avoid making statements ("Q. What well known persons have you met at the Dieterles? A. I don't remember everybody - most everybody is famous"),[51] or ascribed to himself risky political opinions that he did not wish to attribute to someone he knew: "Q. You were in agreement with his [Hanns Eisler's] political views? A. I didn't talk with him about politics. Q. But my question was, were you in agreement or in sympathy with his political views? A. I don't know his political views because I was not interested in the political views. I was interested in his historical views and his historical views of the Marxist . . . Q. You were in agreement with much of Marxist theories? A. Yes."[52]

A second theme of the interrogations was Feuchtwanger's own writings. The examiners had read carefully only the one book that was repeatedly quoted in the FBI files, *Moscow, 1937*. In this part of the interrogation they adopted first a sarcastic and then an aggressive tone. Asked if he had always opposed Stalin's dictatorship, Feuchtwanger twice replied, "always opposed," whereupon the examiner repeated after him in an ironic tone, "Always opposed to it," then confronted him with the reports on Moscow by André Gide and Feuchtwanger himself. At this point the examiner clearly turned up the pressure: "Q. Would you say your book was favorable or unfavorable to Russia? A. I think it was very objective . . . Q. Your opinion, Mr. Feuchtwanger, would you say your book was favorable or unfavorable to Russia and Stalin? A. That depends on . . . Q. Your opinion."[53] Asked if he had personally attended the Moscow show trials in 1937, the refugee cleverly replied: "Together with American Ambassador Mr. Davies. He had exactly the same explanation as I did and we exchanged our opinions about this."[54] But his best defense, when the examiners tried to use passages from *Moscow,*

1937 to convict him of being a Communist, was to express his views on the historical novel, which he was then putting into a book of theory, *The House of Desdemona:* "I feel I am a historian, not a politician,"[55] "even the contemporary novels are historical novels, not political novels." Consequently, he said, *Moscow, 1937* had as little to do with politics as everything else he had written: "I tried to stay away from politics and I try to emphasize that I contemplate world history and contemporary history only from the view point of the historian."[56]

The third main theme of the interviews was the political and religious views of Feuchtwanger as a petitioner for U.S. citizenship. The tone of the ideological passages is best read rather than summarized: "Q. Were you ever a member of the Communist Party of either Czechslovakia or Germany? A. No, no, no."[57] "Q. Can you state briefly as to what portion of the theories expounded in Marxist economic theories you agree with? . . . A. You see I go with Marx as far as President Roosevelt went with him."[58] "Q. Did you agree with the theories expressed by Lenin? A. I didn't study Lenin enough in order to know that, to me Lenin is very difficult to study."[59] "Q. Do you favor public ownership of all utilities? A. In the same way as England had it, Great Britain, in the sense of the way the British Labor Party wanted it."[60] "Q. Were you an admirer of Stalin's? A. It is a ticklish question. He had—he did a lot in order to rescue the world from Fascism."[61] "Q. Mr. Feuchtwanger, you said you had sent a congratulatory telegram to Stalin; had you ever sent a birthday message greeting to President Truman [or] . . . to President Eisenhower? A. Probably he doesn't know my name. How should I?"[62]

The interviews sometimes touched on transcendental issues: e.g., Feuchtwanger was asked how he felt about the phrase "so help me God"[63] in the oath of allegiance for naturalized U.S. citizens. Almost in the same breath with a political question, "Do you feel that private owners should be compensated for their property that is taken over by the State?" the examiners could abruptly switch to religion: "Dr. Feuchtwanger, do you believe in God?" To this they got the same evasive answers as to questions about Marx, Lenin, Stalin, and East German leader Walter Ulbricht: "'God' is such a many-sided word that I couldn't say yes. . . . I believe that there is 'sense' in the universe." A minor theological dispute arose between the INS agent and Feuchtwanger over the "three forms of Judaism today; the Reformed, the Conservatives, and the Orthodox," when the exile defined himself as an "Extreme Reformist."[64] Finally, not without irony, Feuchtwanger disputed the thesis that the oath "so help me God" presupposed some belief "in a supernatural Being," because, he said, ten percent of loyal Americans were atheists. "Q. Would you classify yourself among this ten percent? A. Not necessarily, because probably I believe stronger in some Sense in the universe which can be called 'God' and which can be wronged through a false statement."

Lion and Marta may have had difficulty suppressing a smile when asked questions of this kind. Irritated by Feuchtwanger's sophistries, the examiners would hastily vacate the territory of God for the firmer terrain of politics: "Kruschev recently announced a Seven-Year Plan."[65] But after his experiences with the German and French authorities, Feuchtwanger of course knew quite well that "a malevolent bureaucracy [had] many means at its disposal . . . to trip one up."[66] What he said about Thomas Mann in 1955 when Mann died, several years after returning to Europe, may have applied to himself as well: "The sensitive writer could not endure the political climate of the McCarthy years. . . . He wrote me about the 'disgusting attacks' that were made against him, wrote me that his 'productive mood was suppressed by the political atmosphere in the country.'"[67] Feuchtwanger also felt surrounded by the "shouting of fools," "silly lies," and the "abysmal stupidity of the mob."[68] To Arnold Zweig, a fellow refugee who had spent his exile in Palestine, he complained: "At the moment, the new semi-Fascist laws admittedly do not yet pose a direct threat to me, but they make it even more difficult for me to take any trip outside the country, and give the authorities convenient excuses for harassment."[69]

As previously mentioned, the Feuchtwangers claimed that the INS interrogations were tiring and annoying but not inhumane. Yet a closer look at the transcripts reveals that the examiners, although they stayed within the law, were unscrupulous in how they applied it. The questions they asked about the political views of other exiles, for example, or prominent figures on the international scene, really had nothing to do with Feuchtwanger's application for U.S. citizenship: "Q. In the event there was an armed conflict would the Dieterles be favorable to Russia, the Soviet Union, or would they be favorable to the United States?"[70] "Q. From your observation and discussions with Thomas Mann, would you say that he was in favor of Communism?"[71] "Q. Does Brecht believe in Communism?" "Q. Did . . . Franz Werfel . . . believe in capitalism?"[72] "Q. Do you think . . . Boris Pasternack . . . should have accepted the Nobel Prize?"[73] The frequent use of rhetorical, leading, and trick questions makes evident that the INS was less interested in finding out what Feuchtwanger really believed than in confirming the information in the FBI files that was used to refuse him U.S. citizenship: "Have you ever attacked anti-Communism as you have the Fascist form of government?"[74] And: "Is it your opinion that a writer who makes a full disclosure of everything he knows to an Un-American Investigation Committee would be jeopardizing his professional standing? . . . supposing you yourself were called before such a Committee and were asked to give the names of persons whom you actually knew were members of the Communist Party, would you disclose the information or would you refuse to answer . . . and . . . stand on the Fifth Amendment?"[75]

The INS men sometimes tried to rattle Feuchtwanger by persistent questioning ("But my question was"),[76] brusque interruptions ("Your opinion"),[77] interpolations like "I think we are getting away from the question,"[78] or intimidating phrases: "It is reported that."[79] Finally, they succeeded in pushing even a man like Feuchtwanger, with his considerable intellectual resources and political experience to draw on, into compromising his moral integrity. The phrases he repeated dozens of times—"I do not remember," "I don't think so," or "I haven't the slightest idea. It is always the same thing with me and organizations. I have no idea about it"[80]—testify to his uneasiness and sense that he was being driven to lie, because of course in most cases he could have given a definite answer had he thought it was safe. He must have felt he was treading a very thin line between denial of his real self and a candor that would perpetuate his stateless condition. Lies were necessary to protect his friends and himself from a bureaucracy that valued the principle of "guilt by association" more than "innocent until proved guilty" and showed less devotion to the Bill of Rights than he did in his interrogations: "Q. Do you know of an organization by the name of 'Bill of Rights Congress'? A. I know about Civil Rights, Bill of Rights, of course I am for the Bill of Rights. Q. My question was, do you know of an organization by the name of Bill of Rights Conference? A. It was in 1792."[81]

Only rarely do we see a flash of paradox, cynicism, or humor in the answers of Lion and Marta Feuchtwanger. If Lion tried to fight back, replying "You must know it better than I," the examiner merely pursued the issue: "I am asking your opinion."[82] When Mr. Gren of the INS asked if Nikita Khrushchev could be trusted, Feuchtwanger answered laconically: "This is a question for Mr. Dulles, not for me."[83] Asked in August 1957 where Brecht was, Feuchtwanger replied unemotionally: "He is dead, unfortunately."[84] Marta turned mocking and defiant when asked if she agreed with her husband in political matters: "Yes, as the Bible says 'where you go, I shall go.' I do not have much opinion of my own. . . . If he says it is right, I say it is right." When the INS gentleman pursued the issue, asking if she really had no "independent feelings," Marta, an avid gardener but childless, played the role of a demure little housewife: "No, just about things about gardening and our kids."[85]

The INS interrogations of Lion and Marta Feuchtwanger confirmed what Hoover had known since 1940–41. The only difference was that now, in 1957–58, the question was no longer whether to deport the refugees but "only" whether to refuse them U.S. citizenship. "The petitioner admitted," says the seven-page "Findings of Facts, Conclusions of Law, and Recommendation" INS examiner Samuel Hozman submitted on 4 December 1957, "that he did permit the use of his name and prestige by several organizations which he considered to be anti-Fascist and that he did not care whether they were pro-Communist . . . that he does not think that capitalism as practiced in the United States is the ideal economic system; . . . that he was photographed with Josef Stalin in Moscow in 1937 . . . , that he discounted the reliability of the American newspapers concerning Russian affairs and was convinced of the true situation in Russia only when Kruschev disclosed it. He refused to comment regarding Russia's part during the recent Hungarian uprising. He admitted that he had been very closely associated with Berthold Brecht."

In summary: "Applicant . . . is an ardent proponent of Socialism. . . . It is apparent that he strongly advocates the discarding of the economic system that has made the American working man the envy of the civilized world. . . . He admits close association with pro-Communists. There is no indication in his testimony before the Naturalization Examiner that he has been as cooperative with anti-Communist organizations as with anti-Fascist groups." "I recommend," Hozman concluded, "that the petition for naturalization of Lion Feuchtwanger be denied on the grounds that he has failed to establish . . . that he has been attached to the principles of the Constitution and well disposed to the good order and happiness of the United States."[86]

Lion Feuchtwanger, already suffering from terminal cancer during his final INS interrogations, died a stateless exile a few months after the INS refused his naturalization. Deprived of his German nationality by the Third Reich in 1933 in what Nazi law defined as a legal process, he found that the Federal Republic did not restore it after 1949; nor did the land where he sought asylum wish to have him. Having witnessed the de facto banishment of his friend Charlie Chaplin from the United States [167, p. 753f], he now saw himself barred from ever visiting Germany again, the land from whose language and culture he was neither able nor willing to separate despite the persecutions he had suffered. To regain his freedom to travel, only two equally unacceptable paths lay open to him: to follow the example of Brecht, Thomas Mann, Döblin, and others who burned their bridges in California when they went back to Europe, or to ingratiate himself with the authorities and turn informer just to get a U.S. passport. The America that spent vast sums of time, money, and ideological zeal to spy on him for more than eighteen years had become too much of a homeland for him to leave. Or was he being ironic when he answered INS agents who asked why he wanted to become an American: "Well, I owe to the United States a lot . . . and I feel very much love for this country. . . . I found here a home where I can write what I wish to write, without restrictions. . . . I ardently believe in the Fifth Amendment, and I feel that here I can have free speech and free writing."[87]

No One Was Forgotten: Werfel, Remarque, Bruno Frank, Ludwig, Leonhard Frank, Döblin, and Others

Thomas Mann, Bertolt Brecht, and Lion Feuchtwanger came under FBI scrutiny for their liberal or "leftist" views because they took a public stand on political issues like the future of Germany, and because of their prominence. Less prominent or unpolitical exiles came under less intensive investigation. Franz Werfel, Erich Maria Remarque, Bruno Frank, Emil Ludwig, and Vicki Baum, although well known, either stayed out of politics or, in Ludwig's case, were active in the conservative camp. Leonhard Frank, Alfred Döblin, Alfred Neumann, Ludwig Marcuse, and Curt Goetz went unnoticed for their literary works and for their political views. But regardless of whether they were successful writers or reduced to publishing their own books, not one completely escaped the attention of the FBI and other agencies.

FRANZ WERFEL

Werfel, an Austrian novelist and playwright driven from his homeland in 1938, was known in the United States for his stageplay *Jacobowsky and the Colonel,* the novel *The Song of Bernadette,* and other works. His FBI dossier no longer holds anything but a "name check," which for unfathomable reasons was carried out nine years after his death. Comprising three pages of text and thirteen official forms, it is a web of errors and distortions of his political views. Whoever in July 1941 fed the FBI the story that Werfel had been "a leader of the Communist Party in Germany," linked "for many years . . . in Vienna, Austria, and Berlin, Germany, . . . with radical activities," was definitely not "reliable," as the reporting agent claimed.[1] Hoover's agents and U.S. naval intelligence were told by an informant in Mexico that a plot was under way there to rescue from Europe a group of "Fifth Columnists . . . closely connected with either Nazism, Fascism or Communism,"[2] one of whom was a certain "Franz Werfel, author of the best seller of six years ago 'The Forty Days of Musa Dagh.'"[3] The FBI also quoted information on Werfel from the 20 August 1940 issue of the Communist-affiliated *Daily Worker.* The attempts, commonplace later in the McCarthy era, to discredit people by linking them to organizations blacklisted by the attorney general or California's House Un-American Activities Committee look ineffective in Werfel's case ("national sponsor for the Joint Anti-Fascist Refugee Committee . . . designated by the Attorney General . . . persuant to Executive Order 10450").[4] It remains a mystery why the FBI, having completed the "name check," suggested to the unknown official who requested the check that military intelligence should be asked what they had on Werfel.[5] The OSS took only a marginal interest in him, describing Werfel as a "former close friend of Chancellor Schuschnigg. Has always been very active on behalf of Austria's independence."[6]

No INS file survives, but the sparse FBI material on Werfel is supplemented by a small State Department dossier on "Alma Maria Mahler-Werfel" containing letters exchanged in 1947 between a Harry Freidenberg, formerly with the U.S. occupation forces in Germany, and the State Department in Washington, about legal problems in transferring Werfel's posthumous papers to the University of California at Los Angeles. Alma Mahler-Werfel's petition to be allowed to travel to Vienna as soon as possible after the war to retrieve her family's confiscated property and her husband's manuscripts ("those holdings have been partially siezed by former members of the Nazi party, who justified their seizures by the fact that Mrs. Mahler-Werfel, a Catholic, had twice married Jews [Mahler and Werfel]"),[7] was rejected by U.S. occupation forces citing the usual excuse of "shortage of food, transportation, and housing,"[8] until the Austrian government sent a formal invitation: "Dr. Renner, Pres Aus and Dr. Hurdes, Aus Minister of Education both indorce need for presence of Mrs. Werfel in Vienna in connection with litigation now pending Aus Supreme Court with regard to this property."[9] Shortly after, Alma Mahler-Werfel traveled to Vienna and brought her husband's Austrian archive back to California.

ERICH MARIA REMARQUE

The file on Erich Maria Remarque, best-selling novelist of *All Quiet on the Western Front* and *Arch of Triumph*, both made into popular films, is as slender as Werfel's, comprising only a few pages in the INS archive plus an anonymous letter addressed to "Mr. J. Edgar Hoover."[10] The reason may be that Remarque kept away from exile organizations, did not contribute to refugee magazines, rarely gave interviews, and was more noted for his elegant lifestyle and his liaison with Marlene Dietrich, who had her own FBI dossier, than for his political engagement. Or it may have to do with the sizable income that made him a welcome guest in various nations. Either way, the FBI's appetite for information was whetted neither by Remarque's wide circle of acquaintances in Hollywood and New York, where he frequented the Stork Club, a favorite nightspot of Hoover, nor by the vogue his novels enjoyed in the United States. Not even an anonymous denunciation signed "I am just a true American"[11]— normally a sure way of getting the FBI on the scene—had any effect. "Dear Edgar" ignored the warning from his concerned fellow American ("I hope it's not a crime to be suspecious, . . . but . . . these german men what are they doing here in our country")[12] and was not moved to act even when Remarque's lawyer in 1946–47 underpinned his client's petition for citizenship by appealing to personal contacts in Washington and by a reference to President Roosevelt, who was not popular with Hoover: "If you get up to New York . . . don't forget to give me a ring because I would like to show you some correspondence I had with FDR in regard to legislation which . . . the President called a 'plan to End all Aliens.'"[13]

Certificate of Naturalization 6710597 is proof that the Justice Department official through whom Remarque's lawyer pushed his plea to the INS office in New York to process Remarque's naturalization "as expeditiously as possible"[14] was successful. Six years after he had entered the United States at San Ysidro, California, with the status of "permanent resident," and shortly before he moved back to Switzerland as his main home, the prominent writer ("complexion fair, . . . color of hair brown, height 5 feet 10 inches, . . . married")[15] was awarded citizenship by the District Court in New York

City, apparently without any further investigation. Unlike many of his fellow exiles, he continued to express positive views about his second country years later, when he said in an interview with *Newsweek:* "I am very happy to have become an American. . . . Americans have an innate sense of freedom, whether they realize it or not" [165, p. 108].

BRUNO FRANK

The Bruno Frank case is remarkable because there is so little of it. The FBI claims to have found nothing in its files but a series of letters from 1942–45, although Frank seems a prime candidate for investigation. Successful in the American book, stage, and film worlds, the screenwriter of *The Hunchback of Notre Dame* was not an especially political man but, nevertheless, was among the first refugees to speak against Martin Dies's recently revived House Un-American Activities Committee, at a rally of Hollywood's Anti-Nazi League soon after his arrival in the United States in August 1938.[16] With his wife, Liesl, he worked for years for refugee aid groups, supported the European Film Fund, and in March 1942, when the National Defense Migration Hearings were held by a House committee in Los Angeles, he testified publicly and in a far more impassioned tone than fellow witness Thomas Mann against a plan to "evacuate" the exiles: "I am told, that at first the refugees should be evacuated as enemy aliens, and that later on, by and by, individual readmission might be granted. Sir, that would never do. Such a procedure would spell disaster. . . . The bitterest and most consistent foes of nazi-ism and fascism won't be treated the same way as Nazis and Fascists themselves. Not in this country."[17] His public statement against the equation of Germans with Nazis— "One thing I'm clear about: Nowhere are the German people confused with the mad counterfeiter who is trying to drag them into the abyss"[18]—did not mobilize the FBI against him either.

Frank's name did appear as a cross-reference to other files because he and his wife kept open house for visitors at their handsome villa on Camden Drive in Beverly Hills. Apart from this, the FBI took an interest only in the business correspondence between Frank and El Libro Libre publishing house in Mexico, when the German exiles south of the border tried to involve him more in their political work. They failed, in part, because the Office of Censorship destroyed even harmless pieces of mail like a five-dollar donation for a Free Germany Movement brochure, on the grounds that "As participation of European refugees, residing in the U.S., in free discussion outside the U.S. on controversial issues of international politics may be falsely interpreted abroad, and may tend to contribute to dissension within the U.S., the communication is condemned."[19]

Bruno Frank ("eyes grey, color of hair brown, height 5 feet 10 inches, weight 180 pounds")[20] became a naturalized citizen in Los Angeles on 12 January 1945. Neither the FBI nor the INS tried to prevent it, apart from filing a one-page document with the usual blend of facts, allegations, and half-truths: "He has been reported as pro-Nazi, a close associate of known Communist Party members and is possibly communistic himself."[21] Evidently this summary did not lead to any action against him. And when OSS man John Norman dropped in at Frank's "fine Beverly Hills home" for an interview on 10 December 1944 while canvassing other southern California exiles, he came not to question Frank's loyalty but to ask "what should be done with Germany."

Frank's replies to Norman show that the new American, a man with "bushy eyebrows, dimples, and a strong square jaw"[22] took a cautious and balanced view of the situation in Europe. "Long-time military occupation . . . without oppression"[23] was essential, he said, whereas a U.S. proposal to partition Germany would be acceptable only if it would effectively prevent a "recurrence of aggression."[24] As for the territorial claims on Germany, Frank hesitated to approve making Bavaria part of Austria but said he would have no problem with ceding territory to France, Denmark, and Czechoslovakia. The reeducation of Germans could be achieved most effectively by the occupation forces, not through Germans like former Reich Chancellor Heinrich Brüning who had already demonstrated their lack of political foresight. Punishment should be meted out to "about one hundred thousand . . . and not all by death," so as to leave "some hope for the German people."[25] Asked about the interests of the Russians, Frank said that their plans for expansion, if they had them, were in Asia, but in the West they were only aiming to secure their borders.

Two years after the expiration of a German reentry permit that was purchased from police headquarters in Stuttgart for eight marks in July 1933, and six months after Frank became a U.S. citizen, an FBI agent closed Frank's file after inserting a clipping from the

New York Times: "Dr. Bruno Frank, expatriated German author of many novels, including 'Lost Heritage' and 'The Man Called Cervantes,' died today of a heart attack in his home at Beverly Hills. His age was 58."[26]

EMIL LUDWIG

Emil Ludwig, like Bruno Frank, was a successful writer who felt comfortable in his California exile. Ludwig's books, especially his biographies of great men, had attracted a wide American audience before his arrival. He had left Germany in 1906 to live in Switzerland, and his public lectures and three books on Germany, *The Germans: Double History of a Nation* (1941), *How to Treat the Germans* (1943), and *The Moral Conquest of Germany* (1945), which explained the Nazis as the outgrowth of German national character, made him popular in the United States; but he was bitterly attacked by fellow exiles who felt that they were spokesmen for a different and better Germany. Ludwig's connections with the White House and with high-ranking government officials like Vice President Harry Truman, Secretary of the Interior Harold Ickes, and Secretary of State Edward Stettinius, and also his testimony before the Foreign Affairs Committee of the House of Representatives and writings like "Fourteen Rules for the American Occupation Officer," enabled him to directly influence American policy on Germany after the war.

But Ludwig held no interest for J. Edgar Hoover, who normally wanted to know everything the exiles had to say about a future Germany. As an author who admired detective-story writer Rex Stout and British diplomat Lord Vansittart for their dislike of Germany, who supported the conservative Society for the Prevention of World War III, and was vilified as a "regular swine" and a "pig"[27] by the left-wing Free Germans and publicly greeted with "violent criticism"[28] from members of the Council for a Democratic Germany, he was an ideological soulmate of the FBI chief and many Washington officials. "No investigation has been conducted by this Bureau concerning the above-named individual,"[29] states a 1954 FBI memorandum, in one of few passages that are not blacked out. Ludwig's MID file is insignificant despite its classification as secret. And of 150 pages with the INS, the State Department, and the counsel to the president, the 149 released to me show nothing of interest but a personal letter to Franklin Roosevelt asking for a recommendation to the U.S. consul in Tijuana so that Ludwig could obtain an immigrant's visa to lecture at the State College of Santa Barbara.

One agency that did pay attention to Ludwig was the OSS, whose Foreign Nationalities Branch devoted two dozen documents to the controversial commentator on Germany's future. The FNB analyses climaxed in a lengthy interview conducted by two OSS agents on 16 December 1944 at "Ludwig's residence at 303 Grenola Street, Pacific Palisades, California." "Ludwig received us in a large, comfortable, slightly disordered room, which boasted a large plate glass window affording a beautiful view of the ocean just below. It reminded one immediately of Hitler's eyrie at Berchtesgaden. Ludwig easily presented a picture of the story-book genius, what with his huge head, his long hair resting on his ears, and extraordinarily big bags under his eyes. . . . He wore elegant paint-splashed trousers and a neatly tailored sport coat."[30] After initial communication problems ("every question I asked him met with such replies as 'I have already written a book on that'"), Ludwig quickly got down to the business of Germany's future: he was as opposed to the "Dismemberment of inner Germany"[31] as he was to the plan of Roosevelt's Treasury Secretary Henry Morgenthau to deindustrialize Germany. But he did recommend that the Americans should behave as "conquerors,"[32] keep a wall around Germany for ten years, and rigorously supervise the reeducation of Germans by anti-Fascist teachers. He would not count on exiles like Thomas Mann to help in the reconstruction ("They would laugh at Thomas

Mann in Germany. He wrote Pan-German things in 1923"), nor rely on Hubertus Prinz zu Löwenstein ("a nobody") or on Americans like Dorothy Thompson ("She is a good writer, but she . . . talks against me"). The only Germans who could serve the Americans with advice, he said, were men like himself, the longtime Vansittartist Friedrich Wilhelm Förster, anti-Prussian polemicist "Kurt Reiss"[33] (by whom he presumably meant journalist Curt Riess), and former Hitler crony Hermann Rauschning ("an honest man"),[34] because unlike the other exiles, they had the courage to speak against Germany.

LEONHARD FRANK

Unlike Ludwig, Bruno Frank, Remarque, and Werfel, Leonhard Frank belonged to that group of writers for whom exile in Los Angeles was a distinctly negative experience. His attempts to gain a foothold as a Hollywood screenwriter were unsuccessful, and he made slow progress on his writing during his years in America. His novel *Mathilde,* a fairy-tale love story set in a farming community, was privately printed in 1943. *Deutsche Novelle,* in which Thomas Mann detected the influence of his novel *Doctor Faustus,* was published years later in Germany. The bibliography of Frank's works [42, vol. 1, pt. 2, p. 42] shows that he published virtually no magazine articles in the United States.

It did not improve Frank's situation that the American Federation of Labor had helped him to escape from France, or that Warner Brothers Studios gave him a one-year emergency "lifesaver" contract when he arrived in the United States [58, p. 209]. The film capital of America, the town where, Frank believed, money decided everything, never acknowledged the poverty-stricken emigré from Europe. Even to his successful compatriots he remained a "bodiless, invisible wraith" [ibid., p. 214].

Leonhard Frank was considered a "leftist," albeit without party affiliations. Or as the FBI put it, quoting the *Encyclopedia Britan-*

nica, which normally was apter in its phrasing, he was "violently pacifist."[35] No evidence survives to tell us if this is why Hoover's agents in Los Angeles, New York, and Bonn, and their colleagues in the CIA and the 66th Intelligence Corps Group of the U.S. Army in Europe, continued to pursue him from April 1941 until March 1962, filling more than one hundred pages with information about him. One feature of Frank's files departs from the norm: the detailed report of a house search in summer 1941, "unknown to subject"[36] as R. B. Hood candidly admits. Besides Frank's books, the FBI was mainly interested in his letters and telegrams: "'State Department asks American Federation of Labor whether it supports granting visas to your family members Stop A.F. of L. hesitant because never heard from you.'"[37] Agents looked at jottings by his telephone for clues to his social life ("[blacked out] . . . couldn't keep date")[38] while he was living at 1924 North Argyle Avenue, and noted which filling station he used in the neighborhood. His address book confirmed how isolated a life he lived in Hollywood: "Subject's address book contained approximately twenty-one names and addresses."[39]

Other parts of his dossier seem routine. For years the FBI offices in Washington, New York, and Los Angeles exchanged memos about whether, why, and how long his name should be kept on a Custodial Detention Card, which would cause him to be interned in the event of a national emergency. Although no INS file survives, the Bureau took from INS archives a statutory declaration by Frank in which he "admits having departed from his Switzerland home and family about April 1937" because of "domestic difficulties . . . and . . . seeking better economic future."[40] When interrogated about his Certificate of Identification, Frank suggested that the FBI interview Thomas Mann ("it is believed that the Bureau has considerable information concerning Thomas Mann"), but the interview did not materialize even though an appointment was made for 14 September 1942: "Dr. Thomas Mann . . . was unavoidably absent when the reporting agent and Special Agent [blacked out] appeared to interview him."[41] Twice, in 1947 and 1954, Frank's file, which had been closed for "paucity of derogatory information,"[42] was reopened after the FBI received anonymous denunciations that were unusually crude in their style and content. One led to an FBI lab analysis, from which "the typewriting . . . was concluded to have been prepared on a machine equipped with a Style of Pica Type . . . normally found on Remington and Underwood Noiseless typewriters."[43]

The last occasion on which Frank attracted FBI attention was in 1962, twelve years after he had returned to Germany and ten years after his German citizenship had been restored ("24 March 1952 - German citizenship reinstated"), when the "Legat" (legal attaché) at the U.S. embassy in Bonn sent Hoover a long report from U.S. Army Intelligence in Germany. Two things are noteworthy about the material collected by "Headquarters, 66th INTC Group, USAREUR, APO 154, US Forces AEUC-OCE (O&R) EE 564 953." First, military intelligence gives a detailed "chronology of Subject," drawing parallels between Frank's conduct in 1919 and 1934 without any consideration for the changes in historical circumstances: "1919 - Participated in the communist revolt in Munich; sought by police because of suspected treason. . . . November 1934 - Deprived of his German citizenship. Sought by Gestapo because of suspected treason."[44] Second, the extensive references to Frank's association with a "left-oriented" writers' group, the Tukan Literaturkreis,[45] and with the Fränkische Kreis, which wanted to keep Germany a nuclear-free zone, shows the extent to which U.S. intelligence agents were mixing into the internal affairs of Germany in the sixties, possibly with active support from their German colleagues. "The Frankische Kreis was designated as a supporting organization of the communist party of Germany by Dr. Schroeder, the West German Federal Minister of the Interior," states the reporting MID agent, who evidently had access to German mail or to the files of the Fränkische Kreis itself. "In his correspondence with Prof. Schneider, . . . secretary of the Frankische Kreis, . . . Subject

SUMMARY OF INFORMATION

DATE
12 March 1962

PREPARING OFFICE
Headquarters, 66th INTC Group, USAREUR, APO 154, US Forces   AEUC-OCE(O&R) EE 564 953

SUBJECT	CODE FOR USE IN INDIVIDUAL PARAGRAPH EVALUATION	
Leonhard FRANK (C)	OF SOURCE: COMPLETELY RELIABLE .... A USUALLY RELIABLE .... B FAIRLY RELIABLE .... C NOT USUALLY RELIABLE .... D UNRELIABLE .... E RELIABILITY UNKNOWN ..... F	OF INFORMATION: CONFIRMED BY OTHER SOURCES 1 PROBABLY TRUE .... 2 POSSIBLY TRUE .... 3 DOUBTFULLY TRUE .... 4 IMPROBABLE .... 5 TRUTH CANNOT BE JUDGED ... 6

SUMMARY OF INFORMATION   WARNING NOTICE - SENSITIVE SOURCES AND METHODS INVOLVED

ACTION

1. (U) Subject is listed in the Degener Who's Who, 1951 edition as born on 4 September 1882 in Wuerzburg, Germany. Prior to his emigration in 1933 he resided in Berlin. He can be reached through Peter Davies Ltd., 99 Graet Russel Street, London WC 1. Until 1933 he was a member of the Berlin Academy of Arts. Among his works are the books: Die Raeuberbande (The Robber Band), Die Ursache (The Cause), Der Buerger (The Citizen), Der Mensch ist gut (The Human is Good), Bruder und Schwester (Brother and Sister), Karl und Anna, Hufnaegel (Hobnails) and others.

2. (C) ▓▓▓▓▓▓ listed the following chronology on Subject:

9 April 1908 - Under observation because of mental illness.

August 1915 - Published the periodicals Pan, Forum and Das Freie Wort described as politically suspect publications.

▓▓▓ 1919 - Participated in the communist revolt in Munich; sought by police because of suspected treason.

29 January 1920 - Indictment for treason dismissed by States Attorney, Munich because of lack of sufficient evidence.

8 March 1920 - Conducted camouflaged communist meetings in Frankfurt. Was active in KPD (Kommunistische Partei Deutschlands — Communist Party of Germany) in ensuing years.

22 October 1929 - Married in Berlin to Elena Peysner born 18 August 1899 in Kiev, Russia. Divorced 18 March 1952.

November 1934 - Deprived of his German citizenship. Sought by Gestapo because of suspected treason.

22 October 1950 - Registered in Munich upon return from the United States.

15 February 1951 - Received residence permit in Munich.

24 March 1952 - German citizenship reinstated.

18 April 1952 - Obtained pass to visit Switzerland.

DISTRIBUTION

DA FORM 568
1 APR 62

ENCLOSURE

has indicated his concurrence with Prof. Schneider's point of view."[46]

Leonhard Frank ("Height 5 feet, 7 inches, Weight 150 pounds . . . Race White - Gentile"),[47] winner of East Germany's National Prize for Literature and "reputed to be a communist,"[48] died in Munich, aged 78, on 18 August 1961, some seven months before U.S. army intelligence attached a notice to their final memo: "Warning Notice - Sensitive Sources and Methods Involved."[49]

ALFRED DÖBLIN

Like Leonhard Frank, Alfred Döblin, famous for the classic urban novel *Alexanderplatz, Berlin,* led a sad and shadowy existence in the United States. The FBI claimed that it kept no file on him, and the thirty-nine pages sent me by the INS look like the usual official forms, which keep parroting the same details about Döblin's entries into the United States (New York, 6 May 1939 and 12 September 1940;[50] Nogales, Arizona, 11 March 1941 with assistance from Heinrich Mann),[51] about his citizenship ("I became a French citizen in 1936"),[52] and his race ("Q. Of what race of people are you? A. I am Hebrew").[53]

But the cool jargon of the visa applications and police character references ("the Los Angeles Police Department . . . found no record to indicate that—Bruno Alfred Döblin . . . is . . . wanted for the commission of any crime")[54] cannot hide the human tragedy of the family scattered across the world by the Nazis and the war they had unleashed. In March 1941, in a barren desert town on the Arizona-Mexico border, Döblin filled out an "Application for Immigration Visa" in which he had to list the whereabouts of his children, at a time when one of his four sons had been reported missing by the French army[55] and a second son, Klaus, had gone into hiding in Marseilles to escape his former German compatriots following the demobilization of the French army. A year and a half later the eldest son had been inducted into the U.S. army, while the desperate attempts of the parents to find Klaus and get him out of Europe led to a detailed interrogation by the INS in Los Angeles. Letters that Döblin sent to the State Department and the President's Advisory Committee on Political Refugees in New York were intercepted by the mail censors, and Döblin's own entry into the United States was placed under review.

But the main concern of the INS was Döblin's relationship with Thomas Mann ("Is Thomas Mann his real name?").[56] Mann, hoping to help Döblin obtain a Mexican visa for his son Klaus, had written on his behalf to the influential director general of the Bank of Mexico, Eduardo Villaseñor, not realizing that Villaseñor was suspected of anti-American activities. "The records reveal," says the Examiner's Note on the Office of Censorship form, "that the addressee was involved in a plot to blow up Boulder Dam, and that he is associated with a German confidential agent of the German-American Bund operating in Southern California."[57]

Alfred Döblin left California at the end of 1945 with a French passport and an American "exit permit"[58] to participate—without success—in a French reeducation mission in Germany.[59] The only sizable trace he left in the files of U.S. intelligence when he departed was the record of a conversation that John Norman of the OSS conducted with him on 12 December 1944.

As in other interviews of this kind, Norman first wrote a personal description, depicting Döblin's Hollywood home as "modest" and the man himself, the author of *November, 1918,* as "a short, grey, old man with very thick glasses" whose English even in 1944 was still so bad "that a good portion of the time he conversed in French."[60] What Norman reported about Döblin's views on Germany and the Germans sounds quite moderate compared with statements from other exiles. More important than a debate about the partitioning of Germany or the ceding of territory, Döblin said, was to construct a "true League of Nations"[61] and to establish a federal system of government on a basis of "non-interference."[62] The Soviet Union, weakened by war, would offer Germany a "soft peace" only if its relations with the Western allies deteriorated. It would be desirable to involve exiles like Heinrich Brüning and Hermann Rauschning in building a new Germany. Since the "roots of Hitlerism"[63] ran very deep in Germany, Döblin, a Jew who had only recently converted to Catholicism, advised that Jews not return to Germany, at least in the beginning.

VICKI BAUM, ALFRED NEUMANN, LUDWIG MARCUSE, CURT GOETZ

Vicki Baum, a successful novelist and screenwriter familiar to Americans since her *Grand Hotel* was made into a play and then a film in the United States, was far less active politically than most of her fellow exiles and played only a peripheral role in files of the FBI, which for unknown reasons carried out a brief "review of the files"[64] in February 1954 and May 1957. "No investigation has been conducted by this Bureau concerning the above-named individual,"[65] the FBI summed up, and the INS, in a letter of March 1988, informed me that "three extensive index searches of our Central Office records systems"[66] brought no documents to light about Baum, who had moved to the United States before 1933 and was naturalized in 1938.

The FBI and INS archives contain nothing but a few biographical details on screenwriter Alfred Neumann, one of whose scripts was made into a highly successful Ernst Lubitsch film [42, vol. 1, pt. 2, p. 544]. He was described as "6 feet 1/2 inches"[67] tall, weight 170 pounds with blue eyes; the Exiled Writers Committee had helped him to escape from Europe; he became a naturalized citizen in December 1947; and the Los Angeles police had no negative information about him.

More informative was the record of a talk that an unnamed OSS agent held with Neumann at the writer's Los Angeles home on 24 May 1945, hoping to gain "information about the Communist political cells in Hollywood."[68] After a few standard questions on international politics—Was it likely that Americans would encounter Nazi "werewolves" in Germany? (Neumann "does not anticipate a very active or successful Nazi underground movement")[69]—the agent came to the point and asked the current views of exiles in southern California. Neumann's answers were short and specific. His friend Thomas Mann was universally regarded as an "outstanding representative of the German-American colony," but Alfred Döblin was also "very highly respected." He could not agree with Emil Ludwig that the Germans should be harshly punished because this would play into the hands of Hitler and Goebbels, who said in their propaganda "that if Germany were defeated the Jews would return to work their vengeance upon the German people." He also kept his distance from Feuchtwanger, who had "the most pronounced pro-Russian tendencies among the writers of his acquaintance in this vicinity," because of a past disagreement between them. Otherwise Neumann claimed to be "out of touch"[70] with developments in the film industry and the political debates of the refugees, and so consciously or unconsciously secured himself from further unpleasant political and personal questions. "It is obvious," an OSS memo states drily, "that either Neumann did not want to talk, or was not asked the right questions."[71]

The file of essayist and university teacher Ludwig Marcuse consists of twenty-nine pages of biographical data from the INS but shows no FBI activity. The refugee, who fled Europe in April 1939, was listed as speaking "little English," gave his race as "Hebrew"[72] on an INS form, and cited "Professor Max Horkheimer, Columbia University" as one who could vouch for his "loyalty."[73]

Curt Goetz, the last writer we will look at from California's emigré community, seems not to have had an FBI file. Instead of copies of his documents, the INS gave me only a written summary stating (among other things) that the author of "'Dr. Praetorius,' 'People Will Talk' and 'The Road to Rome'"[74] was employed for forty weeks by MGM at a salary of $1,000 a week and had a mole on his left cheek.

3

The FBI and the Exiles
in New York

The OSS and the FBI: The "Other Germany"

NEW YORK AND ITS IMMIGRATION station on Ellis Island had been
the gateway for sixteen million immigrants to enter the United
States in the five preceding decades. It was now the entry point for
the comparatively small band of German-speaking refugees trying
to escape Hitler. The gate was framed by the Manhattan skyline on
one side and the Statue of Liberty on the other. "A marvel of superb
beauty" [19, p. 371], "a giant fantastic excrescence risen out of the
sea" [58, p. 209], "a nodule of needle-thin, needle-sharp crystal"
[11, p. 403] was how the political scientist Arnold Brecht and writers Leonhard Frank and Vicki Baum described the fascinating and
bizarre cluster of skyscrapers.[1] Actor Fritz Kortner was awed by the
mountain chains of buildings [104, p. 439], while Bruno Frei saw
the office towers as a symbol of "democratic bustle" [59, p. 234] and
a perversion of the human urge to freedom.

The new arrivals also had mixed reactions to the Statue of Liberty. What some saw as the symbol of rescue and freedom, "a captivating hello to everyone fleeing dictatorship" [19, p. 371], reminded others (as it had George Bernard Shaw) of Dante's inscription on the gates of hell: "Abandon all hope, ye who enter here" [42, vol. 2, pt. 2, p. 1310]. In 1948 the Viennese Herta Pauli would publish a history of the Statue of Liberty, *I Lift My Lamp: The Way of a Symbol*.[2] Hans Marchwitza, who in the twenties began to write journalistic pieces about workers' lives, emphasized the contrast between the "stone lady" with her "torch of victory" and the cold "concrete towers" behind her, "each of them a fortress of devil money" [137, p. 20].

The varied responses to the New York skyline and the Statue of Liberty were colored by the personal attitudes of the newcomers. But all agreed in their aversion to Ellis Island. Officials asking acutely embarrassing questions about income and housing conditions, problems with invalid or missing travel papers, expired visas, rejected permits—most of the fugitives had seen more than enough of all that in the previous seven or eight years in Europe. Gustav Regler, a refugee from the Saar, described the Victorian-style main building on Ellis Island, which resembled a railroad station, as a "prison with iron bars" but "without machine-guns" [164, p. 484]. Bruno Frei saw the "giant hall of glass" as "a sort of greenhouse to grow deportees" [59, p. 235]. Writer-physician Theodor Balk, who like Anna Seghers was refused entry and obliged to travel on to Mexico, talked in his memoirs of "iron bars" in the foreground and behind the bars, "in the background, the Statue of Liberty" [9, p. 249]. Journalist Maximilian Scheer emphasized the "well-organized, technical" and "unfeeling" atmosphere of the "prison" isle [175, p. 114] where suspect Germans had once been interned after 1917 and thousands of "red" foreigners were imprisoned in 1919–20.

No sooner had the refugees arrived than they were cross-examined by immigration officers who did not want to hear anything about their struggles against the Nazis but ardently pursued any ties they might have with the political left: "Were you ever a member of the Communist party? . . . In your writings have you advocated the Communist form of government? . . . Were you ever in Russia? . . . Were you a member of the Loyalist warring forces [in the Spanish Civil War]?"[3] INS officials would not or could not see any difference between ordinary lawbreakers and the inmates of German concentration camps and French internment camps. The fugitives did not understand why officials kept asking their reasons for leaving their homeland. Asked how long they planned to stay in the United States and what they would live on, they had to resort to white lies.

Most exiles managed to leave the "isle of tears" [ibid., p. 108] by the Statue of Liberty not too long after they arrived and without major problems. The lucky ones whose papers were in order and who had traveled as first- or second-class passengers and been cleared by customs while still aboard ship even bypassed the island and went directly to New York City. A small number were interned on Ellis Island for days or weeks until relatives, friends, or representatives of the many refugee aid organizations convinced the INS that their charges neither endangered the security of the United States nor would become a burden to taxpayers. A few were put on board the next ship and sent to some other place of asylum. Except for Communist politician Gerhart Eisler and his brother Hanns, no refugee writers were materially threatened with deportation during or after the war, although in several cases initial steps were taken to try to deport them.

Writers with major reputations or powerful connections like Heinrich Mann, Franz Werfel, or stage director Erwin Piscator would be welcomed (FBI men observed) by colleagues and journalists when they disembarked. Klaus Mann in 1938 went "straight from the harbor" to Madison Square Garden, where his father was speaking against the German occupation of Czechoslovakia [122, p. 388]. Carl Zuckmayer spent several weeks living "like a prince" in the home of Dorothy Thompson in Central Park West [241, p. 473]. Alfred Kantorowicz was helped by Ernest Hemingway. But the majority of the fugitives were, like travel writer Lili Körber, journalist Hans Natonek, and Hans Marchwitza, dependent on charity from an aid organization. Richard Krebs, who arrived in the United States illegally by ship, spent his first nights in New York on park benches. Others wandered aimlessly for days through the streets of Manhattan, fascinated or repelled by the alien metropolis but invariably grateful to have escaped the Gestapo.

Many of the better-known writers soon moved on to southern California, attracted by the lifesaver contracts offered by the big film studios and by the mild Mediterranean-like climate. Those without contacts in Hollywood settled in New York, more similar to European cities, or in other East Coast locations that resembled home in weather and landscape. Besides writers Hermann Broch, Ferdinand Bruckner, Oskar Maria Graf, Hans Marchwitza, Fritz von Unruh, Johannes Urzidil, F. C. Weiskopf, and Carl Zuckmayer, the East Coast group included almost the entire elite of politicians, trade unionists, and journalists driven out by the Nazis. In short, while Los Angeles after 1940–41 quickly became the capital of German exile literature, New York became the center of exile politics.

This development was encouraged by the proximity of the East Coast exiles to the center of political power in Washington and to the government agencies that decided the fate of the refugees and were drafting the future of Central Europe. Exile politicians and journalists were in close contact with Germany experts in the State Department. Members of the Institute for Social Research and exile professors who found shelter at the elite eastern universities served as advisers to the Office of Strategic Services. It was to Washington that Brecht and Hanns Eisler were summoned against their will to testify before the House Un-American Activities Committee. Bureaus like the Office of War Information, and divisions of the armed forces like the Psychological Warfare Division and the

Counter Intelligence Corps, were directed from Washington. Washington and New York were the production sites for the great newspapers that played a critical role in forming public opinion about the exiles and American policy on Germany. Those concerned with the political fate of Germany and the Germans thus were more likely to be in the East than on the Pacific Coast, which at that time was less sophisticated and oriented toward Asia.

New York, the capital of exile politics, was of secondary importance for literature. Carl Zuckmayer, to avoid compromising his literary work, withdrew with his wife to a farm in Vermont after negative experiences in Hollywood and New York. Bavarian Oskar Maria Graf, who normally wrote about peasant life, published the novel *Die Flucht ins Mittelmässige* (Flight to mediocrity), one of few attempts by the exiles to address the phenomenon of New York in literary form. Hermann Broch, who fled from Austria in 1938, may have had difficulty adjusting to his host country right up until his death in 1951, yet he completed some of his most important works, including *The Death of Virgil,* with the aid of prestigious grants in Princeton and New Haven. Thomas Mann, once he moved from Princeton to California, only occasionally visited the East, usually staying at the Bedford Hotel in New York. Ernst Toller, in the United States since 1936 and a successful lecturer who temporarily earned a good living in Hollywood, committed suicide in New York's Mayflower Hotel in spring 1939.

Perhaps the most difficult time of all was had by exiles involved with the theater who tried to gain a foothold on Broadway, or off- and off-off Broadway. Famed director Max Reinhardt, nearing seventy when he came to the United States, managed few successful productions before his death in October 1943. Erwin Piscator tried and failed to break into the American theater with his Dramatic Workshop. Brecht, who for the most part kept to the theory of the epic theater with which Americans were unfamiliar, found most East Coast theaters closed to him right up to the time he went back to Europe, even though he paid five long visits to New York trying to forge contacts. Only a handful of refugee actors, including Elisabeth Bergner and Oskar Homolka, were accepted on Broadway, while the press mercilessly criticized Fritz Kortner for his old-fashioned European acting style: "He is strictly of the old scenery-chewing Continental school, flailing his arms, twitching his fingers, bobbling his head around and frequently speaking in a throaty whisper that can't be heard beyond the first few rows. His acting is so furiously out of key . . . that it becomes ludicrous."[4]

Few plays by Germans ran for more than a couple of weeks in the alien, fast-moving, and highly commercialized world of American theater, and some, like Austrian dramatist Ferdinand Bruckner's adaptation of Lessing's *Nathan the Wise,* were only indirectly the work of emigré writers. There were productions of Friedrich Wolf's *The Sailors of Cattaro* and *Professor Mamlock,* and of Franz Werfel's *Jacobowsky and the Colonel,* adapted by American screenwriter Sam Behrman. American critics accused German and Austrian playwrights of producing complicated and static texts without drama. Language barriers, a growing aversion to German themes, the need of the public in the forties to escape the gray reality of war, and an increasingly overt antipathy to the left-wing or liberal thought of the political refugees from Hitler's Germany all contributed to the unpopularity of German plays.

The publishing situation was also a negative factor for exile literature, even though New York at the time was the undisputed center of publishing in the United States. Aurora, the only new publishing house founded by and for the exiled writers, did not actually begin production until nearly the end of the war, when it printed works like Brecht's *The Private Life of the Master Race* (1944), F. C. Weiskopf's *Die Unbesiegbaren* (1945), Anna Seghers' 1946 story *The Excursion of the Dead Girls,* and the anthology *Morgenröte* (1947) with an introduction by Heinrich Mann. Aurora went out of business after only three years, when publishing head Wieland

Herzfelde returned to East Berlin. West Germany's L. B. Fischer wanted from the beginning to establish itself as an American house, and attempts by G. B. Fischer and Fritz Landshoff to market German books in the New World from their subsidiary in Stockholm produced no more than an occasional succès d'estime despite active support from the daughter of house author Thomas Mann who contacted Archibald MacLeish and various U.S. government agencies on Fischer's behalf.[5] Established American houses like Viking, Knopf, and Doubleday had successfully published translations of Feuchtwanger, Thomas Mann, Stefan Zweig, Werfel, and Vicki Baum even before the authors fled Europe, and book clubs, which guaranteed large editions and fat royalties, accepted only titles that promised success, like Anna Seghers' *The Seventh Cross* and Werfel's *The Song of Bernadette*. Less popular writers often were unable to get publishers to look at their work even with the help of literary agents like longtime New Yorker Maxim Lieber[6] or recently transplanted Europeans Weiskopf and Herzfelde.

Despite these negative factors for exile writers in New York, the city and its near surroundings were key to exile history in America. Nowhere else were the intelligence agencies so active in investigating the emigrés' plans for a new Germany after Hitler. Nowhere else were exiled authors so close to the centers of power in politics and publishing, so able to influence U.S. policy on Germany through government agencies and American patrons. In no other city was there a comparable number of exile organizations and English-language magazines where writers could express their views about a new, liberated Germany, even if their literary works were not printed. New York-based authors like Graf, famed for his lederhosen and vast beer consumption, stayed in touch with German-Americans in Yorkville and the Middle West: a public for the most part less hostile to National Socialism than the refugees, but at least German-speaking and from a similar cultural tradition. Conferences arranged by the PEN Club or the League of American Writers were

held in New York in 1939 and addressed by exiles including Bruck-
ner, Döblin, Graf, members of the Mann family, Remarque, Renn,
Werfel, Weiskopf, and Zuckmayer, some of whom traveled from
Europe for the occasion. Boisterous celebrations took place in New
York, like one for Thomas Mann's seventieth birthday that was at-
tended by the U.S. secretary of the interior, Supreme Court justice
Felix Frankfurter, press correspondent William L. Shirer, and Freda
Kirchwey, editor of *The Nation,* while the OSS sat "in the gallery."[7]
New York was the site of major and sometimes controversial speeches
by emigrés on current issues; the city where the FBI watched suspi-
ciously as Thomas Mann attended an international peace conference in the Waldorf Astoria Hotel in 1949.

The foremost concern of the FBI, OSS, and State Department
studying the German exile scene in New York was the effort of
refugee writers, politicians, professors, and journalists to form an
organization that would be listened to in Washington: if not as the
voice of an exile government, at least as the voice of the majority of
exiles. This effort culminated in the Council for a Democratic Germany. But U.S. government agencies were also suspicious of the
refugee aid organizations, which although they were of varying political stamps had generally a liberal orientation. They included the
Emergency Rescue Committee, whose work was supported by Hermann Kesten and Thomas and Erika Mann; the Exiled Writers Committee, a branch of the League of American Writers backed by
Ernest Hemingway, Vincent Sheean, Donald Ogden Stewart (who
fell victim to Joseph McCarthy), and John Steinbeck, then drifting
toward the right; and the Joint Anti-Fascist Refugee Committee, on
which the FBI compiled more than nine thousand documents. Members of the Institute for Social Research served as a "think tank" for
the OSS, producing expert analyses of individual exiles, the National Free Germany Committee founded in Moscow, and the future
of Germany. Another organization in the FBI files was the Ameri-

can Guild for German Cultural Freedom (Amguild), founded by the Tyrolean nobleman and later member of the German parliament Hubertus Friedrich Prince of Löwenstein-Wertheim-Freudenberg, and supported by Thomas Mann, Feuchtwanger, Neumann, von Unruh, Werfel, and other refugees.

The FBI and OSS read the publications of exile organizations: the *German-American*, published by the German-American Emergency Conference and considered left-wing; the *Neue Volks-Zeitung*, printed by the German Labor Delegation, a Social Democrat group; and *Aufbau*, from the German-Jewish Club/New World Club. Ruth Fischer's mimeographed anti-Communist newssheet *The Network* was consulted especially by the OSS; and agents in the larger FBI field offices studied *Freies Deutschland*, which was printed in Mexico. Hoover's and Donovan's professional intelligence gatherers tracked who wrote or was written about in left-wing American magazines and newspapers like *New Masses*, the *Daily Worker*, and *Anti-Nazi News*, or in politically less controversial publications like *Direction*, the *Nation*, the *New Republic*, and *Saturday Review of Literature*.

Finally, the FBI investigated ties between exiles and well-known figures in American cultural and university life and government. The names Agnes Meyer and Dorothy Thompson appear often in the files. Meyer, wife of *Washington Post* publisher Eugene Meyer, attracted FBI notice when Thomas Mann appealed for her support. The G-men scrutinized Dorothy Thompson because she gave employment to Hermann Budzislawski, former publisher of the liberal emigré magazine *Neue Weltbühne*, because she was active in exile organizations and committees, and because she phoned the INS to tell them that refugee Otto Katz was a "member of the OGPU" and "very closely associated with the Communist cause."[8] Alvin Johnson, director of the New School, founder of the University in Exile, and sponsor of many exile committees; the presidents of the University of Newark and of Smith College, Frank Kingdon and William Allen Neilson; George Schuster of Hunter College, and other prominent Americans drew the attention of the FBI because of their contacts with exiles and exile groups. And agents were especially eager to investigate when whole groups of American sponsors got together to support an exile organization, the way the American Association for a Democratic Germany supported the Council for a Democratic Germany.

The FBI's New York Field Office and the Foreign Nationalities Branch of the OSS held a virtual monopoly on surveillance of the exiles and their American friends. The New York City police had their own political division, the "Red Squad" or "Alien Squad," but although they competed briefly with Hoover when the local police commissioner tried to expand his squad to one hundred officers after war began, they played no major role. A committee of New York state assemblymen led by Senator John McNaboe set out to investigate un-American activities in the state, but their methods were too chaotic to leave records. The OSS and FBI were alike in that they took no interest in literary issues but focused on the internal quarrels of exile groups and the different drafts for a postwar Germany. But the two agencies differed in their mission: while Hoover was expected to confine himself to fact gathering, Donovan's agency was mandated to prepare analyses and background material and, in rare cases, to intervene in emigré activities.

Of numerous OSS analyses of New York–based exile groups, we will look at five examples, all cultural or political societies that aimed to represent an alternative Germany. They are the Council for a Democratic Germany, founded by the liberal Protestant theologian Paul Tillich and regarded by the FBI, OSS, and State Department as a mouthpiece for the refugees' Germany policy; the Exiled Writers Committee and the Emergency Rescue Committee, to which many exiled writers owed their rescue from occupied France; and the American Guild for German Cultural Freedom. Finally we

will look at the small FBI file on the refugees' joint publishing firm,
Aurora Verlag.

COUNCIL FOR A DEMOCRATIC GERMANY

The files make clear how concerned the FBI and OSS were about
the Council, regarding it as the American branch of Moscow's National Free Germany Committee [28]. More than fifty OSS documents were devoted exclusively or primarily to the Council. The
FBI has 735 pages, of which 224 were released to me. One agent appears to have had some psychological empathy with his target:
"Most members of the committee have never lost their fear of the
police. They feel that their activities are continually observed and
under surveillance, which especially hampers the activities of those
members who are not American citizens."[9]

U.S. intelligence was preoccupied with the Council, the most
important exile organization in North America, because although
not an exile government it was representative enough to act as a
"committee of national intercession"[10] able to influence American
policy on Germany. Hoover, Donovan, and their State Department
counterparts Adolf Berle, Frederick Lyon of Foreign Activity Correlation, and Secretary of State Stettinius thought of the Council as
the successor to groups like the Thomas Mann Committee of 1943,
and as a branch of the Free Germany Movement, which had spread
from Moscow to Britain, Sweden, Switzerland, and Mexico. E. E.
Conroy and R. B. Hood, the Special Agents in Charge in New York
and Los Angeles, thus would alternately describe the Council as the
"Comintern Apparatus"[11] or the "Free German Movement New
York City."[12] In December 1944, nine months after the FBI opened
a file on the Council, Hoover sent a long memo to his SAC in
Philadelphia telling him how to classify Free Germany: "Free German Activities in the Area," "Free Germany" "when the data to be
submitted are concerned with the Free Germany Movement in

Moscow, Stockholm, London and Mexico City,"[13] or "Council for a Democratic Germany, also known as The Tillich Committee, Internal Security - C."[14]

Government interest in the refugees' image of Germany and in the formation of exile organizations in the United States was for a long period linked to the figure of Thomas Mann. "Thomas Mann," states an early document dated September 1941 that General Sherman Miles, acting assistant chief of staff, G-2, passed to William Donovan while Donovan was still coordinator of information, "as the most distinguished German writer of this generation, . . . must be enlisted in the propaganda service." An OSS roster of "circles where the German Problem is discussed"[15] mentions that Heinrich Mann, Brecht, and Feuchtwanger have written an "'Open Letter to the German People'" and that Thomas Mann views himself as "superior above party politics."[16] Hoover's Bureau was informed when Thomas and Heinrich Mann, Feuchtwanger, Brecht, and others hailed the founding of the National Free Germany Committee in Moscow: "It is known that in August of 1943 the group of individuals met for the purpose of sending a telegram to Moscow in support of the Free German movement. The meeting of this group was held at the house of Berthold Viertel."[17] Agencies continued to track Thomas Mann even after December 1943, when the OSS buried the Thomas Mann Committee with the joke slogan "Mann overboard."[18]

Although Mann played no role in the Council following the events of 1943, that did not mean that Hoover and the OSS thought it posed no threat. On the contrary, Washington felt that under the leadership of Paul Tillich, "the Council . . . is functioning with the approval of its counterpart in Mexico City and may be endeavoring to become, like that organization, the counterpart of the Free Germany Committee in Moscow."[19] The Los Angeles Field Office report opening the investigation of the Council gives an unusually politicized analysis of an Alfred Kantorowicz essay, "Free Germany in Moscow," published in *Free World*. This analysis (which was grossly mutilated by FBI censors before its release to me) comments on international links among the Free Germans: "It is suggested that in the above paragraph, Kantorowicz has stated what may be the Soviet policy. . . . This policy may be to have a 'gap' in Germany, Italy, Poland, etc., after the war by agreement between Soviet Russia, Great Britain and the United States, in which there will be ostensibly democratic governments cooperating with allied representatives in such countries. This will, however, only preface a later communist government."[20] And the mysterious Source D, whom Special Agent Sidney Thwing asked to find out Brecht's views, reported in September 1944 "that as far as he could learn from Brecht only the following persons residing in this area are interested in the Free German movement: Lion Feuchtwanger, Fritz Kortner, and Heinrich Mann."[21]

The OSS was as concerned about the Council as the FBI ("exit Thomas Mann, enter Paul Tillich").[22] Three factors stood in the way of a "politically viable German committee," said a fifteen-page appraisal of social democratic attitudes toward the Council (like other OSS documents, it is now preserved in the files of the CIA): "The first obstacle is the fact that such a committee cannot in the nature of things become a 'committee of national liberation.' . . . Second . . . is the difficulty of programmatic planning by such a committee within the framework set by the United States and Great Britain in the demand for 'unconditional surrender.' Third obstacle is the traditional hostility between the German Social Democrats and Communists."[23] From Hans Sahl, "author of bad poetry and formerly a Communist, but now an admirer of Ruth Fischer," the OSS received a list of people who might form an "Anti-Tillich Group": "Hermann Broch . . . Alfred Doeblin (?) . . . Bruno Frank . . . Hermann Kesten . . . Erich Kahler . . . *Thomas Mann* . . . Gustav Regler . . . K. A. Wittfogel . . . Fritz v. Unruh (?)."[24] Robert Kempner, who in 1944 worked on a "secret"[25] mission for the Justice Department (probably meaning the FBI)[26] and was later a prosecutor at the Nuremberg War

Crimes Trials, informed the OSS "entirely off the record"[27] that the FBI and U.S. army and naval intelligence had detailed information on German exile organizations including the Council.

The Council for a Democratic Germany, which began with such fanfare and was monitored so closely by the secret services, collapsed at more or less the same moment as the Allies' anti-Hitler coalition. "After the Potsdam Conference," Philadelphia's SAC wrote in February 1946, quoting the German-Jewish publication *Aufbau,* "the Council split inasmuch as the right wing socialists and the conservative groups took issue with the policies set down by the Big Three."[28] Ten months later, an FBI special agent approached the Council's American support group, the American Association for a Democratic Germany, and found a pretext to ask them about the Tillich Committee. A young woman in the outer office told him that the Council had closed down its work some time ago, and as far as she knew had no plans for the future.

EXILED WRITERS COMMITTEE

Members of the Council for a Democratic Germany did not consider it formally representative of exiled Germans but as a platform for policy and for involvement in the political reconstruction of their homeland after the destruction of the Third Reich. The FBI in turn was concerned not only by political groups but also by refugee aid organizations like the Exiled Writers Committee and the Emergency Rescue Committee.

The EWC brought into the United States people whom Hoover and his colleagues regarded as having politically dubious histories and opinions ("is playing a part in the international movement of Communists from Germany to Mexico via the United States, possibly on orders from Moscow").[29] It also was a branch of the League of American Writers, which the FBI had kept under watch as "Communist influenced"[30] since its founding in 1935 and classified under "Internal Security - C." The EWC arranged fifty visas for Mexico, the United States, and Cuba, purchased forty ship's passages from Europe to America, and sent food packages to sixty impoverished writers in Europe. The "Hollywood Chapter" of the EWC was slow to begin operations, as the SAC in Los Angeles noted in his reports; but a supper held in the Beverly Wilshire Hotel with Heinrich Mann and Emil Ludwig as speakers raised a respectable $6,000 for the cause. The EWC and the League of American Writers repeatedly attracted the notice of special agents when league secretary Franklin Folsom and his colleagues tried to assist refugees on Ellis Island, including Anna Seghers, Egon Erwin Kisch, Bruno Frei, and Otto Katz. Folsom gave this description of what happened to Frei: "Bruno hoped that the children could get into the United States, where he thought they would have a better education than in Mexico. That would be possible if a U.S. citizen legally adopted them. Bruno himself could not enter the United States because of his Communist politics. Before long, a Mrs. Miller, a schoolteacher in Evanston, Illinois, volunteered. . . . The children came from Ellis Island, and in the League office I introduced the tense, bright-eyed boy and the timid girl to their new parent."[31]

The FBI sought information on the EWC by all the usual means. An informant supplied somewhat inaccurate lists of writers rescued by the Exiled Writers Committee ("Hans Marchwitza . . . Anna Seghers, her husband and 2 children . . . Franz Pfempffert . . . Alfred Kantorowicz and wife . . . Lion Feuchtwanger, Henirichh Mann . . . Bertold Brecht . . . Alfred Neumann . . . Weiskopf")[32] and records of financial donations made to writers ("Kantoorowitz $30 . . . Kisch $45").[33] The Office of Censorship gave the FBI a copy of a telegram in which the league congratulated Seghers on the success of her novel *The Seventh Cross*. Public sources like news articles and advertising leaflets mention that New York governor Herbert Lehman had withdrawn his support from the EWC when it was accused of Communist links.

FBI interest in the EWC waned in early 1942, when the stream of refugees from Europe dried up. By the time the Bureau reviewed old reports from informants two years later, the League of American Writers had dissolved and the Exiled Writers Committee had merged with the Joint Anti-Fascist Refugee Committee.

EMERGENCY RESCUE COMMITTEE

Surveillance of the Emergency Rescue Committee went on longer than for the EWC. The ERC achieved a certain fame through the personality and publications of Varian Fry, who organized its operations in wartime France [61]. Informants sent ERC advertising material to the FBI, including a brochure with pictures of Heinrich Mann, Franz Werfel, Hans Habe, André Breton, and others among the more than five hundred "distinguished Europeans"[34] whom the Committee claimed to have saved from the Gestapo in its first year. The G-men learned from newspapers that Secretary of the Interior Ickes had attended an ERC fund-raising rally in Washington where he accused the United States of being "'fat, soft and rich'"—"'a perfect prize for Hitler to kill, pluck and roast on a slow fire.'"[35] And in summer 1943, the State and Justice departments replied defensively when the Dies Committee demanded that they supply documents "about the former practice of admitting certain 'intellectual' refugees . . . without investigation . . . of their political affiliation." "Mistakes were made. There is no doubt that certain persons should not have been admitted," answered the State Department, "but . . . we were all interested in the humanitarian phases."[36]

The FBI's 255-page dossier on the ERC, only 98 pages of which were released, includes information on Fry, ERC advisers like Thomas Mann, and the operation to rescue "anti-Nazi writers,"[37] many of whom the FBI considered "extremely questionable applicants."[38] The ERC file becomes especially interesting at the point where the anti-Fascist rescue committee evolves into an anti-Communist organization, once again arousing Hoover's displeasure.

The first signs of a change in political orientation came at the end of the war, when a study by the New York–based National Information Bureau claimed that the former ERC, which had by now merged with the International Relief Association to become the International Rescue and Relief Committee (IRRC), was, "in short," "an anti-fascist-anti-totalitarian-pro-democracy-fight-for-freedom-relief-committee."[39] Then in April 1948, the Committee publicly sponsored a lecture by Arthur Koestler: "Hated and feared by Communists, . . . he knows what makes the madmen in the Kremlin tick" was how the event was advertised in *Alert: The Confidential Weekly Report on Un-American Activities in California*.[40] Among the members of the Southern California Committee of the IRRC that sponsored Koestler were Mrs. Bruno Frank, the composer Ernst Toch, Alma Mahler-Werfel, and film actors Gary Cooper and Ronald Reagan.

Hoover might have been happy that the ERC had evolved from an anti-Nazi organization to one that busied itself with Sudeten German evacuees, refugees from Communist Hungary, and victims of the Berlin Wall—if the new organization, its name now shortened to the International Rescue Committee (IRC), had not been dominated in the fifties by his long-standing rival, former OSS director General William Donovan. When Hoover received IRC invitations to a dinner honoring Berlin mayor Ernst Reuter or a ceremony to confer the Freedom Award on future German chancellor Willy Brandt—an event attended by Hans Sahl, former exile and Fry's colleague at the Centre Américain de Secours in Marseilles—the FBI director turned them down.

Hoover's attitude did not change until after Donovan's death, when his name began to appear on IRC sponsor lists with the names of prominent Americans and former exiles including Martin Luther King, Reinhold Niebuhr (once chairman of the American Friends of German Freedom), detective-story writer and political hardliner

Rex Stout, and Paul Tillich. But we do not know if he attended the Freedom Award dinner in August 1965, which was under observation by his own G-men and where the IRC chairman reviewed the history of the organization, emphasizing the achievements of Varian Fry and praising the group for the rescue of refugees like Lion Feuchtwanger, Hannah Arendt, and Franz Werfel, whom Hoover had treated with deep suspicion.

AMGUILD AND AURORA VERLAG

Two exile groups in which the FBI took little interest judging by the size of their files were the American Guild for German Cultural Freedom and the publishing house Aurora Verlag. The Bureau released twenty-three of its twenty-six pages on Amguild, while the State Department and army intelligence gave me two pages each.

Amguild, created by Hubertus Prinz zu Löwenstein in 1936, was supported by prominent exiles and American sponsors. It only came to the FBI's attention twelve years after it had closed down, when the Bureau claimed to have been "reliably" informed that it was "communistic."[41] (The same happened to the American Committee for Anti-Nazi Literature.) Since further investigation would only bring to light more facts about an already extinct organization, the SAC in New York recommended on 9 December 1952 that the case should be closed, and repeated the suggestion on 30 January 1953.

Equally uneventful was the 1945–46 investigation of Aurora Verlag, classified under "Internal Security - C" and also under "G" for "German." Founded by prestigious writers including Ernst Bloch, Brecht, Ferdinand Bruckner, Döblin, Feuchtwanger, Graf, and Heinrich Mann, the firm was described by the New York Field Office and the OSS as the creation of "leftist emigre Germans, many of whom have reliably reported to be members of the KPD [German Communist Party]."[42] A number of Aurora authors were suspected of being "active in Soviet intelligence work."[43] But the SAC did not want to launch a broad investigation, the firm's activities being too insignificant and the business premises and equipment too shabby to bother with: "From personal observation of the writer, it was determined that it is in a very small booth occupying a floor space of approximately fifteen feet by fifteen feet with a sign on the outside advertising the establishment as the Seven Seas Stamp and Book Shop . . . located in the back part is a fairly large desk where apparently [blacked out] carried on a business of a publishing house."[44] The "subject's" products were "about a dozen German language books, . . . a majority of which were found to contain fiction, . . . by German refugee writers presently residing in this country."[45] Despite their clearly evident criticism of capitalist society, these were found to present no particular threat to the United States.

Dossiers

OSKAR MARIA GRAF

Like Klaus Mann and others, Oskar Maria Graf, author of *Prisoners All,* entered the files of the FBI because of a denunciation. Uncharacteristically not anonymous, it left a clear trail and can be traced back to its source: Leopold Schwarzschild, publisher of the exile magazine *Das Neue Tage-Buch,* printed in Paris.

"Files in the New York Field Division . . . indicate that subject was a member of the German-American Writers' Association, which organization is alleged to have Communistic tendencies,"[1] reads the first sentence of the oldest extant FBI document on Graf, a report by New York SAC E. E. Conroy on 5 May 1943. Membership in the German-American Writers Association may appear a minor offense, as the organization, founded in 1938 as an American offshoot of the German Writers League (Schutzverband deutscher Schriftsteller), never had more than 180 members and disbanded two years later without anyone having noticed its existence. Conroy nevertheless trotted out the big guns for his investigation. Agents of the New York Field Office and the NYPD's notorious Alien Squad, armed with an "Executive Search Warrant," scoured Graf's home on Manhattan's Hillside Avenue on 16 February 1943. When this operation produced no results ("no contraband was found"),[2] agents tried a lengthy interrogation focusing on "Background and Personal History" and "Sympathies and Tendencies."[3] Finally, the recent escapee from Nazi terrorism began to have all his mail examined, although nothing remains to mark this activity but the summary of one letter.

A second report of the SAC in New York gives clues, in the introductory "Synopsis of Facts," to the identity of the informant who denounced Graf, "an individualist, though with strong Communist leanings":[4] "[Blacked out] advised that in a pamphlet entitled 'That Good Old Fool Uncle Sam—A Refugee Sounds a Warning' by Rudolf Brandl, subject, President of German-American Writers Association was labelled as an individual of Bavarian peasant stock who has been built by the Communist propaganda as a high ranking figure in the literary sphere."[5] Dr. Rudolf Brandl, whom the FBI later identified as the former editor of the *Frankfurter Zeitung* (Graf himself referred to Brandl as a "well-paid archivist"),[6] was indeed informed about Graf. In Germany he had worked with Ullstein publishers in the same firm as Graf's brother-in-law, Manfred George, and in the United States he was chief editor of *Aufbau* from 1937 to 1939, until Manfred George took his place. Brandl had access to intimate details about his fellow exile, and he claimed that since Graf had emigrated from Germany, "where Dr. Groebbls found no fault with his printed outpourings," he had several times been "lavishly wined and dined in Stalinland."[7] Graf wrote for Communist publications in Moscow, for example a piece in *Internationale Literatur* for the twentieth anniversary of the October Revolution. Supported by "George and a bunch of other masked Communists of European repute," Graf "is keeping his herd on the proper pasture,"[8] said

Brandl, who in 1943 distinguished himself by producing a "conversation and phrase book" called *Blitz German: A Language Guide for Invasion and Occupation.*[9]

Lies and half-truths of this kind may well have sprung from the pen of Brandl. But the simultaneous attack on Manfred George and the simplistic equation of Nazis with Communists pointed to a different source, as the FBI well knew: Leopold Schwarzschild. Commenting on Brandl's pamphlet *That Good Old Fool, Uncle Sam,* the SAC in New York exclaimed, "How right we have been in exposing the camouflaged gang of red penman was evidenced when the 'Neue Tage-Buch' (the new diary) issue of October 28, 1939 arrived from Paris." Because there, in "Schwarzschild's intrepid paper"[10]— so Conroy proclaimed—the veil had been lifted at last from organizations like the German American Writers Association, which had tried to hide their Soviet features.

Schwarzschild's article in *Das Neue Tage-Buch* in 1939 has been analyzed repeatedly by exile historians. Its hysterical and denunciatory tone, and its consequences for refugees like Graf and Klaus Mann, cannot be dismissed by claiming that Schwarzschild, a former sympathizer with the Soviet Union, was suffering a profound disappointment [230, vol. 4, p. 203], or did not fully realize the effects his article might have. A journalist who would call fellow exiles "hired Soviet agents,"[11] denounce their anti-Fascism as pro-Stalinism, describe the German American Writers Association as a "Russian-pro-Bolshevist . . . deception firm" for "clueless, gullible, bleary-eyed pseudo-intellectuals,"[12] welcome the internment in France of exiles with political views different from his own, and praise the witch-hunters of the Dies Committee in his publication[13] must have been conscious that his opinions might destroy careers and endanger lives.

Graf and George survived the attacks of Schwarzschild and Brandl, although in Graf's case the wounds he received may well have contributed to his increasing withdrawal from public life in the early forties. In July 1943 he wrote to a fellow exile that he wanted nothing more to do with the "eternal" debates in "emigré circles"[14] and their "characterless ambition." "Envy and unhelpfulness" marked many fugitives from Hitler. He could not help "actually hating" their "dirty intrigues."[15]

The success of Schwarzschild and Brandl in inciting the FBI to actions like house searches, interrogations, mail interception, and "background checks" suggests that Graf was not wrong in seeing a potent venom in exile society. In 1943, the FBI—evidently following up Schwarzschild's hint that "'Red = Brown'" (Communist = Nazi) [ibid., vol. 4, p. 104]—observed that Graf spent time with German-Americans who were often conservative if not actually pro-Nazi. An exile who had just had a book accepted by the Book of the Month Club told the FBI that Graf was "a rather stupid writer of popular fiction of no literary merit,"[16] who persistently followed the Communist party line. Others described him as "one of the most cunning Moscow agents under his mask of a harmless, jovial, beer-guzzling Bavarian peasant writer."[17] In September 1948, the INS asked the FBI director for official help in preparing deportation proceedings against Graf. At that time, deportation would no longer have threatened his life, although it would have uprooted him and the existence that he had struggled for a decade to carve out for himself in the alien world of New York. Six years later, just as the era of the infamous Senator Joseph McCarthy was drawing to a close, Hoover instructed his New York office to add the labels "Detcom" and "Comsab" to Graf's Security Index Card. "Detcom" stood for "Detention of Communists," an FBI program that provided for the internment of Communists and so-called subversive elements in an emergency, while "Comsab," or "Communist Sabotage," identified persons considered to have training or a position fitting them to carry out acts of sabotage.

Graf's files with other agencies took a similar line. When the OSS and the British Political Warfare Mission met in New York in autumn 1942 to discuss how to improve Allied propaganda work in Germany, they considered employing the down-to-earth Bavarian: "Dorothy Thompson talks with an American accent and is pretty highbrow. What we need is a man who can appeal to peasants and workers,"[18] and "Graf is a splendid orator, and he knows how to talk to Germans of the lower classes. . . . he would . . . have far more influence on the masses of German people than a man like Thomas Mann whose primary appeal is only to intellectuals";[19] but they did not trust Graf enough to make any concrete proposal. An OSS agent who attended a private fund-raiser of the German-American Emergency Conference in Philadelphia reported that Graf in a speech had said that Thomas Mann was leaning toward the anti-Germany views of Britain's Lord Vansittart ("Mann's broadcast over the BBC . . . did not make it clear whether he still considered himself a German").[20] In the fifties and sixties—the last document on Graf is dated 1 June 1964—Hoover had sources in Germany report to him about Graf's activities whenever the writer revisited his former homeland, even though he only made four trips back to Europe after he was belatedly granted U.S. citizenship. Hoover thus learned of reparation payments to Graf ("DM 5,000 per year for five years and, in addition, a lump sum of DM 20,000"). The 66th Counter Intelligence Corps in Stuttgart and the U.S. embassy in Bonn reported remarks from a former Bavarian Communist Party official ("[Blacked out] stated that during his activity in the KPD LL Bavaria he saw no indication . . . that Subject had . . . maintained connections with that organization or any of its members");[21] and a German Trade Union pamphlet said of Graf that "he is a convinced Socialist."[22]

Oskar Maria Graf ("Height: 6′, Weight: 215 lbs . . . Characteristics: Subject speaks with a decided German accent, has little knowledge of the English language")[23] died on 28 June 1967 in New York as an American citizen. The fact that he had to wait twenty years for his citizenship was partly the result of Hoover's politically motivated pursuit, and the denunciations of Schwarzschild and Brandl: "Because of some extremely ridiculous denunciations . . . I am still a 'stateless person' under suspicion here and everywhere people take me for a rabid Communist."[24] But unlike his friend Lion Feuchtwanger, his long wait for citizenship also stemmed from his own views. As a pacifist, Graf could not swear the oath of loyalty to the United States until the line about defending his new homeland by force of arms if called upon was struck out of the text. Eventually this clause was deleted from the oath he had to swear.

To the end of his life Graf remained grateful to American democracy for this special service. "I must say," he told Lion Feuchtwanger in 1958 when Feuchtwanger, already terminally ill, was still waiting in vain to become a citizen, "that I feel some respect for American democracy, because of *my* naturalization."[25]

BERTHOLD VIERTEL

Berthold Viertel, poet, storyteller, essayist, and stage and film director, was among those refugees who had old ties with America before his experience of exile. A native Viennese, Viertel had worked for Fox and Paramount in Hollywood since 1928, and in 1932 he was issued a quota-based immigration visa in the Mexican border town of Ensenada. His numerous applications for reentry permits prove how often his film and drama work took him to Britain ("Reasons for going abroad to fulfill contract . . . with Gaumont-British").[1] Viertel's wife, the successful screenwriter Salomea Sara Viertel, known as Salka, became an American citizen in 1939. Berthold was granted U.S. citizenship on 10 March 1944 after a prominent sponsor, Hans Kindler, conductor of the National Symphony Orchestra in Washington, wrote several times on his behalf to "My dear Francis,"[2] Attorney General Francis Biddle.

Whether J. Edgar Hoover knew that his boss had intervened in the pending naturalization case is not clear from the 140 pages of

Viertel's plump 214-page FBI file that were released to me. But he cannot have been happy about Biddle's unilateral action, because his agents in New York, L.A., Boston, and Washington had been on the Viertels' trail since January 1942, classifying the case as "Internal Security - R."[3]

The inquiry began with an "employee investigation"[4] when Viertel applied for a job at the Office of the Coordinator of Information, forerunner to the OSS and CIA.[5] Nothing much was learned but a few background facts, not always accurately written ("At the New York Public Library it was ascertained that Berthold Viertel was the author of the following publications: *Gedichte* 'Die Spur' . . . , 'Die Bahn' . . . , *Drama:* 'Die Bacchantinnen Des Suripides'"[6] [Euripides' play *The Bacchae*]). Despite the paucity of information, a large-scale surveillance operation including mail interception and phone-tapping was set in motion that was scarcely smaller than Brecht's. Indeed, the Viertels' relationship with Brecht and Ruth Berlau was the FBI's main concern in years of investigation ranging from Los Angeles to New York.

The scope of the surveillance is evident from the first mention of mail censorship: "On August 1942 [blacked out] Santa Monica Branch Post-Office . . . said that for many years the motion picture actress Greta Garbo received a great deal of mail at . . . 165 Mabery Road, Santa Monica, California."[7] The documents show that a "30 day mail cover" mentioned under "Undeveloped leads" turned into four years of censorship. Copies and summaries of the opened correspondence were kept only rarely, for example when Anna Seghers wrote a year after arriving in Mexico: "I don't miss the United States, not for one moment."[8] Lists of intercepted letters to or from Zuckmayer, Isherwood, Brecht, the Joint Anti-Fascist Refugee Committee, and others, although sometimes several pages long, are mostly illegible because so many names are blacked out.

More interesting is the tapping of Viertel's telephone conversations in Santa Monica and, following his move to the East Coast, in New York. Although copies of the Bureau's notes were not kept, or not released to me, the cross-references and quotations in field-office reports and memoranda give a vivid picture of the methods and aims of the eavesdroppers.

Hoover first obtained permission from the attorney general for a "technical surveillance on the residence of Berthold Viertel" (a formality that was necessary because, for one thing, both the Viertels were already American citizens) on 26 January 1945, listing two grounds. First, Viertel was "a known contact of agents of the Soviet Secret Intelligence (NKVD)." Second, Brecht's mistress Ruth Berlau had "access to the telephone located at 165 Mayberry Street."[9] Brecht and Berlau were central to the surveillance on Viertel's telephone. "It was made known by this informant," Hood reported to his superior when applying for one of several extensions of the wire-tap, "that the subject has had repeated contacts with Berthold Brecht [blacked out] during this period."[10] Relations between Thomas Mann, Feuchtwanger, and Brecht, "all of whom are principals in the Free German group in Los Angeles area,"[11] had been discovered through the wiretap, Hood said, as had the Viertels' dinner dates with Charlie Chaplin and Hanns Eisler, and a party that included Thomas and Heinrich Mann. On another occasion, 25 May 1945, the FBI overheard someone in the Viertels' home talking on the phone about essays by Emil Ludwig in the *Los Angeles Times:* "[Blacked out] stated 'That every one of these articles should be saved and when Ludwig comes back they should be spit into his face. That fellow Ludwig is a regular swine, a stupid pig.' . . . She added that Thomas Mann, or somebody, should answer Ludwig."[12]

Hoover also used "physical surveillance" and informers to monitor the Viertels. Residents of their short, exposed street in northwest Santa Monica told the G-men in 1945 that a 1935 Plymouth and a 1937 Cadillac parked outside the Viertels' house almost daily. The Plymouth's owner was identified (probably wrongly) as Brecht.[13] Marion Bach, Salka Viertel's secretary for many years—

"she does not wish her identity disclosed"—interested the FBI because she stayed in contact with the Viertels and thus was in a position "to know Salka's friends, many of whom are Communists, one of whom is Brecht."[14] The House Committee on Un-American Activities also took a dim view of Viertel's associates in 1947, and of meetings in his home between "German Communist refugees among the movie people in Hollywood" and "known American Communist Party line followers as [blacked out]."[15] At 6:15 P.M. on May 13, R. B. Hood in Los Angeles reported to Washington that following a conversation with Representative Thomas of HUAC, and knowing HUAC's interest, he had sent to Robert Stripling, the Committee's chief investigator (the same whom Brecht encountered at his HUAC hearing later that year), a series of memoranda about Viertel, Brecht, Hanns Eisler, Peter Lorre, and "Communist Activities in Hollywood." "Chairman J. Parnell Thomas" and Stripling "appeared to be very friendly and appreciative of this cooperation afforded them."[16]

The Viertel file ends with two documents relating to the American citizenship of the exile ("height 5 feet 4 inches . . . mole on each cheek")[17] born in Vienna in 1885. The first, dated 1949, states that despite the political indiscretions discovered by the FBI, there were no grounds to institute "revocation proceedings,"[18] that is, to revoke Viertel's citizenship. The second, dated four years later, reported to the State Department that the former exile had regained his Austrian citizenship "prior to his death at Vienna, Austria on September 24, 1953,"[19] and consequently was no longer a U.S. citizen.

"Reds": Weiskopf, Marchwitza, Kantorowicz, Bloch

The FBI had good cause to classify F. C. Weiskopf, Hans Marchwitza, Alfred Kantorowicz, and Ernst Bloch as Communists. Weiskopf, a Prague native who joined the Czech Communist Party in 1920, became a prominent journalist and reporter. Marchwitza from the Ruhr went from mining into the workers' movement, was active against the 1920 Kapp putsch that attempted to overthrow the Weimar Republic, and made a name for himself as a worker-newsman and novelist. In exile and after his return to Germany, Marchwitza, who several times won East Germany's National Prize for Literature, completed the *Kumiak* cycle, a classic of working-class literature. Kantorowicz studied law, met left-wing bourgeois writers like Brecht, joined the Communist Party in 1931 and the Volksfront or United Front coalition in exile in France, and fought for the Republicans in the Spanish Civil War. When he returned from U.S. exile to Germany after World War II, he held a chair at Humboldt University in East Berlin and devoted himself to publishing the work of Heinrich Mann. Disappointed by political developments in East Germany after 1956, he moved to West Germany, as did Bloch, the philosopher and theorist of revolution who, after returning home from U.S. exile, taught in Leipzig and became famous for his book *The Principle of Hope*.

F. C. WEISKOPF

"Frantisek Carl Weiskopf, with aliases, Dr. F. C. Weiskopf; Franz Carl Weisskopf; Franz Carl Weiskopf"[1] arrived in the United States for a short work visit on 1 June 1939, as a guest of the League of American Writers—and returned to Europe as a Czech diplomat under heavy FBI surveillance, ten years later almost to the day.

Weiskopf and his wife, Grete, a children's writer with the pen name Alex Wedding, were greeted in New York by a three-man Board of Special Inquiry ("delivered at Ellis Island, June 12, 1939, 10 A.M.") who asked the usual questions of the visitor and the League of American Writers representative who was also present. His race ("Hebrew"),[2] his reasons for leaving Czechoslovakia ("Did you go away because of the Munich agreement?"),[3] the past lives of the couple ("You don't seem to know very much about Mr. Weiskopf"),[4] and their planned length of stay ("I will guarantee that they will leave the United States at the end of six months").[5] The INS did not know that Weiskopf had been active on the Central Committee of the Czech Communist Party after 1920, belonged to the League of Proletarian-Revolutionary Writers, and had taken part in the great literature congresses held in the Soviet Union in the twenties and thirties.

Hoover's FBI was better informed than the INS. The Bureau's attention was first drawn to Weiskopf in July 1942 by a letter addressed to Egon Erwin Kisch that was intercepted and turned over by the Office of Censorship. By the time Weiskopf left the United States, his file held almost a thousand documents with every category of information. The FBI today is still withholding nearly eight hundred of them, which in all probability concern his activities in the Czech diplomatic service, as a cultural attaché in New York, and as embassy adviser in Washington from 1947 to 1949—"in the interest of national defense or foreign policy."[6] His unusually large FBI dossier is supplemented by eighty-eight pages of INS files and four brief but informative documents from the State Department and the 66th CIC Group of the U.S. Army in Europe from the years 1948 and 1955.

Weiskopf was put on the Confidential Security Index and the FBI's "key list"[7] in 1943–44. Apart from the usual suspicion of Communist activities, his file focuses on his connection to the anti-Nazi resistance group Rote Kapelle ("Red Chapel"), which was active in Germany—exactly what the connection was is not known—and his aforementioned diplomatic activity in New York and Washington. Documents describe him as a "literary GPU chief," "comintern dictator," and "commissar in the 'League of American Writers,'"[8] and accuse him of working as a Soviet agent for the Gestapo during the period of the Hitler-Stalin pact. Without giving reasons, the G-men took handwriting samples from "sub-

ject's Selective Service file"[9]—his U.S. Army registration file—
and the FBI learned that army intelligence was concerned about his
novel *Dawn Breaks* because they felt it placed too much hope in the
Red Army as the liberator of Czechoslovakia. Hoover was indignant
at the real or supposed dawdling of his staff when, in 1946,
Weiskopf's name was linked to the Communist Rote Kapelle, and
seemed indifferent to the fact that Rote Kapelle had been bitter opponents of the Nazis, working at the risk of their own lives to achieve
Allied objectives during the war: "In connection with the further investigation of Weiskopf your attention is specifically directed to my
letter to you dated May 28, 1946, . . . reflecting information received
in connection with the investigation of the Western European So-
viet-espionage networks known as Rote Kapelle."[10]

The FBI tracked Weiskopf's cooperation with Brecht, Bruckner,
Döblin, Feuchtwanger, Graf, and Heinrich Mann in founding Aurora
Verlag, "designed," as one FBI agent erroneously put it, "principally
for German Prisoners of War in the United States."[11] A lengthy catalog of Weiskopf's sins was sent to Hoover by the army's Counter
Intelligence Corps in Europe in April 1955, a few months before the
subject's premature death, and it tells us more about the thought pat-
terns of the U.S. intelligence services than it does about Weiskopf.
He "was listed by the RSHA [Reichssicherheitshauptamt, SS Office
of Internal Security] in 1939 as a communist who had fled from Germany," according to this report, "and . . . was arrested by the French
authorities along with a group of German . . . refugee communists
considered to be security threats to the French nation."[12]

The FBI may have been right in suspecting that Weiskopf,
whose novel *Dawn Breaks* (1942) had achieved some success in a
book club and as a gift volume for G.I.s, became a Czech diplomat
in 1947 because his friends wanted to protect him from "trouble with
the American authorities."[13] Or perhaps Prague wanted a man with
experience of America to serve in the Czech diplomatic corps. In
any case, the FBI, State Department, and U.S. embassy in Prague

avidly followed the progress of Weiskopf's career ("his rapid promotion since coup stressed").[14] The few pages that were released to me from the eight hundred relating to this period do not state exactly what concerned U.S. agencies. One document quotes the head of the Czech press office in New York, who "accidentally"[15] blabbed in the presence of an informant that the freshman diplomat could recite passages from Lenin and Stalin by heart. Shortly afterward, the State Department received "through Liaison Channels" a "Blind Cover memorandum" summarizing a "secret" report from "F. C. Weiskopf, Minister Plenipotentiary of the Czech Embassy, Washington, D.C.," to the Czech Foreign Ministry in Prague, in which Weiskopf quoted private statements by the American head of the Economic Cooperation Administration[16] criticizing the restrictive policy of the Marshall Plan in Central and Eastern Europe.[17] The memorandum did not say how this Czech document, which no doubt had been sent via diplomatic post, actually fell into the hands of U.S. intelligence. Years later, in 1955, the 66th CIC Group sent Hoover memoranda describing the activities of Weiskopf, "1.72 m[eters] tall, has a round face, and is considered handsome," on behalf of Czechoslovakia, and his work in East Germany: "Weiskopf . . . was a communist supervisor of the Czechoslovakian embassy in Washington. He was subsequently Ambassador to Sweden and China. Weiskopf was recalled to Prague in the winter of 1952, and shortly thereafter was arrested. . . . His name appeared on a list of East German authors and journalists who were to be utilized in the Land Hesse KPD election campaign in the fall of 1954."[18] "Subject resides in Berlin-Friedrichshain, Strausbergerplatz 19, in a building occupied by SED [East German Communist party] members."[19]

HANS MARCHWITZA

Like Weiskopf, left-wing worker-writer Hans Marchwitza, "born in Ober-Schlesien . . . a miner by trade, . . . openly a Communist and anti-Nazi . . . , claims that he fought in the Spanish war on the Republican side, but French officials suspect him of being morale commissar,"[20] was an unwelcome guest in the United States. Antagonism marked his first encounter with the U.S. authorities when a Board of Special Inquiry interrogated him on Ellis Island on 28 June 1941, the day after he had arrived on the SS *Acadia*. In a two-hour interview, INS officials cleverly concealed their pursuit of Communist connections amid questions on other topics, repeatedly querying the journalistic pursuits of the worker-reporter in the Weimar Republic: "Q. Did you ever work for a newspaper named Ruhr Echo? A. No . . . Q. Did you subscribe to it? A. No. Q. Did you ever read the newspaper? A. No."[21] Marks in the transcript show that the agents knew Marchwitza was lying. Classified as a case of "doubtful transit"[22] from the start, he was also questioned about his anti-Franco involvement in the Spanish Civil War: "What induced you to join the Loyalist forces in Spain? A. Because this way I had a chance to fight Hitler. Q. And incidentally to help Stalin and his principles of government? A. I had nothing to do with Stalin."[23] But above all the Board of Special Inquiry was worried by Marchwitza's membership in a group being helped by the Exiled Writers Committee of the League of American Writers. This group included disturbing presences Dragutin Fodor (alias Theodor Balk), Hans Benedict (probably a mistaken reference to Benedikt Freistadt, that is, Bruno Frei), Elisabeth Freistadt, Ruth Jerusalem, and Albert Norden.

In fact two days after Marchwitza's interrogation, Franklin Folsom came to Ellis Island representing the league, the same Folsom who sponsored Anna Seghers in her thwarted attempt to enter the United States.[24] But he appeared to know little about Marchwitza and was quickly put on the defensive. Why was his organization interested in these people anyway, the INS men asked Folsom, and how were the exiles selected in France? ("Our interest was humanitarian and literary. . . . We tried to determine first whether they were writers and second whether they were bona fide anti-Nazis.")[25] And would Folsom knowingly bring Communists into the United States? ("I am aware of the fact that there is a ruling in the immigration laws prohibiting those people who advocate the use of force or violence.") The Board made the unanimous and absurd decision to apply to Marchwitza a new regulation that had just come into force in June 1941, that "under no consideration"[26] were German citizens allowed to leave the country again once they entered. Marchwitza did not have the required transit papers to travel through the United States to Mexico, so he was refused entry to the United States. On the other hand, as a German he could not be allowed to leave and go to Mexico by a different route. On top of that he was notified in writing that in the event of deportation, he would be sent back to his country of origin, which was trying to kill him.

Five years after this decision on Ellis Island, in May 1946, Marchwitza applied for the sixth extension of his "temporary stay" in the United States on the grounds that the "exit permit" for his return to Germany had not been approved yet.[27] In the interval, his visa for Mexico had expired, an application to change his status from "transit visitor under Section 3(3) to that of visitor for pleasure under Section 3(2)"[28] was approved, and he was granted a work permit as a "helper in the building trade"[29] and a "painter's helper."[30] Hoover's New York agents, who had Marchwitza's forty-one-page file and were not very enthusiastic about pursuing the case ("extreme delinquency . . . in this matter")[31] were told by the usual "confidential sources" that the writer was "one of the more important individuals in the current German sector of the international Communist picture operating between Mexico and the United States."[32] At the New York Public Library, a special agent copied the "Summary of My Life" from one of Marchwitza's books and translated the introduction to the German edition of his novel *Sturm auf Essen,* written by German Communist politician Alexander Abusch.

Military intelligence was not especially happy to see several

"German Comintern agents,"[33] including Kantorowicz and March-witza, return to Europe in 1946. Hilde Marchwitza wanted to go back as a German without giving up her American citizenship ("which I price dearly"),[34] to which the State Department responded with a mildly sarcastic note in her file: "I want my cake + eat it too." But even the FBI's New York Field Office saw no reason to bar the Marchwitzas from going home, having concluded in an eighteen-page report dated 22 September 1944 that Hans, assigned to "Custodial Detention"[35] and classified as a "Security Matter - C,"[36] was an undesirable character: a contributor to the left-wing publications *Linkskurve, Internationale Literatur,* and *Aufbau;* a prisoner in France ("Subject has never tired to avail himself of a chance to leave internment camps");[37] a member of the German Anti-Nazi Writers League; and the bearer of a heart-shaped tattoo on his left hand.

ALFRED KANTOROWICZ

Like Weiskopf and Marchwitza, Alfred Kantorowicz had problems with the INS when he entered the United States. Carrying a ten-day transit visa issued by the U.S. consul in Marseilles on 7 March 1941 and traveling money from the League of American Writers, Kantorowicz and his wife, Friedel, arrived in New York on 16 June on the SS *Borinquem,* the same vessel as Anna Seghers and her family. Next day they were already being questioned by a Board of Special Inquiry on Ellis Island. What happened then was summarized in an FBI report by the Philadelphia Field Office that in turn was based on INS file 7577100: "After entering the United States the subject and his wife found that they were unable to depart from the United States due to the lack of exit permits required of German nationals by executive order. They then requested an extension of three months to permit them to obtain such documents."

Kantorowicz had no way of knowing that his application for an exit permit was never processed, not just because of the new INS directives for Germans but because of a news article denouncing him in Mexico, which a U.S. naval attaché showed to the authorities. After another INS interrogation, the couple's status was changed from "transits to visitors"[38] in early summer 1942; after being threatened with deportation, they were allowed to reenter the United States via Canada and given "permanent residence"[39] in May 1946. But Alfred Kantorowicz, who (the FBI knew) was supported by Ernest Hemingway in the first weeks after his arrival and carried a supporting affidavit from "noted news analyst" William L. Shirer,[40] did not avail himself of his new privileges. "On 11/9/46 left U.S. for permanent residence in Germany,"[41] the FBI noted in mid-February 1947, one day after the U.S. Army Security Group reported from Frankfurt that the "highly dangerous trouble makers" and "top Comintern agents"[42] Kantorowicz and Marchwitza had illegal contacts in the Soviet occupation zone.

Kantorowicz collided with the INS and State Department one last time in spring 1968 when the former exile, now researching the exile period [92], asked to enter the United States on assignment from West German Radio, but he was refused a visa by the U.S. consul in Hamburg "because of KPD membership 1931–49 and SED from 1949 to 1957." The consulates in Hamburg and Frankfurt changed their minds only when they learned that Kantorowicz had left East Germany in 1957 and was "now anti-communist in his beliefs and writings,"[43] and they sent copies of their reports to the FBI and Secret Service. Kantorowicz himself wrote a statement on the subject, headed "To whom it may concern!": "Concerning item 30 [of the visa form] I have to state that I joined the Communist Party of Germany in autumn 1931 and after I was called to be a professor at Humboldt University, East Berlin and moved to East Berlin, I was admitted into the SED. I have never exercised any sort of official party function. . . . The hopes I cherished in the beginning for the humanization of society through Marxism, and also my disappointments and conflicts with the Party that finally led to my fleeing the country again in 1957, are described in detail in my books: *Deutsches Tagebuch, Das Ende der Utopie* . . . , *Deutsche Schicksale,* . . . *Im 2ten Drittel unseres Jahrhunderts.*[44]

ERNST BLOCH

In April 1943 Kantorowicz applied for permission to visit his friend Dr. Ernst Bloch in Cambridge, Massachusetts. The reason for the visit was not recorded, but the FBI used the same piece of paper to comment again on links between Kantorowicz and the Free Germans in Mexico: "In view of the fact that the original investigation in instant case was instigated by information which indicated subject was the liaison agent between German Communists in Mexico and German Communists in the United States . . . it is deemed advisable to conduct further investigation."[45]

The exile group in Mexico and the Free Germany Movement are also central to the seventy-five-page file on Ernst Bloch, seventy-three pages of which the FBI released to me. An anonymous denunciation in 1940 started a short-lived investigation of the exiled philosopher for espionage and "possible UnAmerican activities,"[46] but it was a February 1942 telegram from Bodo Uhse, who had fled to Latin America, that set off the investigation proper: "Subject received a telegram from Mexico City which was suppressed by the Radio and Cable Censorship at New York, New York. Meaning of telegram not clear but believed possibly to be of subversive nature."[47]

Equally scanty as regards evidence were five FBI reports issued in rapid succession from Boston, where Bloch lived from early 1942, studying philosophy and "writing ten hours a day."[48] The FBI's reporting agent seems if anything bored as he scans Bureau archives, aided by a translator, for articles by and about Bloch in the exile magazine *Freies Deutschland,* including essays that contain "glorification of the Soviet Union"[49] and "sarcastic references to the Second Front."[50] The G-men appear concerned by the report that after Bloch lectured in Boston, the exiles had the notion of founding a "chapter of the 'Friends of Free Germany'" there,[51] which among other things would discuss the role of literature in the reeducation of German prisoners of war. And of course agents in Boston and Washington were interested to learn that the author of "Erbschoft Unserde Zeit" *(Heritage of Our Times)* and a contributor to "Das Wurt"[52] *(Das Wort)* was a signatory to the founding proclamation of Council for a Democratic Germany.

Ernst Bloch, whose height was variously listed on forms as 5 feet 5 inches and 5 feet 8 inches, and his weight as 170 or 190 pounds, "very near sighted and wears thick glasses,"[53] arrived in New York on the SS *Pilsudski* from the Polish port of Gdynia on 13 July 1937. On 17 March 1947 he became American citizen no. 6648940[54]—"The asses thought I had more skeletons in my closet than you," Bloch wrote to the shocked Wieland Herzfelde, "in America I mean, and that's what counts"[55]—and in 1949 returned to East Germany. During this time he does not appear to have had problems with the INS, despite what to American officialdom amounted to a shady past ("is a refugee from Berlin and Moscow where he was an active writer in the interest of Communism").[56]

The INS and FBI then ignored Bloch for a time, until their interest was rekindled in the fifties and again in the sixties. First, the Boston Field Office tried in September 1953, with Hoover's help, to prevent Bloch from reentering the United States by establishing a "National Stop with the U.S. Customs Service,"[57] after they had identified him correctly as a "member of the Eisler Group"[58] in Leipzig, but incorrectly as the director of Leipzig's School of Engineering.[59] Then an FBI man at the U.S. embassy in Bonn reported right after the erection of the Berlin Wall that Bloch had moved to the West but had refused a call to teach at the University of Frankfurt on the grounds "that 'he would not think of serving capitalism.'"[60] And finally Hoover's man in Bonn tracked the "subject,"

Office Memorandum • UNITED STATES GOVERNMENT

CONFIDENTIAL

TO : DIRECTOR, FBI

FROM : LEGAT, BONN   (105-0-481)

SUBJECT: PROFESSOR ERNST BLOCH
IS-EAST GERMANY

DATE: September 29, 1961

1-1

An item in the September 21, 1961, issue of the West German newspaper "General Anzeiger", disclosed that ERNST BLOCH, Professor Emeritus at the University of Leipzig, who was forced into retirement by the East German Communist regime in 1957, and who had been staying in West Germany during the period when Berlin was recently sealed off, has decided to remain in the West and settle down in Tuebingen where he may obtain a professorship at the university. BLOCH sent an open letter to the East Berlin Academy of Sciences in which he set out a detailed philosophical basis for his having remained in the West. Friends of BLOCH explained "his coming over to West Germany is a protest against the East but does not necessarily denote approval of the West."

In 1949 BLOCH answered a call to the University of Leipzig and went to the Soviet Zone of Germany from America where he had been an emigre. He turned down the offer of a professorship at the University of Frankfurt/Main with the comment that "he would not think of serving capitalism." In his letter BLOCH recalled how he had at first been allowed freedom at Leipzig but had later been subjected to many restrictions. In the beginning of 1957, ULBRICHT himself took a stand against BLOCH and attacked him and his students as purveyors of "unrealistic, un-Marxist ideas," which "are directed against the party and the government."

3 - Bureau
1 - Bonn
HDG:eds
(4)

CONFIDENTIAL

Classified by
Declassify on: ADR

REC- 17   65- 31509- 17

OCT 6 1961

64 OCT 18 1961

still classed as an "IS - East Germany," to England in May 1962: "An item in the 5/6 May 1962 issue of the West German newspaper 'General-Anzeiger' indicated that Ernst Bloch has been invited to Oxford University. . . . Ernst Bloch is undoubtedly identical with subject. The following items are enclosed for Legat, London: Bonn letter to Bureau dated 9/29/61. Report of [blacked out] dated 9/29/53 at Boston. Buform 0-7 dated 10/17/61."[61]

Unpoliticals and Fellow Travelers: Bruckner, Piscator, Unruh, Habe, Broch, Zuckmayer

Of the writers in this group, Ferdinand Bruckner, Erwin Piscator, Fritz von Unruh, and Hans Habe came under FBI scrutiny. Bruckner and Piscator were suspected of being "fellow travelers" of Communists because of their connections with Free Germany. Unruh entered the files as an "Aryan Protestant Prussian aristocrat."[1] Habe tried to forestall attacks that might be made on him for his journalistic writings by "turning himself in" to the Bureau personally. Hermann Broch and Carl Zuckmayer, on the other hand, were of interest only to the Immigration and Naturalization Service. Neither appears to have had an FBI dossier, even though Broch was active in refugee aid and had close ties with Alvin Johnson, president of the New School for Social Research. Zuckmayer's name is cross-referenced in other files. He often visited Dorothy Thompson [107] and is said to have written over one hundred "biographical portraits of leading personalities in German cultural life" for the Department of Biographical Records of the OSS in 1943–44 [42, vol. 2, pt. 2, p. 1045].

FERDINAND BRUCKNER

Bruckner, a famous stage director in the Weimar Republic who was also known for his plays, shared the experience of many exiles whose careers collapsed when they fled the Nazis. Only one of eleven plays he wrote in the United States was performed during his stay there, and that only by Erwin Piscator's Dramatic Workshop. A second play, *Simon Bolivar,* was printed in his host country by Aurora Verlag, the publishing house Bruckner had helped to found. Six other manuscripts have never been published to this day. Even after his gradual return to Germany around 1950, the once famed dramatist waited in vain to be rediscovered.

Born Austrian with the name Theodor Tagger to a mother who was traveling in Sofia, Bulgaria, Bruckner's career flourished before he fled overseas. A notarized statement of his income that he prepared for the INS before entering the United States (through the border town of Calexico in October 1936) read, "My income at the present time from Europe from plays and motion pictures in Europe amounts to at least Twenty Thousand Dollars ($20,000.00) per year and will continue indefinitely so long as my plays are being produced," and listed in detail the sources of his earnings: "S. Fischer in Berlin—12,000 Marks," "Albert de Lange—1200 florins," "Thalia-Edition Paris—70,000 francs,"[2] and so on.

But the INS and FBI were not concerned with the finances of the Bulgarian-Austrian who had come to the United States on a quota visa: his political connections were what they cared about. Thus in March 1946, when he applied for citizenship, an INS official questioned him thoroughly about whether he had always been "well disposed to the good order and happiness of the United States"[3] during his ten-year stay there. Asked if he knew "a certain Mr. Piscator" who was "alleged to be a member of the German Communist Party,"[4] Bruckner replied that he did, but that he himself had never attended any meetings of the Communist Party and had always believed in the American form of government. Although he was "vice president"[5] of the German-American Writers Association, the office had nothing to do with politics, he claimed. Articles he had written for *Soviet Russia Today* and *Freies Deutschland* might perhaps sound pro-Russian to an unsophisticated reader but they certainly were not pro-Communist: "I personally describe it that way—that because of the fact that the Communists were the strongest fighters against Hitlerism, they made a lot of friends with anti-Hitler writers. . . . That's why occasionally pro-Russian expressions are considered as pro-Communist."[6]

The INS appeared willing to believe Bruckner. Hoover's special agents were more suspicious, because they relied not just on more or less proven facts but on the principle of guilt by association. For example, the New York Field Office took notes on essays that Bruckner published in *German-American* in 1943–44 even though they were "mostly of a literary nature," simply because they contained words of praise for Heinrich Mann, an "alleged Communist."[7]

"Theodore Tagger, with alias Ferdinand Bruckner, Security Matter - C,"[8] officially known as Ferdinand Bruckner since he became a U.S. citizen ("Height: 6′ Weight: 170 lbs . . . Peculiarities: Speaks with slight foreign accent"),[9] residing at Bregenzerstrasse 7, Berlin 15, "expatriated himself" from the United States in June 1954 "by having a continuous residence for five years in a foreign state other than that of which he was formerly a national or in which his birthplace is situated."[10]

ERWIN PISCATOR

Like Bruckner, von Unruh, and Zuckmayer, Erwin Piscator, a famous stage director in the Weimar Republic, was unable to continue his former successful career in his U.S. exile. The ongoing collaboration between the New School and Piscator's Dramatic Workshop was very fruitful, leading to model stage productions, contacts with writers like Tennessee Williams and Arthur Miller, and workshops attended by actors like Harry Belafonte, Tony Curtis, Rod Steiger, Marlon Brando, and Walter Matthau. But Piscator, a founder of political-documentary theater in the Weimar Republic, never achieved a major success on Broadway or in other centers of American theater.

Piscator fled to the United States as a visitor at the start of 1939 and then reentered the country as an immigrant via Canada. His first contact with the FBI came four years later, when his case was classified as "Alien Enemy Control - G." On 21 October 1943, a group of agents from the New York Field Office arrived with an executive search warrant at 56 West Tenth Street to search Piscator's apartment for "contraband,"[11] although what they meant by that term is not clear. Because resistance was futile and Piscator had no reason to believe he had done anything wrong, he let the men in and also granted them a lengthy interview: "The subject admittedly belonged to the Communist Party in Germany from 1922 until 1923 . . . but became dissatisfied with the Communist movement and in 1923 ceased his membership."[12] His income (he said) was $330 a month and his rent $100. He had additional income of $2,000 a year from a trust fund[13] belonging to his wife, a "wealthy widow"[14] whom he had married in Paris in 1936. The special agents found nothing in his apartment but a large library "consisting of books on philosophy, drama and politics"[15] and a camera for which he had a written permit from the office of the U.S. attorney general.

Various FBI investigations of Piscator carried out between 1945 and 1957 turned up no more evidence against him than the apartment search. In 1945 the FBI was concerned about Bruckner's adaptation of Lessing's play "'Nathan the Wise'" ("Subject . . . stated he was not Jewish").[16] In summer 1947 Hoover tried to supply the INS and Justice Department with informants to help them investigate "Erwin Friedrich Max Piscator, Security Matter - C"[17] with a view to deporting him, but most of the informants had moved away, died, or were no longer in a position to testify.

Piscator applied for American citizenship in July 1944 and was refused. When the House Un-American Activities Committee summoned him to testify in Washington on 7 October 1951, he decided to leave the United States the day before and return to the country that had driven him out in 1933 and not asked him back after 1945. The United States refused to grant him a "reentry permit," which he would need if he wished to revisit America like many of his fellow emigrés. In 1965, the U.S. consul in Berlin had to check with the State Department to decide whether "in view of the compassionate and humanitarian aspects of the case"[18] the former Spartacist, who had made a name for himself in West German theater, might be granted a visa so that he could visit his wife in New York at Christmas.

FRITZ VON UNRUH

Fritz von Unruh, like Bruckner and Piscator, belonged to the great names in German theater before 1933. Driven from Germany by the Nazis, then from his home in Zoagli by the Italian Fascists, Unruh traveled through France and Portugal to arrive in the United States on 10 August 1940, assisted by two passports reportedly obtained for him by French defense minister Edouard Daladier in the names Fred and Frédérique Onof, and a quota visa from Secretary of State Cordell Hull. But nothing could be done to help Unruh's writing career, despite his contacts in the exile community, especially with Piscator and his Dramatic Workshop. Neither in the United States nor in postwar Germany did the public appreciate his style, marked by Expressionist pathos, or the extravagant emotional outpourings of his characters. Of the dramas he wrote in New York in the forties, none was performed. He did not fare much better when, "'a stranger to Broadway'" [42, vol. 2, pt. 2, p. 920], he tried through the Office of Overseas Publications to find a new public by writing novels. The OSS commented on his plight with unusual empathy in September 1943: "Fritz von Unruh is a vigorous and colorful poet. . . . In the last year he developed leanings toward mysticism. His misfortunes and the long years in exile without literary successes have filled his life with bitterness."[19]

Unruh, "5' 9", 218 lbs., with blue eyes, grey hair, fair complexion and no identifying marks,"[20] came into the FBI files by a familiar route: an unnamed "individual" described as a "generally reliable and highly confidential source" wrote a number of similarly phrased letters to Hoover at the start of 1942 denouncing more than one hundred people. This time the accusation was not the usual left-wing activities but a charge very rare in the files of the exiles—"that the above-named subject was connected with the Gestapo."[21] Moreover (said the State Department representative in the INS Interdepartmental Committee when giving reasons why Unruh should not be granted an immigrant's visa), the applicant was in his private life "a typical Prussian militaristic aristocrat related to and connected with the German imperial monarchy."[22] In short, Unruh "will undoubtedly, because of his Prussian character and culture which he possesses in the highest degree, be as undesirable in the United States after the war as he was in France and Germany before the war and for the same reason."[23]

The sizable remainder of Unruh's file, which includes documents from the INS, air force, and army besides the 81 out of 102 released by the FBI, is largely routine or involves passports and living quarters during the period in the fifties when Unruh traveled back and forth indecisively between Europe and the United States. From the *New Republic,* of which Hoover said politely "this publication has been unable to make a harmonious adjustment in a capitalistic America,"[24] the G-men extracted a biographical portrait by a Canadian professor who tried to tell the public who Unruh was: "Without wishing to make invidious comparisons, I must nevertheless point out that, while many of our German exiles left the Third Reich only because they were deprived of their livelihood, Unruh left as a matter of sacred principle, as a living protest against the Nazi Weltanschauung."[25] The FBI also filed an article from New York's *Herald Tribune* dated 30 January 1947, which said that Unruh had accepted an invitation from the mayor of Frankfurt, seconded by letters from four hundred young Germans, to live in a ruined building there and help with the reconstruction. A short time later, Unruh's relations with Germany were the topic of a report from the American consul in Hamburg, who said the writer had given a lecture in St. Paul's Church in Frankfurt that the left-wing newspaper *Hamburger Volkszeitung* dismissed as "a State-Department-sponsored propaganda attempt which backfired" because Unruh had not dared to criticize the discrimination against blacks and Jews in the United States for fear of suffering the same government persecution that had befallen his "fellow-author Gerhard Eisler."[26]

Unruh's file was closed by the FBI provisionally in March 1959 "in view of subject's advanced age (74) and inactivity,"[27] and then closed for good on 29 January 1970, ten months before his death, because he had not set foot in the United States since 1962.

HANS HABE

Hans Habe (really Hans Bekessy), known in Hungary and Austria as a journalist of dubious professional ethics, the author of rapidly churned out popular novels, and the husband of six unusually wealthy and influential women, ran true to form in his dealings with the FBI: he turned himself in to the Bureau as a way to protect himself from possible future attacks, either anonymous or public.

Hoover's G-men first noticed the popular journalist, who described himself as "probably . . . the only foreign writer who is a regular contributor to the American magazine literature,"[28] when he appealed to the FBI for an interview in spring 1942, claiming to be the victim of "threatening letters" and slander. Although a persuasive speaker, he appears not to have gotten very far with the FBI, because the reporting agent in the Washington Field Office, after meeting with Habe on 2 May 1942, wrote drily to headquarters: "There is definitely no extortion violation involved in this case. . . . Mr. Bekessy's principle object in calling at the Bureau appeared to be his desire to counteract any reports which might be received at any time relative to his activities having a tinge of international intrigue rather than the reporting of an extortion violation." The agent seems to have been more embarrassed than anything by Habe's detailed self-portrait, "placing particular emphasis upon the fact that he had just recently married the daughter of Ambassador Joseph E. Davies, and likewise going into some detail relative to his literary successes."[29] Habe turned over to the FBI a vast collection of reviews and quotations from letters sent to him after his lectures, showing that despite the upheavals of his life, he never missed an opportunity to hoard material that could show him in a flattering light if the occasion demanded ("documentary evidence: . . . several hundred reviews . . . and . . . over 3,000 clippings, which are in the possession of the author").[30]

It is a moot point whether the reason the FBI left Habe in peace was that even his bitterest enemies could more easily accuse him of links with Nazis than with Communists ("young Hans Habe was in the service of the fascist Heimwehr Movement in Austria").[31] In any case, Habe (the name being the German "pronounciation of H.B.— Hans Bekessy,"[32] as the Bureau put it) did not appear in the files again until he returned to Germany, when after leaving the army in 1956 he made a negative remark about intelligence services ("true freedom cannot exist as long as intelligence agencies exist")[33] in a lecture in Munich. He earned another file entry in 1964 when in a short article for *Stern* magazine he wrote concerning J. Edgar Hoover: "It is said that Hoover has a dossier on every American citizen. That may well be an exaggeration, but Hoover keeps a terrifying amount of information on file."[34]

HERMANN BROCH

The FBI kept no file on Hermann Broch, and his INS dossier concentrates on the year 1938 when the Austrian novelist, after brief imprisonment by the Nazis, fled through England and Scotland and tried to enter the United States. Central to his file were four testimonials by Thomas Mann, Albert Einstein, the publisher Benjamin

Huebsch, and Edward Blatt, asking John Wiley, consul general at the U.S. embassy in Nazi-ruled Vienna and shortly to be Donovan's candidate for head of the Foreign Nationalities Branch of the OSS, to help Broch get into the United States.

Mann's affidavit speaks for itself: "I have known Mr. Broch intimately for many years and in my opinion he is one of the finest living German writers. . . . His works, the product of a rich and wise personality, have been unanimously acclaimes [acclaimed] by critics as among the outstanding contributions to modern literature. . . . I am convinced that Austria's loss will be America's gain. There can be no question of Mr. Broch's ability to adapt himself to the new coutry [country] of his choice. And there is every reason to believe that in due time he will make valuable and lasting contributions to American culture."[35] Einstein limited himself to a universal moral appeal in which he spoke of the "human duty to offer a refuge to those who are innocently persecuted."[36] Huebsch as a publisher referred to his knowledge of literature and described Broch as a writer of "rare talent."[37] Finally, Blatt promised in a notarized document: "I hereby undertake and agree to maintain and support Mr. Hermann Broch from the time of his arrival in the United States until he should become self-supporting."[38]

But the testimonials from America seem not to have worked in Vienna, because Broch's petition for a U.S. quota immigration visa was not approved until 21 September 1938, when he was already in Glasgow. Broch, "6 feet 1 inch, weight 150 pounds,"[39] "burn mark on neck,"[40] "divorced . . . , race: Hebrew,"[41] arrived in New York on October 9 on the SS *Statendam*. Five years later, on 27 January 1944, he became an American citizen in Trenton, New Jersey, near his home in Princeton.

CARL ZUCKMAYER

Broch received his immigrant's visa no. 18592 as part of the German quota although his passport was issued in September 1929 in

Vienna and the applicant himself, until he became a U.S. citizen, always filled in the "race"[42] or "nationality" blanks on forms with "Austrian"[43] or "German-Austrian."[44]

This issue—how U.S. consular officials in other countries and the INS in the United States interpreted the *Anschluss* that had annexed Austria to the Third Reich—lies at the heart of the more than fifty-page INS file of Carl Zuckmayer, best known for his comedy *The Captain of Köpenick*. How complicated things became is evident from statements made by Carl and Alice Zuckmayer to an INS official who interrogated them separately in June 1943 at their home in Barnard, Vermont. Along with other topics ("Q. Are you of Jewish blood? A. No")[45] the official asked why Zuckmayer's petition for "reclassification" as an Austrian was not accompanied by a document showing his naturalization in Austria: "Q. Wasn't it usual to have a certificate of some kind issued to show possession of Austrian citizenship through naturalization? A. No, I just got a notification that naturalization had been completed and that my Austrian passport would be awaiting me at the Passport office of the Austrian Government in Salzburg, but I was in Vienna at that time and before I could get to Salzburg the invasion of Austria occured, making it impossible for me to go there. I was notified by letter but in the confusion of leaving Austria I left it behind me. It could have been dangerous for me to have it in my possession when crossing the border, too, because the letter congratulated me on becoming a citizen of Austria under the Schuschnigg Government which would have labled me as an enemy of the German Reich."[46]

Alice Zuckmayer, too, made life difficult for the INS. Asked where her parents came from, she answered: "This is complicated. I think . . . my father . . . was born in Bucharest, Rumania, but I am not sure. You see my parents were divorced two months before I was born and I met my father only once . . . he was a citizen of Rumania. I know he was naturalized in Austria and I think it was in 1911 or 1912. . . . Q. Would that have made you Rumanian at birth? A. I think it would, yes, but I am not sure, but I was always treated as an Austrian . . . mother's . . . father and mother were Germans. Then, she became Rumanian by marriage. Then, after she was divorced she became Austrian, in about 1912. The only proof I have is a certificate of naturalization for my mother but it was issued a long time after she became Austrian. I became Austrian when my father was naturalized because I was under twenty-one."[47]

No doubt confused and with some cause to be suspicious, the INS decided, despite the emigré couple's protestations of loyalty ("We intend to become United States citizens and become loyal to it")[48] to pursue their investigation further and to question the witnesses cited by Zuckmayer. Franz Werfel, interviewed by a special inspector in Beverly Hills in September 1943 and asked, "Of what race or people is Mr. Zuckmayer?" replied: "I do not know whether he was of the Jewish religion but his parents were certainly Jewish. . . . Of my absolute knowledge I can say this man is a real Austrian—really got his Austrian citizenship."[49] Friderike Zweig, first wife of novelist Stefan Zweig (who had killed himself in Brazil in 1942), resident at 1 Sheridan Square in New York, informed INS officers who questioned her that Zuckmayer had become Austrian, "because the Nazis said that was why they seized his property."[50] And Guido Zernatto, who in 1938 had been a member of Kurt von Schuschnigg's cabinet and was general secretary of the Austrian nationalist Vaterländische Front [42, vol. 2, pt. 2, p. 998], confirmed in a statutory declaration shortly before his death that "Zuckmayer . . . has been bestowed upon the citizenship of Austria . . . in the course of a regular Cabinet meeting in February 1938."[51]

The FBI seems to have had no interest in Zuckmayer's petition to immigrate, or in his activities in America. To my repeated requests for information, the Bureau official administering the Freedom of Information and Privacy Acts curtly replied in November 1994, "Mr. Zuckmayer was not the subject of an FBI investigation"; but since his name appears in the files of a number of other persons and organizations, the Bureau was willing, he said, to release to me sixty-six of seventy-six pages containing cross-references[52] about Zuckmayer's connection with the Free Germany Movement, the Tillich Committee, and "post-war plans for the European Nations."[53]

Carl Zuckmayer, "5 feet, 8 inches, . . . 192 pounds . . . , black hair and grey eyes,"[54] became an American citizen on 4 December 1945 in Woodstock, Vermont. In the fifties he traveled back and forth between the United States and Europe in a state of indecision, until finally in 1957 the State Department received word from the U.S. consul in Salzburg that "Mr. Karl Zuckmayer profession: author residing at 31 Kreuzbergpromenade, Salzburg, Parsch, Austria (c/o Tomaselli)"[55] who "last resided in the United States at 42 River St., Woodstock,"[56] had given up his U.S. citizenship because he and his family had again become Austrians.

JOHANNES URZIDIL, MAX REINHARDT, ERNST TOLLER

The FBI and INS files of German poet and storywriter Johannes Urzidil of Prague, theatrical director Max Reinhardt, and poet of revolution Ernst Toller are largely insignificant.

Urzidil's files, thirty pages with the FBI of which twenty-six were released to me, and twenty-eight from the INS, mainly involve the potentially grave issue of whether his work for two Czech refugee publications in London put him in violation of the Foreign Agents Registration Act. But Hoover's headquarters, which hardly ever let slip the opportunity for an investigation, gave this case a low priority, patiently explaining to their agent in New York that the Foreign Agents Registration Act of 1938 "requires that all agents of foreign principals must file a registration form with the Attorney General," and suggesting that a "dead 97 file"[57] be opened on the case, with "97" indicating a matter under the Foreign Agents Registration Act and "dead" meaning that no further investigation was anticipated.

The FBI likewise showed little interest in world-famous stage director Max Reinhardt, or in revolutionary dramatist Ernst Toller, who had been in the leftist Bavarian government in Munich in the brief period in 1919 when it was a "Soviet republic." Reinhardt moved to the United States in the thirties, became a citizen in 1940, and died in New York three years later at age seventy. Besides the usual INS forms ("On October 15, 1934 . . . purchased from the Equitable Life Assurance Society . . . $80,000.00 Single Premium Retirement Annuity Policy No. 9624851"),[58] his files contained only two significant documents: a notarized statement from his brother Siegfried in 1935 Berlin, showing a Nazi eagle and swastika design, which certified the date and place of birth of the "Professor Doktor,"[59] and the original plus German translation of a long statement from a Latvian court divorcing Reinhardt from his first wife in 1931.

Besides INS documents including a Polish quota visa issued on 14 April 1937 in Windsor, Canada, the file of Ernst Toller, "5 feet and 7 inches, . . . scar in right cheek,"[60] who hanged himself in a New York hotel in 1939, contained nothing but a birth certificate from Samotschin in Poland. There is another document that the CIA would not release, citing "FOIA exemptions (b)(1) and (b)(3)"[61] — that is, national security.

4

The FBI and the Exiles in Mexico

South of the Border: "Communazis"

HOOVER'S G-MEN ARRIVED IN Mexico hard on the heels of the refugees, whom they branded "Communazis." On 26 May 1940, two months after writer Bodo Uhse, veteran of the Spanish Civil War, had left Hollywood on a bus and crossed into Mexico at Laredo, Texas, Hoover told President Roosevelt that he was preparing to send one of his special agents to Mexico City. Several weeks later, Uhse ("organizer of Stalin immigration into Mexico")[1] had been joined by Ludwig Renn, who had also fought in Spain, and together with others they petitioned the Mexican authorities to help them rescue 189 fellow exiles from southern France. Meanwhile the FBI had set up a Special Intelligence Service (SIS) for Latin America that continued to operate until 1947. By autumn 1940, "roving reporter" Egon Erwin Kisch *(Sensation Fair),* Communist politician Otto Katz (alias André Simone), Austrian journalist Leo Katz, and ex-Communist Gustav Regler had reached Mexico, while the SIS had obtained blanket permission from the Mexican government to monitor mail and cable traffic to and from the country. And on almost the same day in August 1941 when a U.S. naval attaché in the Dominican Republic told his American spy colleagues that Anna Seghers was traveling to Mexico by way of New York, Ciudad Trujillo, and Martinique, Hoover's man in Mexico City, Gus Jones, received official accreditation as civil attaché at the U.S. embassy.[2]

What brought the exiles to Mexico was a generous immigration policy for left-wing people of every shade of opinion, especially if they had fought in the Spanish Civil War. The political climate had been shaped by liberal and socialist governments following the Mexican Revolution of 1910, with active trade unionism, land reform, expropriation of foreign capital, and worker education. Mexico also offered the exiles the opportunity to found organizations, magazines, and a publishing house without interference and occasionally even with support from their hosts. The Liga Pro-Cultura Alemana, the Free Germany Movement (FGM) and its branch the Latin American Free German Committee (LAFGC), the Heinrich Heine Club, the monthly magazine *Freies Deutschland,* and El Libro Libre, at that time perhaps the most important emigré publishing firm in the world, allowed the exiles to expand their influence beyond the borders of Mexico. As an official in the U.S. State Department's Division of American Republics put it, the position of left-wing people in Mexico was "unusual" "because in that country a social revolution has already taken place. . . . Accordingly, Mexican Communists find themselves at a disadvantage because much of their thunder has already been stolen by a nationalistic party disavowing Bolshevism's international theories and aims."[3]

The range, skill, and persistence of the exiles in using their opportunities is well documented [96–99; 159; 146], and the achievements of the little exile band of "barely a dozen"[4] in 1941, and later no more than two hundred, in organization and publishing are rightly considered phenomenal. Allied with aid organizations in New York, prominent exiles throughout the United States, and helpful Mexicans, refugees who themselves had only just escaped Hitler's terror set out in 1940–41 to procure dozens of visas and ship's passages to rescue other refugees still trapped in southern France. The main exile organizations in Mexico—the Liga, the FGM, and the LAFGC—bargained tenaciously, organized fundraisers and political events, represented the interests of the Jewish colony, contacted writers living in isolation in South America, and addressed international issues like German collective guilt, a "soft peace," the opening of a second front in Europe, reparations, and the formation of alliances to defeat Hitler and build a new Germany. At times they perpetuated the internal rivalries that traditionally weakened people of the left. But their choice of honorary governors for the Latin American Committee—moderate leftist Heinrich Mann, anti-Soviet Austrian nobleman Hubertus Prinz zu Löwenstein, Kurt Rosenfeld, who headed the German-American Emergency Conference in the United States, and Karl von Lustig-Prean, leader of a small Free German group in Brazil—demonstrated their will to pursue the broad left-coalition policy of the thirties, and their membership soon numbered thousands. Their repeated efforts to work with other exile groups like "Das andere Deutschland" in South America and the Council for a Democratic Germany in the United States failed not because of political differences alone but because communications between groups were disrupted by mail censorship and the restrictions placed on travel.

The magazine *Freies Deutschland,* a high-risk publishing venture when the exiles began to print it in November 1941, soon became a leading publication of the exile community. By mid-1946 when the colony in Mexico dispersed and *Freies Deutschland* ceased publication, fifty-five issues had been printed in editions of up to four thousand and spread throughout the world. Most well-known exiles had written pieces for it. Literary texts and political analyses, cultural essays, reviews, and news from Germany supplied matter for debate in the large exile centers, giving those struggling in isolation in remote sanctuaries a sense of belonging that sustained them.

As important to the refugees as *Freies Deutschland* was the publishing house El Libro Libre, which printed more than twenty titles totaling over fifty thousand copies, under the most difficult conditions, from 1942 to 1946. Its list included classics like Seghers' *The Seventh Cross,* Feuchtwanger's controversial report of his experiences in France, *The Devil in France* (1941), and novels by Heinrich Mann, Bodo Uhse, Ludwig Renn, and Bruno Frank. The "Black Book on Nazi Terror in Europe" was widely circulated in Spanish translation as *El libro negro del terror Nazi en Europa.* Dismissed by the U.S. embassy as appealing to a "morbid interest,"[5] the translation testifies to the close cooperation between the refugees and their host nation, as does the work of German exiles at Mexican universities, especially the Workers' University (Universidad Obrera) founded by trade-union leader and friend of the exiles Vincente Lombardo Toledano. Paul Merker's *Deutschland— Sein oder Nichtsein?* (1944–45) and Alexander Abusch's *Der Irrweg einer Nation* (1945) joined the debate over blame for the war and Germany's future that was raging especially in the United States.

The Heinrich Heine Club, founded in late 1941, evinced a desire by the exiles to address unpolitical exiles and German-Mexicans in their area by sponsoring lectures, literary evenings, concerts, films, and other cultural events. By early 1946 they had organized nearly seventy such events, often attended by hundreds of people. Club members took an active part in drama performances. Evenings built around the theme of France, Spain, Czechoslovakia, or Mexico helped to build bridges to other exile groups and to Mexican artists.

In contrast to all these public activities was the behind-the-scenes work of Hoover as he expanded his sphere of influence beyond U.S. borders into Latin America, hoping that the FBI could fill what he saw as the need for an agency to gather intelligence in other countries. American fears of a German invasion and of Communist infiltration of their southern neighbor supported Hoover's expansionist aims. Indeed, Roosevelt in the mid-thirties, notwithstanding the "Good Neighbor" policy on Latin America that had just been enacted, ordered his military planners to investigate possible attack and supply routes for German troops who might try to land in South America. In 1939–40, when invasion hysteria hit the United States following the military successes of the Nazis in Poland and France, the simulated exercises "Rainbow I" and "Operation Pot of Gold" were held to test the possibility of sending 110,000 U.S. troops to the projected Axis landing zone at Recife, Brazil. Simultaneously, the State Department instructed its diplomatic representatives in Latin America to report to Washington news of any "subversive activities." In 1939 before war broke out in Europe, Roosevelt gave the ONI, MID, and FBI the assignment of coordinating counterespionage in Central and South America and exchanging information through a joint or interdepartmental intelligence committee under State Department control. Just before the fall of France, Hoover declared abruptly without prior agreement of his colleagues that "upon the instructions of the President" [170, p. 34] he had ordered FBI agents to Mexico and Cuba. The resulting conflicts between the FBI chief and his most important rival on the intelligence committee, General Sherman Miles of the MID, were smoothed over by Roosevelt, who issued an unofficial directive[6] that remained in force until the exiles left Mexico and the CIA was founded: the FBI was assigned the entire Western hemisphere as its zone of operations, working jointly with the State Department, while the MID and ONI had the rest of the world.

Hoover with this partial success of his expansion policy at once set to work with his usual energy, entrusting to P. E. Foxworth, an FBI assistant director in Washington [54, p. 326f], the job of building up the Special Intelligence Service, which soon commanded more than five hundred agents and a budget that grew from $900,000 in 1941 to $5.4 million by 1947. Gus Jones, the SAC in Mexico who was succeeded by Birch O'Neal in 1943 and Robert Wall in 1944, used old contacts with the police chief of Mexico City, Miguel Martinez, to gain access to mail and cable traffic starting in August 1940. In 1942, Hoover successfully defended his Latin American territory from a new competitor in the intelligence trade, Wild Bill Donovan of the recently founded Office of Strategic Services, while SAC Jones and his FBI colleagues were safely under cover, disguised as legal attachés at U.S. embassies in Central and South America. This same cover continued to be used by FBI liaison officers in embassies and legations in Bonn and Paris far into the postwar period, as well as at U.S. Army headquarters in Heidelberg.

Hoover's excursion into Latin America began with the fear of Nazi spies and saboteurs. But it soon became apparent that agents of the Third Reich, who for the most part did not begin moving into Mexico until 1939 through the Soviet Union, were no match for the FBI. Love affairs, alcoholism, money problems, and internal rivalries led the "boys from Ast Berlin"[7] to give themselves away; or if they did not, they were quickly recognized and neutralized by the G-men, as were Nazi spies in the states. But Hoover saw to it that his SIS did not run out of things to do. Instead of following his pattern from 1917–18 and 1920 by first hunting German spies and then Communist subversives, he combined the two by tracking the exiles, tarring them all with the same brush as "Communazis."

The left-wing refugees in Mexico gave the G-men more work during the war years than spies from Berlin. The FBI traded information about visas and travel routes with the INS on Ellis Island, and with MID and the State Department. Agents working out of the legal attaché's office at the U.S. embassy in Mexico City diligently wrote down their impressions of events sponsored by the Heinrich Heine Club, articles in *Freies Deutschland,* and books published by El Libro Libre. They recorded relationships between the exiles and Mexican government and union leaders like Lázaro Cárdenas and Vincente Lombardo Toledano, swapped information with the Secretaría de Gobernación, Mexico's ministry of the interior ("The Honorable Ignacio Garcia Tellez, Minister of Gobernacion, requested our Government to send him the names of . . . Communist or Nazi agents . . . , pledging himself to see that they are arrested"),[8] noted friction with Trotskyites and ex-Communists, filed data on love affairs and homosexual activities. The private and commercial mail of the refugees passed through the U.S. Office of Censorship, where thousands of hours were spent translating letters, manuscripts, and entire issues of *Freies Deutschland,* even if the material had been sent not to the United States but to other countries. And of course Jones, O'Neal, Wall, and their colleagues at the embassy and in State Department headquarters in Washington studied the political positions of the "Communazis," their attitudes about the Second Front and the collective guilt of Germans, their connections to the Soviet Union, relations among the Free Germany Movement/Latin American Committee, the National Free Germany Committee in Moscow, and similar groups in the United States, and especially their views on postwar policy for Germany and German culture.

In her novel *Transit,* Anna Seghers described the life of refugees waiting in southern France for a passage overseas. Uhse, Renn, Frei, and others of the Mexico colony recorded their escape stories in diaries or autobiographies. What they did not know was that long before they arrived in Mexico, almost all of them were under observation by U.S. government agencies. For example, on 15 August 1940 Captain Earl Piper, assistant naval attaché in Mexico City working for the ONI, handed in an error-riddled form labeled "Intelligence Report" in which he said that President Cárdenas of Mexico had instructed his foreign and interior ministries

> to issue orders to our Consulate in Marseilles, France, to give documents to the following persons and their wives and husbands as political refugees:

Grans Werfel	Anna Seghers
Leonard Frank	Adrienne Thomas
Konrad Heiden	Ruth Jerusalem
Alfred Doeblin	Sre. de Hermann Kesten
Dr. Friedrich Wolf	Franz Dahlem
Walter Mehring	Hermann Dunker
Ernst Weiss	Gerhard Eisler
Rudolf Leonard	Andreas Ewerd
Alfred Kantorowicz	Dr. Rudolf Neumann
Hans Marchwitza	Prof. Gumbel.

"It pleases me to add" (Piper went on, translating from Cárdenas's letter to Mexicans, including the union leader Lombardo Toledano who had petitioned for rescue of stranded refugees) "that the admission of those persons to the country, granted as said above, has been a means of satisfaction to the Executive since it concerns people who by their antecedents, represent the tradition of German culture and whose personal qualities are those of people who have struggled for the causes of liberty and justice."[9]

That a U.S. naval attaché would be interested in whether Mexico approved the entry of a handful of German exiles—and that the U.S. embassy would send a report about it to the secretary of state in Washington that very day[10]—seems more logical once one has read the secret files. "It is not known," the ONI agent commented on Cárdenas's decision, "if they are bona fide refugees and really political enemies of the present regime in Germany." It was right to be suspicious, the agent thought, because Mexico admitted not only

Nazi agents and sympathizers but also anti-Fascists and Spanish Loyalists into the country "with comparative ease."[11]

Many similar examples could be cited to show the interest of U.S. intelligence in the movements of refugees from southern France, or those threatened with deportation from the United States. The U.S. naval attaché in Ciudad Trujillo, Dominican Republic, notified his headquarters on 20 August 1941 of the route being taken by Alfred Kantorowicz on his odyssey through the Caribbean. In September 1940, a Dallas oilman named D. Harold Byrd had written a letter that sounds paranoid today but that the State Department took very seriously at the time.[12] Addressed to U.S. Senator Tom Connally, it told how Byrd, worried by developments south of the Texas border, had hired an ex-soldier to track suspicious foreigners ("a threat not only to Texas but to the Western Hemisphere")[13] back and forth through Mexico for months, "covering miles of travel by airplane, boat, burro and automobile." He then passed on the fruits of his research to the authorities: "Mexico is 80% pro-German . . . we are 'Gringos' to them"; and he had read in the newspapers that Mexican visas might be issued to German Communists "Gerhart Eisler, . . . Anna Skher, . . . Hans Marchwitza . . . [and] Dr. Friedrich Wolf," he wrote. "I paid this Colonel's expenses here last week and he testified to Martin Dies in a secret hearing." HUAC and its chairman became notorious in Mexico in 1940 when Dies advised that the Monroe Doctrine should be modified in view of the "Ruso-German penetration" of Mexico, and the Mexican press responded with caustic irony: "In such case we would not have a puppet Government controlled by Hitler and Stalin but one much nearer."[14] Moreover, two years after Germany had attacked the Soviet Union and the United States entered the war, Hoover used the term "Communazi" in a letter addressed to the State Department. The apparently deliberate use of this word, which compressed Communists and Nazis into a single idea at a time when the United States and USSR were wartime allies, implied that the alliance was purely tactical—and laid the groundwork for the totalitarianism theory of the McCarthy era and the Cold War.

FREE GERMANY AND THE LATIN AMERICAN COMMITTEE AS INTELLIGENCE TARGETS

Men like J. Edgar Hoover, whose idea of the world never changed after 1918, reacted like bulls to a red flag when they saw Germans with Communist leanings networking in North and South America, staying in touch with Moscow, and forming their own views about the future of their country after the destruction of the Nazi state. U.S. agencies thus amassed considerable material on the exile colony in Mexico, although it had only a few active members. The FBI and military services kept almost two thousand pages on Anna Seghers, Ludwig Renn, Egon Erwin Kisch, and Bodo Uhse, with smaller files on El Libro Libre publishing house and the Heinrich Heine Club. The State Department and military intelligence wrote and stored long reports from and about Mexico, classified under the names of exiles or topics like *"Freies Deutschland,"* "Free Germany," and "Refugees." Representatives of the FBI, ONI, MID, and State Department met in the U.S. embassy in Mexico City each morning to compare "intelligence information" and "to discuss individual cases and general movements."[15] Reports were routinely exchanged, and it was common for one agency to quote another as a "highly reliable informant." The Office of Censorship made decisions about whether to destroy the mail of the Free Germany Movement or to send it on after it had been recorded, translated, and sometimes photographed.

Files on the Free Germans, their Latin American Committee, and "front organizations"[16] like the Heinrich Heine Club are particularly informative for several reasons. First, the various U.S. agencies operating in Mexico all focused their surveillance on a small group who were concentrated in one city. Second, this group was relatively homogeneous in its organization and ideology, and thus easier to observe than the exile centers on the East and West coasts of the United States. Third, the surviving material is for the most part housed in the National Archives of the State Department, which unlike the FBI, ONI, and MID does not black out passages before releasing material to the public.

Central to intelligence reports out of Mexico was the U.S. effort to establish the organizational links and political platform of the FGM ("obedient to the *Comintern*")[17] and its Latin American Committee. Investigation of Free Germany in Mexico began with two typical memoranda. The first, from Clarence Moore, an FBI agent disguised as a civil attaché, comprises twelve typed pages dated 26 March 1943 and so impressed his superior in the State Department's Division of Foreign Activity Correlation that he wrote a personal note encouraging Assistant Secretary of State Adolf Berle to read it: "I think you will find it worth glancing through. It goes pretty thoroughly into an analysis of the organization, its publications & its leaders, & lists, too, its supporters among the Mexicans. It leaves little doubt as to the purpose of 'Freies Deutschland' & shows that this purpose is well on the way to attainment."[18]

The report indeed warranted careful reading, because the main conclusion of Moore's long-term fact gathering and close evaluation of *Freies Deutschland* magazine was that the Free Germans were a Communist-controlled "United Front" that "uses the old Communist technique of using the names of non-Communists to lend an air of respectability to their organization." Proof that the technique was successful, in "the opinion of one rather well informed individual," was that "Andre Simone, with aliases,"[19] was able in late 1941 to persuade a group of "fifteen of the wealthiest German-Jews in Mexico," none with any interest in Communism, to make financial contributions after he showed them a letter "on White House stationary from Mrs. Roosevelt indorsing the Freies Deutschland Movement and Simone personally." Moore alertly pointed out the difference between the Free Germany Movement in Mexico and another group with the same name led by right-winger Otto Strasser, which the State Department tended to confuse, and described the German-American Emergency Conference in New York, the Deutscher Kulturbund in London, and the "Movimiento de los Alemanes Libres de Brazil" as "'sister organizations.'"[20] He learned through the mail censors that Paul Merker, "fat, jovial . . . with both amoebic dysentery and stomach ulcers,"[21] opposed the Liga Pro-Cultura Alemana because of its "half Trotskyite politics"[22] and that the Liga in turn accused the cash-poor Free Germany Movement of having bought the support of Mexican politician Felix Diaz Escobar with money "to buy himself the Governor's job."[23] Without listing a source for the information, Moore voiced the suspicion that the Austrian Bruno Frei was the real leader of the Free Germans, while Ludwig Renn was only its "titulary head," "taking orders from Frei who in turn takes his orders from the Comintern."[24]

Moore ended his report with a mixture of facts and errors about the "more important German-Communist residents in Mexico,"[25] including Alexander Abusch, "Walter Janke,"[26] Kisch, Renn, and Bodo Uhse. In this survey he mentions the collaboration of Anna Seghers with American author Viola Brothers Shore in writing a stage version of Seghers' novel *The Seventh Cross* in English, a project virtually unknown to Seghers scholars. But sometimes Moore gets things wrong: he describes Austrian novelist Robert Musil as a "radical writer" in his reference to an essay that Kisch wrote in June 1942 after Musil's death,[27] for example, and he quotes the view of unnamed "competent literary critics" who dismissed Kisch's book about Mexico, *Sensation Fair,* "as very mediocre."[28]

A second example of thorough American research on the "Free Germans" is a twenty-five-page single-spaced "Review of the Free Germany (Alemania Libre) Movement in Mexico" with eight addenda and classified "Strictly Confidential," which Third Embassy Secretary W. K. Ailshie sent to his State Department superiors on

25 June 1943. Washington thought the report "excellent" and they were right, because the material that Ailshie patiently assembled on the "Origin of 'Alemania Libre' and Background of its Founders,"[29] "Organization and Principles,"[30] and "Literary and Cultural Activities"[31] was one of the earliest descriptions of the FGM and laid the groundwork for discussion of the exiles' role in plans for postwar Germany, a topic of primary importance to the intelligence agencies and the State Department beginning in the summer of 1943.

Ailshie's familiarity with the past and present of the Free Germany Movement is apparent from the opening lines of his report, where he quotes a "Consulate General's unnumbered dispatch . . . , file no. 820.02/800-C" dating the first public appearance of the FGM's future founders to an "anti-Nazi 'rally'" held in August 1941.[32] Ailshie knows about the attack on Anna Seghers and Lombardo Toledano by "certain conservative elements" in the Grupos Socialistas de la Republica Mexicana, just as he knows the guest list at a banquet that Chilean poet and diplomat Pablo Neruda gave on 24 August 1941 for Lombardo Toledano and for Seghers, who had just arrived from New York. He attaches to his report a copy of a letter by Renn and Simone announcing the founding of the "anti-Nazi movement 'Free Germany'" on 28 March 1942,[33] and a gallery of exiles' photos from the files of the Mexican Gobernación, which was one of the most important sources of information for the U.S. diplomat and his agent colleagues.

Ailshie's report supplies a wealth of valuable information. Concerning the Spanish Communist exile Margarita Nelken, who gave Ailshie a "statement"[34] about KPD official Paul Merker, the report says that after her own expulsion from the Communist Party she "branded Anna Seghers and other prominent 'free' Germans opportunists and weaklings."[35] Ailshie's Addendum No. 7, a "letter of *Alemania Libre* addressed to *Comite Inter-Aliados,*"[36] describes relations between the Free Germans and the Allied Information Office in Mexico, which in a controversial exchange a year later was accused by Renn, FGM secretary Erich Jungmann, and jurist Leo Zuckermann of backing denunciatory attacks on the FGM and the LAFGC in the Mexican press. On the other hand, Ailshie does not comment on the controversy between Free Germany and the U.S. embassy over the FGM's appointment of Roosevelt as an honorary chair of the FGM congress of May 1943, because embassy staff, alerted by a letter from their superiors ("the Department considers it most inadvisable for this organization to be using the President's name"),[37] had to wait for Washington to approve the text of a denial letter to be sent to Alemania Libre, with a copy to the Mexican press: "The Department of State has instructed me to invite the attention of the officers of your organization to the fact that the President of the United States has not given his authorization to the use of his name in connection with your organization."[38]

Ailshie's dispatch "No. 10,984"[39] is important not only for the facts it assembles but for his skill at political analysis. For example, he links the formation of Alemania Libre with the German attack on the Soviet Union; gives several pages to the relations between German exiles and Mexican politicians; and expresses surprise that a foreigner like Seghers' husband Laszlo Radvanyi is allowed to use his "so-called 'Scientific Institute of Mexican Public Opinion'" to investigate matters that involve the "patriotism, national honor and the dignity and pride"[40] of Mexicans. He analyzes the literary production of El Libro Libre and *Freies Deutschland* to show that writers like Thomas Mann who are "always glad to have their views published" were used by the FGM to create a "'prestige' atmosphere."[41] And in a section headed "Political Activities" he attributes to FGM organizers a "well-defined plan of campaign from the beginning." First, he says, they infiltrated the Liga Pro-Cultura Alemana ("the familiar communist tactics of 'penetration'")[42] until it looked as if they could successfully found their own organization; then they distanced themselves from the established German colony, which included Nazi sympathizers; and finally, they formed alliances with Mexican politicians.

EMBASSY OF THE
UNITED STATES OF AMERICA

Mexico, June 25, 1943

No. 10,984

SUBJECT: REVIEW OF THE FREE GERMANY (ALEMANIA LIBRE)
MOVEMENT IN MEXICO

STRICTLY CONFIDENTIAL

THE HONORABLE
THE SECRETARY OF STATE,
WASHINGTON.

SIR:

I have the honor to refer to previous correspondence
regarding the Free Germany Movement in Mexico, and to
submit the following review of this organization. Considerable material on this subject has already been forwarded to the Department by various agencies of our
Government, and it is therefore the purpose of this
report to review and analyze the available data in order
to provide the Department with a single report setting
forth all the facts known to this Mission, and the conclusions it has reached on the basis of the evidence.

For convenience, the report is divided into four
sections: I - Origin and Background; II - Organization
and Principles; III - Activities; IV - Conclusions.

I - Origin of "Alemania Libre" and Background of
its Founders.

The Free Germany Movement in Mexico grew out of the
Liga Pro-Cultura Alemana en Mexico, which was organized
here in 1937 by Enrique Gutmann, Ernesto Toller, Hannes
Meyer, Alfredo Miller, and Paul Elle, ostensibly as a
liberal, anti-Hitler group of friends of Germany. It
was communist in its sympathies, and one of its main
purposes was to assist the immigration into Mexico of
German refugees. Among the active Mexican supporters
of the Liga Pro-Cultura Alemana were the following: Lic.
Alejandro Carrillo; Jose Mancisidor; Lic. Mario Souza;
Lic. Victor M. Villaseñor; and Ermilo Abreu Gómez.

While it was never an important force in Mexico,
it is believed that it was sincerely opposed to the
Hitler regime as may be seen from the attack on it by the
Nazi Deutschen Volksgemeinschaft, which was reported by
the American Consul in Mexico City (Mr. George P. Shaw)
on August 2, 1938 (File no. 820.02.) According to this
report, the Nazi group had this to say about the Liga
Pro-Cultura Alemana:

"Certain of the (Nazi) articles have a special
purpose. They have been written for the Mexican
press to correctly point out the malicious cultural Bolshevik speeches delivered before a small
public by a so-called League for German Culture."
"It

862.01/286

PS/RGB

No subsequent report on the Free Germany Movement equaled the quality of Ailshie's of June 1943. One reason is that after the National Free Germany Committee of Moscow was founded in July 1943, U.S. intelligence was less concerned with the past history of the FGM and LAFGC than with their future, that is, with links between the exiles in Mexico, the Soviet Union, and the United States, and with the question of whether to increase censorship of their mail or block it altogether as a means to destroy communications. The agencies also focused on support for a "soft peace"[43] among the exiles in Mexico, their plans for a post-Hitler Germany, and their intention to return to Europe as quickly as possible.

FREE GERMANY, MOSCOW'S NATIONAL FREE GERMANY COMMITTEE, AND THE U.S. OFFICE OF CENSORSHIP

The State Department praised Ailshie's report partly because it arrived at just the right moment "in the light of the Free German manifesto from the U.S.S.R."[44] Actually Ailshie was lucky that he handed in his analysis on 25 June, because in mid-July Washington was startled by the founding of Moscow's National Free Germany Committee ("a surprise")[45] and wanted to identify quickly any potential NFGC allies in other nations, define their aims, and obstruct them if possible. Ailshie's history of a Free Germany group in Mexico almost identical in name to the Moscow group and dominated by German Communists was important to assessment of the movement, especially because the author, being a diplomat, also gave thought to the international issues: "Assuming that there was a connection between *Alemania Libre* and the *Comintern,*" Ailshie concluded the main part of his report, "the formal dissolution of the Comintern would certainly cause *Alemania Libre* to make some changes in its political dispositions. . . . This is not to say that Ludwig Renn and the leaders of *Alemania Libre* will cease their activities, for undoubtedly they are 'internationalists' in an organizational sense and will continue to work for the creation of a strong international Free Germany Movement, but . . . national patriotism is now the order of the day, rather than the oldfashioned communist 'internationalism.'"[46]

Ailshie's ruminations were echoed by other agents. In April 1942 the OSS dutifully filed a message from a "professional 'anti-Communist'"[47] warning that if the U.S. alliance with the Soviet Union broke down, the exile group in Mexico could prove dangerous not only to their host country but to the United States. A careful analysis of the August and September issues of *Freies Deutschland* by the State Department's Division of American Republics concluded that the majority of the articles contained "glowing references to the Russians' struggle"[48] against their German invaders, suggesting that the exiles, maneuvering between the coalition politics of the LAFGC on one hand and the exiled German Communist Party's bid for command on the other, would end by supporting the KPD demand for "universal leadership of the revolutionary party of the German working class and its central committee in the anti-Fascist resistance" [96, vol. 1, p. 197]. G-2 was irritated that "Renn and Seghers are so esteemed by Moscow that each was requested to radio greetings, at Moscow's expense, to the convention of Soviet writers and artists."[49] And in late June 1943, just before the founding of the Moscow NFGC, Hoover sent a memo to Assistant Secretary of State Berle, "personal and confidential by special messenger," warning with his typical blend of fantasy and foresight "that a provisional German government has been established in Moscow." A "Wilhelm Pick" was to be "Reichs-Chancellor," Hoover said, and "Ernest Thaelmann" would be president, while Thomas Mann, "presently residing in this country,"[50] would be offered the post of minister of culture.

U.S. intelligence and State Department activities stepped up after the Moscow NFGC was founded on 19 July 1943. In the following days, anxious telegrams listing facts and preliminary analyses chased back and forth between the U.S. embassy in Moscow and the State Department in Washington. The United States, although caught off guard by this startling turn of events, quickly sized up the situation correctly. On 23 July the U.S. embassy in the USSR wired home that the NFGC had been founded by the Russians in response to the unilateralist policy of the Western Allies in Italy and France,[51] and when the Moscow Committee promised that Germans could count on peace after the fall of Hitler and would be treated by their adversaries as a "free sovereign nation"[52] in control of their own democratic government, Stalin started trying to gain time to build up a position of strength in Eastern and Central Europe. Washington asked its embassies in London, Stockholm, Bern, and elsewhere to find out how successful the NFGC would be in gaining a foothold in the unoccupied part of Europe and in the Western hemisphere, and the Free Germans in Mexico naturally came up for discussion.

"The first Committee was organized in Mexico City in 1942," Secretary of State Cordell Hull summarized the movement in a background report for the U.S. embassy in Moscow, "and . . . the whole movement is known to have connections in Moscow as evidenced by postal intercepts and other information."[53] OSS agents in New York fanned out to gather "facts" and analyses from, among others, exile politician Gerhart Seger and the Research Department of the American Jewish Committee ("Willi Bredel . . . has visited in the United States and written for the American CP,"[54] "Seger was at once categorical in declaring it a Communist move in psychological strategy").[55] Although Hull thought he already detected a Soviet movement away from the NFGC after the foreign secretaries' conference in Moscow in October 1943 ("a distinct shift away from the 'Free German' committees"),[56] the Office of Censorship still prepared a confidential report in December for the OSS, OWI, MID, FBI, ONI, and other agencies ("information taken from private communications and its extremely confidential character must be preserved"),[57] describing (among other things) the internal quarrels of the emigrés in Mexico: "Regler, Gustav . . . former Communist, now Trotskyist . . . considers that the National Committee of Free Germans, Moscow 'is a camouflaged new Comintern and its members are in the pay of Stalin' and urged political counter-warfare by England, whom he regards as the sole potential saviour of Europe from 'Red Fascism.'"[58]

Cordell Hull was not the only one to play down the importance of the Free Germans in 1943. A member of the Special Branch of the Military Intelligence Service of the War Department showed a trace of humor extremely rare among intelligence agents when he joked about the internal feuding among the "Gray Heads of Bygone Germany": "Though the names of all are significant and symbolic to refugee Germans, few of the leaders are known to outsiders. . . . These aging leaders with their salvaged wreckage of rival parties and factions in a bygone Germany, after a decade of Nazi repression and a Nation-wrecking war, may have little influence or leadership in a resurrected Germany of the future. . . . they might be of passing value to the United Nations if our propaganda could use them for appeals to the German people."[59]

But not everyone in Washington felt so relaxed about the Free Germans. In spring 1943, a controversy critically important to the exiles began between the State Department and the Office of Censorship: Could the Free Germans in Mexico best be curbed by destroying all their mail, or would it be more beneficial merely to open and analyze it? An OSS interoffice memo commented as follows on 10 May 1943.

> It may interest you to note that the United States censorship in the Caribbean has begun to condemn the correspondence of the Communist affiliated Free German group in Mexico City. . . . This correspondence is in itself unobjectionable but its purpose is evidently now considered inimical to the best interests of the United States. I assume that the censorship received the orders to condemn such correspondence from higher up. Apparently it is now considered advantageous to the war effort to throw wrenches where

possible into Communist efforts to organize German refugees abroad or at least in Latin America. Such a censorship policy is obviously an advantage to the Social Democratic and related liberal groups among the German refugees in Latin America. It would appear that this country is therefor already tending to recognize the fight against Communist influence among Germans as related to its war effort.[60]

The debate between government agencies about whether to destroy the exiles' mail continued from spring 1943 to May 1944, and although there is not space to describe its every detail, it tells us more about the mechanisms of mail censorship than any other group of exile files. This "basic policy"[61] debate, which the public knew nothing about, shows the Office of Censorship taking a more liberal view than the State Department.

The controversy began with a series of Special Watch Instructions to radically step up mail censorship of the exile group in Mexico ("Condemn all communications to or from the above names, except those which in no way concern the organizations mentioned").[62] The State Department justified the action as follows: "A well-organized group of enemy nationals, subject to no American control, is engaged in intense political activity aimed at fellow nationals throughout this hemisphere and at American citizens of like descent; . . . this group is motivated by political ideas and dominated by political forces of an alien character, such as may make the group embarrassing to the United States in our formulation of policy towards postwar Germany. If Freies Deutschland is allowed to continue building up a strong organization, influencing not only their fellow nationals but American citizens of German descent, it can easily become . . . a dangerous factor in the case of a peace offensive . . . should there ever be a divergency of national interests, this organization would surely throw its full weight on the side of the Soviet Union."[63]

The Office of Censorship and its allies in the State Department's

SWI/
CONFIDENTIAL

October ,1943.

SPECIAL WATCH INSTRUCTION NO. 8 6

Requested by: State Department.

Names to watch: Below-listed subjects who have headquarters in
Mexico City:

Freies Deutschland (Movimiento Alemania
 Libre)(Alemania Libre) (Free Germany) - Apartado 10214
Latin American Committee of Free Germans
 (Comite Latino-Americano de Alemanes
 Libres)   - Apartado 10214
Organizing Committee of the Free Germans
 (Organizations Komitee der Freien Deutschen)-Apartado 10214
Ludwig Renn (Baron Arnold Veigt von Goelsenau) -
                        Apartado 10214 or Dr. Norma 198-4
Paul Merker   - 124 Calle
 Cuenavaca, Dept. 404, or Apartado 10214, or Tamaulipas 129/6
Bodo Uhse
Bruno (Benno) Frei (Benno or Bruno Freistadt)
 (Bruno Frey)   - Apartado 10214
Alexander Abusch (Fritz Reinhard) - Apartado 10214
George Stibi   - Apartado 10214
Rudolf Neumann
A. Callam
Andre Simone (Otto Katz)(Otto or Willi Breda)
 (Otto Simon)   - Apartado 10214
Egon Erwin Kisch   - Apartado 10214
Leo Zuckermann (Leo Lambert)
Walter Janke
Olga Ewert
Erich Jungmann
Johannes Schmidt (Ladislaus or Laszlo Radvany)
 (Johann L. Schmidt-Radvany)
Frau Dr. Henriette Begun
Alleanza Garibaldi (Alleanza Internazionale Giuseppe
 Garibaldi)   - Apartado Postal 777
Francesco Frola   - Apartado Postal 777
Mario Montagnana   - Calle Bajio 28-10
Vittorio Vidali (Carlos J. Contreros)(Carlos Sormiento)
 (Carlos or Enea Sormenti)   - Calle Loteria
                                     Nacional 1-0 to 6
Leone Olper
Rudolf Feistmann   - Calle Coahuila 106,
                                     Dept. 10

   PUBLICATIONS:

   Alemania Libre
   Freies Deutschland (Free Germany)
   Demokratische Post.   (over)

Recid by telephone 12/20/43-WEg

Quoted Paragraph . . . . to
The Office of Censorship by Messrs. Ludwig Renn
and Paul Merker, Freies Deutschland.

. . . . A considerable number of our letters to the
anti-Fascist German writer Heinrich Mann in Los Angeles,
who is the honorary president of our committee, have not
been delivered to him during the last few months.   This
is also true for other communications sent by our committee
to addressees in different towns of the United States.

There is furthermore the fact that the whole correspondence sent since June 1943 by different Latin American
countries to our committee in Mexico City and which have
to pass through the United States Censorship has not been
delivered to us. However, we positively know that since
June 1943 the affiliated movements in these Latin American
countries are continuously mailing us numerous communications.

For all these facts, we must believe that the non-
delivery of the correspondence is not due to technical
difficulties of wartime but that our letters are being
withheld by the jurisdiction of the United States Censorship.

On the other hand, as there can be no doubt of the
100% pro-Allied content of the mailed material, we cannot
understand why the United States Censorship forbids the
transmission of such material to the addressees among
which are the official information office of the Soviet
Union and non-Fascist organizations and parties.

We can hardly believe that these censors acted on
instructions given by the United States Chief Censor
and should be very pleased indeed to hear that necessary
steps have been undertaken in order to avoid the repetition
of similar mistakes . . . .

/s/   Ludwig Renn, President
Paul Merker, Secretary

Division of American Republics took a different view: "Wholesale condemnation is neither necessary nor desirable. . . . Freies Deutschland [is] not of sufficient importance to justify this action and . . . condemnation will dry up their open correspondences and thus prevent us from keeping a close watch on them."[64] Also, the Office of Censorship was legally empowered to destroy only mail that might damage the Allied war effort, which ruled out Free Germany because the exiles in Mexico were "absolutely anti-Nazi and anti-Fascist and wholeheartedly behind our war effort."[65] A Mr. Healy, head of the

Office of Censorship's Press and Pictorial Division, curtly dismissed the State Department argument that the Free Germans might negatively influence future peace talks: "Office of Censorship 'does not look beyond the end of the war' and . . . the curbing of potential pressure groups even if enemy aliens is not a proper function of the Office."[66] Healy used another powerful argument: "Certain people at least, in the United States, such as writers, publishers, and thinkers on political subjects, had a right to and should be informed on the trend of thinking and public expression in other countries although these opinions might at times be unpleasant to us."[67]

The State Department of course would not let itself be influenced in such a high-level policy debate by the people who were the most directly affected. When Renn and Merker wrote to the Office of Censorship protesting the continual disappearance of their mail, the State Department snubbed them forthwith: "No reply should be made to the protest, as such an organization is not justified in expecting an explanation of measures undertaken in time of war by an agency of the United States Government."[68]

The battle over mail censorship, which went on for a year and was critically important to the exiles in Mexico, came to a sudden and unspectacular end on 11 May 1944 when Cordell Hull curtly told Byron Price, head of the Office of Censorship, that he had withdrawn the State Department's application for "blanket condemnation" of the mail of Free Germany in Mexico, owing to "a considerably altered foreign situation,"[69] of which Hull gave no further explanation. But the State Department did ask to continue receiving summaries of Free Germany's mail.

POSTWAR POLICY AND THE RETURN TO EUROPE

U.S. intelligence reports on the Free Germany Movement and the Latin American Committee suggested from the start that the exiles in Mexico might try to influence postwar policy on Germany. When

DEPARTMENT OF STATE

FOREIGN ACTIVITY CORRELATION

December 28, 1943.

CONFIDENTIAL

Eu: Mr. Matthews
PA/D: Mr. Dunn
A-B: Mr. Berle

Mr. Healy, Chief of the Press and Pictorial Section of the
Office of Censorship, just telephoned to Mr. Jessop (FC) the
underlying letter from Messrs. Renn and Merker, president and
secretary, respectively, of <u>Freies Deutschland</u> in Mexico.
Mr. Healy wished to have the Department's recommendation as to
a reply. He implied that he himself, rather than tell Renn and
Merker that their correspondence was being condemned at the
request of the Department of State, would prefer that henceforth
it all be released. As neither of these alternatives seemed to
me acceptable from the Department's point of view, Mr. Jessop
has, at my suggestion, told Mr. Healy that he would probably
not be able to give him a reply for several days.

Is it necessary that any reply at all be sent to Renn and
Merker? They are enemy aliens, residing outside the United States,
who by their letter are demanding an explanation of measures
undertaken in time of war by an agency of this Government.
Their statement as to the "100% pro-Allied content of (their)
mailed material" is open to considerable question. A study of
such material has usually revealed the contrary as far as the
United States is concerned.

Mr. Healy also implied that he considered a question of
general policy to be involved. I am inclined to agree with him
as no definite agreement on this question has yet been reached
with the Office of Censorship. From Mr. Shaw's underlying
memorandum of December 4, 1943 you will see that "it appeared
the principal opposition to granting our request" (i.e. that
all publications and political correspondence of <u>Freies Deutsch-
land</u>, with a few specified exceptions, be condemned) "would
continue to come from the Press and Pictorial Division of which
Mr. Healy is Chief."

On November 27, Mr. Gordon wrote to Mr. Price requesting
modification of the very broad "exceptions" outlined in Special
Watch Instruction No. 88 of October 27, 1943. (See attached copy)
Mr. Price has not yet replied to this letter.

It seems, from our own observations and from reports from
the Embassy in Mexico, that the restrictions placed upon the

communications

862.01/558

FEB 17 1944

FLW

PS/BCG

246

-2-

communications of _Freies Deutschland_ previous to the re-writing
in October of the Special Watch Instruction were most effective
in controlling the dissemination of the voluminous political
propaganda issued by _Freies Deutschland_. If it is considered
desirable that we continue to maintain control over this
material it will be necessary to reach an understanding with the
Office of Censorship whereby the broad exceptions of Special
Watch Instruction No. 88 are modified as outlined in Mr. Gordon's
letter of November 27. The points for consideration are,
therefore:

(1) whether we wish to continue to restrict the
activity of _Freies Deutschland_ (as well as its
Italian counterpart, the _Alleanza_ _Garibaldi_)
by the only means available, namely condemnation
of their correspondence and publications; and,
if this is considered advisable,

(2) whether the whole question should not again be
taken up, preferably in a discussion with Mr. Price.

_Rw._

Rebecca Wellington

FC:RW:DEF

247

the State Department's Division of American Republics analyzed the first issue of *Freies Deutschland* magazine in autumn 1942, they concluded that in several points the magazine "is rather definitely following the Communist line" on Germany. "FD" clearly called for the establishment of a second front in Western Europe, emphasized the need "for distinguishing between Nazis and Germans," and "the writers are loud and uncompromising in praise of the Soviet Union."[70] Around the same time, an ONI officer noted that Alemania Libre was the most dangerous of all "'Free German' Movements in the Western Hemisphere . . . particularly from the points of view of psychological warfare and post-war activities designed to enable individual groups to secure control in their homelands."[71]

But the issue of the plans and future of the German exiles in Mexico did not become central to the intelligence services until 1944, when Allied military successes presaged victory over Germany. Any agent reporting on the history or activities of the Free Germans would now begin or end his statement along similar lines to Lt. Col. Cantwell Brown, assistant military attaché at the U.S. embassy in Mexico: "Its [Free Germany's] anti-fascist pro-Germany program makes it a nucleus for a potential factor in the international settlement of the post-war German problem. . . . Up to the present, the Free Germany Movement has taken no definite action to propose a post-war plan for the handling of the German situation."[72] "The principal members are imbued with the desire to . . . occupy some post or voice in the government regardless of the form such government may take." Because the organization was controlled by Communists, one had to assume "that any part that its members may take in the future government of Germany will be essentially in the interests of the Soviet."[73]

Brown's political reports may have been substantially correct but were based less on hard evidence than on the opinion of a single observer. Hoover himself gave a better example of just how far his Bureau might go to acquire solid evidence, in a long memorandum on "German Targets" that he sent to the State Department's head of Foreign Activity Correlation on 13 April 1945—that is, before the war ended in Europe. Requesting "official aid" from the department dealing with "European Aspects of Latin American Cases,"[74] Hoover said on page 61:

> At the present time there are located in the Western Hemisphere, particularly in Latin America, various individuals who are reported to have been prominently engaged in Communist and Soviet activities in France and Germany, prior to suppression of such activities by those governments. . . .
>
> It is believed that there will be available from official records maintained in France and Germany information of value with regard to general Communist activities and with regard to particular subjects of investigation who have been or are presently located in the Western Hemisphere. It is believed that attempts should be made to review all files and records of an official nature which would logically contain authentic information concerning Communism and prominent Communist figures who have been the subject of interest to the governments of France and Germany.
>
> In addition to the request for a review of official records in Europe for information of a general nature concerning Communism, separate requests of a specific nature are being made for any information available concerning particular individuals.[75]

This passage bears re-reading. What Hoover has in mind seems to be that State Department employees on his instructions should ransack the files of such government arms as the Gestapo, the SS, Nazi counterintelligence, the Reich Ministry of the Interior, and the Foreign Affairs Office in Germany, and of the political police and the Vichy government in France, for what he calls "authentic information" about left-wing people who are the mutual opponents of the United States, the Nazis, and Vichy.[76] Whoever had trouble with Heydrich and Himmler in Nazi Germany, or was confined in a Vichy internment camp like Le Vernet in France, is regarded by Hoover as suspect. What emerges is the interest of American intelligence, unperturbed by questions of crime and punishment, in collaborating with their colleagues in Nazi Germany and Nazi-controlled France in counterintelligence work against the old and new enemy of both.

The files released to me show no sign that Hoover's data on the exiles were actually supplemented by information from Nazi agencies and police. But we do know that in 1945–46 the FBI in Mexico used its established sources to continue stockpiling information on the plans of the Free Germans. A principal source was the unsuspecting president of the FGM and LAFGC, Ludwig Renn, who in a conversation in late 1945 with an informant known as the "highly reliable Source C" disassociated himself from the Moscow Free Germany movement: "Renn explained that although the Moscow and Mexican Free German groups maintained cordial and sympathetic contact, . . . the aims of the Mexican group were more all-embracing in that they included such matters as the punishment of war criminals, . . . and the eradication of anti-Semitism within Germany. . . . He asserted that even before the news of the dissolution of the Moscow Free Germany Movement the Mexican organization has given thought to changing its name, possibly to 'Neues Deutschland' (New Germany)."[77] And another "Source C, who is closely associated with the members of the German colony in Mexico and especially the leading members of the Alemania Libre,"[78] reported details straight from the last executive meetings of the Free German cell in Mexico in early summer 1946, when members discussed the low morale of U.S. troops in Germany who were disappointed that Fascism was not being wiped out more thoroughly, and the appeal of Alexander Abusch and Paul Merker to their fellow exiles to try to get Soviet authorities to repatriate them into the Soviet occupation zone. To what extent U.S. intelligence may have obstructed the exiles' return to Germany from Latin America cannot be determined from the files now extant; but the FBI, State Department, and military services definitely kept a careful record of the refugees' travel plans. "Source E" reported a meeting of exiles "during the evening of June 2, 1945," where people who wanted to return home could sign up on a list "to be delivered to the Russian Embassy, thence to Moscow, where approval or disapproval would be given for their return."[79] A year later, in April and June 1946, other sources reported that Kisch and Otto Katz had left for New York and that Merker, who first applied for an American transit visa assisted by a letter from the Soviet embassy, had boarded the *Gogol* in Manzanillo headed for Vladivostok. When on 17 February 1947 Ludwig Renn, Bruno Frei, Walter Janka, and the military attaché at the Russian embassy set off for Europe from Coatzacoalcos on the *Marshall Govorov,* the U.S. embassy secretary who reported to Washington even sent along a passenger list from the Russian steamer that he had obtained from the Mexican authorities.

Four months later, on 4 June 1947, the names Leo Zuckermann ("gangster type . . . engaged in false passport and visa racket . . . , one of the two GPU agents who ordered the liquidation of certain members of the International Brigade in Spain"), Rudolf Feistmann ("probably GPU agent"), and Günther Ruschin ("German Communist, . . . refused transit visa for him and family by Department under Public Safety Provisions") were listed in the ship's papers of the *Marshall Govorov*. Whereupon the U.S. embassy reported laconically (and as was so often the case, not quite accurately): "The general exodus to Germany via Russian Ports began on May 17, 1946 (Embassy Despatch No. 29561 of May 22, 1946) . . . there remain in Mexico of the former important figures in the Free Germany Movement only Bobo Uhse and Hannes Meyer."[80]

Dossiers

ANNA SEGHERS

Anna Seghers is one of those writers who do not make life easy for their biographers. For many years little was known about her family background and years growing up in Mainz, although the contrast between her sheltered bourgeois upbringing and her longing for an adventurous, unusual life is key to the prevailing mood of her books.[1] Netty Reiling, a.k.a. Mrs. Netty Radvanyi, alias Anna Seghers played a shell game with her own identity that is reflected in fictionalized form in *Transit,* her novel of exile, in manuscripts where she calls herself Peter Conrad or Eve Brand, and in letters variably signed Netty, Anna, or Seghers-Radvanyi. Even today, veteran Seghers scholars continue to swallow fairy tales that the exile herself made up in the forties about the manuscript of *The Seventh Cross,* claiming that the last copy had disappeared with a translator along the Maginot Line, or in a Nazi raid in Paris, or during a bombing attack, while all along she knew perfectly well that a copy was safely tucked away in New York with F. C. Weiskopf.

But perhaps no chapter in her life has remained as obscure as "Anna Seghers and the USA." Her biographers barely mention the success of *The Seventh Cross* from 1942 to 1946 as a Book-of-the-Month Club best seller, a favorite of U.S. soldiers, a Hollywood film, and a comic strip. Her contracts with Little, Brown in Boston and with MGM in Los Angeles, which could tell us much about the financial situation of the Radvanyi family in exile in Mexico and after their return to Germany's Soviet occupation zone, are ignored or simply unknown. For a long time not even the basic facts were accessible about the route the refugee "Hungarian" (Seghers was married to Hungarian Laszlo Radvanyi) took from Ellis Island to Mexico and thence to Laredo, Texas, and back to Berlin, even though copies of the travel forms are available from the INS. Seghers' entry into New York harbor on 16 June 1941 is certified by an official seal, signature, and fingerprint,[2] as is the identity of the vessel, SS *Borinquem*,[3] her departure for Mexico on 25 June aboard the SS *Monterey*,[4] and her return journey out of Mexico via Laredo and New York City on 7 January 1947.[5]

More intriguing than such random facts is the almost thousand-page dossier compiled by the FBI and other agencies in the forties, which Seghers herself can hardly have known existed. Her dossier is interesting, first, because it has all the earmarks of a thriller, replete with intercepted letters, notes written in invisible ink, mysterious coded messages, mail drops, break-ins, murder, and of course—how could it be otherwise when J. Edgar Hoover was involved?—the Red Scare threatening democracy and the American Way. Second, it contains letters and other clues to the living and working conditions of the exiles, and copies of manuscripts, two of which I believe were previously unknown to Seghers scholars.

Emil Moschella, head of the FOIPA section of the Bureau's Records Management Division, reported 833 pages of material on Seghers in the FBI archives, of which 730 were released to me after a long wait. Another hundred-plus pages are lodged with various branches of the National Archives in Washington; and two documents totaling four pages were released by the INS.

FBI headquarters in Washington and the New York and Mexico field offices collected the material on Seghers, with assistance from Boston and Los Angeles. The U.S. embassy in Mexico, the Division of American Republics in the Department of State, the INS, the Office of Naval Intelligence (which simultaneously cooperated and competed with the FBI in Latin America), MID, and after 1945 the CIA were more or less systematically involved in information gathering. The Office of Censorship, in cooperation with the FBI, monitored Seghers' mail and sent almost all intercepted material to the

FBI lab, where envelopes and stationery "were examined for secret ink by means which would not alter their appearance with negative results."[6] Agents burglarized homes; made sketches, blueprints, and photos; tapped phones and shadowed individuals. A small army was occupied in evaluating newspapers and magazines in which Seghers published or to which she subscribed, including the *Daily Worker,* the *New York Times, New Masses* magazine, and *Freies Deutschland* from the Americas, and Russian publications like *Ogonyok, Moscow News,* and *Internationale Literatur.* Other bureaus consulted the local authorities on Martinique about the arrival and departure of the Radvanyi family, investigated refugee aid groups in New York, and attended cultural events sponsored by the Heinrich Heine Club in Mexico to hear Seghers' lectures. Informants, some clearly from emigré circles, gave reports and documents to the FBI: lists of names from the headquarters of the Joint Anti-Fascist Refugee Committee; information on the relationship of Seghers and Kisch ("nothing of particular interest");[7] a clue (which turned out to be false) that Schoenberg's pupil Hanns Eisler was writing the film music for *The Seventh Cross;*[8] and data for analytical background reports like "Source C, who is personally acquainted with Anna Seghers, states that the influence of her husband contributes largely to her remaining a Communist for inwardly she detests violence and fanatical Communist action."[9] And of course the all-powerful Hoover sometimes intervened personally, as he did in other cases. For example, late in 1943 he sent the alien property custodian a memorandum with biographical details on Seghers, some inaccurate, and then sprung the clincher: on 7 November 1942 she had sent "greetings to Russia" on the "occasion of the twenty-fifth anniversary of the October Revolution."[10]

The interest of U.S. agencies in Anna Seghers began in 1940 with the public controversy over attempts by Mexican union leader Vincente Lombardo Toledano to furnish emergency visas to a group of German exiles in France and bring them to Mexico. Eight months later, FBI headquarters informed the New York office that they had learned through "information received confidentially" that Seghers and other "camouflaged Communist agents" were on their way to the United States. Three months after that, the U.S. embassy in London passed on the anonymous letter denouncing Klaus and Erika Mann, which also accused "Dr. Ratvanij and his wife Anna Segers" of being "camouflaged Communist agents."[11] The "bi-monthly report on Communist Activities" from the U.S. consulate general in Mexico City increased government suspicions by attaching a "list of all the individuals who . . . are mentioned as being part of this group of Communists," naming virtually all the prominent exiles in Mexico including "Anna Seghers (or Segers) aliases: Netty Hatwanny, Netty Radvaniji," "Anna Skher (writer)," and "Dr. Radvaniji."[12]

Turning to the U.S. refusal to let Seghers enter the country, letters written by the Radvanyis from France and Ellis Island to F. C. Weiskopf and Wieland Herzfelde tell us that Anna Seghers originally thought of fleeing to the United States. That the Radvanyi family ended up in Mexico instead is due, first, to the fact that the Joint Anti-Fascist Refugee Committee and the League of American Writers, although able to buy ship's passages for refugees, could not guarantee them U.S. entry visas; and second, Seghers and her traveling companions were listed as "camouflaged Communist(s)"[13] in official files, including those of the Special Inspections Division of the INS in New York, making it difficult if not impossible for her to be granted asylum. The official reason the INS gave for refusing her entry, the "defective vision of the child, Ruth Radvanyi,"[14] may have been just an excuse to keep the politically suspect family out of the country. Franklin Folsom, sent by the League of American Writers to support the Radvanyi family on the "Isle of Tears," recalled: "On Ellis Island I watched her sign the contract for her book . . . *The Seventh Cross* . . . and learned why she was being detained. An Immigration Service doctor had said her teenage daughter has 'an incurable disease of the central nervous system.' . . . The fact was that the girl, who had been a hunted—and haunted—refugee for years, had a tic. Her face twitched a little. The examining doctor observed this from a distance of twenty feet, never closer, and the result was that she and her left-wing mother could not take asylum in the United States."[15]

Normally, the FBI file on Seghers should have been closed when the Radvanyis were barred from entering the United States. But because the Bureau had meanwhile obtained from Roosevelt permission to expand its area of operations to the entire Western hemisphere, Seghers and her fellow exiles in Mexico remained under the scrutiny of Hoover's information gatherers, and everything that came into FBI hands was collected, analyzed, and cataloged from then on.

A U.S. embassy attaché in Mexico diligently reported that on 18 August 1941, Seghers lectured in the Bellas Artes Theater on the theme "German Writers Look at the War": "The audience, consisting of about five hundred people, principally American tourists who appeared to be of Jewish extraction."[16] In New York, a "confidential source at 381 Forth Avenue, NYC, headquarter of the Exiled Writers Committee," supplied the FBI with a list of names that included "Anna Seghers . . . , her husband and two children."[17] W. K. Ailshie, the U.S. embassy secretary in Mexico City, recalled in his outstanding review of the Free Germany Movement that Pablo Neruda had given a banquet for Seghers immediately after her arrival in Mexico, but that the Mexican Gobernación, although it kept a file on her husband, had no record of her entry into the country.[18] Documents showed that "Dr. Ladislao Radvanny, alias Dr. Lazlo Radvanyi, alias Johannes Schmidt," a man of "cultured mannerisms, pleasing appearance,"[19] ran a public opinion institute in Mexico and was accused by "Source C" of having raided a meeting of Trotskyites in April 1943 along with Otto Katz, Leo Zuckermann, and the Swiss Bauhaus architect Hannes Meyer.[20]

But however thorough the surveillance of Seghers in her first years of Mexican exile, it looks routine compared to the 1943–45 investigation of the Alto Case.[21] Beginning in summer 1942, the FBI intercepted a series of twenty-four letters mailed from various Latin American countries and, later, Mexico to New York. Written in invisible ink, they contained coded messages interspersed with Russian and Spanish words, and were sent to cover addresses or delivered by courier, and then handed on in New York by a chain of different people. Their contents, which were partly decoded by FBI experts, were not included in the files released to me but seem to have involved the real or suspected activities of the "NKVD" and "Comintern apparatus"[22] in trying to free the murderer of Trotsky, Ramón Mercader, alias Frank Jackson.[23]

Seghers became a key target of investigation in the Alto Case when several coded letters from an Anne Sayer, address Insurgentes 338, Mexico, D.F., were intercepted. The FBI suspected that Anne Sayer was a pseudonym for Anna Seghers; "the address 338 Insurgentes was the private apartment of Laslo Radvanyi."[24] But the Alto investigation led nowhere, at least as far as Seghers was concerned. Of all the letters from her and to her that were opened, analyzed, and tested with "non-staining treatment" in FBI labs in the next two years, not one showed signs of coding or secret writing.[25] The Bureau spent some time searching for a key to the code in the English, German, and Spanish editions of *The Seventh Cross*, which was widely read in the United States at the time [189, pp. 179ff], but found nothing, and seriously considered a plan to investigate all forty thousand books in the Russian language that were then in the New York Public Library, looking for the same code.[26] Agents forced their way into the homes of suspects, stole their letters from Seghers,[27] and photographed bookshelves where they found copies of *The Seventh Cross*. One report of a house search in Mexico City expresses disappointment that instead of secret ink, agents found only stomach drops, a remedy that Europeans in Mexico liked to keep on hand.

An informant who visited Seghers' apartment at Rio de la Plata 25 in spring 1943, under the pretext of offering her a publishing project, gives us a more or less accurate portrait of the writer ("Hair: Very grey, formerly black; Height: About 5'4"; Weight: About 120 lbs; Peculiarities: Extremely nervous and suspicious"),[28] but adds an inventive hypothesis straight from a paperback thriller: "It has been noted that Anna Seghers does not like to have persons whose political background is not well known to her visit her apartment. When she was interviewed, under pretext, it was observed that on three occasions a door bell in the apartment was rung from some place other than at the apartment door. On each occasion, subject jumped up hurriedly and went to the hall as though in order to intercept a visitor before he could come to the apartment. Her actions were so obvious that even [blacked out] remarked that apparently she was expecting someone. It was apparent that she did not want her expected visitor to enter the apartment while the writer was there. It has been ascertained that at the present time subject keeps almost no books in her apartment at Rio de la Plata, #25."[29]

The zeal and meticulousness of the FBI in investigating Seghers and the mysterious letters in the Alto Case appear grotesque and overblown against the background of the military conflicts going on in Europe and the Pacific. The unwarranted scale of the investigation at a time when resources were needed elsewhere confirms the stereotype of Hoover as a man who, since his apprenticeship as a Communist witch-hunter in the Justice Department, thought no cost too great when it came to containing the Red menace. Financial considerations and statutes of limitation could no more curb his pursuit of the Seghers case than firm admonitions from the attorney general's office or discreet inquiries from the State Department. In July 1943, Hoover's men impassively filed away a letter from Assistant Attorney General Hugh Cox that described the FBI's danger classifications as "inherently unreliable," "inadequate," "defective," "impractical," and "unwise"[30] and ordered their immediate cancellation. The FBI likewise ignored the suggestion from the State Department and the SIS agent at the U.S. embassy in Mexico that the costly surveillance of Seghers should be ended and her name struck off "Special Watch List No. 8."[31] And despite the notation made in her file, "subject has been definitely eliminated as a suspect in the ALTO CASE,"[32] the FBI continued to track Seghers, by then a naturalized Mexican citizen, after she returned to Europe. In 1962 when Hoover wrote a memo on "East German Propaganda" to the CIA director with copies to Bonn, he referred to an FBI report dating back to 24 October 1945, even though it had acquitted Seghers of any participation in espionage operations.

A whole curiosity shop could be filled with bureaucratic anomalies from Hoover's reign, but it would add nothing to the picture we already have. Instead, it is more useful to review Seghers' FBI file for what it can tell us about her professional and private activities. Its main feature is a collection of almost one hundred letters written by and to her, many completely preserved in English translation and the rest roughly summarized by the censors. The file also contains more than twenty other letters and telegrams that mention her, plus reports from informants, notes on publications, and several manuscripts in English translation, two of which were unknown to Seghers scholars until recently. One describes her flight from France and the aid she received from the Joint Anti-Fascist Rescue Committee, and the second, the reeducation of Germans after 1945.

The correspondence in the Seghers files mainly revolves around two themes: business details of publishing projects, contracts, and royalties, and personal communications about health, family, and homesickness. Both give us insight into the working and living conditions of her exile.

The second letter in the collection, dated 19 January 1944, is especially informative. It contains her grateful acknowledgment that Metro-Goldwyn-Mayer has begun filming *The Seventh Cross,* refers to Portuguese, Swedish, and French translations of the novel, and says that in a few days she plans to mail out the manuscript of her novella masterpiece *The Excursion of the Dead Girls*. In the near future, she says, she intends to write "a new novel of the same significance and approximately of the same size as 'The Seventh Cross'" (apparently *The Dead Stay Young*) and will begin it in the next week and complete it in approximately two years. She has another project in mind that she had already mentioned in the late thirties but only now (she believes) has the "technical ability"[33] to carry out: a collection of thirty or forty short stories in the style of *The Decameron* or *The Thousand and One Nights,* and would like to arrange an immediate contract with Boston publisher Little, Brown.

Thanks to FBI censorship of her letters, we know that at the last moment Seghers rewrote the last two critically important pages of *Transit.* "I would have changed these two pages a long time ago, but my illness interfered," she wrote on 19 January 1944. "Of course this means new work for the translator, but it is absolutely necessary to substitute these new pages for the old ones. I shall send these two new pages this week and I ask you to give them to the translator immediately. I ask you, also, to send me the English translation for . . . I should like to review the translation."[34] Ten days later, the censors intercepted the manuscript of *The Excursion of the Dead Girls,* and—a rarity in the history of literature—made the first translation, and not a bad one despite their criticism of the original ("this is a very free translation due to lack of clarity in the text"):[35] "'No, from much further away. From Europe.' The man looked at me smiling as though I had said 'from the moon'. He was the landlord of the tavern on the outskirts of the village. He walked back from the table and began to observe me, leaning negligently against the wall of the house, as though he were looking for traces of my fantastic journey. It suddenly seemed equally fantastic to me as it did to him that I should have blundered into Mexico from Europe."[36]

A special find was a letter dated 23 April 1944 in which the Federation of Organizations for Aid to the European Refugees gave an unknown addressee in New York permission to publish an attached manuscript by Anna Seghers. The subject of this short and long-vanished essay[37] was Seghers' experience escaping from France, her gratitude to the Mexican government and the Joint Anti-Fascist Refugee Committee, and a pledge to fight Fascism. With a harshness unusual for her and reminiscent of Feuchtwanger and other exiles in France, she contrasts the "Gaullist friends" who got her and her family through German lines to southern France without any permits with the inhumane guards at Le Vernet internment camp "who . . . searched our pockets, seizing for themselves the bread which the children had gathered in that breadless winter for the starving Vernet." She talks about "Sr. Gilbert Bosques," the Mexican consul general in Marseilles who himself was interned by the Nazis in France and in Bad Godesberg, Germany, until 1944, and tells how her family was interned on Ellis Island, "so that our experiences of internment on democratic soil were complete."[38]

Even more important, perhaps, than this essay is manuscript RG 59, 862.01/5-1945, filed in the papers of the State Department deposited at the National Archives in Washington. Seghers was assigned by General McClure, head of America's Psychological Warfare Division in Europe, to write this brief text on German complicity with Hitler and the war. Or so it appears from a telegram sent to her in Mexico by Theodore Kaghan, news director at the Office of War Information, on 10 May 1945: "General McCletre [McClure?] . . . has requested us to obtain from you a brief statement for immediate publication in German newspapers. . . . Statement should be in a form you feel will be helpful in convincing the German people of the truths from which they have so long been insulated and should be addressed directly to them."[39]

The internal correspondence between the OWI and the State Department indicates that Washington did not wish Seghers' manuscript to reach either General McClure or the German public, who, given the current debate about Germany's future, were bound to be interested in what she said. First, the essay denies that all Germans were Nazis: the same view that had led the State Department to conclude that the Free Germany Movement was pro-Soviet. Second, Seghers invoked with almost biblical pathos the two issues that she had long regarded as central, "whether Germany can rise again as a people, honored and respected among the peoples of the earth," and the positive tradition of "German literature . . . , German music . . . , German science and . . . German labor; and the unspoiled potential of the children."[40]

The FBI collection of Seghers' correspondence contains many details that would enhance our mosaic of exile life in Mexico, but it may be more useful to concentrate on letters relating to *The Seventh Cross*, which earned the exile her reputation and drew special attention from FBI agents when they tried to decode the messages in the Alto Case. The FBI filed letters confirming that Viola Brothers Shore traveled to Mexico in late 1942 to work with Seghers on a stage version of the novel.[41] A woman reader in distant Palestine wrote to her saying that the foreword to the Hebrew translation of the novel, published by the Zionist Labor Youth Group, failed to mention Seghers' political orientation and the fact that she was Jewish.[42] Many of the business letters naturally discuss money matters: delays in the transfer of royalties from the United States, or a request for reprinting rights from the Communist Party newspaper the *Daily Worker* for a fee of twenty-five dollars a month. Some items led the FBI to suspect "that a substantial share of the royalties of Ana Seghers' best seller . . . were channeled into the working funds of Alemania Libre"[43] or went into Party coffers in exchange for "information from the Communist underground."[44]

A letter of 6 July 1944 speaks in detail about the filming of *The Seventh Cross*. The writer, possibly director Fred Zinnemann but in any case a Hollywood insider, states that in his opinion the film was a success and the usually critical lead actor, Spencer Tracy, and the studio bosses thought so too, but that it did not do justice to the book, for one thing because so much was left out. The emphasis on the escape sequence meant that characters like Kress, Mettenheimer, Schulz, Bachmann, and, "after the first cut," Hellwig had to be dropped. The letter-writer says he agreed, "after immense consideration," to cut to a minimum the scenes in Westhofen concentration camp, because the American public was "very tired of these things." On the other hand, he tried but failed to delete the love scene with Toni the waitress, "which was dragged in by the hair at the very end." And of course (he writes) the Rhineland took on a fairly American atmosphere in the film, partly because the most important roles next to Spencer Tracy's had to be given to American actors "in order to achieve a homogeneous effect." All of which did not mean that the project directors had not struggled to preserve the book's basic idea, "that in the final analysis human kindness is indestructible."[45]

Turning from Seghers' business correspondence to the personal letters in her FBI files, we see how little students of her life and work actually knew about the complicated relationships of the Reiling, Fuld, Cramer,[46] and Radvanyi families. For this reason alone, it is impossible to reconstruct the blacked-out names of her correspondents in Martinique, Bolivia, Switzerland, and the United States; but we can trace two main themes.

First is her attitude toward Mexico, her place of asylum. Throughout her stay she felt a mixture of incurable homesickness and interest in her new and alien surroundings. "I should like to spend my old age, if I live to see it very uneventfully in my home town Mainz on Forster Street, lined with old trees,"[47] Seghers wrote on 28 January 1944 to a woman she addresses as "Dear Aunt" in Port de France, Martinique. Three months later, writing to a woman in Iowa about her story *The Excursion of the Dead Girls,* which she had just completed, she recalled childhood experiences and teachers that the two of them had shared and noted tersely: "The older I become, and the greater the surge of people about me, the more real everything appears to me which happened in former times."[48] When postal traffic with Europe was restored, it brought an increasing number of letters that talk about the possibility of her returning to Europe, and questions of where and how to locate vanished friends and relatives in Switzerland, France, and Germany. One example is a letter dated 27 March 1945, addressed to St. Gallen, Switzerland, which was preserved by the Office of Censorship in the form of a summary interspersed with quotations: "In conclusion she states that although she likes Mexico with its rich cultural background, she is essentially European, and much closer to the European cultural pattern. She adds: 'It is possible, that, once at home, I will write something worthwhile, something beautiful about Mexico.'"[49]

A second main theme, closely linked with that of exile and return to Europe, was for a long time barely mentioned by Seghers scholars: her concern about the fate of her mother, who in spring 1942, aged sixty-two, was deported from Mainz in one of the last transports of Jews to Piaski ghetto near Lublin [229]. "I have already written you about mothers fate," Seghers says in a 1 January 1944 letter to La Paz, "although I telegraphed [for] a Mexican visa and she got a Swiss visa, too. I have heard nothing more from her or about her for a long time now."[50] Four months later, her anxiety began to turn to certainty: "Sometimes I read the five, six letters which I have received from my mother and each time I fall into an indescribable state of rage and grief, but there is nothing to be gained by sustaining it."[51] Finally she can no longer hold back "the frightening, horrible news we have from there":[52] "Mother . . . has been declared missing from a camp near Lublin."[53]

Her mother's deportation, a car accident with resulting memory loss, and the Radvanyi family's plan to return to Germany: the central themes of the correspondence blend in late 1944 into the plan to adapt *The Excursion of the Dead Girls* into a film or stage version as "reconstruction and educational material"[54] for the postwar period.

Because of the blacked-out names, we cannot tell with whom Seghers exchanged hasty and anxious telegrams and letters about this project in autumn 1944. But one correspondent whom she addresses with the formal pronoun *Sie* lives in Santa Monica, is in the film industry, and wants to exploit the current success of the film *The Seventh Cross* to promote her new project. She writes to California:

> I have set up for the "Excursion of the Dead Maidens" (or whatever they may call it. So far I am quite pleased with the title) only one possibility, to build it up as a post-war play. It would go something like this, as I see it: I return home, the city is completely changed, here traces still of the bombardment, there disfiguring reconstruction. Where my school was, there is something else entirely. I looked for the girls of my class. They are not to be found. I seek them through the police station etc. Not to be found. I strike out somewhere perhaps on the Rhine steamer to the place where we always went to one of our former teachers, old even then and now aged. The young folks are apparently dead, the old folks apparently tough. I question the old teacher. Now the trend of life before the war, during and after the war is unfolded. Approximately the same failures, instability, and testimonies as appeared in the story. Here in the film or dramatic version in any case a girl must have been saved, perhaps one who was at that time very much endangered, very broken, and perhaps in this way or that way through a completed action which must be connected with the beginning of the story, must come through to us and show her new situation.[55]

Not long after this exchange between Mexico and Santa Monica about a postwar play on Germany, the FBI added to the Seghers file an article from the *New York Times* telling of the exodus of German exiles from neighboring Mexico.[56] As if to prove the saying that once someone is in the FBI's files they never leave him alone again, the New York and Boston field offices issued further reports in summer 1947 with news clippings on Seghers' activities in Germany and references to the English edition of *The Dead Stay Young* published by Little, Brown in Boston,[57] and in 1972, the flyer "Save Angela Davis," "signed by members of the German Democratic Republic,"[58] Anna Seghers among them.

How Seghers fared on her return to Germany, her relations with her native city of Mainz where in 1946 people still remembered quite well what had happened to the Reiling family,[59] and how, after surviving the mountainous hardships of exile, she dealt with the hardships of the plains in everyday life under socialism are matters not documented in the files of the FBI. A different set of agencies with their own zealous army of spies and informers, their own mail censors and surveillance teams, their own archive of surmise and suspicion took over from there. Because one thing we certainly know from the FBI files on Seghers: those in our time who think differently from the majority and who make their views public will not escape monitoring by modern states, not in Mainz or Mexico, not in New York or Berlin.

Free Germans? Egon Erwin Kisch, Bodo Uhse, Ludwig Renn

Three writers besides Anna Seghers principally shaped the exile community in Mexico: the "roving reporter" Egon Erwin Kisch, ex-Nazi Bodo Uhse, and Spanish Civil War veteran Ludwig Renn. Other active members of the colony like Walter Janka, Otto Katz, and Paul Merker worked more in the area of organization, or as Communist Party officials. Still others like B. Traven and Gustav Regler stayed detached from exile activities, or were sympathizers with Leon Trotsky, who came to Mexico in 1937 and was murdered three years later in his heavily guarded home in Coyoacan.

EGON ERWIN KISCH

Kisch's FBI file comprises 169 pages, 157 of which were released to me directly or through other agencies to which I appealed (such as the Defense Intelligence Agency). An additional 47 pages came from the INS, which withheld some documents "compiled for law enforcement purposes" without giving details. The State Department and the CIA each hold one document of unspecified length, which neither would release.

Kisch's dossier, as one might expect from a travel writer and reporter, is most interesting when it relates to his international contacts. Kisch, whose files were classified under "Internal Security - C,"[1] "R,"[2] "Custodial Detention,"[3] "Mexico Subversive Activities,"[4] and "Security Matter - C,"[5] was known in the United States for books like *Changing Asia, Secret China,* and *Australian Landfall.* He first entered the files when a Board of Special Inquiry asked him on Ellis Island on 28 December 1939 why he wanted to spend two months in the United States before completing his transit to Chile: "Q. Why do you have to remain in the U.S. 60 days? . . . A. The latest work I was working on is a book called 'Crawling in the Inky River.' . . . I sent the manuscript to Knopf and they were not satisfied and wanted me to make some changes. . . . I come now to . . . find out in what manner my book can be published in the best taste of the American public. Q. That doesn't sound good. . . . Where will you live while in the U.S.? A. I found out by calling up a friend yesterday that I will live with Mr. William E. Dodd, ex-Ambassador to Germany, in New York City."[6]

The suspicious INS officials then questioned Kisch about his relations with Chile ("Q. How did you connect with this University? A. I know several writers from Chile and one of them, Mr. Neruder [no doubt Pablo Neruda] . . . invited me")[7] and drew the usual conclusions about the political views of the interviewee: "Q. Did you ever belong to any political party? A. No. I am a left-wing writer, so to speak, but I have nothing to do with politics. Q. How far left did you go? A. As far as most American writers, e.g. Theodore Dreiser, Ernest Hemingway, Lewis Sinclair [meaning either Upton Sinclair or Sinclair Lewis]."[8] They pass over without a trace of humor the fact that the book Kisch cited as evidence of being a writer was *Paradise in America*, "which is based upon Ellis Island, although I was not on Ellis Island previously, except for a visit."[9] A second interrogation on Ellis Island makes clear how little the INS understood or wished to understand the people fleeing from Hitler: "Q. [W]hy is it not possible for you to leave the United States, at least to return to Czechoslovakia? A. That is impossible. I am a Jew and a writer. Q. Do you mean that your writings influenced the Czechoslovakian Government so that you could not return there? A. The Hitler Government, of course."[10]

Kisch, who by virtue of his Czech citizenship could not be detained in the United States even after war broke out, was one of few exiles who departed from America more or less when he chose to. But his case was not closed when he left the country; the FBI continued to track this suspicious character even in Mexico ("Inclined to be unkempt; shaggy hair. Very amiable and courteous; easily approached. Walks with a slight limp when climbing stairs due to broken leg incurred in Australia").[11] The U.S. embassy was told by "Mexican political sources" and the "Polish Minister in Mexico" that Kisch was a member of the Czech Communist Party and the GPU, assigned "to undertake certain work here in Mexico."[12] Hoover's G-men recorded concerning their "spy colleague" "that at the age of 21 Kisch discovered one of the most interesting cases of world espionage, notably that of Col. Redl, who while chief of Austrian counterespionage, was at the same time the most important spy in the service of the Russian Czar."[13] The FBI lab confirmed to agents in Mexico that a form filled out there bore "the known type-writing and handwriting of Egon Erwin Kisch."[14]

The most important source of information about Kisch's life and work is, once again, the Office of Censorship, whose reports make up about one-quarter of the material in his FBI files. His mail was intercepted regularly, partly under the "Special Watch Instructions"[15] of 1943 that were contested by Hoover's rivals. An alert examiner knew of a questionnaire sent via the Soviet embassy in Washington to Johannes Becher in Moscow asking him what he and other German writers exiled in Russia were doing in the propaganda war against Germany, and the examiner linked this to a statement from Bodo Uhse, exiled in Mexico, "about Becher's paper."[16] The censors were also suspicious when they read the offer from a Chicago businessman friend of Kisch to send the German exiles in Mexico "any service and information you might require from the United States."[17] FBI special agents learned from the U.S. naval attaché in Mexico and the Office of the Mexican Cable Censorship that Kisch had had problems with Australian immigration back in 1934: "Subject tried to jump ship in Australia but was apprehended by police guards and placed back on board."[18] "His case made legal history . . . , and the resulting change in the statutes of that country is known as the 'Kisch Law.'"[19]

In 1946, the civil attaché at the U.S. embassy in Mexico telephoned Washington to say that Kisch was leaving the country "at 1:00 P.M. on February 14" carrying Czech passport no. 217298 and a U.S. transit visa obtained by the Czech consul from U.S. embassy staff, to travel in "Car No. 226"[20] via Laredo to New York. Soon after, on 4 April 1946, the State Department told the U.S. embassy in Prague to make discreet inquiries as to whether Kisch, who "received a letter from Klement Gottwald . . . that he was needed at home,"[21] was actually being appointed to a high diplomatic post in Latin America, which Hoover believed Czech consul Eduard Beneš had earmarked for Kisch in July 1944, when Beneš met with Eisler and Brecht in Los Angeles.[22]

Unlike F. C. Weiskopf, who rose to become Czech ambassador to China, Kisch died (the FBI learned from the *Daily Worker*) on 31 March 1948, without representing Czechoslovakia in a diplomatic post. The FBI did not therefore end its investigation. A multipart report on master spy Richard Sorge in 1951 also contained a four-page summary of Kisch's life, because the "roving reporter" while researching his book *Secret China* had ended up in the files of the city police of Shanghai and the documents did not reach American hands until much later, after a detour through the Japanese occupation forces in China. Then in 1956, an agent reporting on the uprising in Hungary that autumn said that a colleague recording details on the "Comintern/Apparatus, IS-R"[23] had observed Kisch and his wife in New York on 24 February 1946, visiting the apartment of someone whose name is blacked out.[24]

BODO UHSE

The file of Bodo Uhse ("unattractive, sly, shifty-eyed")[25] was drastically mutilated by the FBI, which gave me 167 almost completely blacked-out pages while withholding 354; and 57 documents were withheld by the army. Yet the FBI and INS both claim to have no material from the period of Uhse's stay in America. Admittedly, the bulk of the censored documents stems from the early sixties and probably has less to do with Uhse than with his American wife, Alma, who after separating from Uhse left East Germany and returned to the United States [153].

Alma, who met Uhse in Mexico in spring 1941, seems to have kept the FBI as busy over the years as her husband, editor of *Freies Deutschland* and member of the KPD colony in Mexico. This may be partly because before she met Uhse, Alma was married to American writer James Agee, known in the states as a successful journalist, screenwriter, and author of the experimental prose volume *Let Us Now Praise Famous Men* (1941), which accompanied the photographs of Walker Evans. ("It is possible that the investigation of Mrs. Agee originated in conjunction with one of her ex-husbands," according to the file).[26] But agencies were probably more concerned with whether German Communists-in-exile had found in Alma Uhse an American citizen who could be used for propaganda work and to make potentially illegal contacts in the United States.

The earliest telegram in the Uhse file comes from the "Director, FBI" and mentions not only Uhse but a certain "she" who has contacts on the East Coast ("the New York office is being requested to make inquiries among its Communist Party informants")[27] and is connected to a "1938 Chevrolet Coach bearing Pennsylvania license [blacked out],"[28] a car that belonged to Alma Agee and was observed going into Mexico via Laredo, Texas. Agents dutifully recorded telephone conversations between an unidentified "she" in Laredo and Bodo Uhse in Mexico City "for the purpose of checking any possible violation of the espionage or other related statutes"[29]—even if the conversations were only about whether Agee's son Joel had slept well and finally gotten over his cold. Other documents certify that "Mrs. Alma Agee who . . . has been the mistress of Uhse for the past several years, on August 28, 1944 arrived at Brownsville, Texas, from Mexico to renew her tourist permit for Mexican residence."[30] When Mrs. Agee protested to the U.S. embassy about FBI methods, including a nine-hour search conducted at the Mexican border, her protests naturally fell on deaf ears. An FBI report from San Antonio said that border patrols in Laredo found in the travelers' luggage—along with Lawrence Sterne's *Tristram Shandy,* Katherine Anne Porter's *The Leaning Tower,* and Elizabeth Woody's *The Pocket Cook Book*—a news clipping about the death of German Communist Alfredo Miller, a.k.a. Alfred Fortmüller,[31] who had been expelled from the United States. And in June 1947 Uhse complained in a letter to Weiskopf that despite the intervention of an attorney in Washington, Alma had "not yet received the passport that she applied for a long time ago and that several times has been promised and complained about" [214, p. 299].

Compared with the case of Alma Uhse, what agencies collected about Uhse's political and literary activities in Mexico from 1941 to 1948 looks pretty routine. FBI SACs in New York and Mexico knew that Uhse had fought beside the Republicans (who included Communists) in the Spanish Civil War, he was said to have been interned in Le Vernet camp in France ("where the French interned the most dangerous German Communists"),[32] and "since his arrival in Mexico Uhse has occupied a high position among Communists."[33] In the records of Mexico's Secretaría de Gobernación U.S. agents found "file . . . 4/-355.1/120690,"[34] which revealed that Margarita Nelken had helped Uhse to obtain a visa. The Office of Censorship recorded Uhse's communications with the USSR and with suspicious persons in the United States like Maxim Lieber: "The Mexican cable censor suppressed this message with the notation 'Because consignee is highly suspicious . . .' Maxim Lieber is known to Source B as the New York literary agent for Uhse, Anna Seghers, Egon Erwin Kisch, Ludwig Renn, Andre Simone, and the other Alemania Libre characters."[35]

More interesting to Hoover's agents than standard information of this kind was the denunciation of Uhse by the Grupos Socialistas, whose claim that Uhse was a "'Communazi' agent"[36] did not seem so farfetched considering his Nazi past. In 1939 he admitted to the Board of Special Inquiry on Ellis Island that he had been a member of the Nazi Strasser faction in Germany in 1927–28, and he gave up his Nazi Party membership only when Strasser split from the Nazis. Other sources, whose identity has been blacked out in the FBI files, claimed that Uhse came "from 'German military stock,'"[37] that he had been a prominent member of the Nazi Party until 1930 before joining the KPD, and "that he was even once the temporary mayor of [the small northern German town] Itzehoe in the capacity of a Nazi politician."[38] And in October 1946 the FBI files still hinted that Uhse was writing a book about the Nazi movement and "that due to . . . Nazi affiliations, Uhse is not considered by the veteran members of the German Communist group in Mexico as dependable."[39]

The rest of Uhse's file involves Alma Uhse's return to the United States from East Germany at the start of the sixties. Predictably, two issues are raised. First, "whether subject's activities are such that it can be concluded clearly and unmistakably that she is a dangerous individual who could be expected to commit acts inimical to national defense and public safety of the United States in time of emergency."[40] And, second, whether now that she had returned home, she could be exploited as a source of information about East Germany: "If the subject is cooperative, no affirmative steps will be taken during the initial interview to direct her activities . . . the Bureau will be requested to authorize recontact with the subject as a potential security informant."[41]

The interrogations of Alma Uhse were not released to me, but they probably were not very helpful to the agencies. Alma in any case was not listed on the infamous Security Index, nor did agents pursue an attempt through the IRS to convict her of tax fraud. When the suspicion "that subject is or has been engaged in foreign intelligence activities"[42] likewise proved unfounded, the FBI closed the file on the wife of Bodo Uhse, "German communist writer" and "currently a communist official . . . in East Germany"[43] in May 1963.

LUDWIG RENN

Of a 290-page file on Ludwig Renn ("speaks English awkwardly and stutters"),[44] the 183 pages released to me by the FBI and U.S. Army Intelligence in Fort Meade, Maryland, have no apparent central theme.[45] But reports by the postal censors and the U.S. embassy's legal attaché in Mexico, and the correspondence between FBI headquarters in Washington and their branch in Mexico, show features that help to complete our picture of the FBI's work and the activities of the exiles.

Most significant is the unusual interest the Bureau took in Renn's personal and political biography. His real name was Arnold Friedrich Vieth von Golssenau, and the FBI listed as aliases "Vieth Von Golzenau, Veidt Von Goltzenau, Veith Von Goelsenau, Arnold Frietrich Vieth Von Golssenau."[46] Hoover, himself an alleged closet homosexual, was not concerned with Renn's rumored homosexual proclivities as the army had been with those of Klaus Mann ("It is common talk among the Mexican foreign colony that in his personal behavior Renn is a homosexual"),[47] but rather with the "Communazi" traits that Renn shared with Bodo Uhse.

An FBI agent in Mexico reported that Arnold Vieth von Golssenau had served "as a captain on the German Imperial Military Staff" in World War I but later became a dedicated Communist, taught "Military History in the Marxist Workers' School in Berlin"[48] in the late twenties, and, according to a report that Spain's foreign ministry made to the U.S. State Department in 1948, went "to Spain during the Civil War and was immediately made a Major in the Red Army."[49] "Espionage" and "counter-espionage"[50] are the key words in the investigation of Renn, which began with a denunciation.

Hoover got the War Department involved, and asked his SIS agents 239 and 909 to reconnoiter how best to break into Renn's office at Calle Dr. Rio de la Loza 86[51] should the need arise: "The building is under constant care of an armed watchman who neither drinks nor has proved amenable to bribery, . . . is soundly constructed and at least four or five locks probably intervene between the street and the private files of Ludwig Renn. . . . Both in the block in which the building is located and in adjoining blocks, it was noted that numerous signs such as 'Vive la U.S.S.R.,' 'Relaciones con la U.S.S.R.,' etc., are crudely painted on the sides of buildings and walls."[52] "His espousal of Communism and loyalty thereto may well be a cloak of opportunism,"[53] the U.S. "naval attaché" in Mexico surmised at the start of 1943, while Hoover's office informed their SIS man "via diplomatic air pouch" "that Renn, although ostensibly engaged in furthering the 'Free German Movement,' is in reality working in behalf of the Nazis."[54] SIS agents reported rumors about Renn that were being spread in private and in public by the Austrian anti-Communist "Silvio Pizarello von Helmsburg y Tofulotte" and the Polish ambassador to Mexico: that he was "a German Agent" and "leader of the Seventh Column in Mexico"[55] and thought his enemy was not Hitler but "England and other Imperialistic powers."[56] Finally, a G-2 agent completely lost touch with reality in February 1946 when, musing about the "Communazis'" return to Europe, he became convinced that Renn had been instructed by Moscow to meet with German "Field Marshal von Paulus at his headquarters" during his transit through the USSR and then to fly on to Berlin "in order to negotiate with the German and Russian chiefs who are in the Russian zone of occupation."[57]

Less imaginative but more reliable than the intelligence reports that assistant military attachés in Mexico wrote "for general use by any U.S. Intelligence Agency"[58] were the records of the Office of Censorship about Free Germany's mail in the critical weeks of January and February 1943 when the exiles founded their Latin American Committee. "A letter written in German dated January 13, 1943, from Movimiento Alemania Libre . . . to Sr. Elie Sontag, Soma Settlement, Puerto Plata R.D., Republica Dominicana, was recently intercepted at Postal Censorship Miami," the local SAC reported on 4 February to his "Director." "This letter . . . pleads for a united single encircling front."[59] The three-week interval between the date of Renn's letter and the date of the Miami SAC's report suggests that not only the letter but the photocopy and translation of the attached LAFGC manifesto that the censors made on 20 January had to wait for Hoover's approval before release, producing the same kind of delay that afflicted other Free Germany mailings in Latin America.

How complicated and time consuming it was to petition Hoover to release documents is evident from a letter Renn wrote to a potential member of the LAFGC's honorary board of directors, the writer Balder Olden, who lived in Buenos Aires. Renn's letter is dated 24 March 1943. "Exam. date" is 29 March, "Typing date" 3 April, with copies to be sent to "C.P.C., G-2, PCD, 15th Nav. Dist., G-2, CDC, Civ. Intell., Amer. Emb. Trinidad, Jamaica, Cristobal."[60] Five days later, the chief of the examination section of the Office of Censorship in Washington contacted Hoover personally: "Please let us have recommendation as to final disposition of the original communication within the usual three-day period."[61] Assuming that Hoover and his busy colleagues would need more time, and that the reply would be sent back by official channels through Miami, we can understand why the writers of intercepted letters chafed at the long delays, like one exile in Uruguay who commented: "We here think that there is a censor operating somewhere in Mexico who is disrupting the whole system of communication and is holding back issues [of *Freies Deutschland*]."[62]

The FBI knew that Renn wanted to return to Europe as fast as possible. "He has expressed an intention of returning to Europe as soon as he is able to procure passage," the civil attaché in Mexico reported to Washington in July 1946, "and as soon as he has completed the reorganization of Alemania Libre in Mexico City."[63] But the passenger list of the "Marshall Govorov"[64] shows that Renn did not actually depart from his host country until February 1947 in one of the last transport vessels headed for Europe, together with Bruno Frei and Walter Janka. "A visa stop notice"[65] issued by the U.S. consulate against him and other exiles could no more prevent his leaving than Hoover, who in summer 1946 had already instructed his agent on the scene "that you advise the Bureau at the earliest possible date regarding the departure of Ludwig Renn from Mexico, together with information as to his itinerary, passport data, and also similar information regarding those individuals prominent in Communist or related activities who may have accompanied Renn."[66]

One month after Renn sailed away, civil attaché John Speakes closed the case of "Ludwig Renn, with aliases,"[67] classified under "Mexico Subversive Activities"[68] and "Security Matter - C"[69]—and closed his own office too.[70] The CIA had been founded and Hoover had lost the territory of Latin America that he had conquered in 1940.

5

The FBI Today:
Obtaining the Files

INTELLIGENCE AGENCIES ARE NOT normally willing to release their files. Their sources of information would dry up quickly if they did (they say) and potential enemies would escape their nets. And by their bizarre logic, making files public violates the right to privacy because they hold data on the private lives of subjects, and informants and innocent bystanders too. A secret service that voluntarily reveals its methods is unworthy of the name, because it is then no different from any public agency.

Access to secret files thus can be obtained only under duress, during revolution or war, or when one country conquers another. One of the few exceptions to this rule is the United States, where in the progressive sixties and following the Watergate scandal in the seventies, Congress passed legislation giving restricted access to government files. This right of access is guaranteed by the Freedom of Information Act (FOIA) of 1966 and the Privacy Act (PA) of

1974, of which a leaflet published by the House Committee on Government Operations says: "The Freedom of Information Act . . . is based upon the presumption that the government and the information of government belong to the people. . . . With the passage of FOIA . . . the burden of proof was shifted from the individual to the government: the 'need to know' standard was replaced by the 'right to know' doctrine and the onus was upon the government to justify secrecy rather than the individual to obtain access" [26, p. v].

How seriously members of Congress took the need to make public the work of government is shown by the fact that FOIA was expanded and strengthened in 1974–75 over the veto of President Gerald Ford when it became clear that the first version of the law was not strong enough. Since this legislation, anyone, including non-Americans, may apply to the FBI, the INS, the State Department, and on a more limited basis the CIA, MID, and ONI, using a clearly defined procedure and without proving cause. Congress ordained that agencies must answer within ten days, even if the only reply sent is a receipt. Each application is given a FOIPA number: for example, 266,988 for Klaus Mann. The applicant pays no charges for copies provided that the release of documents is in the public interest. Where the files applied for are not the applicant's own, he must prove that the subjects of investigation are deceased or that they consent to the release of their documents.

Agencies have the right but not the obligation to withhold information ("delete" in FBI jargon, "sanitize" in the MID) in any of nine categories defined by law. If this occurs, the applicant can either submit an appeal to the agency itself within a specified period or bring legal proceedings, for which his costs will be reimbursed if his suit is found to have merit. Each file from which information is deleted is accompanied by an "Explanation of Exemptions" listing the numbers of exemptions under the Freedom of Information Act. Exemptions range from (b)(1)(A), "specifically authorized under criteria established by an Executive order to be kept secret in the interest of national defense or foreign policy" and (b)(2), "related solely to the internal personnel rules and practices of an agency," to (b)(9), "geological and geophysical information and data, including maps, concerning wells." The two most frequently cited exemptions, for the German exile writers, are vague enough to allow agencies to use their own discretion: (b)(1), national defense, and (b)(7), which under subheading (D) exempts information that "could reasonably be expected to disclose the identity of a confidential source, including a State, local, or foreign agency or authority or any private institution which furnished information on a confidential basis," and under (E), anything that "would disclose techniques and procedures for law enforcement investigations." In other words, the FBI will black out the names of people who are still living or whose deaths cannot be reliably established; data on the staff and methods of the Bureau; anything relating to national security; data about informants, voluntary or coerced, whose identity is normally protected even in the original field office reports by abbreviations ("T-2") or paraphrases ("confidential" or "highly confidential source").

How flexibly the FBI interprets exemptions is evident in the case of (b)(1), which the Bureau routinely applies to refugees suspected of being Communists, enemy aliens, and potential spies or subversives with international contacts. What should be classified as "secret" and where national security begins and ends depends largely on the ideological preferences of whoever is president at the time. Truman, for example, believed that information should be classified as "top secret," "secret," "confidential," or "restricted." Jimmy Carter, in his Executive Order 12065, ruled that in doubtful cases the lower level of security should be assigned and, if possible, all documents should automatically be declassified after six years. Reagan and his attorney general William French Smith ranked national security far above freedom of information in the early eighties, on the grounds that the public needed more protection from terrorists. And Bill Clinton, who in autumn 1993 reminded people that

EXPLANATION OF EXEMPTIONS

SUBSECTIONS OF TITLE 5, UNITED STATES CODE, SECTION 552

(b) (1) (A) specifically authorized under criteria established by an Executive order to be kept secret in the interest of national defense or foreign policy and (B) are in fact properly classified pursuant to such Executive order;

(b) (2) related solely to the internal personnel rules and practices of an agency;

(b) (3) specifically exempted from disclosure by statute (other than section 552b of this title), provided that such statute (A) requires that the matters be withheld from the public in such a manner as to leave no discretion on the issue, or (B) establishes particular criteria for withholding or refers to particular types of matters to be withheld;

(b) (4) trade secrets and commercial or financial information obtained from a person and privileged or confidential;

(b) (5) inter-agency or intra-agency memorandums or letters which would not be available by law to a party other than an agency in litigation with the agency;

(b) (6) personnel and medical files and similar files the disclosure of which would constitute a clearly unwarranted invasion of personal privacy;

(b) (7) records or information compiled for law enforcement purposes, but only to the extent that the production of such law enforcement records or information (A) could reasonably be expected to interfere with enforcement proceedings, (B) would deprive a person of a right to a fair trial or an impartial adjudication, (C) could reasonably be expected to constitute an unwarranted invasion of personal privacy, (D) could reasonably be expected to disclose the identity of a confidential source, including a State, local, or foreign agency or authority or any private institution which furnished information on a confidential basis, and, in the case of a record or information compiled by a criminal law enforcement authority in the course of a criminal investigation, or by an agency conducting a lawful national security intelligence investigation, information furnished by a confidential source, (E) would disclose techniques and procedures for law enforcement investigations or prosecutions, or would disclose guidelines for law enforcement investigations or prosecutions if such disclosure could reasonably be expected to risk circumvention of the law, or (F) could reasonably be expected to endanger the life of physical safety of any individual;

(b) (8) contained in or related to examination, operating, or condition reports prepared by, on behalf of, or for the use of an agency responsible for the regulation or supervision of financial institutions; or

(b) (9) geological and geophysical information and data, including maps, concerning wells.

SUBSECTIONS OF TITLE 5, UNITED STATES CODE, SECTION 552a

(d) (5) information compiled in reasonable anticipation of a civil action proceeding;

(j) (2) material reporting investigative efforts pertaining to the enforcement of criminal law including efforts to prevent, control, or reduce crime or apprehend criminals, except records of arrest;

(k) (1) information which is currently and properly classified pursuant to Executive Order 12356 in the interest of the national defense or foreign policy, for example, information involving intelligence sources or methods;

(k) (2) investigatory material compiled for law enforcement purposes, other than criminal, which did not result in loss of a right, benefit or privilege under Federal programs, or which would identify a source who furnished information pursuant to a promise that his/her identity would be held in confidence;

(k) (3) material maintained in connection with providing protective services to the President of the United States or any other individual pursuant to the authority of Title 18, United States Code, Section 3056;

(k) (4) required by statute to be maintained and used solely as statistical records;

(k) (5) investigatory material compiled solely for the purpose of determining suitability eligibility, or qualifications for Federal civilian employment or for access to classified information, the disclosure of which would reveal the identity of the person who furnished information pursuant to a promise that his identity would be held in confidence;

(k) (6) testing or examination material used to determine individual qualifications for appointment or promotion in Federal Government service the release of which would compromise the testing or examination process;

(k) (7) material used to determine potential for promotion in the armed services, the disclosure of which would reveal the identity of the person who furnished the material pursuant to a promise that his identity would be held in confidence.

FBI/DOJ

FOIA was important to strengthening the democratic form of government,[1] tried through Executive Order 12958 to release all secret documents more than twenty-five years old.[2] Even for the most well-meaning employees of the FOIPA sections of the various agencies it is hard to define the limits of national security and the meaning of phrases like "unwarranted invasion" and "personal privacy" in exemptions like (b)(7)(C). Whether a document is released or blacked out thus depends not only on the mood in Washington, which shifts with each new administration issuing new executive orders [26, p. 55], but on the personal judgment of the officials in charge, over which the public has no control.

Agencies have other ways to try to get around the Freedom of Information Act. The FBI, for example, obtained blanket permissions from the National Archives and Records Service to destroy records in its field offices, and in cases that did not lead to any legal action, in 1945–46 and again after the Freedom of Information Act was amended in the seventies. But until 1975 the Bureau made only selective use of this permission because Hoover did not want to part with his files.[3] The FBI may delay the release of files for years after acknowledging receipt of a request, claiming that the volume of requests (10,800 cases involving over two million pages in 1998, according to the Bureau) makes it impossible for the two hundred full-time FOIPA staff members to deal with them more quickly. Researchers like Herbert Mitgang, who recently investigated the surprisingly meager dossiers on American writers [143; 166], say that complaints and legal proceedings achieve little more than further delays. The INS and CIA block applicants by requiring them to fill out complicated forms on each individual target of investigation, and to supply documentary sources in English to prove details like the date of the subject's death: a demand that is virtually impossible to meet in the case of many exiles. The FBI has removed numerous State Department documents relating to FBI matters from the National Archives, where for the most part they would have been available to the public without restriction (although not especially well cataloged), leaving no record of what it has taken away.

Applications for files must be made in writing to the FOIPA section of an agency, which in the FBI's case is the Freedom of Information/Privacy Acts Section, Federal Bureau of Investigation, Ninth Street and Pennsylvania Avenue, N.W., Washington, D.C. 20535. Applications are passed to the so-called Search Unit of the Records Service, whose staff checks the sixty-eight million file cards of the General Index[4] to find if the person or institution has a "Main File" or a "see references" note listing cross-references to other files. Next, members of the Initial Processing Unit make copies of the original files, which are given to the Disclosure Section. If the material is "classified"—that is, if it belongs to one of the listed exemptions, as is often the case for exile writers—a Classification Review Unit decides which documents to withhold. The rest go to a specially trained "analyst" [220, p. 4] who reads each document line by line, removes pages or parts of files, blacks out words, sentences, or paragraphs with a special pencil that makes the text illegible only in the photocopy, and fills in an attached form with numbered abbreviations (b)(1) to (b)(9), or makes notes in the margins, indicating the reason for blacking something out. Because the law requires that all information, if not withheld, must remain legible, the grotesque situation arises that an entire text may be blacked out with the exception of a single word, like the subject's name or the notation "Strictly Confidential." The applicant of course never meets the professional FBI blackout artists whose identities are indicated in shorthand: for the documents on Anna Seghers by the abbreviations "Sp2Tap/dd" and "9145 Web/dd." Like Kafka's visitor from the country who stands before the "Door of the Law," once you enter the J. Edgar Hoover Building in Washington you find that the gate between the bare reception hall and the main building is guarded by electronic gatekeepers and that the threshold cannot be crossed by a hapless scholar any more than by a TV crew or by tourists.[5]

Asked "whether a public right to know is merely political rhetoric or is an unenumerated constitutional right protected by the Ninth Amendment" [118, p. 781], Bill Clinton's Justice Department roundly replied: "In sum, the FOIA is a vital, continuously developing mechanism which, with necessary refinements to accommodate ... society's interests in an open and fully responsible government, can truly enhance our democratic way of life."[6] Notwithstanding these brave words, FOIPA does not aim to give unrestricted access to government files allowing subjects of investigation, as well as researchers, to personally examine official archives and work with original documents. This is why, despite the generous provisions of the law, the millions of pages that have been released, and the efforts of agencies to maintain friendly relations with the public through leaflets like *Conducting Research in FBI Records,*[7] many applicants cannot help suspecting that individual documents or entire dossiers are being withheld. Moreover, the fact that civilian and military agencies, the INS, Office of Censorship, and the State Department spent substantial resources of personnel and money over a long period both abroad and at home, in both hot wars and cold, to observe a little group of refugees from Hitler, and that they drew up some fourteen thousand documents reporting these operations that today they not only preserve but censor before their release, says disturbing things about the needs and insecurities of the world's leading Western democracy.

There is no reason to assume that the FBI is intentionally or maliciously withholding material on German exile writers. The forties were too long ago for that, and the scattered handful of exiles not prominent enough to interest the Bureau today. Moreover, the U.S. Congress took a clear (if belated) stand against a national-security state by making government records accessible to a degree unknown elsewhere. No exile writer was seriously harmed by agency operations, which cannot always be said of Americans in the same period; nor can it be said of the victims of secret agencies in other nations and other times. Not one was murdered, tortured, deported back to Europe and turned over to the Gestapo. Communist Party official Gerhart Eisler was the only one to be interned, and even in his case this treatment immediately raised a storm of protest. Attempts to strip former exiles of their American citizenship did not lead to concrete results in any case I know of. Nor do the files indicate that agency interrogations or loyalty hearings had a direct negative influence on a writer's career as happened to thousands of Americans,[8] although this does not mean that the refugees escaped self-censorship in the repressive political climate of the McCarthy era.

The visible catalog of sins committed by the agencies is remarkably small given the size of their operations. Anna Seghers and several others had to spend their exile in Mexico instead of the United States; Lion Feuchtwanger was denied U.S. citizenship and, although aged and ill, could not leave to visit Germany one last time; questions put to Brecht by HUAC suggest that the FBI laid the groundwork for political harassment; Thomas and Erika Mann felt compelled by the American political climate to go into a second exile in Switzerland; Klaus Mann was hounded by interrogators asking embarrassing questions about his private life; many exiles found their names published in blacklists drawn up by the anti-Communist Tenney Committee; letters were destroyed or delivered late; and refugees who had already suffered intense political persecution were made to continue feeling intimidated and anxious.

But the relatively venial nature of agency sins is no reason to dismiss their observation of the German exiles as past history that should now be forgotten. Because as long as thinking people continue to be monitored by secret agencies in New York and Berlin, Los Angeles and Cologne, Moscow and Zurich and their files are not available to examine and correct, and as long as the bad example of other countries does not lead to reflection on our own excesses, we still have a way to go. The starting point might be the dissenting opinion of Justice Louis Brandeis, who in the famous Supreme Court case of *Olmstead v. United States* (1928) was outvoted by his colleagues over whether telephone tapping should be regarded as an invasion of the private life of citizens:

> Decency, security, and liberty alike demand that government officials shall be subjected to the same rules of conduct that are commands to the citizen. In a government of laws, existence of the government will be imperiled if it fails to observe the law scrupulously. . . . To declare that in the administration of the criminal law the end justifies the means . . . would bring terrible retribution. . . .
>
> The makers of our constitution . . . sought to protect Americans in their beliefs, their thoughts, their emotions and their sensations. They conferred, as against the government, the right to be let alone—the most comprehensive of rights and the right most valued by civilized men. To protect that right, every unjustifiable intrusion by the government upon the privacy of the individual, whatever the means employed, must be deemed a violation of the Fourth Amendment. . . .
>
> Experience should teach us to be most on our guard to protect liberty when the government's purposes are beneficent. . . . The greatest dangers to liberty lurk in insidious encroachment by men of zeal, well-meaning but without understanding [17, pp. 575, 572f].

Notes

Preface

1. The names J. Edgar Hoover and Jack B. Tenney, for example, appear just twice each in the 868 pages on the California exiles in Volume 1 of the standard *Deutsche Exilliteratur seit 1933* [42]: in Hoover's case, with reference to the Palmer Raids of 1919–20. In Part 2 (ibid.), 1,817 pages about the exiles in New York name the FBI twice, Hoover not even once. Eike Middell's *Exil in den USA* [141], published in the GDR, and Helmut Pfanner's *Exile in New York: German and Austrian Writers After 1933* [158] do not mention the FBI boss either.

1
J. Edgar Hoover's America
THE RED SCARE AND ENEMY ALIENS

1. Klaus Mann, Letter to Draft Board, 15/4/42, in FBI Report, N.Y., 18/6/46, p. 5 (FBI file, K. Mann).
2. J. Edgar Hoover, Letter to [blacked out], 12/4/56 (FBI file, B. Brecht).
3. Anna Seghers and Viola Brothers Shore, *The Seventh Cross* (unpublished play), p. 2, Viola Brothers Shore Collection, American Heritage Center, U. of Wyoming, Laramie.
4. Anthony Summers caused a stir with his somewhat adventuresome theory that Hoover was himself a closet homosexual and transvestite [205, esp.

pp. 80–95 and 253–58]. Cf. the documentary film "The Secret File on J. Edgar Hoover," based on Summers's book, shown on PBS's *Frontline* in 1993.

5. Hoover, "Brief on the Communist Party: Status of the Communist Party Under the Act of Congress Approved October 16, 1918" [quoted in 89, p. 288].

6. General Intelligence Division Report, quoted in U.S. Congress, House of Representatives, *Hearings Before the Committee on Rules,* 66th Congress, 2nd session, part 1, 1920, p. 142.

7. Ibid., p. 174.

8. *New York Times,* 17/12/19 [quoted in 65, p. 85].

9. *Washington Post,* 3/7/19 [quoted in 65, p. 78].

10. "A Study of 'Witch Hunting' and Hysteria in the United States" (Papers of George M. Elsey, Harry S. Truman Library, Independence, Mo.).

11. Truman, ms. of an address to the U.S. Congress, 8/8/50, p. 5 (President's secretary's file, Harry S. Truman Library, Independence, Mo.).

12. Eugene Tillinger, "The Moral Eclipse of Thomas Mann," *Plain Talk,* December 1949, quoted from a copy in Mann's FBI file.

13. Eugene Tillinger, "Thomas Mann and the Commissar," *New Leader,* 18/6/51, p. 6, quoted from a copy in Mann's FBI file.

14. Stefan Heym did not allow me access to his FBI and MID files. That he himself has the documents is evident from his memoirs, *Nachruf* [78].

SECRET AGENCIES, GOVERNMENT BUREAUS, SURVEILLANCE METHODS

1. Special Agent Elmer Linberg, assigned to Communists and exiles in Los Angeles, says that the FBI, to gain access to Kheifetz's papers, installed a secret door to the L.A. hotel room where the diplomat used to meet a woman friend [cf. 226, p. 109]. Like other agents active in the forties with whom I spoke, Linberg believes that the FBI's interest in the German exiles stemmed at least in part from Kheifetz's attempt through Jewish refugees from Germany to make contact with Robert Oppenheimer and other scientists working on the U.S. atomic bomb project (interview with Linberg, Bridgeport, Calif., 18/9/94). Linberg's recollections are confirmed by the memoirs of Kheifetz's superior in the NKVD, Pavel Sudoplatov: "Kheifetz persuaded Oppenheimer to share information with 'antifascists of German origin,' which provided a rationale for taking Klaus Fuchs to Los Alamos" [204, p. 190]. Atomic spy Klaus Fuchs in turn was recruited by the Soviet embassy through "German Communist Juergen Kuczynski" (ibid., p. 193), an acquaintance of the liter-

ary exiles. Sudoplatov claims that Moscow agent Kheifetz was less successful with another project: "Gregory Kheifetz, our NKVD resident in San Francisco, was trying to recruit agents in the United States to be used in intelligence work for us in Germany, but failed because his connections were
mostly in the Jewish community" (ibid., p. 174; cf. [76]). For contrary views
by historians and former KGB agents, cf. [203; 172; 15]. The link between
atomic espionage and exile writers moreover seems very weak, because the
files virtually never refer to this theme aside from occasional passing references, such as the relationship between Brecht and UCLA professor Hans
Reichenbach, who was interested in the civilian uses of atomic energy.

2. FBI Report, L.A., 5/9/44, p. 15 (FBI file, H. Mann).
3. FBI Report, L.A., 30/3/43, p. 5 (FBI file, B. Brecht; Brecht Archiv, Stiftung
   Archiv der Akademie der Künste, Berlin). Here and wherever I quote this
   report, I refer to the copy in the Brecht archive in Berlin, which has fewer
   blacked-out passages than the copy the FBI supplied to me.
4. T/3 Friediger, Memorandum to Bjarne Braatoy, 12/10/45, p. 1 (OSS,
   1707).
5. FBI Report, L.A., 21/10/44, p. 3 (FBI file, Free German Activities in the
   Los Angeles Area, quoted in National Archives 862.01/11-1144).
6. FBI Report, N.Y., 2/8/45, p. 4 (FBI file, F. C. Weiskopf).
7. Director, FBI, Memorandum to SAC, N.Y., 19/5/47 (FBI file, Erwin Piscator).
8. J. Edgar Hoover, Letter to [blacked out], 26/2/46 (FBI file, Aurora Verlag).
9. FBI Report, N.Y., 10/11/47, p. 16 (FBI file, Lion Feuchtwanger).
10. Undated, unclassified document (FBI file, Ludwig Renn).
11. *Zur Archäologie der Demokratie in Deutschland* [242] is based on OSS
    "Research & Analysis Reports" but shows no familiarity with the FNB ma-
    terial. R&A is also the focus of more recent studies [94; 6].
12. Notice of the first William J. Donovan Memorial Award, conferred on Ed-
    ward Teller, 17/11/59 (FBI file, Emergency Rescue Committee).
13. Brecht, Bertolt, 28/9/43, p. 2 (OSS, 850).
14. Interview with Mr. Kurt Wolff, 12/6/45, p. 1 (OSS, 1576).
15. Ibid., p. 3.
16. Interview with Mr. Ullstein, 28/4/45, p. 1 (OSS, 1485).
17. Pat McCarran chaired the Senate Internal Security Subcommittee and pro-
    duced the McCarran Internal Security Act "requiring the registration of all
    Communists and Communist organizations, establishing a registration
    agency, the Subversive Activities Control Board, and providing for 'inter-
    nal security emergencies' and the detention of suspected 'subversives'"
    [33, p. 362].

18. Herschel V. Johnson, American Legation, Stockholm, Sweden, Memorandum to Secretary of State, 1/9/44, p. 1 (862.01/9-244). In October 1943, Brandt had sent the secretary of state a comprehensive report on "Oppositional Movements in Germany" (National Archives, RG 59, Box 5359).

19. Weiskopf, Frantisek Carl aka Franz, Headquarters, 66th CIC Group, US-AREUR, APO 154, U.S. Army, 7/10/55 (F. C. Weiskopf, Army).

20. WDG Idaho REURAD, Telegram to Asst. Chief of Staff, 11/2/47, p. 1 (Alfred Kantorowicz, Army).

21. Executive Order No. 8985 [79]. This material, comprising three microfilms, includes documents on the founding of the Office of Censorship and reports of its branches, 1941–45. It gives no sources or page numbers, so quotations refer in general terms to the *History of the Office of Censorship*.

22. FBI Laboratory Report, 30/9/44 (FBI file, Ludwig Renn).

23. FBI Report, L.A., 30/6/45, p. 21f (FBI file, B. Brecht).

24. Only a brief description of HUAC is given here because so many studies have already been done on this topic.

25. Attorney General Francis Biddle defined as "fronts" organizations that "were represented to the public for some legitimate reform objective, but actually used by the Communist Party to carry on its activities pending the time when the Communists believe they can seize power through revolution" [29, p. 265].

26. [163, p. 9]. Tenney is quoting from Hoover's speech to graduates of Holy Cross College on 29/6/44, three weeks after American troops landed in France.

27. FBI Report, L.A., 21/10/44, p. 2 (FBI file, Free German Activities in the Los Angeles Area, quoted in National Archives 862.01/11-1144).

2
The FBI and the Exiles in Los Angeles
WITCH HUNTS IN PARADISE

1. FBI Report, L.A., 2/10/44, p. 23 (FBI file, B. Brecht).

2. "Findings and Recommendations" (1940 Report) [29, p. 701].

3. J. Edgar Hoover, "Communism in the United States," in *Confidential—from Washington* (June 1948) [quoted in 88, p. 80f].

4. SAC, L.A., Memorandum to Director, FBI, 24/2/48, p. 2 (FBI file, B. Brecht).

5. Ibid., p. 5.

6. *Hollywood Now,* 26/8/38 [quoted in 10, p. 5].

7. Tenney's newspaper column "Commu-Nazism" has been mentioned above. His book *Red Fascism* was published in 1947 [163].

8. "Findings and Recommendations" (1943 and 1947 reports) [29, p. 498f].

9. Ibid., p. 507.

10. Foreign Nationalities Branch, "Foreign Nationalities Groups in the United States," Memorandum to the Director of Strategic Services, 18/1/45, p. 2 (OSS, 33GE-75).

11. Ibid., p. 4.

12. Ibid., p. 7.

13. There is a scarcity of documents because the INS office in Los Angeles has so far been uncooperative in releasing material.

THE MANN FAMILY FILES
Thomas Mann

1. J. Edgar Hoover, Memorandum to Legal Attaché, Paris, France, 21/8/50.

2. 811.001-Roosevelt, F. D./4583.

3. William E. Dodd, Letter to Secretary of State, 17/12/36, Attachment, p. 1f (862.00 P.R./211).

4. Albert Einstein and T. Mann, Telegram to Cordell Hull, 8/10/38 (840.48 Refugees/796).

5. T. Mann and Dorothy Thompson, Telegram to President of the United States, 13/5/39, p. 1 (752.00114/87).

6. George T. Summerlin, Chief of Protocol, Letter to John Dorfman, 4/1/39, p. 1 (811.001 Roosevelt, F. D./6156).

7. Douglas Parmentier, Letter to John Simmons, 25/4/34 (811.111 Mann, Thomas).

8. Damon C. Woods, Consul, American Consulate General, Toronto, Canada, Letter to Secretary of State, 6/5/38 (811.111 Mann, Thomas).

9. Mrs. Eugene Meyer, Letter to Secretary of State, 2/4/38 (811.111 Mann, Thomas).

10. Cordell Hull, Letter to Mrs. Eugene Meyer, 8/4/38, p. 1 (811.111 Mann, Thomas).

11. Emmy Rado, Memorandum to DeWitt Poole, 29/10/43, p. 1 (OSS, 841).

12. Emmy Rado, Memorandum to DeWitt Poole, 8/11/43 (OSS, 847).

13. T. Mann, Letter to Mr. Berle, 18/11/43, p. 1 (862.01/523).

14. Herbert Lehnert has given a fairly comprehensive portrait of Mann's role in creating the "German Committee," although without knowing the OSS materials or the full scale of the internal debate in the State Department [42, vol. 1, pt. 1, pp. 77ff].

15. Note 11.
16. Note 12, p. 1.
17. Cf. Irving Sherman, Memorandum to Hugh R. Wilson, 6/11/43 (OSS, 847).
18. Ibid.
19. Smith called the founding of the Foreign Nationalities Branch "another OSS intrusion into the diplomatic process" [183, p. 25].
20. DeWitt Poole, Letter to Mr. Berle, 10/11/43, p. 1f (OSS, 855). Cf. correspondence of T. Mann with Agnes Meyer [135, p. 993], ed. Hans Rudolf Vaget, who is unfamiliar with the OSS and State Department documents.
21. A.A.B. [Adolf A. Berle], Memorandum of Conversation, 25/11/43 (FW 862.01/523). Cf. *The Adolf A. Berle Diary, 1937–1971* [14]. On the other hand, the names Thomas Mann, Paul Hagen, Paul Tillich, et al. do not appear in *Navigating the Rapids, 1918–1971: From the Papers of Adolf A. Berle* [152].
22. Siegfried Beer describes Friediger as a "conservative, monarchical Austrian former journalist" [12, p. 136].
23. C. B. Friediger, Memorandum to DeWitt C. Poole, 8/1/44, p. 1, 3f (OSS, 940).
24. Franz Neumann, Memorandum to H. C. DeWitt Poole, 4/1/44 (OSS, 934). Neumann, a leader in the OSS Research & Analysis section, was known for his book *Behemoth: The Structure and Practice of National Socialism* [154], published in 1942. He took over the German Research Section in the State Department after the OSS was dissolved.
25. A[dolf] A. Berle, Memorandum, 26/1/44 (FW862.01/548).
26. Hoover, Letter to Adolf A. Berle, 25/6/43 (862.01/362).
27. Ernst Reuter, Letter to Thomas Mann, 17/3/43, in Burton Y. Berry, American Consulate General, Istanbul, Turkey, Letter to Secretary of State, 13/11/43 (862.01/501).
28. Attachment to Herbert Solow, Memorandum to President [Alvin] Johnson, 19/10/42, p. 1f, and Herbert Solow, Letter to Mr. Davis, 8/9/43 (OSS, 789).
29. John Norman, Report of Conversation with Thomas Mann in Pacific Palisades, California, 8/12 [1944], Memorandum to DeWitt C. Poole, 14/12/44, p. 1 (OSS, 1302). This conversation was previously unknown to Mann scholars (according to T. Mann Archiv, Zurich, Switzerland).
30. Ibid., p. 1f.
31. Ibid., p. 2.
32. Ibid., p. 7.
33. Ibid., p. 2. Mann wrote to Agnes Meyer on 16/6/42 that Haushofer, a major general and supporter of German "geopolitics" at the University of Mu-

nich, "deserves to be shot before many others as soon as we have won" [135, p. 410]. Ewald Banse was mentioned in Mann's diary in June 1942 when Mann criticized the "monstrous publication by a Columbia professor" [128, p. 438] who in a map of postwar Europe showed the territory of Germany enormously expanded.

34. Note 29, p. 6.

35. "Five German Writers Discuss What to Do with Germany," Foreign Nationalities Branch, Memorandum to the Director, OSS, 18/1/45, p. 1 (OSS, 33GE-75).

36. "Who's Who? Thomas Mann," Memorandum of 4/8/42, p. 1 (OSS, 1718).

37. John Norman, Conversation with Emil Ludwig in Pacific Palisades, California, 16/12/44, Memorandum to DeWitt C. Poole, 4/1/45, p. 4 (OSS, 1324).

38. An otherwise unidentified document on Thomas and Heinrich Mann, 28/9/43, stamped "Hollywood, California," p. 4f (OSS, 867).

39. SAC, L.A., Memorandum to Director, FBI, 8/7/48, p. 3 (FBI file, B. Brecht; Brecht Archiv, Berlin, Germany).

40. [Blacked out], Letter to Thomas Mann, Imperial Censorship Bermuda, 4/10/41.

41. Conversation with Elmer Linberg, Bridgeport, Calif., 18/9/94. Cf. Linberg's statement in my television documentary *Im Visier des FBI* [190]: "We talked with him about the German emigré colony in Los Angeles . . . because Thomas Mann was considered to be the dean of the emigré colony . . . we were received in a friendly manner. . . . Thomas Mann knew quite a lot about Hanns Eisler. . . . He was cooperative and we talked with him about three hours."

42. Memorandum to Mr. Nichols, date illegible, probably 29/10/47.

43. Herbert Mitgang, who was first to describe Mann's files, overinterprets the word "references" when he writes: "Eight hundred pages! The effort and treasure that must have been expended to accumulate such a thick file. . . . I was able to obtain only about one hundred pages" [143, p. 57]. Natalie Robins speaks of a "153-page file, consisting of 'approximately 800 references.'" She adopts a Bureau typing mistake when she states, "The FBI 'first became suspicious of him in 1927 when information was received that he was a member of the American Guild for German Cultural Freedom'" [166, p. 434]. The correct year is probably 1937, because the guild (of which Mann chaired the European board of governors) was not founded until 1936.

44. SAC, L.A., to Director, FBI, 25/5/50, p. 1f.

45. [Blacked out], Letter to Hoover, 16/6/51.

46. SAC, N.Y., Memorandum to Director, FBI, 4/9/51, p. 1. Hans Rudolf Vaget [224, p. 193] suggests that the *New Leader* article may have been sent by its author, Eugene Tillinger, but the blacked-out passages make it impossible to specify the source. It is clear, however, that the FBI was somewhat suspicious of their informant: "Bureau files contain considerable data of a controversial nature concerning the correspondent" (Memorandum of 2/7/51, names of sender and receiver are blacked out). The FBI consequently was not interested in the material he offered: "This case is being placed in a closed status, and [blacked out] will not be requested to furnish his material for photostating UACB [unless advised to contrary by the Bureau]." (SAC, N.Y., Memorandum to Director, FBI, 4/9/51, p. 2.) On the controversy between T. Mann and Tillinger, see Mann, *Tagebücher, 1951–1952* [132].

47. Liaison Representative, Heidelberg, Germany, Memorandum to Director, FBI, 11/1/55.

48. David Bruce, U.S. Foreign Service, Paris, Memorandum to State Dept., 17/5/50 (751.001/5-1750).

49. D. Bruce, Telegram to State Dept., 15/5/50 (751.00/5-1550).

50. A letter from G. B. Fischer, which is also in State Department file 511.62A21/5-2752, indicates that the publisher appealed to the department for advice because of the international aspects of the legal dispute. Cf. the dispute between Fischer and Aufbau [126, esp. pp. 579–601] and the comments and notes of Inge Jens in [132].

51. S. Fischer Verlag, Letter to the Börsenverein Deutscher Verleger- und Buchhändler-Verbände, 5/5/52, p. 2 (511.62A21/5-2752).

52. Walter Janka, Letter to Thomas Mann, 22/3/52 [93, p. 288].

53. Application for a Certificate of Arrival and Preliminary Form for a Declaration of Intention, 3/11/38 (INS).

54. Declaration of Intention, 2/5/39 (INS).

55. U.S. Department of Justice, Immigration and Naturalization Service, L.A. District, Form 16-4, 4/1/44, p. 1 (INS).

56. Ibid., p. 3.

57. Ibid.

58. Statement of Facts to Be Used by the Clerk of Court in Making and Filing My Petition for Naturalization, n.d. (INS).

59. Certificate of Naturalization, 23/6/44 (INS).

60. U.S. Department of Justice, Form 16-21, 13/1/44, p. 1f (INS).

61. Report of Investigation of Paul Thomas Mann, 7/4/44 (INS).

62. Ibid., 6/4/44 (INS).

63. Ibid., 8/4/44 (INS).

64. [219, p. 11726] Mann describes the hearing in *Tagebücher, 1940–43:* "Extremely pleasant and flattering treatment. . . . A few questions, personal details. Was glad when it was over" [128, p. 402].

65. Apart from summaries of press reports from *Counterattack,* the *Los Angeles Herald-Express,* et al., the extant FBI files on Mann contain remarkably few concrete traces of the personal courage and moral outrage he demonstrated publicly and privately in opposing HUAC after the war ended. Many of his statements were readily accessible in publications and through the postal censors. He sharply criticized HUAC on the radio in 1948, for example: "As an American citizen of German birth . . . I testify that I am very much interested in the moving picture industry and that . . . I've seen a great many Hollywood films. If Communist propaganda had been smuggled into any of them, it must have been thoroughly hidden" [133, p. v]. Not long after, speaking to the Peace-Group in Hollywood, he responded with fury to the Mundt-Nixon Bill, formulated with the help of his former State Department contact Adolf Berle, which proposed to curb the alleged Communist threat by a registration procedure that Mann interpreted as "one powerful and threatening step closer to an American Fascism" [130, p. 926]. And in response to the trial of the Hollywood Ten, he gave a statement in October 1948 to Rev. Stephen H. Fritchman, pastor of the First Unitarian Church of Los Angeles who baptized four of Mann's grandchildren, in which he said, among other things: "The case of the Los Angeles Ten is but one symptom—if a very outstanding and a particularly shocking one—of the incipient decline of legal security which we have of short been witnessing in this country. . . . [T]he American people . . . have never known, never experienced, fascism, and may not recognize its maturing features in what is happening here. As an American citizen of German birth and one who has been through it all, I deem it not only my right but my solemn duty to state: We—the America of the Un-American Activities Committee; the America of the so-called loyalty checks . . . —are well on our way towards the fascist police state" (ibid., p. 953f).

66. W. F. Kelly, Asst. Commissioner, Enforcement Division, Central Office, Memorandum to District Director, L.A., California, 2/4/51 (INS).

67. FWW, Index Card, 4/5/51 (INS).

68. T. Mann, Form 16-21, 26/4/51, p. 2 (INS).

69. H. R. Lanton, District Director, L.A. District, INS, Letter to Richard B. Hood, SAC, L.A., 26/4/51, p. 2 (INS).

70. Information from 1600-37 obtained May 21, 1951, p. 1f (typescript with no listed source, addressee, or date) (INS). Cf. Hanns Eisler's FBI dossier [199].

71. Thomas Mann, Deferred Action Case, 9/3/55 (INS).
72. Handwritten file note, 21/1/53 (INS).
73. Note 71.
74. Clare H. Timberlake, Consul General, American Consulate General, Hamburg, Germany, Memorandum to Dept. of State, 19/6/53, p. 1f (811.41 Mann, Thomas/6-1953).
75. Handwritten file note, 10/8/56 (INS).

Heinrich Mann

1. T. Mann, "Brief über das Hinscheiden meines Bruders Heinrich" [134, p. 336f].
2. Biographical sketch, no title or author, 25/9/43, p. 2f (OSS, 867).
3. H. Mann, Letter to Wolfgang Bartsch, 3/2/49 [quoted in 120, p. 331].
4. Note 2, p. 3.
5. R. B. Hood, SAC, L.A., Letter to Director, FBI, 16/3/45 (FBI file, B. Brecht).
6. Hoover, Memorandum to SAC, L.A., 3/1/46.
7. SAC, L.A., Memorandum to Director, FBI, 10/2/49.
8. H. Mann, Letter to Felix Bertaux, 3/4/45.
9. H. Mann, Letter to Herbert Mann, 21/2/44.
10. H. Mann, Letter to Ludwig Renn, 12/6/42.
11. R. Kupferberg, Letter to H. Mann, 30/6/42, p. 1f.
12. Paul Merker of Comite Latino Americano de Alemanes Libres, Letter to H. Mann, 13/5/43.
13. H. Mann, Letter to P. Merker, n.d. [16/3/45] [cf. 96, vol. 2, p. 411].
14. FBI Report, L.A., 5/9/44, p. 1.
15. Ibid., p. 2.
16. Ibid., p. 1.
17. Ibid., p. 7.
18. Ibid., p. 8.
19. Ibid., p. 15. Thomas Mann withdrew his signature from the joint declaration shortly afterward [125, pp. 339ff].
20. Nicholas Alagan, FBI Report, N.Y., 6/10/44, p. 20, attachment to Hoover, Memorandum to Frederick B. Lyon, Chief, Division of Foreign Activity Correlation, State Dept., 19/12/44 (811.00B/12-1944).
21. Note 14, p. 22.
22. Director, FBI, Memorandum to Peyton Ford, Asst. to the Attorney General, 25/10/49, and Hoover, Memorandum to Jack D. Neal, Associate Chief, Division of Security, State Dept., 25/10/49.

23. H. Mann, Letter to F. C. Weiskopf, 19/4/49 (F. C. Weiskopf Archiv, Stiftung Archiv der Akademie der Künste, Berlin, Germany).

24. Hoover, Memorandum to Commissioner, Bureau of Internal Revenue, Treasury Dept., 6/1/50, and FBI Report, L.A., 28/3/50, p. 7.

25. Cf. H. Mann's letter of 18/9/49 in *Allein mit Lebensmittelkarten ist es nicht auszuhalten . . . Autoren- und Verlegerbriefe, 1945–1949,* ed. Elmar Faber, Carsten Wurm (Berlin: Aufbau, 1991), p. 198.

26. Report of European Command, Army, 9/3/50, p. 3. Attachment to [illegible] Smith, General Staff, U.S. Army, Letter to Hoover, [illegible] April 1950.

27. Ibid.

28. Ibid., p. 4.

29. Alien Registration Form, U.S. Dept. of Justice, INS, 19/12/40 (INS).

30. Application for a Certificate of Arrival and Preliminary Form for a Declaration of Intention, U.S. Dept. of Justice, INS, 31/3/41 (INS).

31. Note 29, p. 2.

32. Ibid.

33. Note 30, p. 2f.

34. Note 14, p. 4.

35. FBI Report, L.A., 21/2/45, p. 4.

36. FBI Reports, L.A., 6/12/44, p. 1, and 23/8/45, p. 5f.

37. Note 14, p. 27; and FBI Reports, L.A., 6/12/44, p. 1, and 10/2/49, p. 2.

38. Note 14, p. 14.

39. H. Mann, Letter to Johannes R. Becher, 12/7/45, quoted in FBI Report, L.A., 23/8/45, p. 4.

40. Undated page.

41. FBI Report, L.A., 14/12/49, p. 3.

42. FBI Report, L.A., 28/3/50, p. 1.

43. FBI Report, L.A., 2/6/50, p. 3.

44. SAC, L.A., Memorandum to Director, FBI, 17/4/50.

45. FBI Report, L.A., 16/8/50, p. 2.

46. Ibid., p. 1.

47. Ibid., p. 2.

48. SAC, N.Y., Memorandum to Director, FBI, 28/1/52.

Klaus Mann

1. Undated, anonymous attachment to A. M. Thurston, FBI, Memorandum to Mr. Foxworth, 19/5/41, p. 2. This and all other cited files on Klaus Mann have the FBI classification 65-17395, which for unknown reasons was also assigned to Erika Mann.

2. Ibid.
3. Handwritten note, 10/8/56 (INS).
4. SAC, L.A., to Director, FBI, 13/9/51. This memorandum belongs to Erika Mann's FBI file.
5. Free Germans, Postal Censorship, Memorandum, 20/12/43, p. 49 (OSS, 964).
6. Walter Schevenels, general secretary of the Provisional Executive Board of the International Federation of Trade Unions, in 1940 and 1941 traveled on behalf of the IFTU to the United States, where his delegation was received by President Roosevelt and leading officials of the American Federation of Labor. He had worked for refugee aid in unoccupied France and helped members of his union to resettle in Britain and the United States [176, pp. 282f, 290f].
7. MID, War Dept. (L.A.), Report of 10/6/43, p. 1.
8. For example, the SAC in Washington turned Zurich publisher Emil Oprecht into a "Dr. Ottrecht" (FBI Report, Washington, 26/10/41, p. 2) and the Querido Verlag in Amsterdam into "Kuerido Publishers" (ibid., p. 4). Thomas Mann's *Unordnung und frühes Leid* (Early sorrow) becomes *"'Unrube Und Fruches Leid'"* in a memorandum by the New York SAC, 18/6/42, p. 2.
9. FBI Report, N.Y., 18/6/42, p. 1.
10. FBI Report, L.A., 20/3/42, p. 2.
11. Very few letters have been preserved in Klaus Mann's FBI file (unlike those of Heinrich Mann, Anna Seghers, et al.).
12. Personal Description of Deponent, n.d. (INS).
13. Note 9, p. 9.
14. Ibid., p. 5f. Klaus Mann's diary entry for this date states: "Today, first medical exam. (Way uptown. Civilian doctor. Blood test.)" [123, p. 95].
15. "Report of Investigation Under Immigration Laws," 5/9/40, p. 7 (INS).
16. Note 10, p. 4.
17. Ibid., p. 3.
18. Note 9, p. 1.
19. J. F. Delany, District Director, INS, Baltimore District, Memorandum to Edward J. Shaughnessy, Deputy Commissioner, INS, Washington, 28/5/43, p. 1 (INS).
20. MID, War Dept. (Governor's Island), Report of 9/6/43, p. 1 (MID).
21. Interview with Gerhard Seeger [Seger] and Rudolph [Rudolf] Katz, p. 1 (Memo G) (MID).
22. Interview with Charles Henry Rieber, Report of 9/6/43, p. 1, L.A. (Memo A) (MID).

23. Interview with Eileen Garrett, Report of 31/5/43, Governor's Island (Memo I) (MID).

24. Note 9, p. 9. Cf. Interview with Thomas Quinn Curtiss (Note 20, p. 12f [Memo A] [MID]) with an FBI report (date illegible) that states: "On the evening of 10/23/1942, subject and a soldier were seen in the bar of the Hotel Bedford, [illegible], New York City. When soldier accompanied Mann to his apartment, located in the hotel, he was questioned, and later when detained by local police, stated his name was John C. Fletcher, and admitted that he was a deserter from Camp [illegible], Georgia since November 1941. He also admitted . . . that he had syphilis. It was noted that both Fletcher and Mann were well-known by the Hotel Bedford staff and believed to be homosexuals." In his diaries, Klaus Mann gave a very detailed description of this evening, which ended in a suicide attempt ("I try to slit open the artery in my right wrist. But the knife is . . . pretty filthy" [123, p. 119]).

25. FBI Report, N.Y., 4/2/43, p. 1f.

26. Paul Abrahamson, Interview with Klaus Mann, 30/8/43, p. 2 (MID).

27. Ibid., Report, 7/9/43, p. 1 (MID).

28. Note 26, p. 3.

29. Note 27. "Sewing" = sowing.

30. Interview with Thomas Quinn Curtis, 10/2/43, Note 20, p. 6 (MID).

31. Ibid., p. 7.

32. Ibid., p. 8.

33. Note 9, 18/6/42, p. 13f.

34. Ibid., p. 9.

35. Note 15, p. 8 (INS).

36. Ibid., p. 9.

37. Note 9, p. 13f.

38. MID interview with Thomas Mann, 4/6/43, War Dept. (L.A.), 9/6/43, p. 1f (Memo C) (MID). Interestingly, Mann's diaries mention neither the interview nor the name Dawson.

39. Ibid., p. 2.

40. Memorandum on FBI Report, 20/3/43, p. 1 (Memo E) (MID).

41. Note 10, p. 4.

42. Note 7, p. 2 (Memo E) (MID).

43. Ibid., Interview with Bruno Frank, p. 1 (Memo B) (MID).

44. Ibid., Interview with First Sergeant Merritt, 72nd Training Battalion, Camp Robinson, Arkansas, 20/5/43 (Memo [illegible]) (MID).

45. Note 7.

46. Note 21, 31/5/43, p. 1.

47. Note 1, p. 1.
48. Note 27, p. 2.
49. Note 7, p. 4.
50. Note 27.
51. Certificate of Naturalization, 25/9/43 (INS).

Erika Mann

1. An earlier version of this chapter published in *neue deutsche literatur* (1993) drew strong reactions from the press in Germany and the United States that say much about people's emotions in a time of nonstop revelations about the Stasi and virtually nothing about the FBI file of Erika Mann (with which the commentators were largely unfamiliar). The majority of newspaper reports labeled Erika Mann an "informer" or even a "spy" (*Bild Zeitung,* 13/7/93), evidently based on a widely circulated German press release of which I was unaware and without having read my article, in which I deliberately avoided such terms. Other commentators, including contributors to major national newspapers, expressed doubt that Mann had contacted the FBI, or claimed that the contacts were meaningless; but in any case they were only able to express opinions, since they had not read her dossier or absorbed no new information from it. I have already replied elsewhere to the emotional views of Mann's biographer Irmela von der Lühe [195], who in a study published by Campus in 1993 alluded to the FBI material, curiously enough, only in passing and with phrases like "Erika briefly offered her services to the FBI" [111, p. 159], and who has since repeated this dismissal on several occasions. *Der Spiegel* (29, 19/7/93, p. 144f), the *New York Times* (18/7/93, p. 11), and German television ("Arena," NDR, 19/8/93 and EINS PLUS, 8/9/93) used caution and checked facts with me before reporting the Mann story, although the two print media also felt obliged to use the word "informant." Several radio stations consulted me in live interviews (HR 3 and HR 2 on 13/7/93; BR 2, 14/7/93; Radio Brandenburg, 18/7/93 et al.), while the *Frankfurter Allgemeine Zeitung* and the *Süddeutsche Zeitung* printed various reports on the "case" of Erika Mann but did not give me an opportunity to comment. Elisabeth Mann Borgese and other personal witnesses expressed their views in my documentary film *Im Visier des FBI* [190]. Cf. the distorted reporting by the German press of the cautious and nuanced arguments of American historian William Chase in his essay [37] on Diego Rivera's short-term contacts with the U.S. embassy in Mexico [64; 150].

2. Because FBI headquarters kept a joint file on Erika and Klaus Mann, no

precise records exist to tell us the size of the material on Erika. The joint designation 65-17395 continued to be used even after June 1943, when the FBI stated the intention (which was never carried out) of separating the records: "The title of this case is being changed in order to drop the name of subject's sister, Erica Mann Auden therefrom inasmuch as investigation to date fails to indicate that she is involved in activities inimical to the United States" (FBI Report, N.Y., 18/6/42, p. 2 [FBI file, Klaus Mann]).

3. The INS informed me in a letter dated 29/9/88 that in addition to the 375 pages that they would not turn over to me, Erika Mann's INS file contained 158 pages of "duplicated materials" that they would not release either.

4. E. A. Tamm, Memorandum to Director, FBI, 4/6/40.

5. FBI Report, N.Y., 15/12/41, p. 4.

6. Director, FBI, Memorandum to SAC, L.A., 6/7/51. Thomas Mann's diary entry reveals—and misspells—the name blacked out by the FBI: "Dark morning. Erika visited by FBI about matters concerning Angell-B[odo] Uhse" [132, p. 74]. What Mann does not mention is that the interview had to do above all with the Burgess-MacLean spy case. A two-page telegram sent from the L.A. Field Office at "4-58 PM" that same day to FBI headquarters in Washington says: "Mrs. W. H. Auden, aka. Erica Mann . . . knows nothing of any pro Soviet or pro Communist tendencies of Burgess in addition to Auden, Isherwood, Spender and Howard. She believes that Burgess would possibly be known to Louis McNiece and Cyrill Connolly, both writers who are presently in London, and to Paul Willerd—or Willert-, believed to be Air Attache to the British Embassy in Paris. Willerd described as being quote leftist unquote in political thinking but not to the extent of subscribing to the aims and purposes of the CP as Spender did" (Hood, L.A., Telegram to Director, 19/6/51, p. 1).

7. SAC, L.A., Memorandum to Director, FBI, 15/8/51, p. 2.

8. Director, FBI, Memorandum to SAC, L.A., 13/9/51. File notes labeled "On Yellow Only," written on the yellow carbon paper used at FBI headquarters, held especially controversial information that was not revealed even to field office special agents (e.g., the reference in Feuchtwanger's files to FBI surveillance of U.S. Senator Thomas Kuchel).

9. Francis Biddle later became attorney general and was Hoover's direct superior in 1941–45.

10. Note 4.

11. FBI Report, Washington, 24/10/41, p. 2.

12. E. A. Tamm, Memorandum to Director, FBI, 10/6/40. P. E. Foxworth at the time was assistant director of the Domestic Intelligence Division and shortly after became assistant FBI director and SAC of the New York Field Office.

13. Walter Winchell, long "one of J. Edgar Hoover's favorite leaking journalists" [143, p. 142], had cooperated with Hoover in 1939 in arresting Louis "Lepke" Buchhalter, the boss of an infamous New York extortion ring and head of Murder, Incorporated. In this spectacular operation, Winchell and Hoover, ostensibly without any backup, met the gangster, who turned himself in voluntarily, believing that he would receive a mild penalty. In 1944, Lepke was executed in the electric chair.

14. FBI Memorandum, 11/6/40. The soldier's letter was not preserved in Mann's file.

15. Director, FBI, Memorandum to SAC, L.A., 13/9/51.

16. Note 5.

17. Ibid., p. 5.

18. Ibid., p. 2.

19. Ibid., p. 4.

20. SAC, Boston, Memorandum to Director, FBI, 21/2/45.

21. (FBI) Chicago, Telegram to Director and SACs, 17/6/51.

22. The British press circulated the report that Burgess on the morning of his escape went to Spender trying to learn Auden's address in Italy [cf. 206, pp. 100, 123].

23. Hood, L.A., Telegram to Director, 19/6/51, p. 1.

24. Ibid., p. 2.

25. Erika Mann, "Account of FBI-'Inquisition,'" handwritten ms., n.d., no place, pp. 1–3 (Erika Mann Archiv, Handschriften-Sammlung, Stadtbibliothek München, Germany).

26. An FBI informant commented as follows in spring 1942 on the relationship between Mann and Auden: "Erica Mann had no use for marriage at all and had discussed this point with informant's wife. Also, he stated . . . that this marriage might possibly have been for citizenship purposes" (FBI Report, N.Y., 18/6/42, p. 13 [FBI file, Klaus Mann]).

27. FBI Report, L.A., 9/11/51, pp. 1–3. Mann remembered events differently from the special agents. After meeting with the FBI, she wrote to her New York lawyer Victor Jacobs, who had recently represented her in dealings with the immigration authorities: "I had the extreme pleasure of welcoming . . . two charming gentlemen of the F.B.I. bent, this time, on talking turkey. Our two hour conversation wound up as follows: They: 'You claim that you are not now and have never been a member of any communist party and that you are not now and have never been an agent—paid or unpaid—of the Soviet government or the Comintern?' I: 'I do indeed'" (E. Mann, Letter to Victor Jacobs, 8/11/51 [E. Mann Archiv, see Note 25]. Cf. Thomas Mann's diary entry: "1 1/2 hour inter-

rogation of Erika by the two FBI men. Paid Stalin agent or party member? Unbelievable" [132, p. 124].

28. Note 27, p. 2 [cf. contrary versions in 131, pp. 35, 44, 51, 586, 657].
29. E. Mann, Letter to Duff Cooper, 22/9/48 (E. Mann Archiv, see Note 25).
30. FBI Report, L.A., 16/2/42, p. 1.
31. FBI memorandum, 11/6/40.
32. Anonymous undated attachment to Memorandum from A. M. Thurston to Mr. Foxworth, 19/5/41, p. 2.
33. F. J. Baumgardner, Memorandum to A. H. Belmont, 5/2/51.
34. FBI Report, London, 23/7/54.
35. Erika Mann, "Selbstanzeige: Interview mit Fritz J. Raddatz" (1965), p. 21 (Typescript in E. Mann Archiv, see Note 25).
36. Note 5, p. 3.
37. Note 11, p. 4.
38. Ibid., p. 5.
39. Ibid., p. 9.
40. FBI Report, Newark, 2/7/43, p. 1.
41. Ibid., p. 2.
42. Note 5, p. 6.
43. FBI Report, N.Y., 4/4/51, p. 2.
44. "Dr. Brandt, Erika Mann Don't Agree," *Palo Alto Times,* 27/3/50.
45. Note 30, p. 2.
46. Note 43, p. 3.
47. Ibid., p. 4.
48. Ibid., p. 6.
49. Ibid., p. 8.
50. Note 26, p. 1.
51. Note 5, p. 3.
52. Note 30, p. 2.
53. Note 43, p. 5.
54. Note 20, p. 2.
55. Cf. E. Mann's "Statement Concerning Application for U.S. Citizenship," 30/1/50, written in the third person: "In January 1942 joined the staff of the Coordinator of Information in New York and resigned when her activities as an adviser had become superfluous" (E. Mann Archiv, see Note 25).
56. C. B. Friediger, Memorandum of Conversation with S. Aufhäuser, 1/12/43, p. 2 (OSS, 896).
57. John Norman, Report of conversation with Lion Feuchtwanger at Pacific Palisades, California, on 10 December, Memorandum to DeWitt C. Poole, 19/12/44, p. 4 (OSS, 1308).

58. See Erika Mann's "Statement (concerning the possible reasons for which naturalization is being held up)," 30/1/50, also written in the third person: "When, in the summer of 1947, Miss Mann found it impossible to obtain permission to enter the American zone of Germany, she succeeded in having a Washington friend of hers get a glimpse at her file" (E. Mann Archiv, see Note 25).

59. Note 15. What a thin line separated reality and fantasy in those days is evident from Wysling and Schmidlin's biography of Thomas Mann, which says that Erika, who probably only suspected that deportation proceedings were under way against her but did not know for certain, was rather unstable at the time: "Exhausted as she was, she continued thinking in the old categories and was amazed when her articles were no longer accepted. . . . Besides, the use of drugs had weakened her physically and she inclined to depression. During her stay in Switzerland . . . she deteriorated into psychotic states, believing that the American bloodhounds were waiting for her to come back to intern and dehumanize her." When she traveled to New York and was "simply ignored," that "hurt her again . . . because she had become unimportant while she had felt she was very important" [136, p. 441].

60. James E. Riley, Acting Asst. Commissioner, Enforcement Division, INS, Memorandum to Hoover, 12/6/51 (INS).

61. Note 43, p. 10. Erika Mann's letter to Edward J. Shaughnessy, INS Director, N.Y., is reproduced in [116, pp. 275–80].

DOSSIERS
Bertolt Brecht

1. Henry Marx, "Unterredung mit Bert Brecht," *New Yorker Staats-Zeitung und Herold,* 7/3/43 [quoted in 42, vol. 2, pt. 2, p. 1551].

2. FBI Report, L.A., 6/3/43, p. 1.

3. John Fuegi speaks of a "1,100-page Brecht FBI file" [62, p. 426] but quotes no material that was not released to me. James Lyon was given "a total of 427 pages" of a file that the FBI said contained "approximately 1000" pages [113, p. 362]. No "FOIPA Deletion Page Information Sheets" were attached to the copies released to me, but presumably the thousand pages do not all belong to Brecht's own file. Rather they include cross-references to other files in which Brecht is mentioned, however briefly.

4. R. B. Hood, Letter to Director, FBI, 16/4/43.

5. Ibid., p. 1f. This passage led John Fuegi to identify Ruth Fischer as a possible informant [62, p. 428].

6. Ibid.

7. R. B. Hood, Letter to Director, FBI, 18/5/44.
8. FBI Report, L.A., 2/10/44, p. 13.
9. Brecht, Bertolt, 28/9/43, p. 2 (OSS, 860).
10. C. B. Friediger, Memorandum to DeWitt C. Poole, 7/1/44, p. 3 (OSS, 940).
11. Friediger, Memorandum to DeWitt C. Poole, 22/2/44, p. 1 (OSS, 1000).
12. Note 8, p. 21.
13. Ibid., p. 25.
14. FBI Report, L.A., 21/10/44, p. 3f (FBI file, Free German Movement in the Los Angeles Area, quoted in National Archives 862.01/11-1144).
15. The Eisler brothers' experience was typical: Hanns was deported although he wanted to stay, and Gerhart was interned even though he wanted to return to Europe as soon as possible.
16. A blacked-out source is quoted by the FBI as saying that "in placing his name on the American quota waiting list, he indicated that he possessed a German passport written in New York in 1936" (Note 8, p. 9).
17. Ibid., p. 29.
18. Hood, Letter to Director, FBI, 8/8/47, p. 1f.
19. J. P. Coyne, Memorandum to D. M. Ladd, 5/11/47.
20. Hoover, Telegram to SAC, N.Y., 23/10/47.
21. Hood, Letter to Director, FBI, 5/11/47.
22. SAC, N.Y., Teletype to Director, 20/3/56.
23. W. A. Branigan, Memorandum to A. H. Belmont, 21/3/56.
24. SAC, N.Y., Teletype to Director, 22/3/56. This episode was confirmed by Eric Bentley (my conversation with him, New York, 10/9/94).
25. FBI Report, N.Y., [illegible] August 1945, p. 16.
26. FBI Report, L.A., 30/3/43, p. 6.
27. Note 2, p. 2. "Source A" was "Mr. and Mrs. Fritz Nuernberger" (ibid., p. 11; Bertolt Brecht Archiv, Stiftung Archiv der Akademie der Künste, Berlin).
28. Ibid., p. 1.
29. Ibid., p. 2.
30. Note 8, p. 16.
31. Note 26, p. 1. See also [202].
32. Ibid., p. 4.
33. Hood, Letter to Director, FBI, 18/6/43, p. 1.
34. Hoover, Letter to SAC, L.A., 22/5/43.
35. FBI Report, L.A., 10/7/43, p. 1.
36. A notation indicating that Brecht's file was still active in relation to another, top secret case ("The [blacked out] investigation has been developed along extremely confidential lines" [Hood, Note 4, p. 2]) cannot be deciphered without further information.

37. [62, p. 425]. Ernest J. van Loon, special agent at the Los Angeles Field Office, recalls checking Brecht because of the curfew for aliens (my conversation with him in Phoenix, 18/11/94). That van Loon in fact worked on Brecht's case is attested by (among other things) references in FBI reports from New Orleans and Cincinnati on 11 and 30/11/44 to "Report of Special Agent Ernest J. van Loon [illegible] 10/2/44 at Los Angeles, Calif.," p. 1 (Brecht Archiv, see Note 27).

38. Note 8, p. 19.

39. Ibid., p. 33.

40. Ibid., p. 17.

41. Notation in SAC, L.A., Teletype to Director, 5/11/45.

42. Note 8, p. 19.

43. Hood, Letter to Director, FBI, 21/2/45, p. 1f.

44. Hood, Letter to Director, FBI, 16/3/45.

45. FBI Report, L.A., 1/2/45, p. 4.

46. Hoover, Teletype to SAC, L.A., 9/4/45.

47. Hood, Teletype to Director, FBI, 5/11/45.

48. Hood, Letter to Director, FBI, 5 [illegible] 1945.

49. FBI Report, L.A., 30/6/45, p. 32.

50. Hood, Letter to Director, FBI, 30/6/45.

51. Note 49, p. 31.

52. Ibid., p. 34.

53. Ibid., p. 15.

54. FBI Report, L.A., 24/10/45, p. 7.

55. Ibid., p. 13: "On August 20, 1945," the report continues, "pursuant to information received on August 16, 1945 from CNDI La. BB-1 to the effect that Eugene Tumantsev, Soviet Vice Consul at Los Angeles, had made an appointment with Bert Brecht for 7 P.M. on August 20th, Special Agents [blacked out] and reporting Agent observed Tumantsev arrive in a Consulate car driven by the chauffeur. Tumantsev's arrival at the Brecht residence was at 7:05 P.M., at which time he was observed to enter, where he remained for approximately thirty minutes. At the time of Tumantsev's arrival a green Buick station wagon bearing California license 14 D 565, was observed at the Brecht residence. This car is registered to Elsa Lancaster [Lanchester], 14954 Corona Del Mar, Pacific Palisades, California. Elsa Lancaster is the wife of Charles Laughton, and shortly after Tumantsev's arrival an individual appearing to be Laughton departed in the station wagon."

56. Note 49, p. 31.

57. Hood, Letter to Director, FBI, 17/9/45, p. 2.

58. Note 49, p. 36.

59. This hotel still exists under the name Star Dust Motor Hotel with the slightly changed address 3202 Wilshire Blvd.

60. Hood, Letter to Director, FBI, 18/5/44; Note 8, p. 30; Hood, Letter to Director, FBI, 10/1/45; Hoover, Letter to SAC, L.A., 6/11/45; J.C. Strickland, Memorandum to D. M. Ladd [date illegible, c. December 1945].

61. Note 25, p. 11.

62. Ibid., p. 6.

63. Note 49, p. 5.

64. Ibid., p. 7.

65. Note 45, p. 20.

66. Note 8, p. 21.

67. Note 25, p. 11.

68. Ibid., p. 12.

69. Note 2, p. 2.

70. FBI Report, L.A., 2/1/45, p. 4 (list of names).

71. Note 8, p. 23.

72. Hood, Letter to Director, FBI, 5/4/45, p. 1.

73. FBI Report, L.A., 2/5/45, p. 3.

74. Note 54, p. 6. Marianne Hoppe, a leading actress in Germany, and Gustaf Gründgens, who earned the enmity of many exiles for his career as a theater manager and actor in the Third Reich (cf. Klaus Mann, *Mephisto*, 1936), married in 1936.

75. FBI Report, L.A., [illegible] August 1945, p. 5.

76. SAC, Springfield, Memorandum to Director, FBI, 17/7/52, p. 2.

77. Note 8, p. 15.

78. FBI Report [date and place illegible], p. 4.

79. FBI Report, N.Y., 2/5/45, p. 3.

80. Note 54, p. 5. The names Bronard and Zeiss could not be verified at the Brecht archive in Berlin.

81. Note 8, p. 16.

82. Note 72, p. 1f.

83. SAC, L.A., Memorandum to Director, FBI, 9/5/45.

84. If Alexander Charns is right [36, p. 17] and the FBI in 1945 really carried out only "519 wiretaps and 186 buggings," this would mean that Hoover took Brecht's case very seriously.

85. Note 49, p. 4. The FBI appeared confused by the abbreviation "e.p.e.p." by Brecht's signature in this and other letters from Brecht to Berlau: "et prope et procul," "the same when near or far away."

86. Note 45, p. 14 (Brecht Archiv, see Note 27).

87. Source A is described as follows in a report in the Brecht archive in Berlin

(see Note 27): "A highly confidential source known to Special Agents Daniel F. Cahill and Ernest J. Van Loon" (Note 49, p. 39).

88. Ibid., p. 2.
89. Ibid., p. 18.
90. Ibid., p. 20.
91. Note 25, p. 11.
92. Note 49, p. 21.
93. Ibid., p. 22.
94. Karin Michaelis, Letter to Ruth Berlau, 16/10/44, in FBI Report, Note 54, p. 25.
95. Michaelis, Letter to Berlau, 7/11/44, in ibid., p. 26.
96. Note 49, p. 3.
97. Note 25, p. 2.
98. FBI Report, L.A., 29/5/46, p. 11 (Brecht Archiv, see Note 27).
99. SAC, L.A., Memorandum to Director, FBI, 24/2/48, p. 7.
100. Note 8, p. 24.
101. Note 49, p. 16f.
102. Hood, Letter to Director, FBI, 14/5/47.
103. RE. Bert Brecht, p. 1 (undated and unsigned document).
104. Note 18, p. 1. It seems an irony of history that just when Brecht was being interrogated in Washington, Kheifetz in Moscow was being isolated and then imprisoned in Stalin's campaign against "Jewish cosmopolitanism." Pavel Sudoplatov comments: "Kheifetz, who had performed so brilliantly in obtaining atomic information for us and establishing high-level contacts in the American Jewish community, was suddenly out of favor" [204, p. 294]. On the contacts between Kheifetz and Brecht, cf. the remarks of former FBI agent Elmer Linberg in my video documentary *Im Visier des FBI:* "During this time Brecht was contacted by Gregori Kheifetz, the head of the KGB on the West Coast. . . . Did the Soviet Union pass messages to Brecht to write certain things?" [190].
105. Note 103, p. 5.
106. Undated, unsigned document.
107. Director, CIA (undated memorandum), p. 3.
108. Hoover, Memorandum to Director, CIA, [illegible] 1962, p. 5f (Brecht Archiv, see Note 27).

Lion Feuchtwanger

1. Feuchtwanger, Lion, Ph.D., 30/9/45, p. 3 (OSS, 862).
2. Henry M. Hart, Letter to Eliot B. Coulter, 6/8/40 (811.111 Refugees/22).

3. Lion Feuchtwanger, in *What Will Happen with Germany? The Creation of the National Committee Free Germany,* no page, Attachment to Emmy Rado, Memorandum to DeWitt Poole, 19/8/43 (OSS, 763).
4. Transcript of INS Interrogation of Lion Feuchtwanger, 20/11/58, p. 18.
5. FBI Report, N.Y., 8/5/42, p. 1. The reference is to the pseudonym "Wetcheek" (the English translation of Feuchtwanger's name), which he used during his escape from France.
6. FBI Report, L.A., 24/1/45, p. 16.
7. FBI Report, L.A., 2/10/46, p. 3.
8. FBI Report, L.A., 18/11/42, p. 10.
9. FBI Report, N.Y., 10/11/47, p. 13.
10. FBI Report, L.A., 3/7/47, p. 7.
11. FBI Report, Washington, 27/5/48.
12. Memorandum, SAC, L.A., to Director, FBI, 16/3/48; FBI Report, Washington, 6/5/48; FBI, Laboratory Work Sheet, 22/3/48, and FBI, Laboratory Work Sheet, 7/4/48.
13. Memorandum, [blacked out] to [blacked out], 27/7/55, p. 1.
14. FBI Report, L.A., 30/10/45, p. 3.
15. Note 9, p. 12.
16. Sworn Statement of Paul Crouch made to Investigator Oral K. Chandler, INS, 16/9/52, p. 2f. Crouch was among the "professional witnesses," in the pay of the Justice Department, who remained on call to testify at trials, deportation proceedings, and congressional hearings [cf. 171; 151].
17. FBI Report, L.A., 9/3/56, p. 3.
18. Report of [blacked out], FBI, L.A., 21/1/59.
19. Feuchtwanger, Telegram to [illegible], Stockholm, 11/4/44.
20. Feuchtwanger, Telegram to Europa Verlag, Zurich, 26/2/43.
21. [Illegible], Letter to Feuchtwanger, n.d. [c. April 1945].
22. Hoover, Memorandum to L. R. Schofield, 4/6/41.
23. Hoover, Letter to E. J. Connalley, 4/6/41, p. 2.
24. Hoover, Letter to SAC, L.A., 8/5/43.
25. Director, FBI, Memorandum to SAC, L.A., 9/6/53.
26. SAC, L.A., Memorandum to Director, FBI, 31/12/53.
27. FBI Report, L.A., 22/6/53, p. 31.
28. [Blacked out] to [blacked out], 14/4/54.
29. Typed notation on a letter from J. Edgar Hoover to Thomas H. Kuchel, 18/3/54, p. 1f. This passage is marked "Note on Yellow" indicating that it is to be read only by FBI headquarters.
30. District Director, INS, Letter to Richard Nixon, 29/5/52.
31. John Norman, Report of conversation with Lion Feuchtwanger at Pacific

Palisades, California, on 10 December, Memorandum to DeWitt C. Poole, 19/12/44, p. 1 (OSS, 1308).

32. Ibid., p. 4.
33. Ibid., p. 1.
34. Ibid., p. 3.
35. Ibid., p. 1.
36. Ibid., p. 6.
37. Ibid., p. 7.
38. Ibid., p. 4.
39. Supplemental Sheet to Lion Feuchtwanger's Application for Certification of Identification (Dept. of Justice), 5/2/42, p. 1.
40. Ibid., p. 2.
41. Statement of Lion Feuchtwanger, Petitioner for Naturalization, L.A., 5/3/48, pp. 1ff.
42. Ibid., p. 5.
43. Ibid., p. 4.
44. Whether this was the FBI man Marta Feuchtwanger described later is unclear: "And there was usually also a man with them. I had the feeling he was from the FBI. He was sitting in a corner and looking very lugubrious" [56, p. 1573].
45. Ibid., p. 1571.
46. Feuchtwanger, Letter to Ben Huebsch, 1/12/58 [quoted in 182, p. 294].
47. Note 4, p. 29.
48. Ibid., p. 26.
49. Ibid., p. 20.
50. Statement of Lion Feuchtwanger, Petitioner for Naturalization, L.A., 5/3/48, p. 5.
51. Transcript of INS interrogation of Lion Feuchtwanger, 8/8/57, p. 3.
52. Ibid., p. 5.
53. Ibid., p. 11.
54. Ibid., p. 16 [cf. 40].
55. Transcript of INS interrogation of Lion Feuchtwanger, 24/11/58, p. 47.
56. Transcript of INS interrogation of Lion Feuchtwanger, 8/8/58, p. 20.
57. Note 55, p. 44.
58. Note 51, p. 10.
59. Ibid., p. 11.
60. Ibid., p. 26.
61. Ibid., p. 13.
62. Ibid., p. 29f.
63. Note 55, p. 46.

64. Ibid., p. 45.
65. Ibid., p. 46.
66. Feuchtwanger, Letter to Arnold Zweig, 23/7/57 [55, vol. 2, p. 361].
67. Lion Feuchtwanger, "Gedenkrede für Thomas Mann," L.A., 15/10/55 [quoted in 182, p. 272].
68. Feuchtwanger, letters to Thomas and Katja Mann, 16/12/52, 10/2/53, and 25/8/52 [quoted in 182, p. 272f].
69. Feuchtwanger, Letter to Arnold Zweig, 23/10/50 [55, vol. 2, p. 88].
70. Note 51, p. 7.
71. Note 4, p. 21.
72. Ibid., p. 24.
73. Note 55, p. 42.
74. Note 51, p. 20.
75. Note 4, p. 14f. Cf. the Warner Bros. film *Guilty by Suspicion* (1991).
76. Note 51, p. 5.
77. Ibid., p. 11.
78. Ibid., p. 9.
79. Ibid., p. 39.
80. Transcript of INS interrogation of Lion Feuchtwanger, 13/11/58, p. 7.
81. Note 51, p. 43.
82. Ibid., p. 7.
83. Ibid., p. 28.
84. Ibid., p. 37.
85. Transcript of INS interrogation of Marta Feuchtwanger, 8/8/57, p. 2.
86. "In the Matter of the Petition of *Lion Feuchtwanger* to be Admitted a Citizen of The United States of America, Findings of Facts, Conclusions of Law; and Recommendation of the Designated Naturalization Examiner," 4/12/57, pp. 2ff. Despite the negative decision in 1958, Feuchtwanger was interrogated again by the INS. It is unclear whether Hozman's decision was withdrawn or whether Feuchtwanger filed an objection. Also, the files I have do not indicate whether Feuchtwanger had a realistic chance of obtaining U.S. citizenship eventually.
87. Note 51, p. 45f.

NO ONE WAS FORGOTTEN: WERFEL, REMARQUE, BRUNO FRANK, LUDWIG, LEONHARD FRANK, DÖBLIN, AND OTHERS

1. Franz Werfel, Name Check, 12/5/54, p. 2.
2. Naval Intelligence Report, Mexico, 2/6/41, quoted in "Memorandum Re: Gerhart Eisler and Others," 24/7/41, p. 4 (862.20211/3242).

3. Earl S. Piper, Asst. Naval Attaché, Mexico, Intelligence Report, 15/8/40, p. 1 (840.48 Refugees/2253).
4. Note 1, p. 1.
5. Ibid., p. 3.
6. List of politically active Austrians in America [accompanied by brief biographies], 14/4/42, p. 15 (INT-4AU, 38).
7. Harry A. Freidenberg, Letter to Major General Hilldring, Dept. of State, 23/6/47, p. 1 (FW 363.115 Mahler-Werfel, Alma Maria/6-2347).
8. J. H. Hilldring, Letter to Mr. Freidenberg, n.d. (FW 363.115 Mahler-Werfel, Alma Maria/6-2347).
9. COMGENUSFA, Vienna, Telegram to HQ European Command, Frankfurt, 30/6/47 (363.115 Mahler-Werfel, Alma Marie/6-3047).
10. Anonymous letter to Hoover, 10/6/42, p. 1.
11. Ibid., p. 3.
12. Ibid., p. 1.
13. Morris L. Ernst, Letter to Ugo Carusi, Executive Asst. to Attorney General, 7/3/46.
14. Ugo Carusi, Commissioner, Letter to Morris L. Ernst, 2/4/46.
15. Erich Maria Remarque, Certificate of Naturalization, 7/8/47.
16. *Hollywood Now* reported this event on 26/8/38 under the headline "'Red' Scare Fails to Scare Speakers" [cf. 42, vol. 1, pt. 1, p. 369].
17. [219, pp. 11731 and 11728]. T. Mann described Frank's testimony as follows in his diary: "Frank too loud and not always edifying . . . A rather hysterical excitement from Frank, whom I singled out for this favor, which he has not put to the best use" [128, p. 402].
18. Bruno Frank, "Lüge als Staatsprinzip," unpublished manuscript [quoted in 42, vol. 1, pt. 1, p. 359].
19. D.A.C.'s Note (Federal Emergency Management Agency and National Archives).
20. Bruno Frank, Certificate of Naturalization, 12/1/45.
21. [Illegible], INS memorandum, 17/5/44.
22. John Norman, Conversation with Bruno Frank in Beverly Hills, California, on 12 December, Memorandum to DeWitt C. Poole, 9/1/45, p. 1.
23. Ibid., p. 1f.
24. Ibid., p. 2.
25. Ibid., p. 4.
26. "Dr. Bruno Frank, 58, Expatriated Author," in *New York Times,* 22/6/45 (news clipping in Frank's FBI file).
27. FBI Report, L.A., [illegible] June 1945, p. 4 (FBI file, Berthold Viertel).
28. P., ("'Freies Deutschland'"), Memorandum, 9/8/42, p. 3 (OSS, 381).

29. Emil Ludwig, Memorandum, 5/3/54, p. 1.
30. John Norman, Conversation with Emil Ludwig in Pacific Palisades, California, 16/12/44, Memorandum to DeWitt C. Poole, 4/1/45, p. 1 (OSS, 1324).
31. Ibid., p. 2.
32. Ibid., p. 4.
33. Ibid., p. 3.
34. Ibid., p. 4.
35. FBI Report, L.A., 22/9/42, p. 5, purportedly quoting the 14th edition of *Encyclopedia Britannica* (1936).
36. Ibid., p. 6.
37. FBI Report, L.A., 6/8/41, p. 7.
38. Ibid., p. 6.
39. Note 35, p. 6.
40. Note 37, p. 3.
41. Note 35, p. 7.
42. SAC, N.Y., Memorandum to Director, FBI, 26/4/54.
43. FBI Laboratory Report, Washington, to SAC, L.A., 12/3/48.
44. Summary of Information, 12/3/62, p. 1 (Army Intelligence).
45. Ibid., p. 2. The Tukan Kreis, founded by writer Rudolf Schmitt-Sulzthal in 1930, was described by G-2: "Subject is active in the Tukan Kreis, a literary association which was banned during the Third Reich and reorganized in 1950. It is an association of authors, editors, publishers and newsmen which frequently acts as host to speakers from East Germany. Among other festivities scheduled was a memorial meeting in honor of Berthold Brecht, a prominent German man-of-letters who spent his last years in East Germany. The Tukan Kreis is comparable to the Komma Klub in Munich which advocates an all-German interchange of cultural activities and maintains close ties to East German cultural groups and personalities" (ibid.). Whence G-2 derived this analysis is unknown. In any case, the twenty-fifth anniversary volume *Dichter und ein grosser Schnabel. 25 Jahre Tukankreis* [44] no more bears out the theory of left-wing bias than does the roster of speakers at Tukan Kreis public events, which included Hans Egon Holthusen, Luise Rinser, Erich Kästner, Eugen Roth, Rudolf Hagelstange, and Alexander Spoerl.
46. Note 44, p. 3. The same report says: "The Frankische Kreis has been active in cultural circles propagandizing against the use of atomic weapons. The Frankische Kreis advocates that neither of the two German states arms its armed forces with atomic weapons . . . and that an atomic free zone (a zone free of atomic weapons) be created in Central Europe."

47. Note 35, p. 4.
48. Note 44, p. 3.
49. Ibid., p. 1.
50. Alfred Bruno Döblin, Alien Registration Form, 7/12/40, p. 1.
51. Heinrich Mann's FBI file says: "In the early part of 1941, Mann was active . . . in assisting Alfred Doblin, a German Jew of French citizenship, in entering the United States" (FBI Report, L.A., 5/9/44, p. 6).
52. Bruno Alfred Döblin, Statutory declaration, 3/3/41.
53. Paul M. Smith, Special Inspector, INS, L.A., Report of Investigation regarding Klaus Döblin, 30/10/42, p. 2.
54. Dept. of Police, L.A., 3/3/41.
55. Wolfgang Döblin committed suicide in France in June 1940 to avoid capture by the Germans [142, p. 181].
56. Note 53, p. 7.
57. Ibid., Examiner's Note, p. 2.
58. Information, Mail and Files Section, INS, Philadelphia, Memorandum to Visa Division, State Dept. (Exit Permit Unit), 17/9/45.
59. Form, 27/8/45, p. 1.
60. John Norman, Report of conversation with Alfred Doeblin in Hollywood, 12 December 1944, Memorandum to DeWitt C. Poole, 6/1/45, p. 1 (OSS, 1325).
61. Ibid., p. 2.
62. Ibid., p. 3.
63. Vicky Baum, Name Check, 15/2/54, p. 1f.
64. Ibid., and Baum, Name Check, 3/5/57, p. 1.
65. Alice Neary, FOIA/Pa. Reviewing Officer, INS, Washington, letter to me, 7/3/88.
66. Ibid., p. 6.
67. Alfred Neumann, Certificate of Naturalization, 26/12/47 (INS).
68. Charles B. Friediger, Memorandum to Bjarne Braatoy, 8/6/45 (OSS, 1571).
69. Martin H. Easton, by Capt. A. D. McHendrie, Memorandum to John O'Keefe, 25/5/45, p. 2 (OSS, 1559).
70. Ibid., p. 1.
71. Note 68.
72. Application for Immigration Visa (Quota), Paris, France, 16/2/39.
73. Supplemental Sheet to Application for Certificate of Identification, L.A., 5/2/42.
74. Robert M. Moschorak, District Director, INS, L.A., Letter to me, 25/4/91.

3
The FBI and the Exiles in New York
THE OSS AND THE FBI: THE "OTHER GERMANY"

1. Helmut Pfanner [158, pp. 36ff] has compiled an extensive collection of quotations by exiles about the Manhattan skyline, the Statue of Liberty, and Ellis Island. My examples are partly from this work.
2. New York: Appleton-Century-Crofts (1948).
3. Board of Special Inquiries, Ellis Island, Interview with Hans Marchwitza, 28/6/41, pp. 9, 4, 6 (INS file, Marchwitza).
4. [?] Cohen, "Herod and Mariamne," *Variety,* 2/11/38, p. 56.
5. Cf. State Dept. file on Fritz Landshoff in the National Archives (862.20211 Landshoff, Fritz H.), especially an undated letter from Erika Mann to John [Farrar?].
6. Maxim Lieber was not American either but had worked as a literary agent in the United States for years.
7. "Thomas Mann Warns U.S. on Misuse of Power," *New York Herald Tribune,* 26/6/45, copy enclosed with Charles B. Friediger, Memorandum to Bjarne Braatoy, 27/6/45 (OSS, 1615).
8. FBI Report (on Otto Katz), N.Y., 15/2/40, p. 2, Attachment to Hoover, Letter to Adolf A. Berle, Asst. Secretary of State, 20/4/40 (800.00B Katz, Otto, 12).
9. Nicholas J. Alaga, FBI Report, N.Y., 6/10/44, p. 47, Attachment to Hoover, Memorandum to Frederick B. Lyon, Chief, Division of Foreign Activity Correlation, Dept. of State, 19/12/44 (811.00B/12-1944).
10. "Volksfront or Isolation? The Dilemma of German Social Democracy," Foreign Nationality Groups in the United States, FNB Memorandum to Director, 10/4/44, p. 2 (OSS, 182).
11. R. B. Hood, SAC, Memorandum to Director, FBI, 21/4/44.
12. E. E. Conroy, SAC, Memorandum to Director, FBI, 13/5/44.
13. Ibid., p. 2.
14. Ibid., p. 1.
15. [Dr. Frank Bohn's 1940 mission to France], Report No. 2, p. 3 (OSS, 4).
16. Memorandum, 4/3/42, p. 3 (OSS, 47).
17. Hood, SAC, Letter to Director, FBI, 15/1/45, p. 1.
18. Emmy Rado, Memorandum to DeWitt Poole, 8/12/43, p. 1 (OSS, 904).
19. Hoover, Memorandum to Adolf A. Berle, Asst. Secretary of State, n.d. (c. 22/7/44).
20. Note 11, p. 1.
21. FBI Report, L.A., 21/10/44, p. 4 (FBI file, Free German Activities in the Los Angeles Area, quoted in National Archives, 862.01/11-1144).

22. Note 10, p. 3.
23. Ibid., p. 2.
24. Friediger, Memorandum to DeWitt C. Poole, 5/5/44, p. 1f (OSS, 1108).
25. Robert M. W. Kempner, "Vorbemerkung" [178, p. 11].
26. Kempner's name appears twice in Brecht's FBI file, once as a Philadelphia special agent who wrote an FBI memorandum, "German Communist Activities in Western Hemisphere" (30/8/43), and again as a "Special Employee of the Philadelphia Field Division" reporting on "Council for a Democratic Germany," 28/4/45 (see FBI Report, L.A., 2/10/44, p. 35, and FBI Report, L.A., 30/6/45, p. 39) [FBI file, Bertolt Brecht; Brecht Archiv, Berlin, Germany].
27. Sanford Schwarz, Memorandum of Conversation with Robert M. W. Kempner, 17/11/44, p. 2 (OSS, 1280).
28. SAC, Philadelphia, Memorandum to Director, FBI, 19/2/46.
29. S. S. Alden, Memorandum to Mr. Ladd, 5/2/42.
30. FBI Report, N.Y., 10/12/41, p. 1.
31. [57, p. 56]. Cf. chapter "Hans and the 32 Grams" in [140, pp. 82–101].
32. FBI Report, N.Y., 18/12/41, p. 3f.
33. Ibid., p. 6.
34. "Saved by America," Brochure of the Emergency Rescue Committee, sent anonymously to the FBI.
35. "Ickes Pleads for Refugees," newspaper clipping, no source, n.d.
36. B.L., Memorandum to Secretary of State and Undersecretary of State, 13/8/43, pp. 1–3 (National Archives, file number illegible).
37. FBI Report, N.Y., 26/11/40, p. 1.
38. [Blacked out], Memorandum to Mr. Ladd, 3/9/42.
39. International Rescue and Relief Committee (IRRC), 4/5/49, p. 3.
40. *Alert,* n.d.
41. Director, FBI, Memorandum to SAC, N.Y., 7/10/52.
42. Cf. Charles B. Friediger, Memorandum to Bjarne Braatoy, 23/5/45 (OSS, 1543).
43. Hoover, Memorandum to SAC, N.Y., 5/12/45.
44. FBI Report, N.Y., 7/2/46, p. 2f.
45. SAC, N.Y., Memorandum to Director, FBI, 2/5/47.

DOSSIERS
Oskar Maria Graf

1. FBI Report, N.Y., 5/5/43, p. 1.
2. Ibid.

3. Ibid., p. 2.
4. P., Memorandum, 4/3/42, p. 3 (OSS, 47).
5. FBI Report, N.Y., 24/4/50, p. 1. Brandl's brochure, published with no date or place except "Printed in the U.S.," was probably printed in May 1940 (cf. FBI Report on Heinz Jacob Pol, N.Y., 1/6/44, p. 16, cited in National Archives, 800.00 Pol, Heinz Jacob). It entered the files of (among others) the OSS (OSS, 617).
6. Oskar Maria Graf, "Rede zum 'Deutschen Tag'" [69, p. 138].
7. Note 5, p. 7.
8. Ibid., p. 8.
9. Harrisburg: Military Service Publishing Company.
10. Note 5, p. 8.
11. Anon., "Affäre des deutschen 'Schutzverbands,'" *Das Neue Tage-Buch* 44, 28/10/39, p. 1025 [cf. 230, vol. 4, p. 105].
12. Ibid., p. 1023.
13. [186]. On the title page of *Das Neue Tage-Buch,* this article is headed "Kommunazis in Amerika."
14. Graf, Letter to Gustav and Else Fischer, 4/10/42 [70, p. 118].
15. Graf, Letter to Kurt Kersten, 24/5/43 [70, p. 171].
16. Note 5, p. 14.
17. Ibid., p. 11.
18. Dr. Heilbrunn, Letter to Major Littauer, 4/6/42 (OSS, 321).
19. L. V. Heilbrunn, Letter to John C. Wiley, 18/9/42 (OSS, 321).
20. Memorandum, n.d. [c. 22/2/44], p. 3 (OSS, 1002).
21. Memorandum of the 66th CIC Group, Stuttgart; Attachment to Legat, Bonn, Memorandum to Director, FBI, 30/9/55, p. 4.
22. Ibid., p. 5.
23. Note 1, 5/5/43, p. 3.
24. Graf, Letter to Thomas Mann, 15/3/49 [70, p. 219].
25. Graf, Letter to Lion Feuchtwanger, 14/5/58 [70, p. 283].

Berthold Viertel

1. Application for Reentry Permit, 8/8/34 (INS).
2. Hans Kindler, Letter to Francis Biddle, Attorney General, 20/8/43 (INS).
3. FBI Report, N.Y., 24/1/42, p. 1.
4. Hoover, Letter to SAC, N.Y., 7/4/42, p. 1.
5. James B. Opsata, Chief, Personnel Division, Coordinator of Information, Letter to D. M. Ladd, Asst. Director, FBI, 31/3/42 (CIA).
6. FBI Report, N.Y., 18/6/42, p. 7.

7. FBI Report, L.A., 3/9/42, p. 2.
8. Anna Seghers, Letter to B. Viertel, 11/7/42.
9. Hoover, Director, Memorandum to Attorney General, 26/1/45.
10. Hood, SAC, L.A., Letters to Director, FBI, 21/2/45 and 9/3/45.
11. Hood, SAC, L.A., Letter to Director, FBI, 10/4/45.
12. FBI Report, L.A., [illegible] June 1945, p. 4.
13. On another occasion, Salka Viertel speaks of Brecht's "battered Ford" [227, p. 283].
14. FBI Report, L.A., 22/5/43, p. 6 (FBI file, Bertolt Brecht; Brecht Archiv, Berlin, Germany).
15. Re: [blacked out], n.d., p. 1.
16. Hood, SAC, L.A., Letter to Director, FBI, 14/5/47.
17. Petition for Naturalization, 13/4/43, p. 1 (INS).
18. L. Paul Winings, General Counsel, Memorandum to W. F. Kelly, Asst. Commissioner, Enforcement Division, 7/10/49.
19. Certificate of the Loss of U.S. Nationality, 9/11/53 (State Dept.).

"REDS": WEISKOPF, MARCHWITZA, KANTOROWICZ, BLOCH

1. FBI Report, Washington, 10/3/43, p. 1.
2. Hearing, Board of Special Inquiry, Ellis Island, 12/6/39, p. 1 (INS).
3. Ibid., p. 2.
4. Ibid., p. 5.
5. Ibid., p. 6.
6. Explanation of Exemptions, Subsections of Title 5, U.S. Code, Section 552.
7. E. E. Conroy, SAC, N.Y., Letter to Director, FBI, 21/3/44.
8. FBI Report, N.Y., 19/3/43, p. 1.
9. SAC, N.Y., Memorandum to Director, FBI, 4/6/45.
10. Director, FBI, Memorandum to SAC, N.Y., 28/10/46, p. 1f.
11. FBI Report, N.Y., 26/2/47, p. 2.
12. Headquarters, 66th CIC Group, USAREUR, 19/4/55, p. 1f (Army Intelligence).
13. FBI Report, N.Y., 1/8/47, p. 2.
14. Dept. of State, Telegram to American Embassy, Prague, 24/12/48, p. 2 (State Dept.).
15. Note 13.
16. File notation, n.d. or sender; probably part of "Summary of Main File 40-12476."
17. How seriously the Marshall Plan was regarded by Soviet intelligence at the time is attested by Pavel Sudoplatov's memoirs, *Special Tasks*. Sudoplatov

recalls that Donald MacLean, who as first secretary at the British embassy in Washington held a position similar to Weiskopf's, caused a sudden change in Stalin's foreign policy when he reported "that the goal of the Marshall Plan was to ensure American economic domination in Europe" [204, p. 231].

18. Note 12, p. 2. The report of Weiskopf's arrest is not confirmed by the author's posthumous papers at Berlin's Academy of Arts.
19. Note 12, 7/10/55 (Army Intelligence).
20. H. Marchwitza, Pan American Express Way dispatch to El Libro Libre, 27/4/43.
21. Hearing of Hans Marchwitza, Board of Special Inquiry, Ellis Island, 28/6/41, p. 8 (INS).
22. Ibid., p. 1.
23. Ibid., p. 9.
24. Surprisingly, Marchwitza is not mentioned in Folsom's book *Days of Anger, Days of Hope* [57].
25. Note 21, 30/6/41, p. 13 (INS).
26. Ibid., p. 15.
27. Application to Extend Time of Temporary Stay, [illegible] May 1946, p. 1f (INS).
28. Marchwitza, Statutory declaration, County of New York, 12/12/41 (INS).
29. Note 27, [illegible] 1945, p. 2 (INS).
30. Note 27, 5/9/44, p. 2 (INS).
31. Hoover, Memorandum to SAC, N.Y., 20/7/44.
32. FBI Report, N.Y., 22/9/44, p. 4.
33. [Blacked out], Memorandum to D. M. Ladd, 12/2/47.
34. Hilde Marchwitza, Letter to Special Projects Division, State Dept., 28/8/46 (711.62115P/8-2846).
35. Hoover, Memorandum to SAC, N.Y., 1/6/43, p. 1.
36. Hoover, Memorandum to SAC, N.Y., 20/7/44.
37. Note 32, p. 6.
38. FBI Report, Philadelphia, 29/7/46, p. 3.
39. Ibid., p. 4.
40. Ibid., p. 6.
41. FBI Report, N.Y., 12/2/47, p. 1.
42. WDG Idaho REURAD, Telegram to Asst. Chief of Staff, 11/2/47, p. 1 (Army).
43. In Re: Alfred Kantorowicz, n.d. [c. May 1968] (INS).
44. Alfred Kantorowicz, "To Whom it may concern!" 23/4/68 (State Dept.).
45. FBI Report, N.Y., 19/10/43, p. 4.

46. FBI Report, Boston, 13/11/40, p. 1.
47. FBI Report, Boston, 11/5/42, p. 1.
48. FBI Report, Boston, 16/2/44, p. 2.
49. FBI Report, Boston, 18/4/44, p. 1.
50. Ibid., p. 2.
51. Note 48, p. 3.
52. Ibid., p. 3.
53. FBI Report, Boston, 4/8/42, p. 2.
54. FBI Report, Boston, 29/9/53, p. 2.
55. Ernst Bloch, Letter to Wieland Herzfelde, 23/4/47 (W. Herzfelde Archiv, Stiftung Archiv der Akademie der Künste, Berlin, Germany).
56. Note 48.
57. SAC, Boston, Memorandum to Director, FBI, 29/9/53.
58. FBI Report, Washington, 22/5/53, p. 2.
59. Ibid., p. 3.
60. Legat, Bonn, Memorandum to Director, FBI, 29/9/61.
61. Legat, Bonn, Memorandum to Director, FBI, 8/5/62.

UNPOLITICALS AND FELLOW TRAVELERS: BRUCKNER, PISCATOR, UNRUH, HABE, BROCH, ZUCKMAYER

1. Interdepartmental Visa Review Committee, N.Y., Minutes of 9/6/43, p. 2 (FBI).
2. Theodor Tagger/Ferdinand Bruckner, Statutory declaration, L.A., 14/10/36 (INS).
3. Joseph Wehler, in Re: Theodor Tagger, 20/3/46, p. 1 (INS).
4. Ibid., p. 4.
5. Ibid., p. 2.
6. [Illegible], Re: Theodor Tagger/Ferdinand Bruckner, 18/2/46, p. 2 (INS).
7. FBI Report, N.Y., 16/5/44, p. 5.
8. Ibid., p. 1.
9. Ibid., p. 6.
10. Certificate of the Loss of U.S. Nationality, Berlin, 4/6/54 (State Dept.).
11. FBI Report, N.Y., 11/11/43, p. 1.
12. Ibid., p. 3.
13. Ibid., p. 4.
14. Ibid., p. 3.
15. Ibid., p. 2.
16. FBI Report, N.Y., 30/5/45, p. 6.
17. FBI Report, N.Y. 4/6/47, p. 1.

18. Cecil Peterson, Acting Officer in Charge, in Re: Erwin Friedrich Max Piscator, 19/11/65 (INS).
19. Unruh, Fritz von, 29/9/43, p. 3 (OSS, 873).
20. FBI Report, N.Y., [illegible] October 1943, p. 2.
21. P. E. Foxworth, Asst. Director, Letter to Director, FBI, 3/2/42, p. 1.
22. Minutes, Interdepartmental Visa Review Committee, 9/6/43, p. 1.
23. Ibid., p. 3.
24. Director, FBI, Memorandum to SAC, Newark, 13/12/56.
25. FBI Report, N.Y., 12/11/43, p. 7.
26. Edward M. Groth, American Consul General, Hamburg, Letter to Secretary of State, 14/7/48, p. 1f (862.00B/7-1448).
27. SAC, Newark, Memorandum to Director, FBI, 26/3/59.
28. "Hans Habe," n.d. This otherwise unidentified c.v. is written in the third person; the many references to "documentary evidence" suggest that it probably was written by Habe himself.
29. [Blacked out], Memorandum to Mr. Rosen, 2/5/42.
30. Hans Habe, n.d., p. 2f.
31. Untitled, undated typed document, p. 1.
32. Ibid., p. 2.
33. FBI, Washington, Re: Hans Habe, 24/10/56.
34. "Hoover" [clipping from Stern, 15/3/65], attachment to [blacked out], Memorandum to Director, FBI, 16/3/54.
35. T. Mann, Letter to John C. Wiley, Consul General, American Consulate General, Vienna, Austria, 15/5/38.
36. A. Einstein, Letter to John C. Wiley, Consul General, American Consulate General, Vienna, Austria, 15/5/38.
37. Ben Huebsch, The Viking Press, Letter to John C. Wiley, Consul General, American Consulate General, Vienna, Austria, 16/5/38.
38. Edward Blatt, Statutory declaration, N.Y., 18/5/38, p. 1f.
39. Declaration of Intention, 15/2/46.
40. Petition for Naturalization [date illegible].
41. Declaration of Intention, 15/2/39.
42. Application for Immigration Visa (Quota), 21/9/38.
43. Certification of Naturalization, 27/1/44.
44. Note 41.
45. A. H. MacGregor, Special Inspector and Examining Inspector, INS Examination of Carl Zuckmayer, Barnard, Vt., 17/6/43, p. 3.
46. Ibid., p. 2.
47. Note 45, INS Examination of Alice Alberta Henriette Zuckmayer, p. 2.
48. Note 45, p. 6.

49. Harold Woods, Special Inspector, INS Examination of Franz Werfel, Beverly Hills, Calif., 11/9/43, pp. 2, 4.
50. [Illegible], Special Inspector, Examining Officer, INS Examination of Friderike Zweig, N.Y., 28/8/43, p. 2.
51. Guido Zernatto, Statutory declaration, N.Y., 30/10/42.
52. J. Kevin O'Brian in his letter to me, 15/11/94.
53. FBI Report, Albany, 8/3/45, p. 2 (FBI file, Lion Feuchtwanger).
54. Alien Registration Form, [illegible] October 1940, p. 1.
55. American Consulate, Salzburg, Austria, Document Attesting the Granting of Citizenship, 7/8/58 (State Dept.).
56. Certificate of the Loss of U.S. Nationality, American Consulate, Salzburg, Austria, 1/10/58 (State Dept.).
57. Hoover, Letter to SAC, N.Y., 26/1/44.
58. Equitable Life Assurance Society, "To Whom It May Concern," 30/3/35.
59. Siegfried Reinhardt, Statutory declaration, Berlin-Wilmersdorf, 8/3/35 (INS).
60. Application for Immigration Visa (Quota), 14/4/37 (INS).
61. Lee S. Strickland, Information and Privacy Coordinator, CIA, Washington, attachment to letter to me, 2/12/87.

4
The FBI and the Exiles in Mexico
SOUTH OF THE BORDER: "COMMUNAZIS"

1. FBI Report, Washington, [illegible] October 1941, p. 3 (FBI file, Anna Seghers).
2. A. A. Berle, Letter to Josephus Daniels, American Ambassador, Mexico, 8/8/41. Daniels had asked for Jones partly because the embassy lacked a specialist "to secure information regarding totalitarian agents" (Daniels, Letter to Secretary of State, 27/5/41 [124.12/110]).
3. E. T. Lampson, "Communism in Mexico," Memorandum, 5/10/43, pp. 1, 2 (81200B/821).
4. [97, p. 279]. Patrik von zur Mühlen estimates a group of "approximately twenty members" [146, p. 170] at the start of World War II.
5. Cantwell C. Brown, Asst. Military Attaché, "Free Germany Movment in Mexico," 26/9/44, p. 3, Attachment to Raleigh Gibson, First Secretary U.S. Embassy, Mexico, 20/10/44 (862.01/10-2044).
6. According to Rout and Bratzel [170, p. 37], Roosevelt in summer 1940 wanted to avoid association with intelligence gathering in Latin America to prevent possible diplomatic complications.

7. Ibid., p. 57. "Ast" is short for "Abwehrstelle," military intelligence in the German Wehrmacht.
8. Josephus Daniels, U.S. Embassy, Mexico, Letter to Secretary of State, 23/4/40, p. 1 (862.20212/1869).
9. Earl S. Piper, Asst. Naval Attaché, Mexico, Intelligence Report, 15/8/40, p. 1f (840.48 Refugees/2253).
10. Josephus Daniels, U.S. Embassy, Mexico, Letter to Secretary of State, 15/8/40 (840.48 Refugees/2219).
11. Note 9, p. 2.
12. "Memorandum Re: Gerhart Eisler and Others," 24/7/41, p. 5 (862.20211/3242).
13. D. H. Byrd, Letter to Tom Connally, 20/9/40, pp. 1–3 (812.00-N/376).
14. *El Universal,* 17/4/40, quoted in Josephus Daniels, U.S. Embassy, Mexico, Letter to Secretary of State, 18/4/40, p. 1f (862.20212/1870).
15. W. K. Ailshie, Third Secretary U.S. Embassy, Mexico, Letter to Secretary of State, 2/3/43, p. 5 (862.20210/2286). One goal of this group was to index the names of suspicious Germans.
16. Clarence W. Moore, Civil Attaché, Memorandum to Raleigh A. Gibson, First Secretary U.S. Embassy, Mexico, 26/3/43, p. 3 (862.01/256).
17. W. K. Ailshie, Third Secretary U.S. Embassy, Mexico, Letter to Secretary of State, 25/6/43, p. 21 (862.01/286).
18. RW [probably Rebecca Wellington of Foreign Activity Correlation in the State Dept.], handwritten note to Mr. Berle, 27/4/43 (862.01/256).
19. Note 16, p. 1.
20. Ibid., p. 2.
21. Junius B. Wood, Memorandum to Carter W. Clarke, 9/6/43, p. 9, Attachment to Wood, Letter to M. J. McDermott, Chief, Current Information Bureau, State Dept., 11/6/43 (862.01/284).
22. Note 16. Moore quotes (without date) a letter from Paul Merker to E. R. A. Caden, alias Gerd Caden, in Havana, Cuba.
23. Ibid., p. 4.
24. Ibid., p. 2.
25. Ibid., p. 6.
26. Ibid., p. 7.
27. Egon Erwin Kisch, "Auf den Tod Roberts [Robert] Musils," *Freies Deutschland* 8/1942, p. 29.
28. Note 16, p. 8.
29. Note 17, p. 1.
30. Ibid., p. 7.
31. Ibid., p. 17.

32. Ibid., p. 2.
33. Ibid., Attachment 1.
34. Note 17, p. 5.
35. Ibid., p. 13.
36. Ibid., p. 25.
37. Cordell Hull, Letter to George S. Messersmith, Ambassador, U.S. Embassy, Mexico, 2/6/43 (862.01/259).
38. Attachment to George S. Messersmith, Letter to Secretary of State, 7/6/43.
39. Note 17, p. 1.
40. Ibid., p. 14.
41. Ibid., p. 18.
42. Ibid., p. 19.
43. Rebecca Wellington, Memorandum, 19/1/44, p. 3 (862.01/561).
44. Memorandum of the Division of the American Republics, State Dept., 30/7/43 (FW862.01/286).
45. Standley, Telegram to Secretary of State, 23/7/43, p. 1 (862.01/300).
46. Note 17, p. 20f.
47. R. R., Memorandum, 9/4/42 (OSS, 71).
48. "Summary of Contents of 'Freies Deutschland,' German-Language Monthly . . . for August and September, 1942, and related comment," Memorandum of the Division of the American Republics, State Dept., 22/10/42, p. 1 (812.00B/768).
49. Note 21, p. 10.
50. Hoover, Letter to Adolf A. Berle, Asst. Secretary of State, 25/6/43 (862.01/362).
51. Note 45, p. 1f.
52. Note 45, 22/7/43, p. 3 (862.01/299).
53. Hull, Telegram to U.S. Embassy, Moscow, 24/11/43, p. 1 (862.01/498A).
54. Mr. Schuster, Head of Research Dept., American Jewish Committee, [illegible] July 1943, p. 1 (OSS, 706).
55. Malcolm W. Davis, Interoffice Memo to DeWitt C. Poole, 28/7/43, p. 1 (OSS, 711).
56. Note 53, p. 4.
57. Byron Price, Director (Office of Censorship), Annotation to "Postal and Telegraph Censorship, 20th December, 1943, Free Germans," p. 1 (OSS, 964).
58. Ibid., Attachment, "Postal & Telegraph Censorship, Index to Report on Free Germany," p. 60.
59. Note 21, p. 15.
60. Captain Ross, Interoffice Memo to Mr. Poole, 10/5/43 (OSS, 679).

61. Geo. P. Shaw, Foreign Activity Correlation, Memorandum to Mr. Gordon, 15/2/44, p. 2 (862.01/616).
62. Byron Price, Director, Office of Censorship, "Special Watch Instruction No. 88," October 1942, p. 2, Attachment to G. E. Brown, Chief, Digest Section, Letter to George P. Shaw, Acting Chief, Division of Foreign Activity Correlation, 20/10/43 (862.01/611).
63. John C. Dreier, Division of the American Republics, "Condemnation of the Correspondence of 'Freies Deutschland' and the 'Allianza Garibaldi,'" 25/6/43, p. 2 (811.711/4253).
64. Note 63, 17/6/43.
65. State Dept., Memorandum of Conversation, 15/2/44, p. 1 (862.01/608).
66. Ibid.
67. Note 61, p. 1.
68. Letter to Byron Price, no sender or date (862.01/559) [cf. 104, vol. 2, p. 443].
69. Cordell Hull, Letter to Byron Price, 11/5/44 (862.01/637a).
70. Note 48, p. 1f.
71. "'Free German' Movements in the Western Hemisphere," Office of Naval Intelligence Report, 22/12/42, p. 12, Attachment to J. W. B. Waller, Office of the Chief of Naval Operations, Memorandum of 24/12/42 (Navy).
72. Note 5, pp. 1, 11.
73. Cantwell C. Brown, Asst. Military Attaché, Memorandum, p. 2, Attachment to Raleigh A. Gibson, First Secretary U.S. Embassy, Mexico, Letter to Secretary of State, 26/6/44 (862.01/6-2645).
74. Hoover, Memorandum to Frederick B. Lyon, Chief, Division of Foreign Activity Correlation, 13/4/45, Foreword, no page (862.20210/4-1345).
75. Ibid., p. 61.
76. [31]. A study by me, "Exile Literature and the Nazi State: Expatriation and Surveillance of German Writers by the Third Reich," is in preparation.
77. Re: Alemania Libre, aka, Free Germany, Freies Deutschland, 7/1/46, p. 19, Attachment to Hoover, Memorandum to Frederick B. Lyon, Chief, Division of Foreign Activity Correlation, 7/2/46 (862.01/2-746). Kiessling [96, vol. 1, p. 256] says that KPD members met on 3–4 November 1945 shortly after the Free Germany Committee dissolved. The meeting decided, among other things, to rename *Freies Deutschland* magazine *Neues Deutschland* at the start of the year and to redefine the work of the Free Germany Movement.
78. Re: Alemania Libre, also known as Free Germany, Freies Deutschland, Nueva Alemania, Neues Deutschland, 15/4/46, p. 1, Attachment to Hoover, Memorandum to Frederick B. Lyon, Chief, Division of Foreign Activity Correlation, 10/6/46 (862.01/6-1046).

79. Note 77, p. 22.
80. S. Walter Washington, First Secretary U.S. Embassy, Mexico, Letter to Secretary of State, 4/6/47, pp. 1–2 (800.00B/6-447).

DOSSIERS
Anna Seghers

1. We now have some help in this regard [see 180].
2. Anna Seghers, Alien Registration Form, 7/3/41 (INS).
3. Cf. John Butler, U.S. Naval Attaché, Intelligence Report, Ciudad Trujillo, Dominican Republic, 26/8/41 (800.00B Ratvanyi, Laslo/4).
4. Note 2.
5. Seghers, Alien Registration Foreign Service Form, 13/11/46 (INS).
6. E.g., FBI Laboratory Report to SAC, N.Y., 5/5/44.
7. Informant's report, 18/8/43, in "Correlation Summary," 8/3/74, p. 21.
8. Report from "highly confidential source," January 1944, ibid., p. 26.
9. "Analysis of the Membership of Alemania Libre," p. 40, Attachment to Raleigh A. Gibson, First Secretary U.S. Embassy, Mexico, Letter to Secretary of State, 26/6/45 (862.01/6-2645).
10. Hoover, Letter to Lee T. Crowley, 25/9/43 (attachment).
11. Attachment to A. M. Thurston, Memorandum to Mr. Foxworth, 19/5/41 (FBI file, K. Mann).
12. "Re: Gerhart Eisler and Others," State Dept., Foreign Activity Correlation, 24/7/41, p. 6 (862.20211/3242, Confidential File PS/BJH).
13. FBI Report, Washington, [illegible] November 1941, p. 6.
14. FBI Report, N.Y., 26/6/43, p. 7.
15. [57, p. 51] and conversation with me, New York, N.Y., 22/11/94.
16. Morris N. Hughes, Consul, American Consulate General, Mexico, Letter to Secretary of State, 18/8/41, p. 1f (740.0011 European War 1939/422).
17. Informant's Report, N.Y., 18/12/41, in "Correlation Summary," 8/3/74, pp. 10–11.
18. W. K. Ailshie, Third Secretary U.S. Embassy, Mexico, Letter to Secretary of State, 25/6/43, pp. 2, 5 (862.01/286).
19. SIS/FBI Report, Mexico, 8/7/43, p. 9.
20. "Re: Hannes Meyer," 17/2/44, p. 1, Attachment to Hoover, Memorandum to Adolf A. Berle, Asst. Secretary of State, 17/2/44 (800.00B Meyer, Hannes/3).
21. The FBI did not reply to my request for a history of the Alto Case. Robert J. Lamphere, an agent assigned to surveillance of Communists, believes that the case involved a courier operation with Mexico in which a certain

Lidia Altschuler was implicated (Lamphere's conversation with me, Green Valley, Ariz., 16/11/94) [cf. 226, pp. 55ff, 109f].

22. E. E. Conroy, N.Y., Letter to Director, FBI, 29/1/44, pp. 13, 16.

23. "From the decipherment of some of the messages it appears that the subjects of this case are presently trying to free Frank Jacson from his Mexican prison," states one report to Hoover, "RE: Alto Case, Internal Security-R, Censorship Matters" ([blacked out], Letter to Director, FBI, 5/5/45, p. 1). Cf. Conroy, Note 22.

24. Memorandum, sender, and addressee blacked out, probably September 1946, p. 4.

25. However, Anna Seghers did have contact with one suspect close to the Hiss-Chambers case in the mid-forties: her literary agent Maxim Lieber, who during the McCarthy era fled to Mexico and then back to his native Poland. In the late sixties, anti-Semitism in Eastern Europe drove him back to the United States. Several conversations I had with Lieber's widow, Minna Lieber, in Hartford, Conn., since 1994 led me to believe that I had initially exaggerated the extent of his political activity [193, pp. 247–49]. See Sudoplatov [204, pp. 227ff] for relations between Alger Hiss and Soviet diplomat Konstantin Umanski, who after he transferred from Washington was ambassador to Mexico, 1941–45, and in contact with the exile group there. On Seghers' relationship with Lieber, see the unpublished correspondence between Seghers and F. C. Weiskopf in the Akademie der Künste, Berlin, Germany.

26. FBI Report, N.Y., 31/5/44.

27. E. E. Conroy, N.Y., Memorandum to Director, FBI, 22/3/43 and 21/8/43.

28. Note 19.

29. Ibid., p. 10.

30. Attorney General, Memorandum for Hugh B. Cox, Asst. Attorney General, and J. Edgar Hoover, Director, FBI, 16/7/43 (Dept. of Justice).

31. Hoover, Letter to Byron Price, Director of Censorship, 28/10/44.

32. SIS/FBI Report, Mexico, 24/10/45, p. 2.

33. Seghers, Letter to [blacked out], 19/1/44, Attachment to Office of Censorship, 16/2/44.

34. Seghers, Letter, 19/1/44 (Office of Censorship). The emendations to *Transit* have unfortunately not been preserved, although papers held by Little, Brown show that Seghers did mail her corrections to them in January 1944: "Please wire whether or not received the three last pages of my novel Transit which I rewrote and sent in January" (Seghers, Telegram to Little, Brown, Publishers, 3/3 [1944]). Cf. the letter from translator James Galston to D. Angus Cameron at Little, Brown dated 26/2/44: "I am sending

you enclosed the translation of the amended final pages of Anna Seghers'
'Transit.' . . . I wonder why the author considered this changed ending im-
perative, and I also wonder whether it is an improvement over the original
shorter version" (Archive of Little, Brown, Publishers, Boston). Pierre
Radvanyi recalled in conversations with me that his mother had to decide
between two or three versions of the ending.

35. Censor's note to Seghers, Letter to "Dear Aunt," 28/1 [1944], Attachment
    to FBI Laboratory Report, 5/5/44.
36. Anna Seghers, "The Excursion of the Dead Girls," Attachment (Note 35).
37. A translation of this text back into German, with commentary, may be found
    in [189, pp. 125–30].
38. Attachment to FBI Laboratory Report, 15/5/44.
39. Theodore Kaghan, Chief, Basic News Division, OWI, Telegram to Mme.
    Netty Radvanti [Radvanyi] Anna Seghers, 10/5/45 (filing code illegible,
    probably 862.01/5-2645 or 5-1945). A reproduction of this ms. is in [189,
    pp. 172–78].
40. Ibid., p. 174.
41. Telegram to A. Seghers, 19/11/42, quoted in FBI Report (Note 26) [cf. 191;
    198; 181].
42. Letter to Seghers, 1/11/44, quoted in Office of Censorship Report, 25/1/
    45.
43. "Report by Office of the Naval Attaché of this Embassy concerning Ale-
    mania Libre," 12/4/43, p. 3, Attachment to W. K. Ailshie, Third Secretary
    U.S. Embassy, Mexico, 29/4/43 (862.01/261).
44. Note 9, p. 41.
45. [Blacked out], Letter to Seghers, 6/7/44, Attachment to FBI Laboratory
    Report, 26/7/44.
46. Note 42. Cf. the recently rediscovered "Chronik der Familie Herz Salomon
    Fuld, Frankfurt am Main v. 1.1.1944 durch Heinrich Benjamin," now in the
    Seghers archive (Stiftung Archiv der Akademie der Künste, Berlin, Ger-
    many), and various pieces in *Argonautenschiff,* the yearbook of the Anna
    Seghers Society.
47. Seghers, Letter, Note 35.
48. Seghers, Letter to [blacked out], 21/4/44, Attachment to FBI Laboratory
    Report, 9/6/44.
49. Seghers, Letter to [blacked out], 27/3/45, quoted in Office of Censorship
    Report, 26/4/45.
50. Seghers, Letter to [blacked out], 1/1/44, Attachment to FBI Laboratory Re-
    port, 24/4/44. Notably, the FBI had already stated in one of its biweekly

reports on the Alto Case in autumn 1943: "Her father died some time ago, and her mother is believed to have been deported to Poland" ("Re: Anna Seghers with aliases," p. 3, Attachment to FBI Report, N.Y., 14/12/43). Two years later, the joint report "Re: Netty Radvanyi, with aliases" (24/10/45) said that her father, "70 years of age was frequently molested by the German authorities," p. 1.

51. Seghers, Letter to [blacked out], 5/5/44, Attachment to FBI Laboratory Report, 9/6/44.
52. Seghers, Letter to [blacked out], 21/9/44, Attachment to FBI Laboratory Report, 17/10/44.
53. Seghers, Letter to [blacked out], 19/3/45, quoted in Office of Censorship Report, 26/4/45. A letter from an unknown person in Mexico to an unknown addressee in New York, dated 12/9/44, says: "Anna Seghers wanted to know whether we can possibly locate her mother, Hedwig Reiling. She was kept in a camp in Piscki, near Lublin. I am afraid it is a hopeless undertaking" (FBI Report, N.Y., 7/12/44).
54. Seghers, Letter to [blacked out], 4/9/44, Attachment to FBI Laboratory Report, 23/9/44.
55. Ibid.
56. *New York Times,* 23/7/46, in "Correlation Summary," 8/3/74, p. 35.
57. *Washington News,* 5/9/51, ibid., p. 51: "The 9/5/51 issue of the 'Washington News' contained an article captioned 'Little, Brown & Co Seems Sure You Can Do Business With Stalin.'"
58. Ibid., p. 67.
59. Cf. H.R. (Review of Anna Seghers, *Das siebte Kreuz*), in *Neuer Mainzer Anzeiger,* 31/8/46.

FREE GERMANS? EGON ERWIN KISCH, BODO UHSE, LUDWIG RENN

1. Hoover, Letter to E. J. Connelley, 9/5/41.
2. FBI Report, L.A., 31/8/42, p. 1.
3. [Blacked out], L.A., Letter to Director, FBI, 6/4/43, p. 1.
4. [SIS/FBI Report], Mexico, 14/10/43, p. 1.
5. [SIS/FBI Report], Mexico, 12/5/45, p. 1.
6. Board of Special Inquiry, Ellis Island, N.Y., Hearing on Egon Ervin [Erwin] Kisch, 28/12/39, p. 5 (INS).
7. Ibid., p. 4.
8. Ibid., p. 5.
9. Ibid., p. 2

10. G. S. German, Immigrant Inspector, INS, Ellis Island, N.Y., Interview with Egon Erwin Kisch, 11/5/40, pp. 4–6 (INS).

11. Re: Egon Erwin Kisch, p. 1.

12. Geo. P. Shaw, Consul, American Consulate General, Mexico, Letter to Secretary of State, 22/8/41, pp. 1–2 (861.20212/7).

13. SIS/FBI Report, Mexico, 8/11/45, Attachment, p. 1. Cf. Kisch's description of this event in 1913, in *Der Fall des Generalstabschefs Redl* (1924).

14. FBI Laboratory, Report for Mexico City, 7/11/44.

15. "Special Watch Instruction No. 88," October 1943, Attachment to G. E. Brown, Chief, Digest Section, Office of Censorship, Letter to George P. Shaw, Acting Chief, Division of Foreign Activity Correlation, State Dept., 20/10/43 (862.01/611).

16. Egon Erwin Kisch, Letter to [blacked out], Press Division of the Embassy of USSR, Washington, 4/1/43, p. 1. The reference evidently is to Uhse's article in *Internationale Literatur* published under the title "Das kann nie vergessen werden" in *Freies Deutschland,* no. 2 (1943).

17. [Blacked out], Letter to [blacked out], 15/4/45.

18. FBI Report, L.A., 4/3/44, p. 2.

19. Note 4.

20. C. H. Carson, Memorandum to D. M. Ladd, 14/2/46.

21. [Dept. of State] to [U.S. Embassy, Prague], 4/4/46, p. 2.

22. Hoover, Memorandum to Adolf A. Berle, 31/7/44, p. 1 (862.01/7-3144): "It has likewise been learned by the source mentioned above that Consul Benes informed Hanns Eisler and Bert Brecht that Egon Erwin Kisch is assured of a position in the future government of Czechoslovakia."

23. FBI Report, N.Y., 9/10/56, p. 13.

24. Ibid., p. 7.

25. "Bodo I. Uhse, alias Bodo Uhse," p. 8, Attachment to Hoover, Memorandum to Adolf A. Berle, Asst. Secretary of State, 9/10/43 (862.2021 Uhse, Bodo I./7).

26. Edward G. Trueblood, Second Secretary U.S. Embassy, Mexico, Letter to Secretary of State, 12/5/42, p. 2 (800.20210 Agee, Alma [Mrs.]).

27. [Blacked out], Memorandum for [blacked out], 15/12/41, p. 1.

28. FBI Report, Philadelphia, 11/3/42, p. 2. The SAC in Philadelphia refers to a report by his colleague in San Antonio, 18/12/41 [cf. 153, p. 86].

29. Hoover, Letter to SAC, San Antonio, 4/1/43.

30. Re: Bodo I. Uhse, 2/7/45, p. 2f, Attachment to Hoover, Memorandum to Frederick B. Lyon, Chief, Division of Foreign Activity Correlation, State Dept., 26/7/45 (812.00B/7-2645).

31. Concerning the adventurous journey of Alfredo Miller (Alfred Fortmüller)

from Germany to the United States to Mexico, cf. Bodo Uhse, "Ein Leben: Zum Tode Alfred Millers," *Freies Deutschland* 2/1944, p. 22f, and [97, p. 166f].

32. Note 25, p. 4.
33. Ibid., p. 2.
34. Note 30, p. 4.
35. Note 25, p. 2.
36. Ibid.
37. Ibid., p. 1.
38. Ibid.
39. Re: Bodo I. Uhse, 19/9/46, Attachment to Hoover, Memorandum to Frederick B. Lyon, Chief, Division of Foreign Activity Correlation, 14/10/46 (862.01/10-1446).
40. Director, FBI, Memorandum to SAC, N.Y., 20/12/62, p. 1.
41. SAC, N.Y., Memorandum to Director, FBI, 4/10/62, p. 1.
42. Director, FBI, Memorandum to SAC, N.Y., 7/5/63, p. 1.
43. Ibid., p. 2 [cf. 153, pp. 156ff; 3].
44. Re: Ludwig Renn, n.d., no sender, p. 1.
45. The INS claims to have no files on Renn, which is surprising even though he was a Spanish citizen when he first arrived in the United States in 1937 [97, p. 142]. After difficulties with French intelligence, Renn traveled to America again via England in June 1939 to participate, like Bodo Uhse, in a congress of the League of American Writers. At the start of September, Wolfgang Kiessling says, he journeyed on to Mexico, partly because of the "anti-Communist hysteria" in the states "following the German-Soviet nonaggression pact" [98, p. 279] and partly because of Party orders he received through Johannes Schröter, who was active in the German-American community from 1938 on.
46. SIS/FBI Report, Mexico, 5/4/44, p. 1.
47. SIS/FBI Report, Mexico, 3/10/45, Attachment, p. 2.
48. Note 46, Attachment, p. 1.
49. "Transmitting Information Concerning Alleged German Communists," p. 1, Attachment 1 to Edward P. Maffitt, Second Secretary U.S. Embassy, Madrid, Letter to Secretary of State, 18/3/48 (862.00B/3-1848).
50. [Blacked out], Letter to Director, FBI, 22/9/43, p. 2.
51. Civil Attaché, Mexico, Letter to Director, FBI, 22/11/43, p. 1.
52. Ibid., p. 2f.
53. "Report by Office of the Naval Attaché of this Embassy Concerning Alemania Libre," 12/4/43, p. 1, Attachment to W. K. Ailshie, U.S. Embassy, Mexico, Letter to Secretary of State, 29/4/43 (862.01/261).

54. Hoover, Letter to [blacked out], SIS, Mexico, 13/2/43.
55. Cmdr. Silvio P. de Helmsburg, Letter to [blacked out], 10/12/42, p. 2.
56. Note 46, Attachment, p. 4.
57. James H. Walker, Military Attaché, Mexico, Intelligence Report, 19/2/46, p. 1f (Army).
58. Ibid., p. 1.
59. A. P. Kitchin, Letter to Director, FBI, 4/2/43.
60. L. (Ludwig) Renn, Letter to Balder Olden, 24/3/43.
61. A. G. Kay, Chief, Examination Section, Office of Postal Censorship, Washington, Letter to Hoover, 8/4/43.
62. Anneliese Hirschfeld, Letter to Anselm Glücksmann, 16/2/44 [quoted in 97, p. 348f].
63. Civil Attaché, Mexico, Letter to Director, FBI, 17/7/46, p. 2.
64. S. Walter Washington, First Secretary U.S. Embassy, Mexico, Letter to Secretary of State, 1/4/47, Attachment (800.00B/4-147).
65. Robert Wall, Civil Attaché, Mexico, Letter to Director, FBI, 14/6/45, p. 2.
66. Director, FBI, Memorandum to Civil Attaché, Mexico, 4/6/46.
67. Civil Attaché, Mexico, Letter to Director, FBI, 14/9/44.
68. Civil Attaché, Mexico, Letter to Director, FBI, 20/9/43, p. 1.
69. [Blacked out], Memorandum to [blacked out], 16/12/59.
70. Rout and Bratzel report that Hoover's SIS was replaced between July 1946 and April 1947 by the new Central Intelligence Group (CIG), which shortly afterward became the CIA [170, p. 455]. Dirk Raat, in "U.S. Intelligence Operations and Covert Action in Mexico, 1900–1947" [162] dates the SIS closedown to 31/3/47.

5
The FBI Today: Obtaining the Files

1. "President's Memorandum for Heads of Departments and Agencies Regarding the Freedom of Information Act" [quoted in 221, p. 3].
2. *Der Spiegel* no. 38, 15/9/97, p. 168. Recently, the FBI has started to make important files available on the Internet.
3. On the destruction of FBI files, see [7].
4. Natalie Robins [166, p. 17] reports that at the end of the eighties, computerized records were kept of only around 27 million of these cards.
5. I was not permitted to film the area of the General Index while making the documentary film [190] that is a companion to this book. The guided tours that the FBI organizes for tourists are not very informative either.

6. "Introduction" [221, p. 10].
7. The update of this publication can be ordered free of charge from the FBI's Office of Public Affairs. It lists the addresses of FBI field offices and useful clues to the history of the files and to the Central Record System Classifications. Buitrago and Immerman's guide [26; cf. 54; 143, pp. 242–49; 74; 208] is slightly dated, but an important aid.
8. Cf. the Irwin Winkler film starring Robert De Niro, *Guilty by Suspicion* (1991).

Bibliography

1. Aaron, Daniel, *Writers on the Left*. New York: Avon, 1961; repr. New York: Columbia University Press, 1992.
2. Adamic, Louis, *Dynamite: The Story of Class Violence in America*. New York: Viking, 1931.
3. "Affäre des deutschen 'Schutzverbands.'" In *Das Neue Tage-Buch*, no. 44, 28/10/39, p. 1025.
4. Agee, Joel, *Twelve Years: An American Boyhood in East Germany*. New York: Farrar, Straus and Giroux, 1981.
5. Albrecht, Richard, "Das FBI-Dossier Carl Zuckmayer." In *Zeitschrift für Literaturwissenschaft und Linguistik* no. 73, 1989, pp. 114–21.
6. *American Intelligence and the German Resistance to Hitler: A Documentary History*, ed. Jürgen Heideking and Christof Mauch. Boulder, Colo.: Westview, 1996.
7. *Appraisal of the Records of the Federal Bureau of Investigation: A Report to Honorable Harold H. Greene, United States District Court for the District of Columbia*, ed. National Archives and Records Service and Federal Bureau of Investigation. Washington, 1981.
8. Arendt, Hannah, "The Ex-Communists." In *Commonweal*, no. 24, 20/3/53, pp. 595–99.
9. Balk, Theodor, *Das verlorene Manuskript*. Berlin: Dietz, 1949.
10. Barrett, Edward L., *The Tenney Committee: Legislative Investigation of Subversive Activities in California*. Ithaca, N.Y.: Cornell University Press, 1951.

11. Baum, Vicki, *Es war alles ganz anders: Erinnerungen*. Cologne: Kiepenheuer & Witsch, 1987.

12. Beer, Siegfried, "Exil und Emigration als Information: Zur Tätigkeit des Foreign Nationalities Branch (FNB) innerhalb des amerikanischen Kriegsgeheimdienstes COI bzw. OSS, 1941–1945." In Dokumentationsarchiv des österreichischen Widerstandes, *Jahrbuch, 1989*. Vienna: Österreichischer Bundesverlag, 1989, pp. 132–43.

13. Belfrage, Cedric, *The American Inquisition, 1945–1960: A Profile of the 'McCarthy Era.'* New York: Thunder's Mouth Press, 1989.

14. *The Adolf A. Berle Diary, 1937–1971*. Hyde Park: Franklin D. Roosevelt Library, 1978.

15. *Beyond the Hiss Case: The FBI, Congress, and the Cold War*, ed. Athan G. Theoharis. Philadelphia: Temple University Press, 1982.

16. *Biographisches Handbuch der deutschsprachigen Emigration nach 1933/ International Biographical Dictionary of Central European Emigrés, 1933–1945*, 3 vols., ed. Werner Röder and Herbert A. Strauss. Munich: Saur, 1980, 1983.

17. Brandeis, Louis D., in *The Supreme Court Reporter*, vol. 48. St. Paul: West Publishing, 1929, pp. 570–75.

18. Brandl, Rudolf, *That Good Old Fool, Uncle Sam: A Refugee Sounds a Warning*. No place, n.d. (ca. May 1940).

19. Brecht, Arnold, *Mit der Kraft des Geistes: Lebenserinnerungen, Zweite Hälfte, 1927–1967*. Stuttgart: Deutsche Verlags-Anstalt, 1967.

20. Brecht, Bertolt, *Große kommentierte Berliner und Frankfurter Ausgabe*, ed. Werner Hecht et al. Berlin: Aufbau; Frankfurt: Suhrkamp, 1988.

21. ———, *Versuche 1–12*. Frankfurt: Suhrkamp, 1977.

22. *Bertolt Brecht Before the Committee on Un-American Activities: An Historic Encounter*, ed. Eric Bentley. New York: Folkways Records, FD 5531, 1961.

23. *Brecht in den USA*, ed. James K. Lyon. Frankfurt: Suhrkamp, 1994.

24. Budenz, Louis Francis, *Men Without Faces: The Communist Conspiracy in the U.S.A.* New York: Harper, 1950.

25. ———, *The Techniques of Communism*. New York: Arno, 1977.

26. Buitrago, Ann Mari, and Leon A. Immerman, *Are You Now or Have You Ever Been in the FBI Files: How to Secure and Interpret Your FBI Files*. New York: Grove, 1981.

27. Bunge, Hans, *Fragen Sie mehr über Brecht: Hanns Eisler im Gespräch*. Munich: Rogner & Bernhard, 1972.

28. Bungert, Heike, *Das Nationalkomitee und der Westen: Die Reaktion der Westalliierten auf das NKFD und die Freien Deutschen Bewegungen, 1943–1948*. Stuttgart: Steiner, 1997.

29. California Legislature, *Fifth Report of the Senate Fact-Finding Committee on Un-American Activities*. Sacramento, 1949.

30. Carr, Robert K., *The House Committee on Un-American Activities, 1945–1950*. Ithaca: Cornell University Press, 1952.

31. *A Catalog of Files and Microfilms of the German Foreign Ministry Archives, 1920–1945*, 4 vols., ed. George O. Kent. Stanford: Hoover Institute, 1962–72.

32. Caute, David, *The Great Fear: The Anti-Communist Purge Under Truman and Eisenhower*. New York: Simon & Schuster, 1978.

33. Ceplair, Larry, and Steven Englund, *The Inquisition in Hollywood: Politics in the Film Community, 1930–1960*. Garden City, N.Y.: Anchor Press, 1980.

34. Chamberlain, Lawrence H., *Loyalty and Legislative Action: A Survey of Activity by the New York State Legislature, 1919–1949*. Ithaca: Cornell University Press, 1951.

35. Chambers, Whittaker, *Witness*. Washington: Regnery Gateway, 1952.

36. Charns, Alexander, *Cloak and Gavel: FBI Wiretaps, Bugs, Informers, and the Supreme Court*. Urbana: University of Illinois Press, 1992.

37. Chase, William, "The Strange Case of Diego Rivera and the U.S. State Department: A Research Note" [ms.]; first printed in Spanish in *Zona abierta suplemento de economía, política y sociedad*, supplement to *El financiero*, vol. 2, no. 61, 19/11/93, pp. 8–11.

38. Cook, Fred J., *The FBI Nobody Knows*. New York: Macmillan, 1964.

39. Cushman, Robert E., *Civil Liberties in the United States: A Guide to Current Problems and Experience*. Ithaca: Cornell University Press, 1956.

40. Davies, Joseph E., *Mission to Moscow*. New York: Simon & Schuster, 1941.

41. Davis, James K., *Spying on America: The FBI's Domestic Counterintelligence Program*. New York: Praeger, 1992.

42. *Deutsche Exilliteratur seit 1933*, vol. 1, parts 1–2 (California), and under the title *Deutschsprachige Exilliteratur seit 1933*, vol. 2, parts 1–2 (New York), vol. 4, parts 1–4 (Bibliographies), ed. John M. Spalek et al. Bern: Francke, 1976, 1989, 1994.

43. Diamond, Sigmund, *Compromised Campus: The Collaboration of Universities with the Intelligence Community, 1945–1955*. New York: Oxford University Press, 1992.

44. *Dichter und ein großer Schnabel: 25 Jahre Tukan-Kreis*, ed. Rudolf Schmitt-Sulzthal. Munich, n.d., no publ. [1955].

45. Dick, Bernard F., *Radical Innocence: A Critical Study of the Hollywood Ten*. Lexington: University of Kentucky Press, 1989.

46. Dies, Martin, *The Trojan Horse in America*. New York: Dodd, Mead, 1940.
47. Döblin, Alfred, *Schicksalsreise: Bericht und Bekenntnis*. Frankfurt: Knecht, 1949.
48. Donner, Frank, *The Age of Surveillance: The Aims and Methods of America's Political Intelligence System*. New York: Knopf, 1980.
49. ——, *Protectors of Privilege: Red Squads and Police Repression in Urban America*. Berkeley: University of California Press, 1990.
50. Dorwart, Jeffery M., *Conflict of Duty: The U.S. Navy's Intelligence Dilemma, 1919–1945*. Annapolis: Naval Institute Press, 1983.
51. Dunlop, Richard, *Donovan: America's Master Spy*. Chicago: Rand McNally, 1982.
52. Eliot, Marc, *Walt Disney: Hollywood's Dark Prince, A Biography*. New York: Birch Lane, 1993.
53. *The European Emigrant Experience in the USA*, ed. Walter Hölbling and Reinhold Wagnleitner. Tübingen: Narr, 1992.
54. *The FBI: A Comprehensive Reference Guide*, ed. Athan G. Theoharis. Phoenix: Oryx, 1999.
55. Feuchtwanger, Lion, and Arnold Zweig, *Briefwechsel, 1933–1958*, 2 vols., ed. Harold von Hofe. Berlin: Aufbau, 1984.
56. Feuchtwanger, Marta, *An Emigré Life: Munich, Berlin, Sanary, Pacific Palisades*. Los Angeles: University of Southern California, 1976 (typescript).
57. Folsom, Franklin, *Days of Anger, Days of Hope: A Memoir of the League of American Writers, 1937–1942*. Niwot: University of Colorado Press, 1994.
58. Frank, Leonhard, *Links wo das Herz ist*. Munich: Nymphenburger, 1952.
59. Frei, Bruno, *Der Papiersäbel: Autobiographie*. Frankfurt: Fischer, 1972.
60. Fried, Richard M., *Nightmare in Red: The McCarthy Era in Perspective*. New York: Oxford University Press, 1990.
61. Fry, Varian, *Surrender on Demand*. New York: Random House, 1945. Abridged as *Assignment Rescue*. New York: Four Winds, 1968.
62. Fuegi, John, *Brecht and Company: Sex, Politics, and the Making of the Modern Drama*. New York: Grove Press, 1994.
63. *The Gallup Poll: Public Opinion, 1935–1971*, vol. 1 (1935–1948), vol. 2 (1949–1958). New York: Random House, 1972.
64. "Geheimagent Rivera?" In *Frankfurter Allgemeine Zeitung*, 30/11/93.
65. Gentry, Curt, *J. Edgar Hoover: The Man and the Secrets*. New York: Plume, 1992.
66. Goetz, Curt, and Valérie von Martens, *Wir wandern, wir wandern . . . : Der Memoiren dritter Teil*. Stuttgart: Deutsche Verlags-Anstalt, 1963.

67. Goodman, Walter, *The Committee: The Extraordinary Career of the House Committee on Un-American Activities.* New York: Farrar, Straus and Giroux, 1968.

68. Graebner, William S., *The Age of Doubt: American Thought and Culture in the 1940s.* Boston: Twayne, 1991.

69. Graf, Oskar Maria, *Reden und Aufsätze aus dem Exil,* ed. Helmut F. Pfanner. Munich: Süddeutscher Verlag, 1989.

70. *Oskar Maria Graf in seinen Briefen,* ed. Gerhard Bauer and Helmut F. Pfanner. Munich: Süddeutscher Verlag, 1984.

71. Grosshut, F[riedrich] S[ally], "Heinrich Mann." In *Books Abroad,* no. 4, 1950, pp. 356–59.

72. *Guide to the Microfilm Edition of the FBI File on the House Committee on Un-American Activities,* ed. Kenneth O'Reilly. Wilmington: Scholarly Resources, [1986].

73. Gumprecht, Holger, *"New Weimar" unter Palmen: Deutsche Schriftsteller im Exil in Los Angeles.* Berlin: Aufbau Taschenbuch Verlag, 1998.

74. Haines, Gerald K., and David A. Langbart, *Unlocking the Files of the FBI: A Guide to Its Records and Classification System.* Wilmington: Scholarly Resources, 1993.

75. Haynes, John Earl, *Red Scare or Red Menace: American Communism and Anticommunism in the Cold War Era.* Chicago: Dee, 1996.

76. ———, *Venona: Decoding Soviet Espionage in America.* New Haven: Yale University Press, 1999.

77. Heilbut, Anthony, *Exiled in Paradise: German Refugee Artists and Intellectuals in America from the 1930s to the Present.* New York: Viking, 1983.

78. Heym, Stefan, *Nachruf.* Munich: Bertelsmann, 1988; repr. Berlin: Buchverlag Der Morgen, 1990.

79. *History of the Office of Censorship,* 7 vols. Washington: University Publications of America, n.d.

80. Hoover, J. Edgar, *Masters of Deceit: The Story of Communism in America and How to Fight It.* New York: Holt, 1958.

81. ———, *A Study of Communism.* New York: Holt, Rinehart & Winston, 1962.

82. ———, "Fifty Years of Crime." In *Vital Speeches of the Day,* vol. 5, no. 16, 1/6/39, pp. 505–9.

83. ———, "A Nation's Call to Duty: Preserve the American Home." In *Vital Speeches of the Day,* vol. 8, no. 18, 1/7/42, pp. 554–56.

84. ———, "The Battle on the Home Front: Protection for Home and the Hearthside." In *Vital Speeches of the Day,* vol. 9, no. 23, 15/9/43, pp. 734–36.

85. ———, "Our 'Achilles' Heel': Loyal Americans Must Stand Up and Be Counted." In *Vital Speeches of the Day,* vol. 13, no. 1, 15/10/46, p. 10f.

86. ———, "Speech Before the House Committee on Un-American Activities." In U.S. Congress. Senate. *Congressional Record*. 80th Congress, 1st session, vol. 93, pt. 2, 1947, pp. 2689–92.

87. ———, "How to Fight Communism." In *Newsweek*, 9/6/47, pp. 30–32.

88. ———, *J. Edgar Hoover on Communism*. New York: Paperback Library, 1970.

89. ———, *J. Edgar Hoover Speaks Concerning Communism*, ed. James D. Bales. Washington: Capitol Hill Press, 1970.

90. *Inside the FBI Secret Files: Star Magazine* Special (1993).

91. Janka, Walter, *Schwierigkeiten mit der Wahrheit*. Reinbek: Rowohlt, 1989.

92. Kantorowicz, Alfred, *Politik und Literatur im Exil: Deutschsprachige Schriftsteller im Kampf gegen den Nationalsozialismus*. Munich: Deutscher Taschenbuch Verlag, 1978.

93. Katz, Barry M., *Foreign Intelligence: Research and Analysis in the Office of Strategic Services, 1942–1945*. Cambridge: Harvard University Press, 1989.

94. ———, "German Historians in the Office of Strategic Services." In *An Interrupted Past: German-Speaking Refugee Historians in the United States After 1933,* ed. Hartmut Lehmann and James J. Sheehan. Washington: German Historical Institute, 1991, pp. 136–39.

95. Keller, William W., *The Liberals and J. Edgar Hoover: Rise and Fall of a Domestic Intelligence State*. Princeton: Princeton University Press, 1989.

96. Kiessling, Wolfgang, *Alemania Libre in Mexiko*, 2 vols. Berlin: Akademie, 1974.

97. ———, *Exil in Lateinamerika*. Leipzig: Reclam, 1980 (1st ed.), 1984 (2nd ed.).

98. ———, *Brücken nach Mexiko: Traditionen einer Freundschaft*. Berlin: Dietz, 1989.

99. ———, *Partner im 'Narrenparadies': Der Freundeskreis um Noel Field und Paul Merker*. Berlin: Dietz, 1994.

100. Klehr, Harvey, John Earl Haynes, and Kyrill M. Anderson, *The Soviet World of American Communism*. New Haven: Yale University Press, 1998.

101. Klehr, Harvey, John Earl Haynes, and Fridrikh Igorevich Firsov, *The Secret World of American Communism*. New Haven: Yale University Press, 1995.

102. Klehr, Harvey, and Ronald Radosh, *The Amerasia Spy Case: Prelude to McCarthyism*. Chapel Hill: University of North Carolina Press, 1996.

103. Koch, Stephen, *Double Lives: Spies and Writers in the Secret Soviet War of Ideas Against the West*. New York: Free Press, 1994.

104. Kortner, Fritz, *Aller Tage Abend*. Munich: Kindler, 1959.

105. Krohn, Claus-Dieter, *Intellectuals in Exile: Refugee Scholars and the New School for Social Research.* Amherst: University of Massachusetts Press, 1993.

106. Kroll, Frederic, *Trauma Amerika, 1937–1942.* Wiesbaden: Blahak, 1986.

107. Kurth, Peter, *American Cassandra: The Life of Dorothy Thompson.* Boston: Little, Brown, 1990.

108. Lamphere, Robert J., and Tom Shachtman, *The FBI-KGB War: A Special Agent's Story.* New York: Random House, 1986.

109. *Litigation Under the Federal Open Government Laws,* ed. Allan Robert Adler. Washington: American Civil Liberties Union Foundation, 1991.

110. Lowenthal, Max, *The Federal Bureau of Investigation.* New York: Sloane, 1950.

111. von der Lühe, Irmela, *Erika Mann: Eine Biographie.* Frankfurt: Campus, 1993.

112. Lyon, James, *Bertolt Brecht in America.* Princeton: Princeton University Press, 1980.

113. ———, "Das FBI als Literaturhistoriker." In *Akzente,* no. 4, 1980, pp. 362–83.

114. Mahler-Werfel, Alma, *Mein Leben.* Frankfurt: Fischer, 1965.

115. Manchester, William, *The Glory and the Dream: A Narrative History of America, 1932–1972.* New York: Bantam, 1990.

116. Mann, Erika, *Briefe und Antworten,* vol. 1., ed. Anna Zanco Prestel. Munich: Ellermann, 1984.

117. Mann, Everett E., *The Public Right to Know Government Information: Its Affirmation and Abridgement.* Ph.D. diss., Claremont Graduate School, 1984. Ann Arbor: University Microfilms International, 1989.

118. ———, "Freedom of Information Act." In *Encyclopedia of the American Constitution.* New York: MacMillan, 1986, p. 781.

119. Mann, Heinrich, *Ein Zeitalter wird besichtigt.* Berlin: Aufbau, 1973.

120. *Heinrich Mann, 1871–1950: Werk und Leben in Dokumenten und Bildern,* ed. Sigrid Anger. Berlin: Aufbau, 1977.

121. "Heinrich L. Mann, Novelist, Was 79." In *New York Times,* 13/3/50.

122. Mann, Klaus, *Der Wendepunkt: Ein Lebensbericht.* Reinbek: Rowohlt, 1984.

123. ———, *Tagebücher 1940 bis 1943,* ed. Joachim Heimannsberg et al. Munich: edition spangenberg, 1991.

124. Nelly Mann, Brief an Friedel Kantorowicz, 21/10/42. In *Das Schönste* (March 1960), p. 54.

125. Mann, Thomas, *Briefe, 1937–1947,* ed. Erika Mann. Frankfurt: Fischer, 1963.

126. ———, *Briefwechsel mit seinem Verleger Gottfried Bermann Fischer, 1932–1955,* ed. Peter de Mendelssohn. Frankfurt: Fischer, 1973.

127. ———, *Die Entstehung des Doktor Faustus: Roman eines Romans.* Frankfurt: Fischer, 1967.

128. ———, *Tagebücher, 1940–1943,* ed. Peter de Mendelssohn. Frankfurt: Fischer, 1982.

129. ———, *Tagebücher, 1944–1.4.1946,* ed. Inge Jens. Frankfurt: Fischer, 1986.

130. ———, *Tagebücher 28.5.1946–31.12.1948,* ed. Inge Jens. Frankfurt: Fischer, 1989.

131. ———, *Tagebücher, 1949–1950,* ed. Inge Jens. Frankfurt: Fischer, 1991.

132. ———, *Tagebücher, 1951–1952,* ed. Inge Jens. Frankfurt: Fischer, 1993.

133. ———, "Foreword." In Gordon Kahn, *Hollywood on Trial: The Story of the Ten Who Were Indicted.* New York: Boni & Gaer, 1948, p. v.

134. Mann, Thomas, and Heinrich Mann, *Briefwechsel, 1900–1949,* ed. Ulrich Dietzel. Berlin: Aufbau, 1977.

135. Mann, Thomas, and Agnes E. Meyer, *Briefwechsel, 1937–1955,* ed. Hans Rudolf Vaget. Frankfurt: Fischer, 1992.

136. *Thomas Mann: Ein Leben in Bildern,* ed. Hans Wysling and Yvonne Schmidlin. Zurich: Artemis & Winkler, 1994.

137. Marchwitza, Hans, *In Amerika.* Berlin: Tribüne, n.d.

138. Marcuse, Ludwig, *Mein zwanzigstes Jahrhundert: Auf dem Weg zu einer Autobiographie.* Munich: List, 1960.

139. Marquardt-Bigman, Petra, *Amerikanische Geheimdienstanalysen über Deutschland, 1942–1949.* Munich: Oldenbourg, 1995.

140. McWilliams, Carey, *Witch Hunt: The Revival of Heresy.* Boston: Little, Brown, 1950.

141. Middell, Eike, et al., *Exil in den USA.* Leipzig: Reclam, 1979 (1st ed.), 1983 (2nd ed.).

142. Minder, Robert, *Dichter in der Gesellschaft: Erfahrungen mit deutscher und französischer Literatur.* Frankfurt: Insel, 1966.

143. Mitgang, Herbert, *Dangerous Dossiers: Exposing the Secret War Against America's Greatest Authors.* New York: Ballantine, 1989.

144. Morley, Michael, "The Source of Brecht's 'Abbau des Schiffes Oskawa durch die Mannschaft.'" In *Oxford German Studies,* no. 2, 1966, pp. 149–62.

145. Morros, Boris, *My Ten Years as a Counterspy.* New York: Viking, 1959.

146. Von zur Mühlen, Patrik, *Fluchtziel Lateinamerika: Die deutsche Emigration, 1933–1945: Politische Aktivitäten und soziokulturelle Integration.* Bonn: Verlag Neue Gesellschaft, 1988.

147. Murphy, Walter F., *Wiretapping on Trial: A Case Study in the Judicial Process*. New York: Random House, 1966.

148. Murray, Robert K., *Red Scare: A Study of National Hysteria, 1919–1920*. New York: McGraw-Hill, 1964.

149. *The Muses Flee Hitler: Cultural Transfer and Adaptation, 1930–1945*, ed. Jarrell C. Jackman and Carla M. Borden. Washington: Smithsonian Institution Press, 1983.

150. "Der Mythos vom revolutionären Maler und die Spitzeldienste." In *Frankfurter Rundschau*, 27/11/93.

151. Navasky, Victor S., *Naming Names*. New York: Penguin, 1980.

152. *Navigating the Rapids, 1918–1971: From the Papers of Adolf A. Berle*, ed. Beatrice Bishop Berle, Travis Beal Jacobs. New York: Harcourt Brace Jovanovich, 1973.

153. Neuman, Alma, *Always Straight Ahead: A Memoir*. Baton Rouge: Louisiana State University Press, 1993.

154. Neumann, Franz, *Behemoth: The Structure and Practice of National Socialism*. Toronto: Oxford University Press, 1942.

155. O'Reilly, Kenneth, *Hoover and the Un-Americans: The FBI, HUAC, and the Red Menace*. Philadelphia: Temple University Press, 1983.

156. Oshinsky, David M., *A Conspiracy So Immense: The World of Joe McCarthy*. New York: Free Press, 1983.

157. *Österreicher im Exil: USA, 1938–1945. Eine Dokumentation*, ed. Peter Eppel. 2 vols. Vienna: Österreichischer Bundesverlag, 1995.

158. Pfanner, Helmut, *Exile in New York: German and Austrian Writers After 1933*. Detroit: Wayne State University Press, 1983.

159. Pohle, Fritz, *Das mexikanische Exil: Ein Beitrag zur Geschichte der politisch-kulturellen Emigration aus Deutschland, 1937–1946*. Stuttgart: Metzler, 1986.

160. Powers, Richard Gid, *Secrecy and Power: The Life of J. Edgar Hoover*. New York: Free Press, 1987.

161. *Public Opinion, 1935–1946*, ed. Hadley Cantril. Princeton: Princeton University Press, 1951.

162. Raat, Dirk W., "U.S. Intelligence Operations and Covert Action in Mexico, 1900–1947." In *Journal of Contemporary History*, no. 4, 1987, pp. 615–38.

163. *Red Fascism*, ed. Jack B. Tenney. New York: Arno Press, 1977.

164. Regler, Gustav, *Das Ohr des Malchus: Eine Lebensgeschichte*. Cologne: Kiepenheuer & Witsch, 1958.

165. "Erich Maria Remarque, Violent Author . . . Quiet Man." In *Newsweek*, 1/4/57.

166. Robins, Natalie, *Alien Ink: The FBI's War on Freedom of Expression*. New York: Morrow, 1992.

167. Robinson, David, *Chaplin: His Life and Art*. New York: MacGraw-Hill, 1985.

168. Rohrwasser, Michael, *Der Stalinismus und die Renegaten: Die Literatur der Exkommunisten*. Stuttgart: Metzler, 1991.

169. Rothmiller, Mike, *L.A. Secret Police: Inside the LAPD Elite Spy Network*. New York: Pocket Books, 1992.

170. Rout, Leslie B., and John F. Bratzel, *The Shadow War: German Espionage and United States Counterespionage in Latin America During World War II*. Frederick, Md.: University Publications of America, 1986.

171. Rovere, Richard H., "The Kept Witnesses." In *Harper's Magazine* 210 (May 1955), pp. 25–34.

172. "Russian Intelligence Denies Oppenheimer-KGB Link" (Reuters press release, 5/5/94).

173. Sayer, Ian, and Douglas Botting, *America's Secret Army: The Untold Story of the Counter Intelligence Corps*. London: Grafton, 1989.

174. Schebera, Jürgen, "The Lesson of Germany: Gerhart Eisler im Exil: Kommunist, Publizist, Galionsfigur der HUAC-Hexenjäger." In *Exilforschung*, no. 7. Munich: edition text + kritik 1989, pp. 85–97.

175. Scheer, Maximilian, *Paris—New York*. Berlin: Verlag der Nation, n.d.

176. Schevenels, Walther, *Forty-Five Years International Federation of Trade Unions*. Brussels: Board of Trustees der IFTU, n.d. [ca. 1956].

177. Schneider, Sigrid, "Die FBI-Akte über Oskar Maria Graf." In *Text + Kritik* (special issue, 1986), pp. 131–50.

178. Schneider, Thomas, *Robert M. W. Kempner: Bibliographie*. Osnabrück: Universität Osnabrück, 1987.

179. *The Secrets War: The Office of Strategic Services in World War II*, ed. George C. Chalou. Washington: National Archives and Records Administration, 1992.

180. *Anna Seghers: Eine Biographie in Bildern*, ed. Frank Wagner et al. Berlin: Aufbau, 1994.

181. Seghers, Anna, and Viola B. Shore, "Viola Brothers Shore: Auszug aus einer Dramatisierung von Anna Seghers' Roman *Das siebte Kreuz* für das amerikanische Theater," trans. Alexander Stephan. In *Argonautenschiff* 5. Berlin: Aufbau, 1996, pp. 56–60.

182. Skierka, Volker, *Lion Feuchtwanger: Eine Biographie*. Berlin: Quadriga, 1984.

183. Smith, Bradley F., *The Shadow Warriors: O.S.S. and the Origins of the C.I.A.* New York: Basic, 1983.

184. Smith, R. Harris, *OSS: The Secret History of America's First Central Intelligence Agency.* New York: Dell, 1972.

185. Soley, Lawrence C., *Radio Warfare: OSS and CIA Subversive Propaganda.* New York: Praeger, 1989.

186. Souvarine, Boris, "Die andere Unterwelt" ("Kommunazis in Amerika"). In *Das Neue Tage-Buch,* no. 51, 16/12/39, pp. 1184–87.

187. *Staatsschutz der Stadt Zürich: Bericht der Untersuchungskommission an den Gemeinderat von Zürich,* ed. Untersuchungskommission Politische Polizei des Gemeinderates von Zürich. Zurich, 1991.

188. Stephan, Alexander, *Die deutsche Exilliteratur, 1933–1945.* Munich: Beck, 1979.

189. ———, *Anna Seghers im Exil: Essays, Texte, Dokumente.* Bonn: Bouvier, 1993.

190. ———, *Im Visier des FBI.* Video documentary, Sender Freies Berlin, Westdeutscher Rundfunk, Mitteldeutscher Rundfunk, 1995 (with Johannes Eglau).

191. ———, *Anna Seghers: Das siebte Kreuz. Welt und Wirkung eines Romans.* Berlin: Aufbau, 1997.

192. ———, "Pläne für ein neues Deutschland: Die Kulturpolitik der Exil-KPD vor 1945." In *Basis: Jahrbuch für deutsche Gegenwartsliteratur,* no. 7. Frankfurt: Suhrkamp, 1977, pp. 54–74, 229–33.

193. ———, "Ein Exilroman als Bestseller: Anna Seghers' *The Seventh Cross* in den USA. Analyse und Dokumente." In *Exilforschung,* no. 3. Munich: edition text + kritik, 1985, pp. 238–59.

194. ———, "Erika Mann und das FBI: ' . . . a liaison which might be of possible value.'" In *neue deutsche literatur,* no. 7, 1993, pp. 124–42.

195. ———, "Nach-Bemerkung zur 'Akte Erika Mann.'" In *Neuer Nachrichtenbrief der Gesellschaft für Exilforschung,* no. 2, 1994, pp. 17–19.

196. ———, "Das FBI und die deutschsprachigen Exilanten in Mexiko." In *Mexiko, das wohltemperierte Exil,* ed. Renata von Hanffstengel et al. Mexico: Instituto de Investigaciones Interculturales Germano-Mexicanas, 1995, pp. 127–35.

197. ———, "Österreichische Autoren und die amerikanischen Geheimdienste: ein Archivbericht." In *Geschichte der österreichischen Literatur,* ed. Donald Daviau and Herbert Arlt, pt. 1. Ingbert: Röhrig Universitätsverlag, 1996, pp. 207–19.

198. ———, "Nachrichten aus Laramie, Wyoming: Zu zwei verschollenen Theaterfassungen von Anna Seghers' Roman *Das siebte Kreuz.*" In *Argonautenschiff* 5. Berlin: Aufbau, 1996, pp. 61–73.

199. ———, "Enemy Alien: Die Überwachung des exilierten Komponisten

Hanns Eisler durch FBI, HUAC, und INS." In *Brecht Yearbook*, no. 22. Madison/Waterloo: University of Wisconsin/International Brecht Society, 1997, pp. 180–93.

200. ———, "Personal and Confidential: Geheimdienste, Alfred Döblin und das Exil in Südkalifornien." In *Internationales Alfred-Döblin-Kolloquium, Leiden 1995*. Bern: Lang, 1997, pp. 181–209.

201. ———, "'Der Paß ist der edelste Teil von einem Menschen.' Bertolt Brecht, Gestapo, Reichsaußenministerium und FBI." In *Theater der Zeit* (special issue, 1997), pp. 133–36.

202. ———, "'. . . advocates Communist world revolution by violent means.' Brecht, Eisler und 'The Measures Taken' in den Dossiers von FBI und HUAC." In *Massnehmen: Bertolt Brecht/Hanns Eislers Lehrstück 'Die Massnahme': Kontroverse, Perspektive, Praxis*, ed. Inge Gellert et al. Berlin: Theater der Zeit, 1998, pp. 115–31.

203. Streitfeld, David, "The Book at Ground Zero: They Published a Soviet Spy's Allegations. Then Came the Fallout." In *Washington Post*, 27/5/94.

204. Sudoplatov, Pavel, and Anatoli Sudoplatov, *Special Tasks: The Memoirs of an Unwanted Witness—a Soviet Spymaster*. Boston: Little, Brown, 1994.

205. Summers, Anthony, *Official and Confidential: The Secret Life of J. Edgar Hoover*. New York: Putnam & Sons, 1993.

206. Sutherland, Douglas, *The Great Betrayal*. New York: Penguin, 1982.

207. Tenney, Jack B., *The Tenney Committee . . . the American Record*. Tujunga: Standard Publications, 1952.

208. Theoharis, Athan G., *The FBI: An Annotated Bibliography and Research Guide*. New York: Garland, 1994.

209. Theoharis, Athan G., and John Stuart Cox, *The Boss: J. Edgar Hoover and the Great American Inquisition*. New York: Bantam, 1990.

210. *Thirty Years of Treason: Excerpts from Hearings Before the House Committee on Un-American Activities, 1938–1968*, ed. Eric Bentley. New York: Viking, 1971.

211. Tillinger, Eugene, "Thomas Mann's Left Hand." In *The Freeman*, 26/3/51, p. 397.

212. Toledano, Ralph de, *J. Edgar Hoover: The Man in His Time*. New Rochelle, N.Y.: Arlington House, 1973.

213. Troy, Thomas F., *Donovan and the CIA: A History of the Establishment of the Central Intelligence Agency*. Frederick, Md.: Central Intelligence Agency, 1981.

214. Uhse, Bodo, and F. C. Weiskopf, *Briefwechsel, 1942–1948*, ed. Günter Caspar. Berlin: Aufbau, 1990.

215. "... und leiser Jubel zöge ein." Autoren- und Verlegerbriefe, 1950–1959, ed. Elmar Faber and Carsten Wurm. Berlin: Aufbau, 1992.

216. U.S. Congress. House of Representatives. Committee on Government Operations. *A Citizen's Guide on Using the Freedom of Information Act and the Privacy Act of 1974 to Request Government Records.* 100th Congress, 1st session, 1987, House Report 100-199.

217. U.S. Congress. House of Representatives. Committee on Un-American Activities. *Hearings Regarding the Communist Infiltration of the Motion Picture Industry, October 20, 21, 22, 23, 24, 27, 28, 29, and 30, 1947.* 80th Congress, 1st session, 1947.

218. U.S. Congress. House of Representatives. Committee on Un-American Activities. *Interim Report on Hearings Regarding Communist Espionage in the United States Government.* 80th Congress, 2nd session, 1948.

219. U.S. Congress. House of Representatives. *Hearings Before the Select Committee Investigating National Defense Migration.* 77th Congress, 2nd session, part 31, 7/3/42.

220. U.S. Department of Justice, Federal Bureau of Investigation, Research/Drug Demand Reduction Unit, Office of Public Affairs. *Conducting Research in FBI Records.* Washington, 1990.

221. U.S. Department of Justice, Office of Information and Privacy. *Freedom of Information Act Guide and Privacy Act Overview.* Washington, September 1994.

222. *United States Intelligence: An Encyclopedia.* Ed. Bruce W. Watson et al. New York: Garland, 1990.

223. U.S. Office of Strategic Services. *Foreign Nationalities Branch Files, 1942–1945.* 2 vols. Bethesda, Md.: Congressional Information Service, 1988.

224. Vaget, Hans Rudolf, "Vorzeitiger Antifaschismus und andere unamerikanische Umtriebe." In *Horizonte: Festschrift für Herbert Lehnert zum 65. Geburtstag,* ed. Hannelore Mundt et al. Tübingen: Niemeyer, 1990, pp. 173–204.

225. Vaughn, Robert, *Only Victims: A Study of Show Business Blacklisting.* New York: Putnam, 1972.

226. *Venona: Soviet Espionage and the American Response, 1939–1957,* ed. Robert Benson, Michael Warner. Washington: National Security Agency and Central Intelligence Agency, 1996.

227. Viertel, Salka, *The Kindness of Strangers.* New York: Holt, Rinehart & Winston, 1969.

228. Völker, Klaus, *Brecht-Chronik: Daten zu Leben und Werk.* Munich: Hanser, 1971.

229. Wagner, Frank, "Deportation nach Piaski: Letzte Stationen der Passion von Hedwig Reiling." In *Argonautenschiff* 3, 1994, pp. 117–26.

230. Walter, Hans-Albert, *Deutsche Exilliteratur, 1933–1950,* vols. 2–4. Stuttgart: Metzler, 1978–88.

231. *War Report of the OSS (Office of Strategic Services),* 2 vols. New York: Walker, 1976.

232. *Wartime Censorship of Press and Radio,* ed. Robert E. Summers. New York: Wilson, 1942.

233. *Was aus Deutschland werden sollte: Konzepte des Widerstands, des Exils und der Alliierten,* ed. Reinhard Kühnl and Eckart Spoo. Heilbronn: Diestel, 1995.

234. *Weimar am Pazifik: Literarische Wege zwischen den Kontinenten, Festschrift für Werner Vordtriede zum 70. Geburtstag,* ed. Dieter Borchmeyer and Till Heimeran. Tübingen: Niemeyer, 1985.

235. Weinstein, Allen, *Perjury: The Hiss-Chambers Case.* New York: Knopf, 1978.

236. Whitehead, Don, *The FBI Story: A Report to the People.* New York: Random House, 1956.

237. Williams, David J., *Without Understanding: The FBI and Political Surveillance, 1908–1941.* Ph.D. diss., University of New Hampshire, 1981.

238. Wills, Garry, *Reagan's America: Innocents at Home.* Garden City, N.Y.: Doubleday, 1987.

239. Winks, Robin, *Cloak and Gown: Scholars in the Secret War, 1939–1961.* New York: Morrow, 1987.

240. Wyman, David S., *Paper Walls: America and the Refugee Crisis, 1938–1941.* Amherst: University of Massachusetts Press, 1968.

241. Zuckmayer, Carl, *Als wär's ein Stück von mir: Horen der Freundschaft.* No place, Fischer, 1966.

242. *Zur Archäologie der Demokratie in Deutschland,* 2 vols., ed. Alfons Söllner. Frankfurt: Europäische Verlagsanstalt, 1982; Frankfurt: Fischer, 1986.

243. *Zwischen Befreiung und Besatzung: Analysen des US-Geheimdienstes über Positionen und Strukturen deutscher Politik, 1945,* ed. Ulrich Borsdorf and Lutz Niethammer. Weinheim: Beltz Athenäum, 1995.

Index

351